CHILDREN & MOVEMENT

Physical Education in the Elementary School

Second Edition

CHILDREN & MOVEMENT

Physical Education in the Elementary School

Jennifer Wall
McGill University

Nancy Murray
Brock University

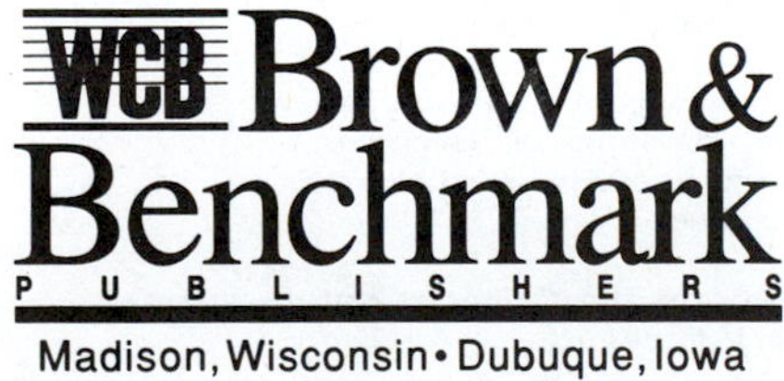

Book Team

Executive Editor *Ed Bartell*
Editor *Scott Spoolman*
Production Editor *Michelle M. Campbell*
Designer *Kristyn A. Kalnes*
Art Editor *Kathleen Huinker Timp*
Photo Editor *Robin Storm*
Permissions Coordinator *Gail I. Wheatley*
Visuals/Design Developmental Consultant *Marilyn A. Phelps*
Visuals/Design Freelance Specialist *Mary L. Christianson*
Marketing Manager *Pamela S. Cooper*
Advertising Manager *Susan J. Butler*

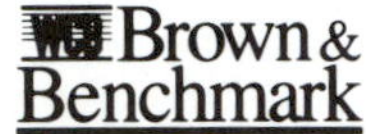

A Division of Wm. C. Brown Communications, Inc.

Executive Vice President/General Manager *Thomas E. Doran*
Vice President/Editor in Chief *Edgar J. Laube*
Vice President/Sales and Marketing *Eric Ziegler*
Director of Production *Vickie Putman Caughron*
Director of Custom and Electronic Publishing *Chris Rogers*

Wm. C. Brown Communications, Inc.

President and Chief Executive Officer *G. Franklin Lewis*
Corporate Senior Vice President and Chief Financial Officer *Robert Chesterman*
Corporate Senior Vice President and President of Manufacturing *Roger Meyer*

Cover image by © David Leach/Tony Stone Images

Consulting Editor A. Lockhart

Unless otherwise noted, all photos © Jennifer Wall and Nancy Murray.

Children's drawings on cover and interior by Geoffrey Campbell, 7; Justin Harms, 9; Jenny Harms, 7; and Lindsey Harms, 4.

A Times Mirror Company

Library of Congress Catalog Card Number: 93-70463

ISBN 0-697-12666-8

Printed in the United States of America by Wm. C. Brown Communications, Inc., 2460 Kerper Boulevard, Dubuque, IA 52001

10 9 8 7 6 5 4 3 2 1

Table of Contents

4 Developing a Quality Program

Section 2
Dance

5 The Dance Program

6 Teaching Dance

7 Learning Experiences in Dance

Section 3
Games

8 The Games Program

9 Teaching Games

10 Learning Experiences in Games

Section 4 Gymnastics

11 The Gymnastics Program

12 Teaching Gymnastics

13 Learning Experiences in Gymnastics

Preface

Children and Movement is written to meet the needs of students in professional programs which prepare teachers for elementary schools, and it is also for teachers already in the schools and teaching physical education. The intent is to provide a solid foundation for the development of an effective physical education program. In such a program, we try to meet the needs of every child, rather than the few who are highly skilled. We also wish to promote a balanced program, which develops skills in dance, games, and gymnastics. To do this we must

1. know the children,
2. understand the movement material in the lessons,
3. become versatile in our teaching methods,
4. be competent long- and short-term planners and evaluators.

As teachers, therefore, we need to be knowledgeable about *children, movement,* and *teaching*.

Children and Movement presents *one* way of developing and implementing a physical education program in elementary schools. Because of the range of abilities and interests found in a class of children, we believe that it is essential to provide learning experiences which allow for variations in response. We must, therefore, be able to design a variety of learning experiences which encourage all children to become skillful to the limit of their individual abilities. We need to ensure that the children are appropriately challenged, become successful, and gain a sense of achievement. Children's innate love of movement must be fostered so that they develop positive attitudes toward an active life-style.

The book has four sections; Foundations, Dance, Games, and Gymnastics. The nonlinear relationship between the chapters comprising these sections is visually represented in the following figure.

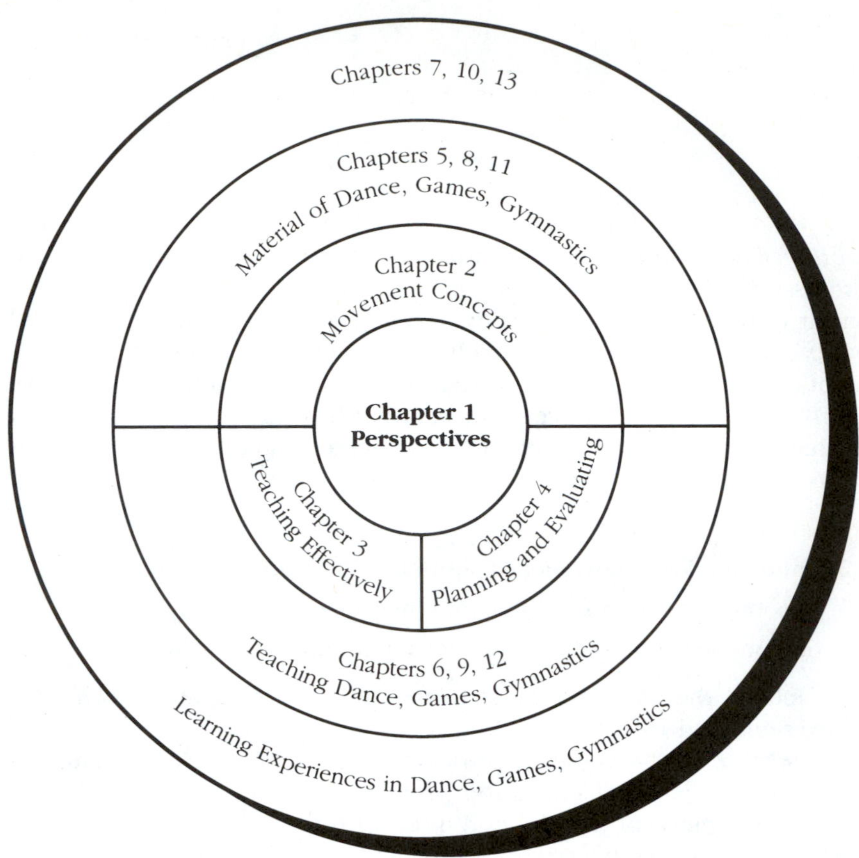

Section 1: Foundations

The foundations of the elementary school physical education program are introduced in this section. Chapter 1 outlines the importance of physical education for the child, and provides information on physical, cognitive, and social developmental sequences. The movement concepts, which form the content of the program, are introduced in chapter 2; teaching skills, appropriate for any physical activity, are discussed in chapter 3. Planning and evaluating, essential for the development of a quality program, are the focus of chapter 4.

After reading Section 1, you should be able to discuss

1. the characteristics and goals of a quality physical education program,
2. the movement concepts derived from Rudolf Laban's study of human movement,
3. various teaching skills which contribute to effective teaching and result in positive learning experiences for the children,
4. ways in which physical education programs may be planned and evaluated.

Section 2: Dance

This section presents the dance component of the elementary school physical education program, focusing on singing games, folk dance, and creative dance. Chapter 5 discusses the material of dance in terms of the movement concepts presented in chapter 2. Chapter 6 highlights some teaching skills and strategies that are specific to the dance context, and chapter 7 provides sample lesson plans and progressions.

After reading section 2, you should be able to discuss

1. the types of dance experiences that should be included in the program,
2. the application of the movement concepts in the dance context,
3. teaching skills that are specific to the dance lesson,
4. how dance lessons are developed so learning may be progressive.

Section 3: Games

The games component of the elementary school physical education program is discussed in this section. Chapter 8 presents the material of games, and distinguishes between low-organization, lead-up, and formal games. Chapter 9 focuses on teaching skills and strategies employed in games lessons, and chapter 10 provides sample lesson plans and progressions.

After reading Section 3, you should be able to discuss

1. the types of games experiences that should be included in the program,
2. how the movement concepts are applied in the games context,
3. teaching skills specific to games lessons,
4. how games lessons are developed so learning is challenging and progressive.

Section 4: Gymnastics

This section presents the gymnastics component of the elementary school physical education program. Chapter 11 discusses the movement material of gymnastics lessons; chapter 12 focuses on selected teaching skills specific to gymnastics lessons, and chapter 13 provides sample lesson plans and progressions.

After reading section 4, you should be able to discuss

1. the types of gymnastics experiences that are appropriate for the children,
2. how the movement concepts apply to gymnastics activities,
3. teaching skills that are relevant in gymnastics lessons,
4. the development of gymnastics lessons.

Throughout the text, there are boxes providing additional information. The "To Do" boxes reinforce an idea being discussed and they may be used for in-class activities or as mini-assignments. "Remember That" boxes are just that—small pieces of information we should keep in mind when we are preparing to teach or are actually teaching. "Fitness Facts" highlight a fitness element related to participation in dance, games, and gymnastics lessons. "Safety Tips" provide help with some organizational need during lessons.

The text and the accompanying *Lesson Plans for Dance, Games, and Gymnastics,* are linked by the inclusion of the relevant "Theme Index" at the end of chapters 5, 8, and 11.

We hope to stimulate your interest in teaching physical education to children. We have tried to make the book easy to read by writing in a personal style. Photographs, figures, tables, chapter summaries, review questions, and related readings have been included to clarify, reinforce, and extend the content.

Acknowledgments

We particularly wish to thank our friends and colleagues, Paulette Côté-Laurence, Valerie Drake, and V. Jean Wilson, for their detailed lesson plans which are in the accompanying *Lesson Plans for Dance, Games, and Gymnastics.* We hope these plans, together with the text, will provide you with the information you need in order to plan and implement your program.

In preparing this second edition of *Children and Movement,* we are indebted to many people who have provided us with a considerable amount of feedback. It is not possible to name everyone, but included are the many student teachers we and our colleagues have taught since the first edition was published. They have provided us with considerable information, and we hope they will accept our thanks in this general form.

Special recognition and thanks go to our reviewers, who provided us with much valued feedback:

M. Louise Humbert, *University of Saskatchewan*
Marliese Kimmerle, *University of Windsor*
Monica A. Magner, *Morehead State University*
Lynda E. Randall, *California State University—Fullerton*

We are particularly indebted to Jane Wardle, McGill University, Montreal, Quebec, for her detailed comments and encouragement.

We also thank Michelle Campbell and Scott Spoolman, our editors, who have been so supportive and ready to answer our questions; and the following principals, who allowed us to take photographs of children in their schools:

Bob Davis (Director of Athletics and Services), *Brock Sports School, Brock University, St. Catharines, Ontario*
Vern Johnstone, *Davin School, Regina, Saskatchewan*
Richard McGrail, *Spring Gardens Elementary School, Dollard des Ormeaux, Quebec*
Del Needham, *Douglas Park School, Regina, Saskatchewan*
James Taylor, *Richmond Street School, Thorold, Ontario*

We appreciate the generosity of Anne Brown, Ginette Gingras, and Sayla McCowan, teachers in the schools listed, for giving up their lesson and lunch times; Maureen Pritchard's class at Massey School, Regina, Saskatchewan, for the drawings used for the section opener collages; and the children, for their participation.

We wish to extend special appreciation to our families and friends for their support during this project.

Section 1

Foundations

What is important in physical education today is that we increase the number of people who are skilled in working with children in a loving, caring environment and in helping them learn about physical education.

Source: D. Siedentop, J. Herkowitz, and J. Rink, Elementary Physical Education Methods. *Copyright © 1984 Prentice-Hall, Inc., Englewood Cliffs, NJ.*

Chapter 1
Perspectives

Teaching physical education to children in elementary school is a stimulating, interesting, and satisfying challenge. It is a situation where both the teacher and the children can interact in a lively and fun manner. The lessons should be enjoyable, happy times for both you and the children.

> *Making discoveries about what one's body can do, becoming skilled, inventing ways of getting on and off an obstacle, creating one's own dance, maybe sharing the creation with a friend, are all rewarding experiences (Wall, 1981).*

Children love to move. They love to learn. As we observe children playing in the street or playground, we see that they move with total involvement. Movement is often enjoyed for the sheer pleasure of the sensations arising rather than for the specific purpose of "doing" something. Because movement is at the very core of our being, it is vitally important that all children have the opportunity to both learn to move and move to learn. As teachers, we have a responsibility to foster a love of physical activity so that children develop worthwhile skills and form a basis and appreciation for movement that will last throughout their lives.

Physical education is a time for doing. All children would rather do than watch or listen. Children naturally enjoy the lively atmosphere of the gymnasium or outdoors, and the freedom from the confines of the classroom. Equipment and other stimuli provide new challenge in movement, and children look forward to the opportunity to work alone or with others. As a classroom teacher, you have the advantage of children being naturally eager to participate in your lessons.

This chapter is intended to provide you with a basic understanding of how we can meet children's educational needs through physical education. We will first consider why physical education is important as a school subject.

The Importance of Physical Education

Physical education makes a unique contribution to a child's education because it promotes an appreciation of their body, the acquisition of physical skills, and increased physical abilities. Rich experiences in dance, games, and gymnastics provide children with the joy of acquiring skills in both expressive and functional movement, in cooperative and competitive situations, with other children and alone. Skills are explored, practiced, and mastered without equipment, with small equipment, and on large apparatus. Children will develop economy and efficiency of movement. The acquisition of skill may elicit in the child a feeling of the kinesthetic—the powerful feeling that the movement was "right."

Children naturally enjoy physical education.

Physical education is vital in the elementary school program as it has a paramount role in maintaining and/or enhancing children's fitness levels. Children's active, spontaneous play contributes to their growth and health (Bailey, Martin, & Howie, 1986). Frequent physical education classes are also important for wellness and the establishment of a healthy life-style. Every child should be offered the opportunity to benefit from engaging in regular, vigorous physical activity.

Most children, including those who are developmentally delayed, enjoy moving and want to become more competent and versatile as they plan and work with different challenges in different environments. Possession of physical skill is important for social reasons. Skillful movers are usually highly sociable children, so they are readily accepted into peer groups. Children recognize and appreciate competency in their peers and wish to be identified with competent children. Movement skills, therefore, may influence the friendships children develop. Children's abilities or inabilities may affect their popularity, self-confidence, self-image, and the competency to pursue new challenges and goals.

Because we pursue only those goals we feel are attainable, it is vital that children experience success in physical education. In order for them to develop motor skills and wholesome attitudes toward physical activity, a well-rounded program that provides for individual differences and encourages each child to succeed is extremely important. This implies that children are not to be expected to perform at the same level. Teachers set problem-solving tasks to which there are numerous ac-

Table 1.1

Goals of Physical Education

A quality program should help children do the following:

1. Acquire useful physical skills
2. Enhance physical growth and development
3. Maintain or enhance physical fitness
4. Acquire knowledge and understanding of movement
5. Apply movement knowledge in varied situations
6. Develop positive lifelong attitudes toward physical activity
7. Gain self-esteem and self-worth
8. Acquire desirable social skills
9. Enhance their creative abilities
10. Develop an aesthetic appreciation for movement

ceptable movement responses. As part of this process, it is vitally important that each child receives feedback and reinforcement in every class.

As long ago as 1951, Van Hagen, Dexter, and Williams wrote:

> *Educators have long recognized the need for a thorough program of physical education during the early years of childhood. These are the years of rapid growth and development when strength and stamina are acquired to form a healthy body. These are the years when posture habits are being formed and fundamental motor skills are being learned to give the individual poise, grace, and bodily efficiency. Physical education, with its many kinds of activities offered to develop the whole child, has an important place in the program of the elementary school.*

The goals of physical education programs are varied and diverse (table 1.1), and a quality physical education program will strive to meet them.

Our aim as teachers is to provide worthwhile physical activities that encourage children to become skillful movers in a variety of situations. Movement tasks that are challenging, fun, and rewarding will promote positive lifelong attitudes toward personal fitness, physical education, and leisure pursuits. We want to educate children to be physically literate, as Morison writes:

> *To be physically literate one should be creative, imaginative and clear in expressive movement, competent and efficient in utilitarian movement, and inventive, versatile and skillful in objective movement. The body is the means by which ideas and aims are carried out and, therefore, it must become both sensitive and deft (Morison, 1969).*

Children learn by doing.

To Do

Think back as far as you can to your earliest school experiences. What did you learn by *doing*?

Where Have We Come From?

To explain some of the diversity in today's literature about elementary school physical education, it may be valuable for you to understand a little of its recent history.

European gymnastic systems, the emergence of sports, and an emphasis on the military were characteristics of physical education at the beginning of the twentieth century. Termed physical training, students performed routine exercises in order to become physically fit. The teaching method most commonly employed was a command style, where the teacher set specific skills or exercises to be learned, and the class was expected to meet specific standards.

Several factors contributed to the transition from physical training to physical education. Immigrants from Germany had been influenced by the German gymnastic clubs; the Swedish and Danish brought to North

America their systematic exercises; and all immigrants contributed to the cultural mosaic with their national folk dances. The additional influence of strongly emerging games and sports in North American society accelerated progress toward "education" rather than "training."

Before the Second World War, Rudolf Laban, an Austrian dancer, escaped from Nazi Germany and fled with some of his colleagues to England, where he pursued his interest in "dance for all."

> *He postulated that, in addition to the fact that human movement was governed by physical laws, it also contained four principles which could best be comprehended by movement experiences (Hill, 1979).*

These four principles—body concepts, effort concepts, spatial concepts, and relationship concepts—deal with what the body does, where it moves, how it moves, and with whom or what it moves. (See chapter 2 for a thorough discussion of these principles.)

Laban was an inspiring individual who ". . . began to have profound influence on the teaching of physical education in general and dance and gymnastics in particular" (Wall, 1981). In Britain, many of the male teachers of physical training had gone to war and women (who were largely untrained) replaced men in educational settings. Some of these women had trained with Laban and employed his movement principles when teaching children.

There began a growing concern

> *. . . about the value of teaching isolated, unnatural movement patterns to children, children who, when left to play alone, exhibited exciting movement phrases (Wall, 1981).*

The countryside of wartime Britain, scattered with commando equipment, offered children new challenges.

> *They swung and balanced, climbed, dropped from improbable heights and extremely important, if left to themselves and not interfered with by adults, were sensible about taking safety precautions. Such equipment could be modified, set up in playgrounds and school halls, and in this way, physical education would be in a position to provide its own materials for learning. . . .*
>
> *So, these three quite diverse happenings—teachers with an understanding of Laban's principles, changes in philosophy about how children learn and the introduction of much freer forms of activity, all became consolidated into what was to result in a new thrust in physical education (Hill, 1979).*

Exchanges between Britain and the United States also influenced the changes in physical education. Many teachers who had studied with Laban immigrated to Canada and the United States, employing his movement concepts in their programs. At the same time, American teaching methodology was evolving, and American teachers who had traveled to Britain offered their insights into effective teaching methods. Thus, the marriage began—the use of Laban's concepts for content, with an array of teaching styles to create a positive learning environment to meet all children's needs. The result was much more effective physical education programs.

Where Are We Now?

Today's elementary school physical education programs vary greatly. While some schools boast large modern gymnasia with numerous and diverse equipment and ample funding, other schools have virtually no facility other than a tiny outdoor area or a dingy basement room with a few hoops and deflated balls for the children. Some school principals highly value their daily, quality physical education program, while others treat it as "time off" for the teacher to merely "referee" the children's play.

There is ample evidence that physical activity, physical fitness, and leisure activities are being recognized as important factors in a quality life-style for both children and adults. Thus, teachers of physical education are encouraged to incorporate these factors in their programs through regular, varied, enjoyable, and relevant movement experiences with children. This implies that movement activities are ***developmentally appropriate.***

A number of other positive developments have influenced physical education since you were in elementary school. These developments include a heightened appreciation for ***difference*** among students and their talents, increased appreciation for ***physical fitness,*** the importance of ***students' understanding*** and ***conceptualizing movement,*** an expansion of ***scientific knowledge*** of skill acquisition, the need for ***students' self-identity*** and ***self-worth*** and the value of ***aesthetic appreciation*** for movement. Each of these trends has influenced programs as teachers incorporate this knowledge to varying degrees in their programs. Thus, we may find programs that stress fitness, motor development, skill acquisition, social behavior, learning skills, and creative movement.

This text advocates an ecclectic, commonsense approach to teaching physical education. We believe that this approach, which focuses on ***children*** and ***movement,*** is particularly attuned to the recent concerns in the field and can incorporate these values in a unified program. Children should be the focus of our teaching in physical education; therefore, we need to be sensitive, open, and knowledgeable to meet students' needs.

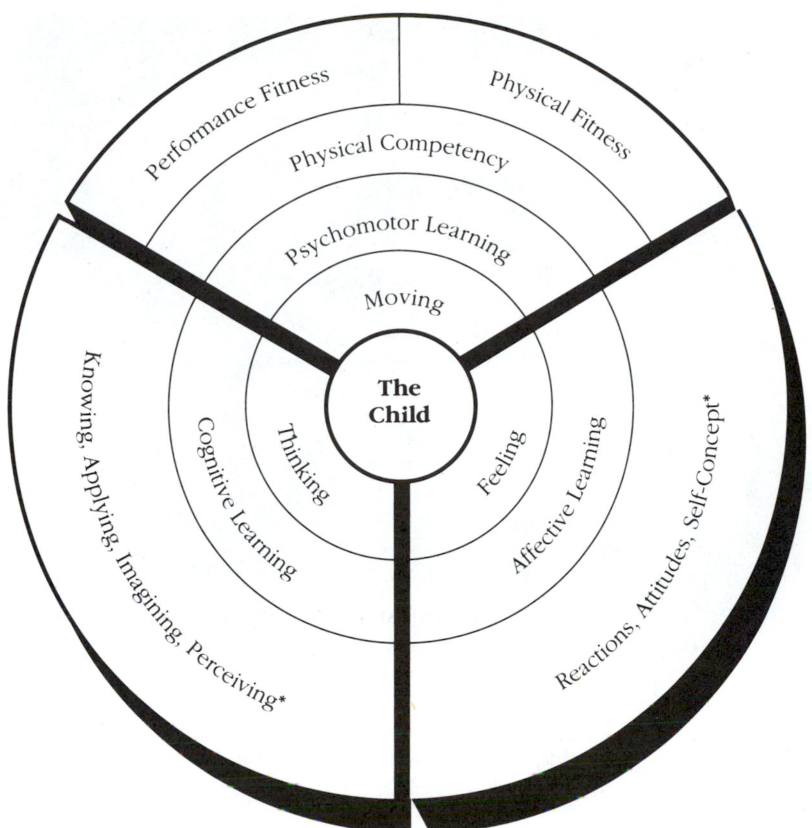

Figure 1.1 The moving, thinking, feeling child.

* Not all concepts are stated here.

The Moving, Thinking, Feeling Child

Children are complex beings whose thoughts, feelings, and actions are constantly in a state of flux. Because of the dynamic nature of children as they grow and mature, change in one element often affects the others. Thus, it is a "whole" child whom we must educate, not merely the physical or bodily aspect of the child (figure 1.1).

You will very likely study, or may have already studied some child psychology, so only a cursory overview on cognitive or affective development will be included here. While some important points will be dis-

a.

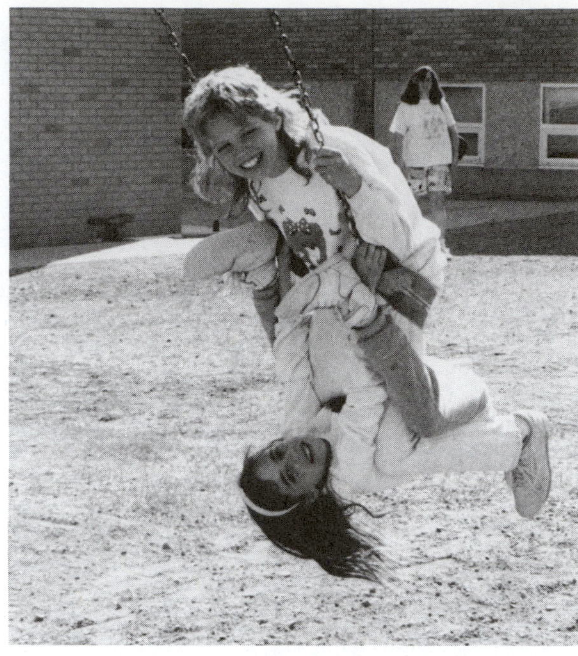

b.

We are concerned with both (*a*) cognitive abilities and (*b*) affective abilities, as well as physical abilities.

cussed briefly in this chapter, you will see how we apply cognitive and affective development theory in the teaching chapters on dance, games, and gymnastics.

The Moving Child

Our primary goal as teachers of physical education is, of course, to educate children as they move, termed the **psychomotor development** of the child. In order to understand psychomotor development, we need to appreciate some basic concepts that affect children's progression through various stages in the process of acquiring movement competency.

Each of us grows and matures in much the same way under healthy conditions. Our growth and development is largely predetermined by our bodies. Most of us learn to walk at about twelve months, run at age three, and skip at age six. Despite our individual differences, we can predict that children of the same age will move quite similarly. This is particularly true of younger children performing **fundamental movements.** Fundamental movements are those movements which are fundamental to refined, sport-specific movements. The fundamental movements include basic locomotor patterns, such as walking, running, jumping, skipping, and galloping; skills of balancing, weightbearing, stretching, curling, and twisting; and manipulative activities, such as

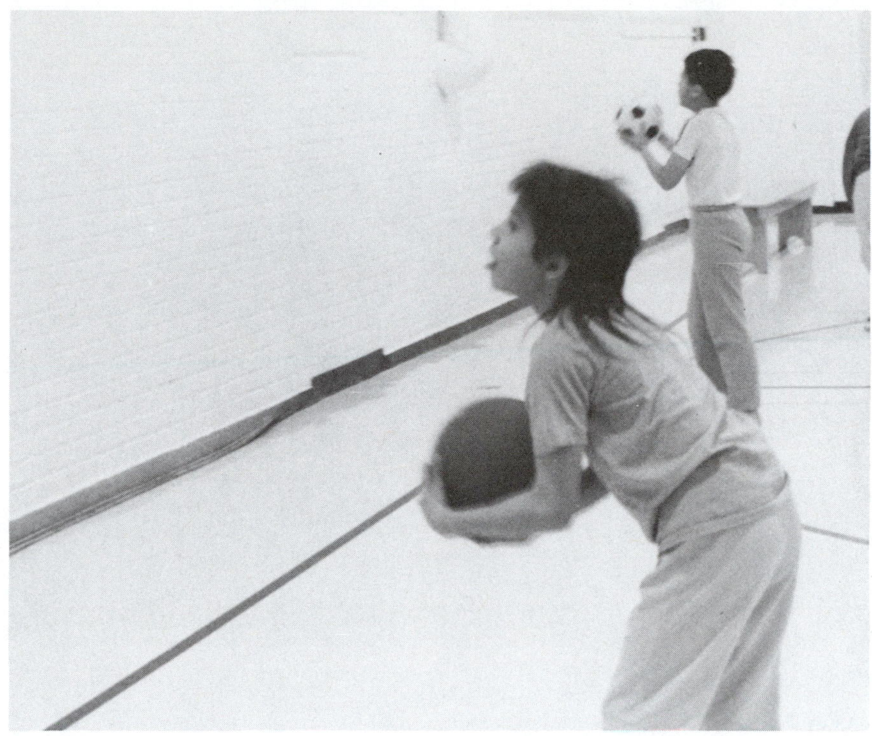

We are concerned with psychomotor abilities.

throwing, catching and striking. For example, the lay-up in basketball is a refined skill but is comprised of numerous fundamental movements including running, dribbling, skipping, jumping, stretching, and throwing.

You will find that children's locomotor patterns and manipulative patterns are characterized by similar qualities, which we group in particular **stages.** For example, as the preschooler learns to run, strides are short and the feet are placed wide apart, rather than one in front of the other. As children mature, the whole body becomes involved in the action. Young children use the fewest body parts possible to throw or catch a ball. No steps are taken, and their bodies are firmly planted on the ground. As children mature, they tend to involve more of their upper body, so trunk rotation occurs. Years later, at about age seven or eight, they will take a step as the ball is thrown and then may perform the mature pattern in upper elementary school, providing there has been sufficient correct practice.

When the child is born, the head constitutes about one quarter of the total length of the body. Thus, the center of gravity is high, making balancing difficult from infancy through preschool. The trunk develops prior to the limbs and extremities. As a result, children are able to gain

Balance is difficult for young children because of their physical proportions.

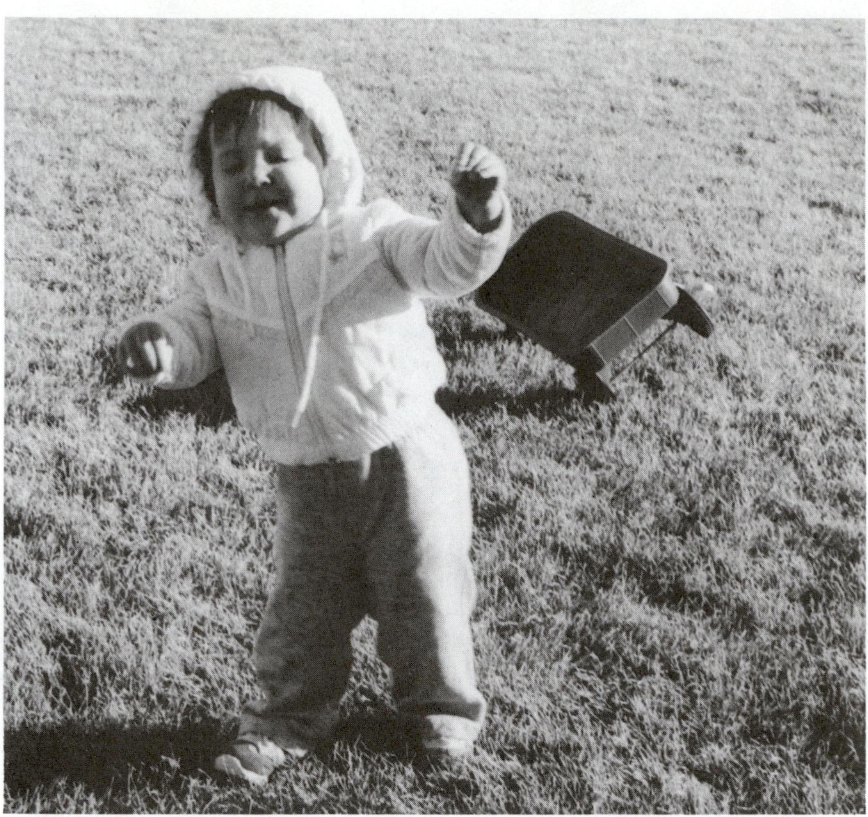

control over the trunk of their body before limbs, hands, and feet. This concept infers that control proceeds from mass or **gross** muscles to specific or **fine** muscles. For a child, large movements are much easier than fine, precise movements.

When a child enters kindergarten, an array of gross motor skills have been mastered and many others are being acquired. The delight these children experience in gross motor activities is obvious. They seem to speak and react with their entire body. Running, jumping, climbing, hopping, leaping, skipping, and galloping engrosses their whole being. Fine motor skills, such as cutting, pasting, printing, drawing, coloring, and tracing, are much slower to develop and require much practice.

A quality elementary physical education program will take both gross and fine motor control into account. Gross motor activities slowly give way to skills that require both gross and fine muscle control. When children gain control over their bodies, they will want to spend more time handling objects, called **manipulative activities.** The simple skill of running and stopping emerges to be used later in a game situation where the child runs, stops, dodges an opponent, catches, and then aims

Each child is unique.

the ball at a target. Gross motor skills demonstrated without equipment progress to a combination of gross and fine motor skills with equipment. The skills demanded of the child should always proceed from simple to complex.

There will be some children who are advanced in their motor development and skills, while others will lag behind. This is due to many factors. Some children may have experienced a growth spurt. These children are constantly accommodating their movements to rapidly changing physical proportions. Still others may be small and physically immature when compared to their peers. Often these smaller children are agile and quick, excelling at dance and gymnastics activities. An eight-year-old child highly skilled in catching and throwing will not necessarily be equally adept at striking or kicking skills. Although some of the movement patterns and spatial strategies may be similar, direct transfer does not usually occur.

> **A Quality Physical Education Program** provides all children with frequent and age appropriate opportunities that help them develop competence and confidence (COPEC , 1992).

The Process of Skill Acquisition

It is quite remarkable that despite all of the obvious differences between children, the process of skill acquisition is relatively predictable as children grow and mature. Table 1.2 outlines this process, in which basic movements progress to complex movements and finally to refined movement skills. In the elementary years, gross motor activities that require primarily large muscle control are developed through locomotion, balancing, and weightbearing. As some degree of proficiency is acquired, children will be challenged by manipulative activities, most of which

Remember That

Some children may be developmentally delayed in relation to their peers. While this, of course, depends on their condition, children may "catch up" in due time or reach a plateau at some point in the continuum of skill acquisition.

Table 1.2

Process of Skill Acquisition

BASIC → Gross motor activities		COMPLEX → Fine motor activities		REFINED Specialized skills
Require large muscle control		*Require small muscle control*		*Require fine and gross muscle control*
Arms	Shoulders	Fingers	Toes	Balancing on hands
Legs	Hips	Hands	Feet	Cartwheeling
Trunk	Back	Wrists	Ankles	
		Neck		
NONMANIPULATIVE ACTIVITIES		**MANIPULATIVE ACTIVITIES**		**MANIPULATIVE ACTIVITIES**
Develop control of the body		*Develop control of objects*		*Ability to control both the body and objects*
1. Locomotion:		1. Projecting:		Tennis serve
walking	running	throwing	rolling	Lay-up
rolling	skipping	bouncing	kicking	Slap shot
jumping	climbing	2. Receiving:		
galloping	sliding	catching	trapping	
leaping	hopping	3. Retaining:		
2. Balancing		dribbling	carrying	
3. Weightbearing:				
hanging	stretching			
swinging	twisting			
gripping	contracting			

require a degree of fine motor skill. Specialized skills emerge as children discover efficient and effective movements in dance, games, and gymnastics.

Many researchers, such as Gallahue (1987), Roberton and Halverson (1984), and Wickstrom (1983) have studied children's movement patterns extensively. This material is extremely valuable for your understanding of developmentally appropriate activities for particular age groups or other groupings of children. Because it is beyond the scope of this text, we encourage you to seek the information for more detail or when you are planning activities for children.

Remember That

Practice makes permanent! Make sure the children are practicing *correctly*.

The process of learning new skills is complex. What do we need to know to run, catch a baseball, or serve a tennis ball? Perhaps you are adept at all of these skills; perhaps not. What we know is that it is not maturation alone that makes us adept at particular skills, but there is a

Table 1.3

Developmental Considerations for Planning Children's Movement Experiences

Skill	Easier	More difficult
Running	Alone	In a tag game
Galloping	Forward	To music, sideways
Twist, jump sequence	On a mat	On a bench with a partner
Catching	Tossed beach ball	Thrown tennis ball
Throwing	Tennis ball	Basketball
Batting	Plastic ball off a tee	Batting a pitched baseball
Kicking	Kicking a stationary soccer ball	Running and kicking a passed soccer ball
Balancing	Balancing on one foot	Jumping and landing on one foot

complex interplay of cognition, movement, and emotion. Researchers in **perceptual development** (Fleishman, 1978; Kerr, 1982; Magill, 1989; and Schmidt, 1991) study how we process movement information. This literature offers much relevant information about the spatial and temporal (space and time) decisions a child must make in movement activities. When you plan movement activities for children, you will need to consider the complexity of both the skill and the environment. Some considerations to help you are presented in table 1.3.

> **A Quality Physical Education Program** gives every child the opportunity to practice skills at high rates of success adjusted for his or her individual skill level (COPEC, 1992).

Physical Competency

Quality physical education programs ensure that physical competency is developed while the children develop movement skills. Physical competency may be divided into two components: physical fitness and motor abilities (figure 1.2).

Physical Fitness

One of the primary objectives of the physical education program should be to increase—or at least maintain—each child's level of fitness. Our level of fitness is influenced by our diet and our genetic inheritance, as well as our exercise patterns. Our level of fitness is enhanced through regular, vigorous activity. Because our fitness level is temporary, it is vitally important that children experience vigorous activity in physical education at least three times a week. It is also important that the movement experiences we design for the children are fun and rewarding for the children, so they will develop an appreciation and love of movement, whatever form it takes.

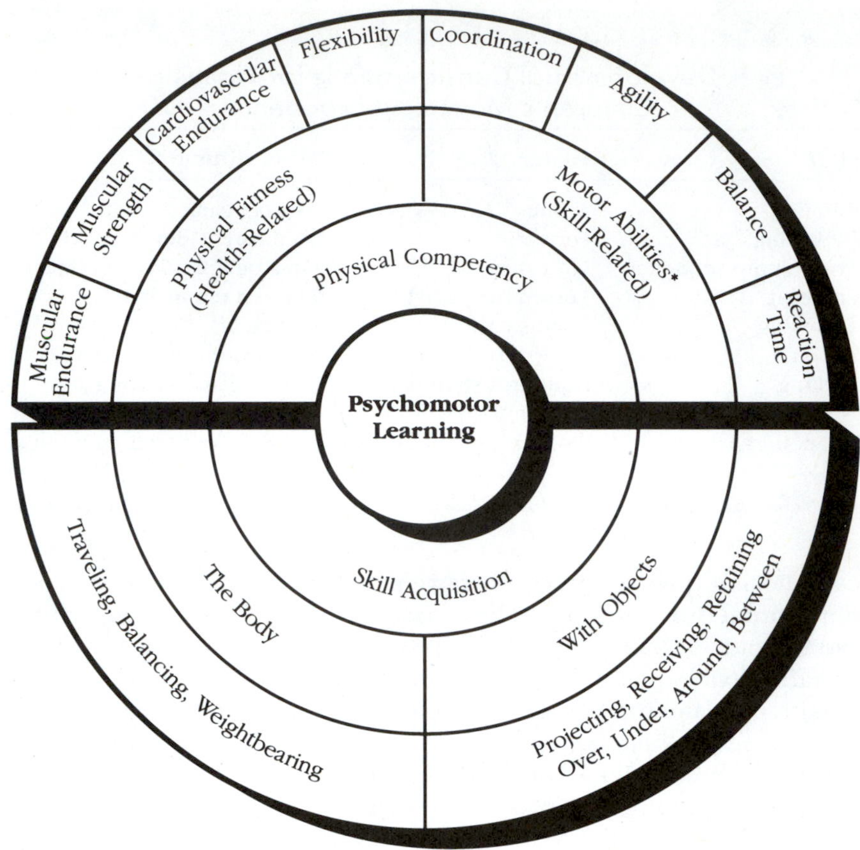

Figure 1.2 The psychomotor domain.

Within any typical class, there will be a child who runs the fastest, another who is declared the strongest, and possibly another who boasts being able to do the "splits." Each child is demonstrating an admirable ability in one of the following four components of fitness:

1. Cardiovascular endurance
2. Muscular endurance
3. Muscular strength
4. Flexibility

In order to maintain or increase one's fitness level, at least twenty minutes of activity three or four times a week, which increases the heart rate significantly, is necessary. Regular physical education classes are essential if this objective of increased fitness is to be realized.

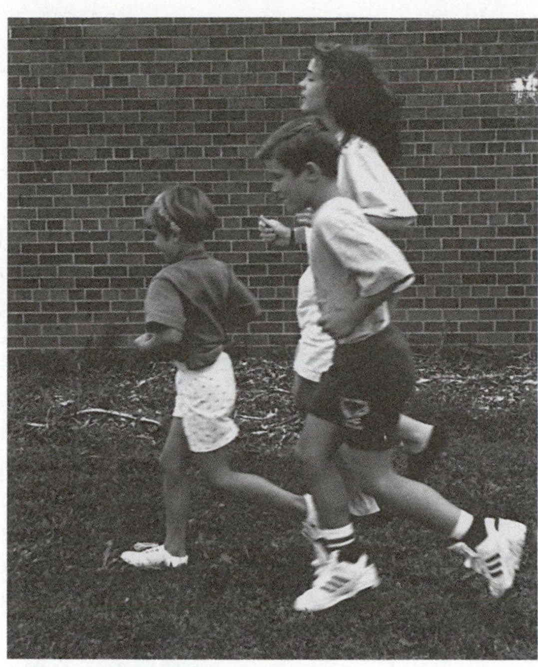

Jogging promotes cardiovascular endurance.

1. **Cardiovascular endurance.** This refers to the body's ability to pump blood from the heart to supply the muscles with oxygen over a long period of time. Any strenuous activity engaged in over three minutes that significantly increases the heart rate is considered beneficial to the cardiovascular system. This is aerobic activity. Examples of these low-power output activities are running, swimming, skipping, or biking for an extended period of time.

   In the physical education lesson, the introductory activity warms up the student—a vitally important component of fitness. Cardiovascular activity may also be found in games and folk dance lessons where a great deal of running or jumping is involved.

2. **Muscular endurance.** This refers to the individual's ability to use particular muscles repeatedly. Most activities that tax the cardiovascular system also tax the particular muscles necessary to complete the exercise. Examples of these high-power output activities include practicing a handstand or cartwheel repeatedly, climbing a high rope, or jumping over and over again.

   Gymnastic activities that involve taking weight on the hands promote muscular endurance of the arms. In the games lesson, the repeated serving of a volleyball or throwing and catching of a playground ball require muscular endurance of the upper body.

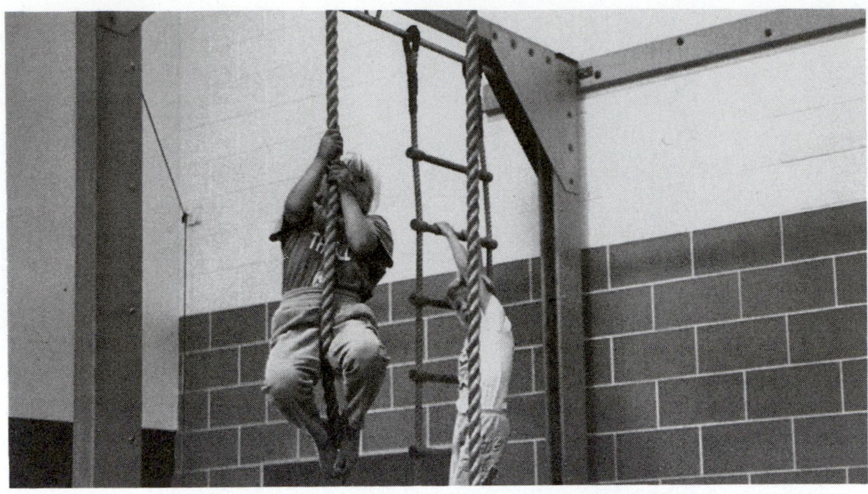

Rope climbing requires muscular endurance.

Leaping, jumping, and balancing activities in the dance lesson require muscular endurance of the legs.

3. **Muscular strength.** Strength refers to a muscle's ability to work over a short period of time (ten seconds to three minutes). This is anaerobic activity. Muscular strength refers to the maximum force exerted by a muscle when contracted maximally. Examples of activities that require muscular strength are sprinting a short distance, lifting a heavy object, and opening an uncooperative jar.

   In dance, games, and gymnastics, the ability to jump high and with ease is an asset. This requires strength. Whether Cossak dancing, maintaining an unusual body shape in dance, balancing on the hands in gymnastics, or holding a defensive position in games, strength is an important aspect of fitness to consider.

Handstands require muscular strength.

4. **Flexibility.** This term refers to the range of motion about a particular joint of the body. Touching your toes is a common exercise. This is an indication of hip and lower back flexibility. While children are extremely flexible, it is evident that the body loses some flexibility due to the growth and maturation process. It appears that our level of flexibility may be in part due to genetic endowment, as well as environmental factors or the activities in which we engage. If, for example, a child has been involved in gymnastics, ballet, wrestling, or diving, a higher level of flexibility may carry over into his or her adult life. Males are usually less flexible simply because typically male-oriented activities do not require good flexibility and thus flexibility is not worked on during training. If movements that increase flexibility are not practised, then a reduced level of flexibility may be anticipated. It

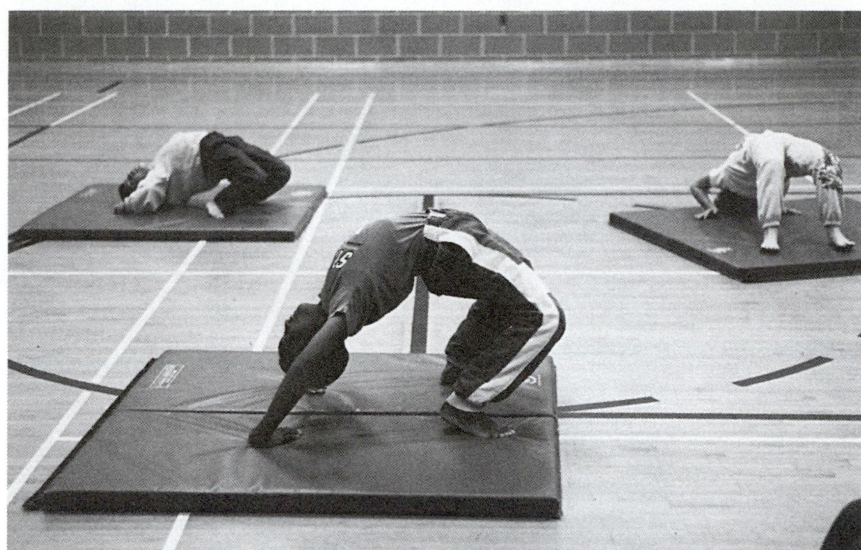

Hip and back flexibility are required to arch backward.

is important for every teacher to include activities that promote flexibility both to increase range of motion and reduce the possibility of injury.

Flexibility is primarily developed in physical education through dance and gymnastic activities that stretch the muscles.

> **In A Quality Physical Education Program,** "children participate in activities that are designed to help them understand and value the important concepts of physical fitness and the contribution they make to a heathy life-style" (COPEC, 1992).

To Do

1. Run up and down a set of stairs until you are tired. Was it your legs that "gave out"? If so, the muscular endurance of your legs wasn't equal to your cardiovascular endurance. If your chest hurt and you had "no air," it was your cardiovascular system that couldn't keep up to the muscular endurance of your legs.
2. Place one hand on the back of your neck and your other hand on your back. Slowly move your hands toward each other. Can you touch your fingertips together? If so, you have good shoulder flexibility.
3. How many unassisted sit-ups can you do in thirty seconds? How many push-ups can you do in thirty seconds? These exercises will test your muscular strength and endurance. If you can do 12–15, give yourself a pat on the back!

This is an indication of good shoulder flexibility.

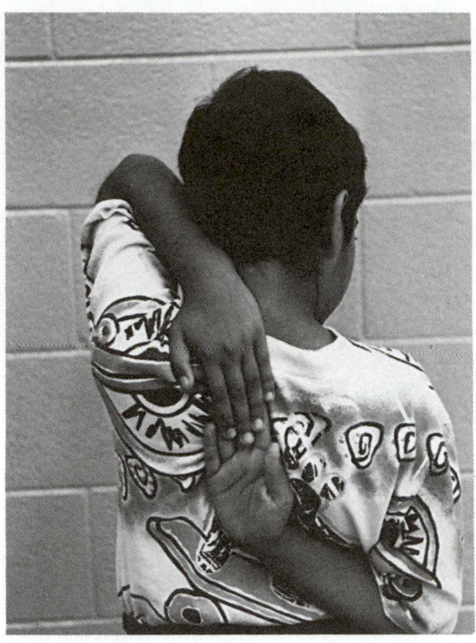

Fitness Programs

The importance of physical fitness was demonstrated in the United States through the unification of the President's Challenge and the Physical Best Program into the President's Youth Fitness Program. The joint program features the Physical Best test items and educational materials, while the President's Challenge award system was adapted to criterion-referenced assessment standards (AAHPERD, 1992). In Canada, The Canada Fitness Awards Program has been replaced with The Active Living Challenge Program, which reflects a shift away from performance and awards to supporting a developmental learning process for active living. The objective of the new program is to encourage and enable daily, enjoyable physical activity throughout life and will consist of four programs, each aimed at a particular age group and emphasizing a particular theme (CAHPER, 1992).

Motor Abilities

Motor ability refers to "a capacity of the individual that is related to the performance of a variety of tasks" (Fleishman, 1978). This directly affects our quality of performance and relates to our ability to participate with ease and efficiency. Motor abilities include coordination, power, agility, balance, and speed.

We enhance these motor abilities in children through varied and challenging activities. For example, when children are encouraged to run into the empty spaces and change direction in the gymnasium, they are taxing their agility, power, and coordination. In gymnastics, motor abilities are developed in activities where timing is crucial, for example, when matching a partner's movements or in balancing activities where the supporting surface is small.

The Thinking Child

Physical education has a special role in cognitive development. We call the subject physical *education,* which implies the transmission and reception of knowledge and thought, and the application of concepts. Thought (conscious or subconscious) should accompany all motion, and difficult movements and sequences require refined thought.

In physical education, we focus on the specific concepts of body, space, effort, and relationships (see chapter 2). Because of their relevance to all movement, these concepts form the basis of the subject. One of the objectives of physical education is for children to understand the principles governing movement because this understanding promotes progression in physical skill.

The physical education program should promote cognitive development in many ways. Even as the class enters the activity area or outdoor setting, children adapt to a new learning environment—one of large spaces, various equipment, and a modified set of behavioral guidelines.

As learning begins, a specialized vocabulary is used and language is developed. Because the aim is to structure lessons around a specific movement concept, all activity should pertain to that concept. Children will gain insight by responding to the task and receiving feedback as movement concepts are studied.

> **A Quality Physical Education Program** offers "experiences which encourage children to question, integrate, analyze, communicate and apply cognitive concepts, as well as gain a multicultural view of the world, thus making physical education a part of the total educational experience" (COPEC, 1992).

The range of task structure, from closed (with little or no choice of response) to open (which allows for much individual interpretation), encourages the child to think as the problem is solved (see chapter 3). Although the task may be wide in scope, "practice what you learned yesterday," or more specifically, "work with your ball at a high level," in both the child must consciously decide which movements are appropriate. Questioning often helps to reinforce and clarify facts and concepts, and assist children in applying new movement ideas. Some examples follow:

1. Where should you look if you are pressing?
2. What would your pathway look like if you were to meander?

The child must use cognitive abilities in movement activities.

3. Can you clap to this music?
4. Change your punching action so that it is very s-l-o-w. What word can you use to describe this new movement?
5. We absorb force when we bend our arms in catching a ball. How can you absorb force when you jump?
6. How should you use your arms to jump higher?
7. How can you use space more effectively when you are passing the ball around an opponent?
8. Which rolls, a ball or a box? What body shape do you need to roll smoothly?
9. How should you place your hands so that you have a firm base in a headstand?
10. What kind of a body shape is best when you want to be very stable?

Thus, the cognitive domain is developed. Quality movement is a major objective of any physical education program and is the result of creating, analyzing, memorizing, concentrating, and applying knowledge.

The Feeling Child

Attitudes, moods, self-concept, and social awareness affect all of our feelings. Sometimes called "gut reactions," the source of our feelings may be very spontaneous or may be the result of expertise or experience. While the affective domain has been largely ignored in the educational curricula of the past, educators are becoming increasingly aware of the vital importance of enhancing the child's self-awareness.

The environment of the physical education class affects the feelings of every child. Teachers who encourage and appreciate individual differences will foster desirable attitudes towards physical education. Our ultimate goal is to develop a positive class environment in which everyone may be prepared to risk without fear of ridicule.

For this reason, teachers must aim to treat all children as unique human beings. The teacher who praises positive efforts helps create a friendly atmosphere where children feel welcome. Thus, children's self-esteem and social skills are enhanced.

Positive teacher behavior includes calling children by name, ensuring that various children take on leadership roles, and ensuring children are not singled out for negative reasons. Therefore, such activities as elimination games are unacceptable as they draw attention to the lesser skilled children and punish them through exclusion from the activity. All children, regardless of ability, need as much opportunity for skill acquisition as possible. The process is cyclical in nature, as illustrated in figure 1.3.

Because children learn from observing and interacting with their peers, observation and close student interaction (e.g., "help your friend improve the end of her sequence") is of tremendous value for skill development. Teachers may stop a class to have them observe quality movement or a unique response to the task. We do not expect every child to work at a specified skill level nor respond in the same manner, so it is possible for every child in the class to be offered the opportunity to demonstrate occasionally.

Appropriate social groupings are very important. A positive learning environment will be the result of careful planning of which children work together, how many children are in the group, as well as how they are spatially placed. A space overcrowded with gymnastic apparatus and lacking in safety is not conducive to positive or happy peer interaction. When a game is played with too many children it restricts activity, and the children's resulting boredom may lead to negative peer interaction. In dance, creating groups that are too large will result in lack of cooperation, because of the children's difficulty of dealing with too many people and ideas. Thus, the teacher must be cognizant of age appropriate social groupings (table 1.4).

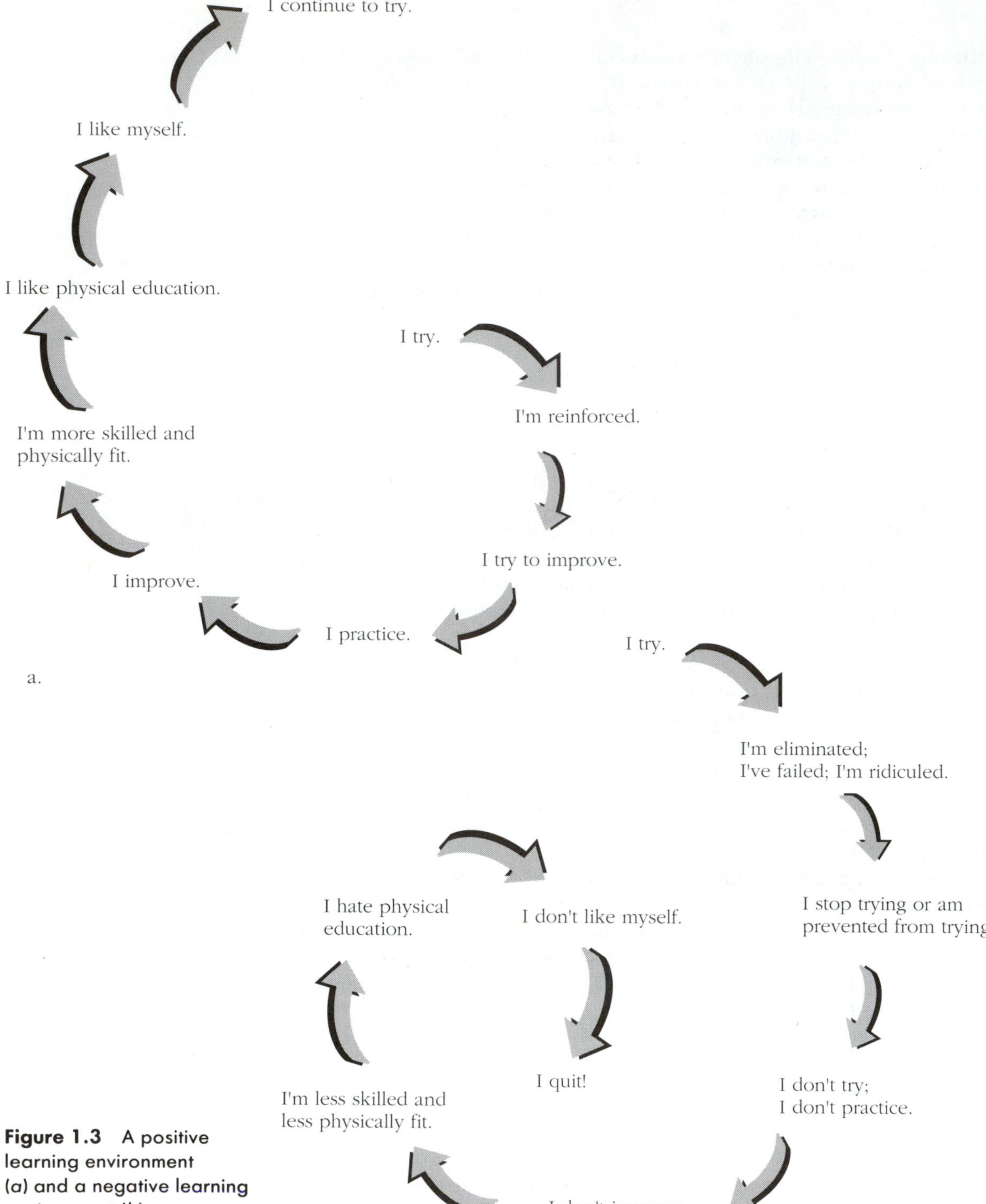
I continue to try.
I like myself.
I like physical education.
I try.
I'm reinforced.
I'm more skilled and physically fit.
I try to improve.
I improve.
I practice.
a.
I try.
I'm eliminated; I've failed; I'm ridiculed.
I hate physical education.
I don't like myself.
I stop trying or am prevented from trying.
I quit!
I'm less skilled and less physically fit.
I don't try; I don't practice.
I don't improve.
b.

Figure 1.3 A positive learning environment (*a*) and a negative learning environment (*b*).

Table 1.4

Physical, Cognitive, and Social Development of Children, as Related to Age

AGE 5		
Physical development		
Characteristics	***Implications***	***Activity suggestions***
Children need vigorous activity.	Daily lessons of twenty to thirty minutes will promote healthy growth and development.	Every child should engage in maximum activity for a maximum amount of time.
Growth rate is decreasing.	General movement abilities are improving.	Body awareness activities should be used—body parts, weightbearing, locomotion.
Percentage of muscle mass is increasing; body fat is decreasing.	Children are becoming stronger, more agile, and are very flexible.	Dance, gymnastic, and locomotor activities promote agility and flexibility.
Children lack muscular endurance.	Children tire easily and may require moments of rest.	Alternate periods of intense activity with periods of a less strenuous nature.
Center of gravity is still high.	Sense of equilibrium is developing; balance is sometimes difficult.	Rolling, hopping, leaping, jumping—weightbearing on various body parts promote good balance.
Energy is directed toward mastering bodily control and, to a lesser extent, control of objects.	Activity without equipment is important.	Locomotor activities in dance, games, and gymnastics should be stressed.
Gross motor skills are much easier than fine motor skills.	Locomotor skills are easier than manipulative skills.	Gross motor activities, nonmanipulative activities.
Most can run with adult form.	Running may be used in activities.	Stopping, starting, dodging, changing direction, pathways, and speed in running—chasing games are a favorite.

Physical development		
Characteristics	***Implications***	***Activity suggestions***
Some locomotor movements are still being acquired.	Much time should be spent on locomotor activities.	Rolling, jumping, hopping, leaping, skipping, and galloping, presented in various ways.
Beginning of object handling.	Manipulation of objects is difficult: may throw and strike (project) with some proficiency; may catch and trap (receive) with difficulty; may bounce and dribble (retain) with difficulty.	More time should be spent on nonmanipulative skills than manipulative skills. Throw with small balls; strike with a large bat or hand at a stationary ball. Catching and trapping is easiest when rolled or bounced with a large ball. Large balls should be used. A predictable surface, such as the wall or floor, should be used in initial development of ball skills.
Children may excel in one skill and find another difficult.	Teacher should allow for and anticipate individual differences.	Skilled children should be given additional challenges; lesser skilled children should be encouraged but not pressured.
Cognitive development		
Children have a short attention span.	Change activities/tasks often.	Directions for and duration of activities must be brief. Children may need to be reminded of task.
Amount of concentration varies.	Children are prone to accidents, may forget easily, can't work alone for lengthy periods.	Remind children of task and safety procedures.
Repetition is enjoyed and provides security.	Routines are necessary; favorite activities are enjoyed repeatedly.	Establish routine; repeat favorite activities; and repeat mastered skills.

Cognitive development		
Characteristics	***Implications***	***Activity suggestions***
Children always want to be involved.	A variety of equipment should be supplied for every child.	Children should be as active as possible with their own equipment.
Children are eager to learn.	Children enjoy solving problems and discovering.	Problem solving is ideal with much exploration and time to discover. Apply Laban's concepts of body, effort, space, and relationships.
Children enjoy music and rhythmic activities.	Children keep good time to rhythmic music and create their own rhythms.	Music and percussion instruments may be used extensively in dance.
Children are imaginative and love dramatics.	Children enjoy the expressive nature of dance.	Foster use of the imagination, creativity, and dramatics.
General lack of fear exhibited by children.	Children should work within their capabilities.	Children should be taught safety rules and procedures to prevent injuries.

Social development		
Children are very egocentric.	Cooperation with a partner may be difficult.	Working alone is best; short periods of working with a partner.
	Children have difficulty in seeking a team goal.	Team games present a problem because the child is not always active.
	Scores are not important.	Racing and chasing games (tag) are appropriate.
Children need approval and much praise.	Provide experiences that will challenge the child yet foster success.	Give praise for quality work, good efforts, and recent accomplishments.
Children are learning to share and take turns.	Children will share and take turns if the activity is appropriate.	Children should not be forced to work with others.

AGES 6 AND 7		
Physical development		
Characteristics	***Implications***	***Activity suggestions***
Children need vigorous activity.	Daily lessons of thirty minutes will ensure healthy development.	Every child should engage in maximum activity for a maximum amount of time.
There are steady gains in height and weight.	Health improves and children are stronger and more physically adept.	Much repetition of previously acquired skills is required in new and varied situations.
Legs are still short in relation to trunk; however, legs are growing rapidly.	Children may appear awkward at times and adept at others.	Much activity is needed to enhance control of the body and, to a lesser extent, control of objects.
Center of gravity is near adult location.	Activities requiring balance are important.	Repeat simple challenges requiring good balance; introduce new ones on floor and apparatus.
Children have improved ability to focus eyes and track objects.	Manipulation of objects is steadily improving.	Catching, trapping with feet, dribbling with hands or feet are appropriate activities.
Children enjoy constant activity and have sudden bursts of energy.	Children should have maximum activity within a lesson.	Directions should be short, each child should have equipment.
Children are mastering or have mastered most locomotor movements.	Running, skipping, galloping, hopping, leaping, jumping, and rolling play a large role in the program.	Much repetition of locomotor activities in dance, games, and gymnastics is needed.
Skill and control is developing in gross motor activities.	Repeat gross motor skills acquired; practice new gross motor skills.	Create new balances, shapes, or ways of traveling on body parts, in new directions and pathways, on or with various equipment.

Physical development		
Characteristics	***Implications***	***Activity suggestions***
Manipulative skills are slowly developing.	Children vary in their ability to manipulate equipment. Most can kick, bounce a ball, throw, and catch.	Manipulate equipment with various body parts. Extensions, such as paddles, sticks, and racquets, are often too difficult. Batting is appropriate if the ball is stationary.
Fine motor skills are slowly developing.	Activities requiring small muscle control are difficult.	Ball activities are important, but bean bags, hoops, and skipping ropes should be used as well to encourage fine muscle control.
Abilities of males and females are not different.	Differences in ability due to gender are not apparent.	All children should be encouraged to participate to their best ability.
Cognitive development		
Attention span is still short.	Lessons should be short with varied activities.	Change activities/tasks often. Keep directions short and simple.
Children have improved reasoning powers.	Children may be reasoned with effectively.	Children will understand clear, short directions and explanations.
Children discourage easily and have strong desire to please others.	Children need praise, encouragement, and understanding.	Each child should receive positive reinforcement; children should not be singled out for negative reasons.
Chidren are imaginative and creative, enjoy dramatics.	Activities should foster creativity and imagination.	Create games, dance, and gymnastics sequences. Dramatic movement is enjoyed.
"Why?" is often asked.	The program should encourage reasoning, problem solving, and memory.	Set tasks using problem-solving and limitation methods of teaching.

Physical development		
Characteristics	***Implications***	***Activity suggestions***
Memory is improving, though it may lapse.	A well-planned program should provide continuity by building on previous work.	Children may require reminders for safety, sequence work, and previous activities.
Children have a greater purpose in work than at age five.	Children have a tremendous desire to learn new skills and master others.	Repeat body and space concepts without equipment. Provide much time for work with equipment in various ways.
Concepts of time, weight, and space are developing.	Concepts of time, weight, and space should be included.	Concepts of fast and slow, heavy and light, directions, pathways, and levels should be explored.
Responds well to rhythmic music.	Various kinds of recorded music, as well as percussion instruments, are enjoyed.	Dance activities should involve the use of music.
Social development		
Sense of humor is not mature.	Children will laugh at silly situations—slapstick humor.	Sarcasm will be perceived as ridicule.
Transition period is required between individual and group play.	Would rather play alone or with one other, but groups of three or four may be suitable at times.	Children should work primarily alone or with one other; groups of five or more are ineffective.
Friendships shift continually.	Teacher should allow for spontaneous groupings.	Sensitivity to children's social preferences is important.
There is little differentiation between friends of same or opposite sex.	Children will gladly play with a member of the opposite sex.	Pairing children is not a problem due to gender.
A child will recognize that some children are more skilled than others.	Program should allow for individual differences.	Children should be openly praised for skill, although every child needs praise and reinforcement.

Social development		
Characteristics	***Implications***	***Activity suggestions***
Children are usually in awe of teacher and may be intimidated by teacher who knows all.	Teacher should be aware of this responsibility.	Children should be free to ask questions, and the teacher should openly admit mistakes or lack of knowledge.
	AGES 8 AND 9	
	Physical development	
Children need vigorous activity.	Lessons should be thirty to forty-five minutes long, at least three times a week.	Maximum amount of children should participate for a maximum amount of time.
Height and weight gain is strong and steady.	Children have good balance, agility, flexibility, and strength.	Previously learned skills may be used in more challenging ways.
Upper body is in good proportion to lower body.	Balance is excellent and should be applied in dance, games, and gymnastic activities.	Balance activities that challenge the student in both body and object handling should be included.
Usually, there is little difference in physique of males and females, though there may be some early maturing 9-year-olds.	Males and females should engage in all activities together.	Both males and females should be exposed to a wide range of activities.
Physiological growth changes occur in females from eight to twelve years of age and in males from nine to thirteen years of age.	Some early maturers experience hormonal imbalances.	Plan activities that provide for differences in physical and emotional maturity, such as creating games, gymnastic and dance sequences, and playing cooperative games.
Distinct individual differences occur due to physical maturation and past experience.	Children need a well-balanced program.	Choose challenging, success-oriented activities in dance, games, and gymnastics.

Physical development		
Characteristics	***Implications***	***Activity suggestions***
Children are active and energetic and may be overactive with hurried carelessness.	Children need much activity and encouragement to tenaciously pursue new skills and sequences.	Children work alone or in pairs to maximize activity and skill development.
Eye-hand and eye-foot coordination is quite good.	Skills with equipment can begin to progress to being sport specific.	Practice ball control with feet and hands alone, with a partner, and in small groups.
	Include such extensions as racquets, paddles, sticks, and scoops in program.	Children work alone and with a partner, cooperatively and competitively, with extensions.
Locomotor skills are being refined.	Activities in dance, games, and gymnastics become more dissimilar and complex.	Locomotion involving apparatus, equipment, and other children will be challenging.
Fine motor control is developing.	Choose activities that require use of small muscles of hands, wrists, feet, ankles.	Gestures, balancing, body parts leading the action in dance is appropriate. Work on gripping, releasing with feet and hands, balancing in gymnastics with children. Throwing, catching, kicking, striking, controlling different objects with different implements in games offers a diversity of skill development.

Cognitive development		
Characteristics	***Implications***	***Activity suggestions***
Children desire quality approval and want to do things well.	All children should experience success.	Employ success-oriented teaching methods with encouragement. Children should not be made to conform to set standards and expectations nor singled out for lack of ability (as in relays).
Memory sharpens.	Children can concentrate, maintain interest for longer periods of time.	Lessons should be from thirty to forty-five minutes in length.
Egocentricity decreases.	Children can appreciate and empathize with others.	Children can work well in pairs or groups up to four in dance, games, and gymnastics.
Thought processes begin to be adultlike.	Problem-solving and concept development may be more complex.	Children enjoy creating sequences and game strategies. Combinations of concepts make lessons both mentally and physically demanding.
Distinct individual differences in personality and interest appear.	Children are aware of their own abilities and interests; self-concept is being established.	Personalities may harmonize or clash; teacher should carefully structure groups.
Social development		
Winning and losing are of tremendous importance.	May be aggressive, quarrelsome; may argue over fairness.	Rules must be established and adhered to; disciplinary measures should be consistent and fair.
Children are between childhood and adolescence.	Children want responsibility and adult privileges but may not have maturity to handle it.	Teacher's guidance and supervision is crucial.

Cognitive development		
Characteristics	***Implications***	***Activity suggestions***
Awareness of peers is increasing.	Peer acceptance and pressure may be more important than adults' approval.	Activities should reinforce the self-image of both males and females.
Clubs and gangs begin to form of one sex.	Children enjoy being a member of a group or team.	Children may work well in groups of four in games activities; in dance and gymnastics, partner work is best.
Friendships are almost exclusive to same sex.	Teacher needs sensitivity when forming groups and teams so all children feel accepted.	Children should not be forced into working with partner of opposite sex if they don't wish to (i.e., folk dancing).
Children are becoming aware of sexual roles, separate interests of sexes.	Boys tend to enjoy rough play and strong vigorous movement; girls tend to enjoy social interaction, fine motor movements, and attention to details.	Dance activities should appeal to boys' masculine nature; games activities should be structured so that girls will experience and progress in their skill. Avoid playing "boys against girls."
Role models from the community, television, or movies become important.	Children may attempt to emulate the behavior of role models.	Role models may be used to the teacher's advantage to develop or provide impetus to an activity (i.e., "Sugar Ray Leonard jumped rope to train, Let's all jump rope").

AGES 10 THROUGH 12

Physical development

Characteristics	*Implications*	*Activity suggestions*
Children need vigorous activity.	Lessons should be thirty to sixty minutes long and at *least* three times per week.	Children should experience maximum activity for a maximum amount of time.
Individual differences become obvious.	Wide differences in physical stature and abilities occur within the class.	Children should be able to work at their own level and progress at their own rate.
Rapid development in strength and control of gross and fine muscles.	Complex skills are being refined and may be applied to specific sports.	Judicious instruction and expected level of performance in sports skills must account for individual differences.
Girls tend to be taller and heavier than boys.	Girls are usually more mature both physically and socially.	Girls may need extra encouragement at times to participate fully due to self-consciousness.
Flexibility may begin to decrease, especially in boys who naturally tend not to pursue activities which promote flexibility.	Girls may begin to show greater ability than boys in activities that require flexibility.	Teacher needs to be persistent for both males and females to pursue dance and gymnastic activities that require flexibility. Teacher should encourage challenging balances, shapes, transference of weight, and unique use of body parts to promote flexibility.

Cognitive development		
Characteristics	***Implications***	***Activity suggestions***
Children enjoy some intellectual activities and appreciate applying abstract concepts. Fact retention increases.	Program should be intellectually stimulating.	Children can readily apply and use concepts learned previously, such as biomechanical factors and movement concepts. Teacher may discuss fitness principles and their implications in the program. Children may wish to pursue learning about the history of particular sports, professional athletes, etc. Rules become increasingly important.
Children enjoy contests.	Contests may be used more frequently in games activities.	Large- and small-group contests are appropriate occasionally, when children have mastered the skills required.
Interest in hobbies and extracurricular activities increases.	Some children may be highly skilled in specific sports.	Additional challenges should be provided for the highly skilled. This may include having the highly skilled help the lesser-skilled children.

Social development		
Egocentricity decreases.	Usually conforms well to authority, though children may sometimes find conflicting reactions to adult standards.	Rules and procedures should be well-established and enforced. Some adults are highly respected; teachers must earn children's respect.

Social development		
Characteristics	***Implications***	***Activity suggestions***
Definite groups form according to age and gender.	May display antagonism towards opposite gender.	Groups should be created with prudence. Classes should be mixed; however, occasionally separating the sexes may increase skill development and productivity.
Children seek group approval.	Children are aware of group reactions and group standards.	Teachers should structure activities with children's preferences in mind.
Role models play an important part in a child's world.	Athletic role models should be incorporated and discussed when appropriate.	Incorporate children's interests in games, dance stimuli, and dance themes.
Children are establishing values.	Children may be swayed easily by the opinions and values of respected others.	Teacher must be fair, encouraging, and positive.
Males and females develop separate interests.	Boys tend to be extremely competitive and value high skill; girls fluctuate in friendships and may value skill to a lesser degree.	Boys may need encouragement to play fairly and to include others; girls may need encouragement to participate fully.
Children desire to be popular and need to assert themselves.	Program should use problem-solving teaching methods and provide for individual differences where all can succeed.	Peer observation should be used, but children should not be forced to demonstrate if they would prefer not. Every child should be recognized for achievements at all levels of skill.

Research has resulted in greater understanding of the cognitive, affective, and psychomotor development of children, helping us to identify needs of different stages, as well as to recognize that children do not have the same likes, abilities, motivation, and skills. We are more accepting of individual differences; indeed, we often encourage variations in performance more than discourage them. The "miniature adult" idea has long since passed, but we must avoid falling into the trap of underestimating children's capabilities. This may result in our underchallenging them and/or accepting poor quality performance.

When skilled teachers combine the following elements, they are able to offer exciting lessons in dance, games, gymnastics, and other movement forms:

1. Theoretical knowledge of growth and development
2. Knowledge of the individual children they are teaching
3. Movement knowledge
4. Teaching knowledge

Characteristics of Children

Despite obvious individual differences within a class of children, various age groups are often similar in many ways. A sequential physical education program based on an understanding of the general characteristics of particular age groups is most valuable. Table 1.4 illustrates characteristics, implications, and activity suggestions for ages five through twelve.

Summary

A quality physical education program has tremendous value for all children. While gaining useful physical skills and improving fitness, children may learn movement concepts and other cognitive skills that increase their ability to participate in groups and get along with others. The rich variety found in dance, games, and gymnastics experiences allows all children to benefit from a diverse program.

Contemporary physical education has evolved from physical training programs, which stressed calisthenics, to a focus upon movement concepts and individualized learning. The physical education program should promote useful physical skills, enhance physical fitness, promote an understanding of movement principles, and increase the child's self-esteem. The content of physical education is based upon four movement concepts as postulated by Rudolf Laban. The teaching method should be varied according to the needs of the children.

Teachers should be aware of educating the "whole" child through dance, games, and gymnastics activities that enhance the child's cognitive, affective, and psychomotor skills. While most children progress through similar periods of physical growth and development, individual children progress differently.

Review Questions

1. Why should physical education be included in the elementary school program?
2. What are some of the objectives of the elementary school program?
3. What contribution did Rudolf Laban make towards physical education?
4. What is the affective domain? How may it be enhanced in physical education?
5. What is the psychomotor domain and its component parts?

References

American Alliance of Health, Physical Education, Recreation and Dance (AAHPERD). (1992, April) *Update,* p. 1.

Bailey, D., Martin, A., & Howie, J. (1986). Physical activity, nutrition, bone density and osteoporosis. *Australian Journal of Science and Medicine in Sport,* 18 (3), 3–8.

Canadian Association for Health, Physical Education and Recreation (CAHPER). (1992, Summer). *In Touch,* p. 3.

Council on Physical Education for Children (COPEC). (1992). Developmentally appropriate physical education for children: A position statement. Reston, Virginia: AAHPERD.

Fleishman, E. (1978). Relating individual differences to the dimensions of human tasks. *Ergonomics, 21,* 1007–1019.

Gallahue, D. (1987). *Developmental physical education for today's elementary school children.* New York: MacMillan Publishing Company.

Hill, R. (1979). Movement education: What's in a name? *CAHPER, 46* (1), 18–24.

Kerr, R. (1982). *Psychomotor learning.* Philadelphia: Saunders College Publishers.

Magill, R. (1989). *Motor learning: Concepts and applications* (3rd ed.). Dubuque, IA: Wm. C. Brown Publishers.

Morison, R. (1969). *A movement approach to educational gymnastics.* London: J. M. Dent and Sons Limited.

Roberton, M., & Halverson, L. (1984). *Developing children: Their changing movement.* Philadelphia: Lea & Febiger.

Schmidt, R. (1991). *Motor learning and performance. From principles to practice.* Champaign, IL: Human Kinetics Publishers.

Van Hagen, W., Dexter, G., & Williams, J. (1951). *Physical education in the elementary school.* Sacramento: California State Department of Education.

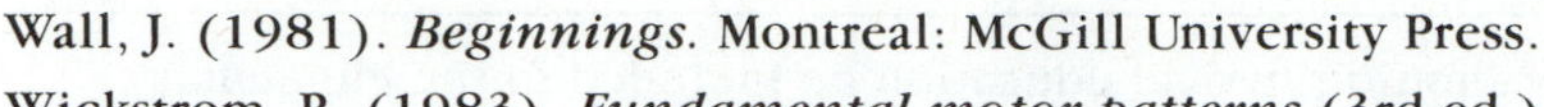

Wall, J. (1981). *Beginnings.* Montreal: McGill University Press.

Wickstrom, R. (1983). *Fundamental motor patterns* (3rd ed.). Philadelphia: Lea & Febiger.

Related Readings

Bredekamp, S. (1992). What is "developmentally appropriate" and why is it important? *JOPERD, 63* (6), 31–32.

Bressan, E. (1986). Children's physical education designed to make a difference. *JOPERD, 57* (2), 26–28.

Graham, G. (1990). Physical Education in U.S. Schools, K–12. *CAHPER Journal, 56* (1), 8–11.

Grineski, S. (1992). What is a truly developmentally appropriate physical education program for children? *JOPERD, 63* (6), 33–35, 60.

Robbins, S. (1990). An Overview of Physical Education in Canadian Schools. *CAHPER Journal, 56* (1), 4–7.

Rupnow, E. (1980). Eliminating sex role stereotyping in elementary physical education. *JOPERD, 51* (6), 38.

Verabioff, L. (1986). Can we justify daily physical education? *CAHPER Journal, 52* (2), 8–11.

Whitehead, J. (1992). A selected annotated bibliography for fitness educators. *JOPERD, 63* (5), 53–64.

Chapter 2 Understanding Movement

The physical education program we propose for children in elementary schools is based on *movement concepts* which are studied in the context of three distinct movement forms: *dance, games,* and *gymnastics.* This is a skill oriented program, dependent on our understanding and recognizing individual differences in performance levels. We try to help all children maximize their different movement abilities, and the expectation is that children will have different levels of competency (indeed, they may develop quite different skill vocabularies), in the areas of dance, games, and gymnastics.

One of our responsibilities is to help children develop positive attitudes towards an active life-style. We hope that children will enjoy their physical education lessons and will wish to be active at other times. We hope this enjoyment will continue throughout their lives. The need for specific fitness programs should, therefore, be reduced. In today's society, the question has been whether children are taught physical skills in order to improve their level of fitness, or whether children are fit because they enjoy participating in various movement forms. We believe children should be fit because they enjoy physical activity.

> In **A Quality Physical Education Program,** "teachers help all children to experience satisfaction and joy which results from regular participation in physical activity" (COPEC, 1992).

The Movement Concepts

Rudolf Laban 1879–1958.
Source: The Laban Archives, University of Surrey, England.

Our physical education program is based on Rudolf Laban's *descriptive analysis of human movement.* Laban was interested in the conscious control of human movement, the ability we have to develop a variety of movement responses and, unlike the animals, to select and change these responses at will. The concept of humans as thinking, feeling, doing beings is central to his movement analysis.

Over the years, many educators in Britain, Canada, and the United States have used his movement concepts as the *content* of their physical education programs for students at all levels of education. When Laban's movement concepts form the basis of a physical education program, a conscious attempt is made to help the students understand the movement concepts so they can

1. apply the concepts in dance, games and gymnastics;
2. become skillful in dance, games, and gymnastics activities;
3. appreciate different movement forms.

These are three major long-term objectives of our program.

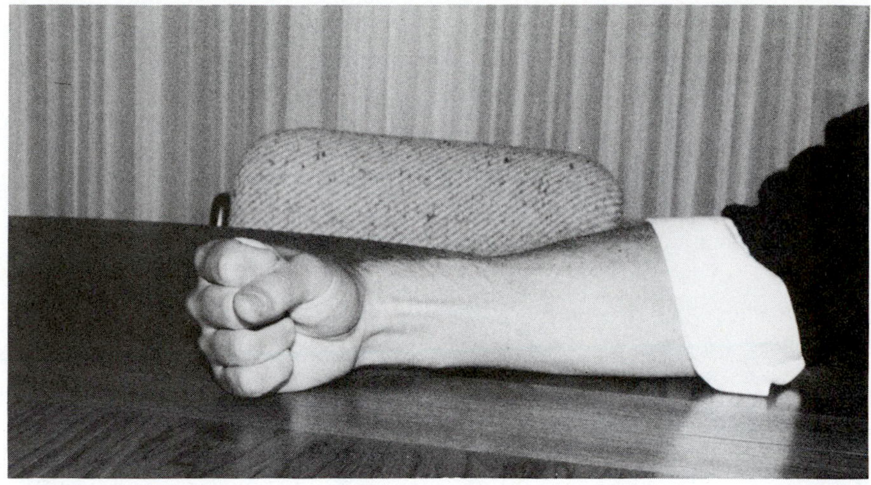

Figure 2.1 Is this gesture expressive or functional?

Functional and Expressive Movement

Functional and expressive movement are two important concepts in Laban's descriptive analysis of movement. In reality, the two are inseparable; but in order to discuss them, it is necessary to present them as two distinct ideas.

When, for example, is running dancelike or expressive? What differentiates it from the very functional activity used when trying to catch a bus? Do we consciously select the running skill appropriate for each situation? Laban's analysis of human movement helps us to understand, observe, distinguish between, select, and classify actions.

The descriptive analysis begins with the premise there are two dimensions to our movement lives:

1. "The *doing,* which encompasses all those movements necessary for the development and preservation of life in an objective way" (Wall, 1983).
2. The *dancing,* including all movements concerned with feelings, expression, communication, personality, and the subjective component of our being.

The factor that differentiates between one movement activity and another is our intention as we move. An action can be functional in one context and expressive in another. To illustrate this idea, make a fist and pound the table with it. (figure 2.1). What is the intention behind the activity and the context in which the activity occurs? It could be that you are trying to make a stamp stick on an envelope, a very functional action; or you may be making a very dogmatic statement, and this gesture is used to reinforce what you are saying, in which case the action is expressive (figure 2.2).

Figure 2.2 The expressive and functional aspects of movement and suggested criteria for classification of actions according to intention(s) behind the movement.

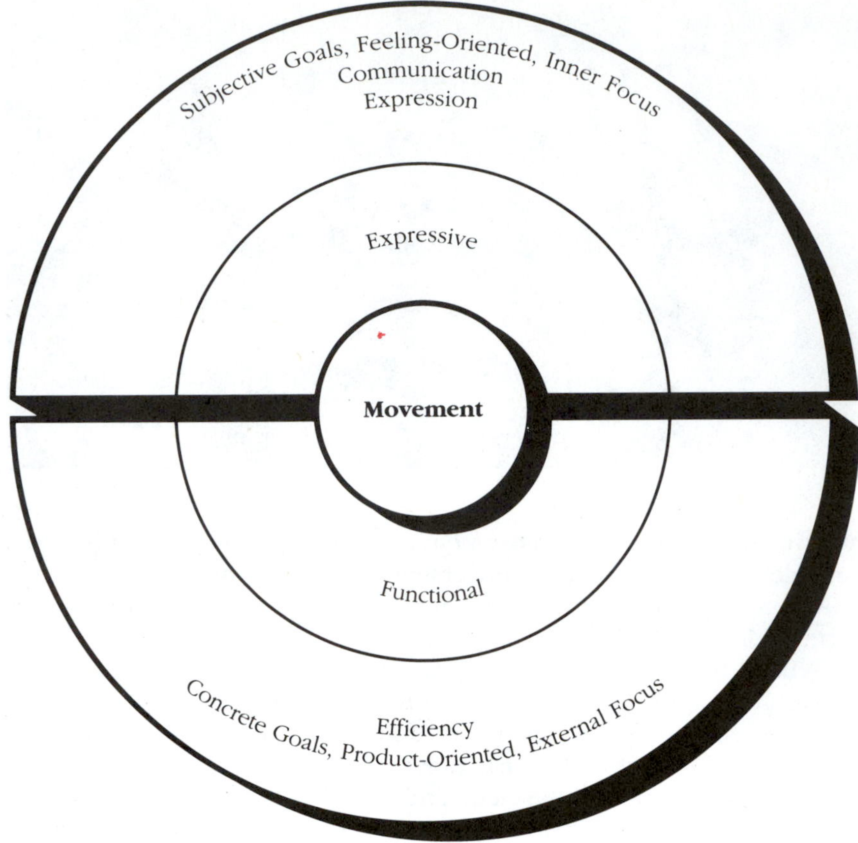

To Do

The following actions may be **functional** or **expressive,** depending on the intention behind them and the context in which they are used. Suggest situations in which they are first employed functionally and then expressively.

Stamping a foot

Clapping your hands

Walking backwards

A sudden turning action

A Quality Physical Education Program "includes a balance of skills, concepts, games, gymnastics and dance experiences, which enhance the cognitive, motor, affective and physical fitness development of every child" (COPEC, 1992).

Why is it important for us to distinguish between functional and expressive movement? Understanding functional and expressive movement helps us to do the following:

1. Appreciate the nature of the movement forms we are teaching
2. Define more specific objectives for our lessons
3. Elicit from the children movement responses appropriate for the context/situation
4. Select vocabulary related to the different movement forms (table 2.1)

Table 2.1

A Semantic Comparison of Dance, Games, and Gymnastics

Movement form (perception)	Body concepts—Verbs		Effort and spatial concepts—Adverbs
Dance (expressive)	Neutral:	Descriptive:	Qualifying:
	run	flee	smoothly
	walk	creep	angrily
	jump	bounce	hesitatingly
	turn	spin	forcefully
Games (functional)	Nonmanipulative:		Quantifying:
	run		quickly
	jump		slowly
	guard		faster
	pivot		stronger
	swerve		
	Manipulative:		
	catch		
	throw		
	kick		
	strike		
	volley		
Gymnastics (functional)	Neutral:		Quantifying/qualifying:
	hang		quickly
	balance		smoothly
	jump		slowly
	roll		strongly

In dance lessons, we are trying to develop skillful use of the body as an instrument of expression, a carrier of ideas and abstractions. There will be a decided qualitative and aesthetic stress in our teaching. Games and gymnastics are movement forms in which the skills are used in very functional, concrete ways—to catch a ball, avoid an opponent, walk along a narrow bar, jump over a box. Beyond this, the two movement forms differ considerably. In games, the body is employed as a tool, a means to the end of scoring in some way. In gymnastics, the activities are ends in themselves. The gymnast asks, "Can I balance on two different body parts or hang upside-down suspended by one knee or leap across this gap?" When teaching games and gymnastics, we are concerned with improving the efficiency of each movement and increasing the versatility and adaptability of the children. Our teaching will have a quantitative, functional stress.

Table 2.2

Laban's Four Movement Concepts

Body concepts: activity-oriented

Telling us what the whole body and/or specific parts are doing

Effort concepts: quantity/quality-oriented

Telling us what the movement is like, what dynamics are used

Spatial concepts: place- and pattern-oriented

Telling us where the movement is, how it moves through the environment

Relationship concepts: people- and things-oriented

Telling us what interaction is occurring between people and objects in the environment

The Four Movement Concepts

Laban's descriptive analysis of human movement allows us to describe any human activity in terms of four major concepts (table 2.2). These concepts give us the answers to the following four questions:

1. What is the body doing? (**body concepts**)
2. What is the dynamic content or quality of the movement? (**effort concepts**)
3. Where is the movement occurring? (**spatial concepts**)
4. With whom or to what is the mover relating? (**relationship concepts**)

Besides being able to describe any movement, we can also teach a new skill, and develop and/or change existing skills by using the movement concepts to modify and refine the movement patterns of the learner. The concepts provide us with the framework to do the following:

1. **Structure** learning tasks in all aspects of the physical education program
2. **Observe** and **analyze** movement
3. **Communicate** with others by using an accepted terminology
4. **Evaluate** the content of the physical education program (Logsdon et al., 1984)

A number of authors (Holbrooke, 1973; Logsdon et al., 1984; Russell, 1975; Stanley, 1977; Wall, 1983) have developed schema to illustrate, explain, and clarify the components of the movement concepts. Initially, they appear to be very simple ideas; however, do not be deceived by the apparent simplicity of Laban's descriptive analysis. You will understand the potential of the ideas only if you have used the movement concepts for your own skill development in the areas of dance, games, and gymnastics. Your own movement experiences are key factors in the development of your teaching skills.

The four major concepts will be introduced separately and discussed as they relate to movement in a general way. In chapters 5, 8, and 11, you will find the same concepts explained as they relate specifically to the three movement forms—dance, games, and gymnastics—that are the core of the physical education program.

Body Concepts

Awareness of the body concepts provide us with an understanding of our physical selves. Being familiar with our physical structure is a prerequisite for the acquisition and refinement of all motor skills. Very young children spend much time "discovering" their bodies. Babies open and close their hands, carefully watching the action. They hold onto their feet and put them into their mouths. From an early age many playful activities involve identifying and naming different body parts.

You may like to think of the body as a puppet or doll with the same number and types of joints as humans. You can manipulate these inanimate objects in many ways, making them "do" many humanlike actions and activities. Unlike the puppet or doll, we learn through experience, to control our bodies so that we can consciously produce a specific action or combination of actions. To do this, we must know what is possible, either through discovery or by being told. Figure 2.3 shows four components of body concepts, each of which can be subdivided further.

The Body in Action

The structure of our bodies is such that every movement we make, or posture we assume, is some combination of three basic actions: bending, stretching, and twisting. These words describe what we observe when the joints move in a particular way.

Bending Bending is the result of a joint, or series of joints, flexing. The body becomes rounded or angular as the extremities are brought nearer the center of the body; there is an accompanying inward focus. Some authors use the word *curling* interchangeably with *bending*. Curling has a rounded connotation; bending is more angular. Maybe bending relates more to an action at an isolated joint, whereas "curling represents a more total involvement of many joints" (Logsdon et al., 1984).

Stretching When we stretch, the joint extends, and the body parts move away from the body center, highlighting either the length and linear quality of the body, or the width and flatness of the body. There tends to be an outward focus when stretching.

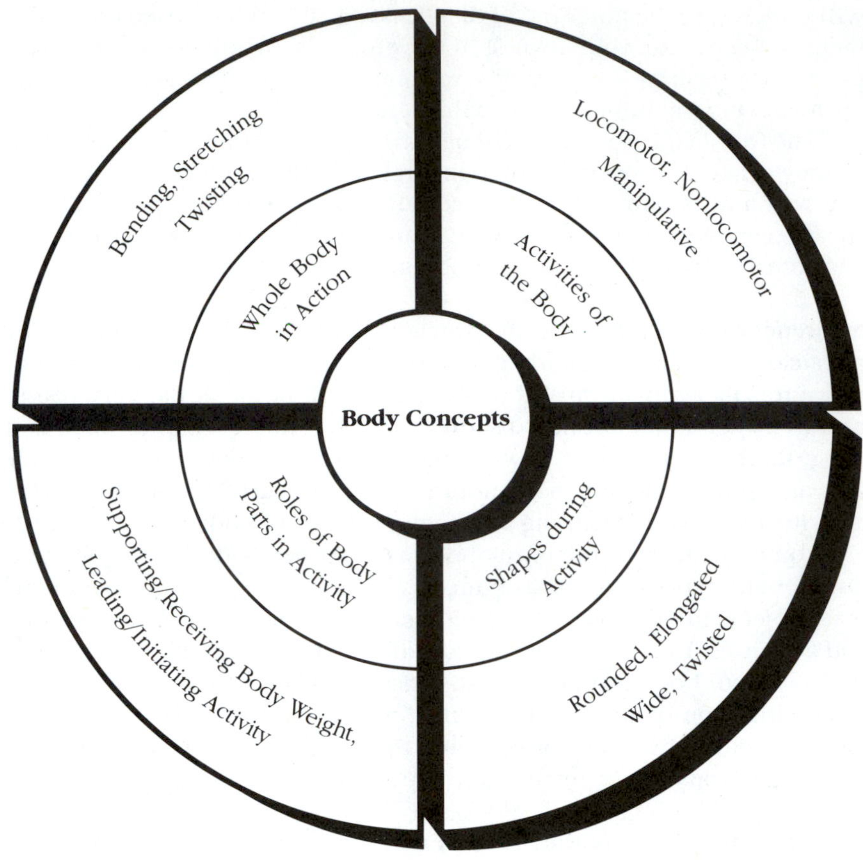

Figure 2.3 Components of the body concept of movement.

To Do

1. Slowly lower your weight onto a chair, focusing on the bending actions occurring at your knee and hips. Feel the relaxation of the muscles when your weight is shifted from your feet to your hips.
2. Turn to look at someone or something behind you as you are sitting. What action occurs in your spine? Be aware of the counteraction in the hip region. If you look over your left shoulder, what do you feel happening in your left thigh (knee to hip)? Right thigh?

Twisting The joint action of rotation can result in twisting, but only when one body part is fixed and kept still, and other body parts rotate to face a new direction. To illustrate this, take a short length of paper, about the length of a finger, and hold it at each end between finger and

Table 2.3

Some Locomotor and Nonlocomotor Activities

Locomotor	Nonlocomotor
Cartwheeling	Balancing
Climbing	Hanging
Jumping	Rocking
Rolling	Stopping
Skipping	Swinging

thumb. Rotate both hands evenly away from you and towards you; the paper does not change. Now keep one hand still and rotate the other; the paper will twist. It will twist even more if you simultaneously rotate both hands in opposite directions.

Activities

As the body bends, stretches, and twists different *activities,* or skills, arise. These can be grouped into three categories:

1. Locomotor activities
2. Nonlocomotor activities
3. Manipulative activities

These activities are the basic skills, which are modified and refined according to the context in which they are used. Dance and gymnastics each has a specialized vocabulary of locomotor and nonlocomotor skills; games has its specialized vocabulary of locomotor, nonlocomotor, and manipulative skills. Chapters 5, 8, and 11 discuss these skills in greater detail.

Locomotor Activities These are activities concerned with traveling, or moving the body from place to place (table 2.3). The purpose of locomotion is to "go somewhere" through the general space. In our everyday lives, we probably use the action of walking more than any other form of locomotion. Young children may choose to skip along the sidewalk, or they may have to run to keep up with their adult companion. Today, we see more adults running as they jog to keep fit. When jogging, the focus of attention is less on the *where* of running and more on *how far* or *how long* we can run.

Many forms of locomotion are explored in dance because of the rhythmic nature of the activity. Activities, such as skipping, hopping, and leaping, are incorporated in many folk dances. In creative dance, the expression inherent in those and other locomotor activities, such as creeping, rolling, and sliding, are developed.

To Do

Recall two or three recent everyday situations when you ran (e.g., to catch up with a friend on a busy street). Describe the running skill(s) you needed to be successful. Are the skills the same or different in each situation? How versatile are you when running?

A variety of running skills is developed for playing games, and the variations in the skill depend on the nature of the game and the different roles of the players in the teams. Compare, for example, the running skills of a quarterback with the running skills of a wide receiver, or the running skills of a squash player with those of a soccer player. They are very different.

The gymnastics program really exploits our locomotor potential as we cartwheel, climb, jump, roll, slide, swing over, or go under, across, between, and along various apparatus arrangements designed to challenge and excite.

Nonlocomotor Activities These are activities that occur in our personal space. The everyday activity of changing our position from standing to sitting or lying is nonlocomotor. There are two aspects to this kind of activity:

1. **Supporting** the body weight and the resulting stillness
2. **Transferring** the weight from one body part to another, resulting in changes in position

Both of these ideas are important in dance and gymnastics, and there is a considerable challenge in finding different ways of supporting ourselves and transferring weight (see chapter 11).

Examples of other nonlocomotor activities include the gestures we make as we talk, the way we turn our head or whole body to look in a different direction, and our posture as we sit in a chair. Some may occur as we walk along the street. For example, we may turn to look at someone and use hand gestures as we speak; thus, two or more components of a concept can occur simultaneously.

Manipulative Activities Activities used to control other objects are called *manipulative.* When we are very skilled, we almost forget the object is there; but in the initial stages of learning the skill, our attention is focused exclusively on the object. Professional athletes and magicians are prime examples of people highly skilled in manipulative activities.

When we are very young, there is a large vocabulary of manipulative skills to be learned: managing a spoon, buttoning clothing, tying shoe laces, using scissors, and holding a pencil, to name but a few. We take our ability to perform these activities for granted until we hurt or lose the use of a hand or arm. We then discover how complex and important these skills are. Some amputees and people born without hands learn to use their feet with the same degree of dexterity as those who have hands. Some people paint exquisitely by holding a paint brush in their mouths.

Rounded body shape when jumping.

Widening the body to defend the space.

The games portion of the physical education program includes a large range of manipulative skills, which Mauldon and Redfern (1969) categorized into three groups:

1. Sending away an object
2. Receiving an object
3. Traveling with an object

This categorization is discussed fully in chapter 8.

Body Shapes

This concept may be less obvious in our daily lives than other ideas. There are times when we consciously change the shape of our bodies: when trying to squeeze into an already full elevator or, as children do, going through a hole in a fence to retrieve a ball thrown accidentally into a neighbor's yard.

On very windy and wet days, we round our bodies to protect ourselves from the elements. If someone throws a ball inaccurately in our direction, we dodge to avoid being hit. Shape and the basic actions of bending, stretching, and twisting are interrelated, and shape results from the appropriate selection and combination of these basic actions. Indeed, we often describe shapes in terms of the actions used to achieve them, as in "look at that twisted shape." While in motion, our bodies are constantly assuming and passing through a variety of shapes, to which we may pay little attention.

Role of Body Parts in Activity

The integrated involvement of various body parts during action is often termed *coordination*. Most of our daily activities involve using more than one body part, but when we concentrate on learning a new skill or improving a known skill, it is sometimes necessary to isolate a body part. As teachers, we must be able to recognize the roles the various body parts play.

To Do

Do the following activities, then watch a friend do them. Discuss what you saw and the differences you felt.

1. Sit before a mirror; feel and watch the differences in expression when you make the following gestures:
   a. Palm of hand moving toward the mirror, fingers toward the ceiling
   b. Fingers move toward the mirror, palm toward the ceiling
2. Keeping weight on your feet, crouch low. Begin to rise with the following body parts leading the action:
   a. Head
   b. Elbow

Leading Action In a welcoming or greeting gesture, you can clearly see your hands leading your whole body, similar to reaching out to lift an object. In dance, many different body parts may lead an action. In creative dance, there is considerable emphasis on exploring the varying expressions arising when actions are led by different body parts. Notice how hands lead baseball players as they catch fly balls near fences. In gymnastics, the hands lead the body into a handstand, and once balanced upside down, the feet lead the body into an upright position.

Initiating Activity It may be more difficult to observe which body parts initiate activity than which parts lead. To illustrate the concept, sit on a chair with your weight evenly distributed between your hips and with both feet flat on the floor. Try to stand up, first by pushing your feet against the floor and then lifting your hips off the seat. Do it a second time, initiating the action in your hips. Probably, you will find the second method more efficient and comfortable than the first.

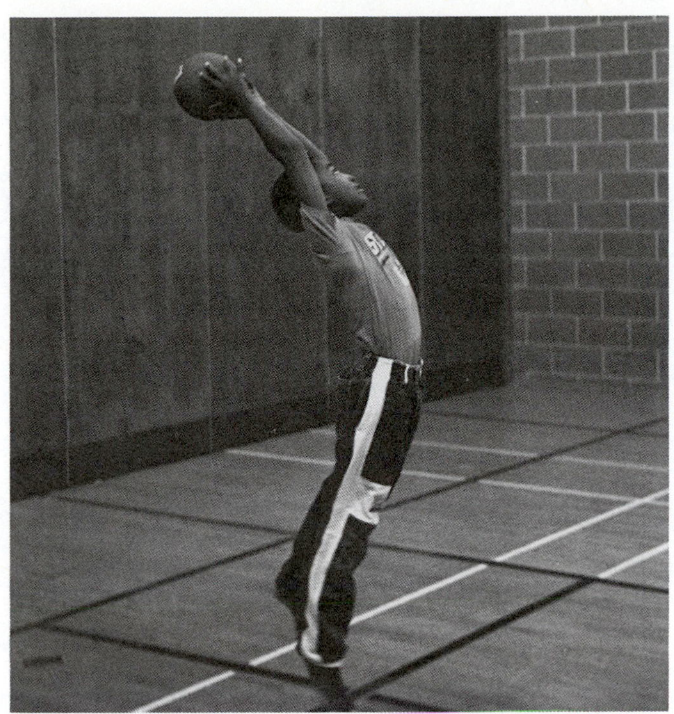

Elongation of body when catching a ball above one's head.

Twisted body shapes.

Use of body parts to suspend weight.

Changes in direction and momentum are produced by initiating activity with different parts of the body. If you have the opportunity to watch highly skilled figure skaters on television, notice how the leg not bearing weight (free leg) is used to initiate turning. In dance, games, and gymnastics, the arms are important when jumping; they are used to add momentum and increase the flight. Insufficient attention is often paid to this component of movement. This may be due partly to our inability to observe accurately.

Supporting and Receiving Weight These two concepts are taken together because, though different in intention, they are closely allied. Once weight is received it must be supported, even if only for a fleeting moment. It is in the area of dance and gymnastics that considerable time is spent improving and extending our ability to support and receive our body weight.

The ability to *support* weight leads to balancing and suspending activities. We need to learn how to *receive* weight, absorb force, and reduce impact after such activities as jumping, transferring weight from one body part to another (as in a cartwheel), or grasping a bar with our hands so that we are suspended.

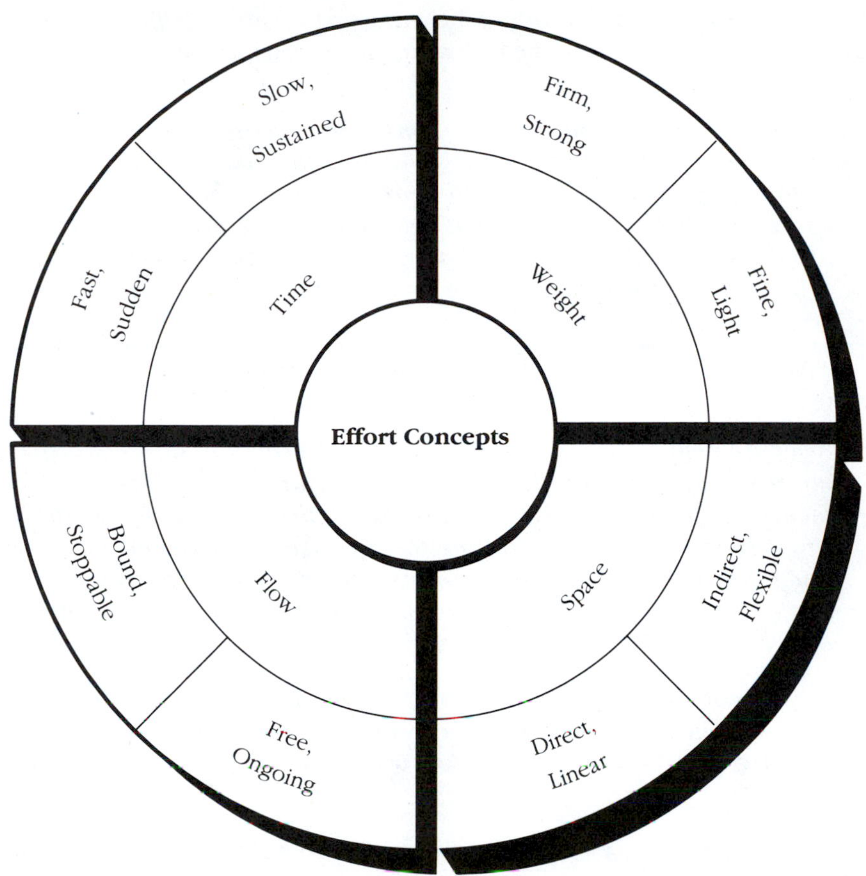

Figure 2.4 The four motion factors and the extremes of each.

There are some situations in both dance and gymnastics where we are responsible for receiving and/or supporting all or part of someone else's weight. These are very challenging situations which demand considerable concentration and respect for other people.

During games activities, we learn to receive balls of various kinds. We have to be able to absorb the impact directly, with our hands, or indirectly, through a glove, stick, or other piece of equipment. Our reaction to the oncoming object depends on the speed with which it has been sent, the level at which it will arrive, and its size, shape, and weight. The appropriate amount of muscle relaxation, together with the controlled bending of the receiving limbs, result in our being able to gain and retain control of the ball.

Effort Concepts

The concepts inherent in the word *effort* are probably the least understood of Laban's principles. Initially, it appears to be a very simple notion: there are four *motion factors* (time, weight, space and flow), and movements may be fast or slow, strong or light, direct or flexible, bound or free (figure 2.4).

You are directed to the original writing on the subject, *Effort* by Laban and Lawrence (1947), but the following quotation may help to reinforce the notion that Laban meant more than simple changes in speed, etc.:

> *Few people realize that their contentment in work and their happiness in life, as well as any personal or collective success, is conditioned by the perfect development and use of their individual efforts. But what effort really is and how this essential function of man could be assessed and adapted to the specific necessities of life remains for most people an unsolved problem (Laban & Lawrence, 1947).*

To relate effort to the physical manifestation, Laban and Lawrence state:

> *A person's efforts are visibly expressed in the rhythms of his bodily motion. A rhythm may consist of strong, quick and direct movements. People who are strong, quick and direct can easily be distinguished from those with fine touch, sustained consideration and a flexible approach to decisions and actions. People thus endowed look and move differently from the strong, quick and direct people (Laban & Lawrence, 1947).*

Effort Attitudes

After years of studying human movement in many different situations, Laban concluded that we have two opposite attitudes towards the motion factors. He called one attitude *indulging* and the other *fighting* (figure 2.5).

Indulging Attitude When we combine some or all of the motion factors in a specific movement in this way, we might consider we are using more of each factor in the activity. This is a satisfactory analogy with time, space, and flow. An activity can be slow and last a long time, therefore incorporating two aspects of the *time* factor: speed and duration. Such quality is termed *sustained.* The less speed and the longer the duration the more sustained the quality.

We indulge in the movement factor *space* if our movement is roundabout and has no apparent focus in its route through space. Watch someone who uses flamboyant gestures; these gestures are most likely to be flexible in quality.

When indulging in the use of *flow,* the sensation is of the body's energy streaming from within to the periphery and beyond. The movements will be fluent and feel free, and the focus will tend to be outside ourselves. Flow is less physical than the other factors and is more related to our emotions and how we feel.

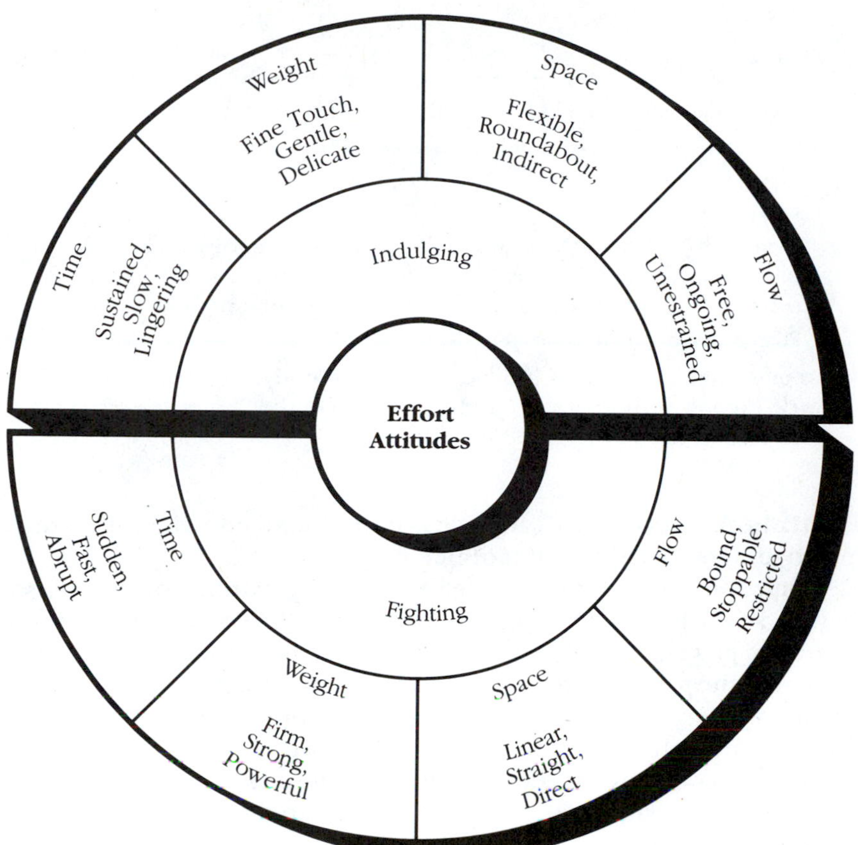

Figure 2.5 Effort attitudes.

The idea of indulging in the *weight* factor may be a little more difficult to understand because indulging in weight means enjoying the sensation of weightlessness, being free from the pull of gravity, and able to use our muscle power with very delicate results. On earth, a good example of indulging in the weight factor is the classical ballet dancer, who is very strong yet able to give the impression of being very light, often seeming to float across the floor. Astronauts actually experience this sensation! In our everyday world, we see people "indulging" in the weight factor when they pick up very delicate objects, thread a needle, or lower themselves delicately onto a rickety chair. In this case, there is very strong muscular action prevents gravity from bringing the full body weight onto the chair all at once. When they do sit on the chair, they may still be holding back some of their weight, and the sitting may appear tentative.

To Do

Contrast indulging (*a* and *b*) with fighting (*c* and *d*) the **weight factor.**

a. Focus on your hands; gently touch your fingertips together.
b. Tap a balloon so that it floats slowly upward; use fingers, elbows, and wrists.
c. Stand tall, feet about shoulder-width apart, arms above your head, and hands clasped; look up to the ceiling. Pull strongly, as if clasping a rope that is trying to pull you upwards. Release and breathe; repeat.
d. Push a heavy piece of furniture (e.g., piano).

In **a** and **c,** the resistance is produced within the body, with opposing muscle groups working against each other. In **b** and **d,** the resistance is from outside the body.

Fighting Attitude This attitude is opposite to indulging and results in very different qualities of movement.

Some functional activities need the fighting extreme of the *weight* factor to be efficient. Shot putters and weight lifters attempt to exert maximum power, which is applied in ways specific to their sport. In these examples, the participants are "feeling" their weight, the accompanying sensations being great power, alertness, and solidity. Gravity helps as they stabilize themselves and pull against its force. It is a very different sensation from complete relaxation when the muscles do not support the body weight, gravity takes over, and the sensation is of heaviness and lethargy.

A fighting attitude towards *time* is seen when we move suddenly, quickly, or abruptly in a way that suggests we wish to finish the action. A fast action of short duration is called *sudden*. Excitement, agitation, nervousness, anger, and frustration are inner states which may be conveyed through sudden movements. Two examples of functional tasks which use this motion factor are the quick footwork needed in many ball games, when unexpected changes of direction occur, and the sudden hand movement (usually following a sustained, approaching gesture) used when trying to swat a fly.

Figure 2.5 will remind you that linear and direct are the qualities of fighting *space*. The limb or body as a whole moves through the space, disturbing it as little as possible. One literally takes the shortest route. Threading shoelaces or a needle are good examples of tasks requiring this quality of movement. There is a two-dimensional aspect with this quality, whereas indulging implies moving into the third dimension as the body parts twist and untwist.

To Do

Contrast indulging (**a** and **b**) with fighting (**c**) the **time factor**.

a. Write the word *time* slowly. Focus on how long you can take to write it. Remember to keep the pen moving because stopping en route changes the dynamics.
b. Make a series of dots (. . . . .) as quickly as possible. Make sure the pen comes off the paper after each dot and that there are no smudges.

Retiring, hesitant, and shy people tend to move in a linear fashion, their movements being more unobtrusive than those of ebullient people, who often use more space as they move. Dogmatic people may also exhibit linear qualities as they move.

To Do

Contrast indulging (*a*, *b*, and *c*) with fighting (*d* and *e*) the **space factor.**

a. Put a screw into a piece of wood.
b. Flick some dust off your clothes.
c. Jump and wriggle in the air. Land on both feet.
d. Pick up a pen, or other thin object, from a table.
e. Walk through a partially open doorway.

Flow is the motion factor responsible for the degree of control that we have as we move. Movement that can be stopped at any moment has the quality of bound flow. The mover is anticipating the need to stop and, therefore, withholds the energy flow. People with poor eyesight exhibit bound flow quality when they move in unfamiliar surroundings, as do many children walking along a narrow ledge, such as a balance beam. During most actions, the degree of flow will fluctuate. As we become more sure of what we are doing, we often increase the flow, and the movement becomes fluid. It is our ability to shift between the extremes of free, ongoing movement and bound, stoppable movement, that determines how much control we have. "The capacity for control increases with the awareness of the degrees of control representing the fine shades between the contrast of fluent flow and bound flow movement" (Laban & Lawrence, 1947).

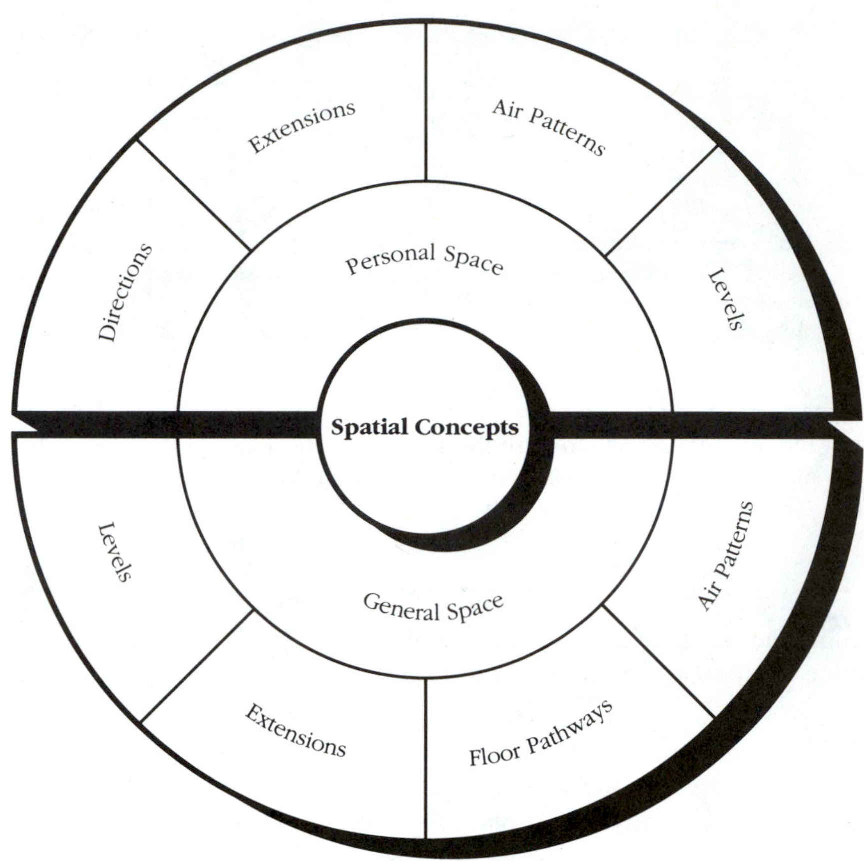

Figure 2.6 Components of the spatial concept of movement.

To Do

Contrast indulging (*b* and *d*) with fighting (*a* and *c*) the **flow factor.**

a. Using children's building blocks, build a tower as high as possible. Be aware of the changing sensation as the tower becomes taller and less stable.
b. Knock the tower down!
c. Walk quickly along a very crowded street.
d. Walk quickly along an empty street.

Spatial Concepts

The focus of our attention now shifts from ourselves, and our physical being, to the environment or space in which we are moving. We are concerned with where we have been and where we are going. In dance, games, and gymnastics, we aim to develop skill and knowledge about using space effectively and efficiently (figure 2.6).

General Space

This refers to the area in which we are; it may be a small room, a large field, or a cafeteria. There may be clearly visible boundaries or none at all; in which case, we may wish to establish some.

The point of reference for all general space is the environment itself. We know where the center of the space is, that *up* is towards the sky or ceiling, and *down* is to the ground or floor.

As we move throughout general space, we can concentrate on one or more of the following four components:

1. Levels
2. Extensions
3. Floor patterns
4. Air patterns

Levels This refers to how close to, or far away from, the floor we are as we move. As individuals, we have level preferences. Some of us enjoy being low and are seemingly earthbound, while others prefer being high and more remote from the earth. This preference may also be a function of age. Watch preschoolers as they play. They spend a lot of time crouching on, sitting on, and scrambling across the floor. In contrast, older children are tempted to climb and reach heights that sometimes scare us as we supervise their play. In gymnastics, we structure different environments that offer different levels, or heights, for the children to explore. Once they feel confident and are skillful at one level, we may encourage them to challenge themselves by doing the same activity at a higher level. In games lessons, children learn to control a ball at different levels. Examples of the tasks are "keep the ball low as you travel" or "send it higher when you hit."

Extensions In general space, the concept of extensions applies mostly to locomotor activities. It describes the amount of space a movement pattern uses. The key words are *small, large,* and *short, long.* The appropriate pair depends on the activity. For example, you can run and trace either a small or a large circle on the floor. A jump may take you a short distance, or you may try for a long distance through the space, as when long jumping.

Floor Pathways All locomotor activities trace a pattern on the floor. When walking along a crowded street, we may trace an erratic pathway as we try to avoid people. In contrast, predictable pathways and accurate designs are practiced for hours by figure skaters. The resulting design is a combination of two kinds of lines: straight and curved. Many folk dances involve intricate pathways as the dancers advance and retire, change places, and cast to the bottom of the set. Football and basketball players learn to run patterns so that plays are predictable.

Air Patterns Air patterns are three dimensional, whereas floor pathways are two dimensional. The concept is exploited in black-light theater productions and artistic films that trace the pathways of movement through the general space. In dance, a group may run in the general space and create an air pattern that gives the impression of a whirlpool. In game situations, children learn to control the pathway of balls as they throw them at different targets. In gymnastics, attention needs to be paid to the pattern/shape made by the body as it is launched into space, as in a dive roll. To encourage an inverted V shape, a rolled mat is sometimes placed near the take-off point.

An understanding of different air patterns, and the skill to produce specific ones, increase the effectiveness of movement in objective and expressive situations.

Personal Space

Laban called our personal space the ***kinesphere***. If you can imagine your sphere of movement being similar to a huge bubble of space surrounding you, the boundaries of which are determined by your fullest reach in every direction, then you will easily understand the concept of personal space.

Our point of reference as we make spatial decisions is now our own bodies. Where is up? Where is down? Astronauts working in a gravity free environment cannot be upside down. For them, as for us when relating to our personal space, ***up*** is always toward the head, ***down*** toward the feet, ***front*** is where we face, and ***back*** is behind us. Figure 2.6 shows four components of personal space.

Directions There are six basic directions in which we can move: forward, backward, left, right, up, and down. We sometimes combine two directions. For example, we need to move our arms forward and upward when taking a free throw in basketball. In a gesture of supplication, we may combine three directions: upward, forward, and sideways. The resulting expression and accompanying sensation are different from those when the hands move upward and sideway—try it.

To Do

Stand naturally and focus on a spot on the floor. Sense the accompanying downward "pull." Then focus upward. Is there any change of sensation throughout your body?

Levels ***Level*** implies an area of space in relation to our body structure. The ***low level*** is below the hips, the area usually occupied by our legs. The ***medium level*** is the area between hips and shoulder girdle. The area above the shoulders is called ***high level*** and is the more natural area for the arms and head. Changing from one level to another is often accompanied by changes in body shape, but it is possible to focus on and imply a specific level with minimal change of position and shape.

In dance, the expression changes when movements are performed at different levels. A low, turning action may appear sinister or express fear, depending on the context. In contrast, a high level turn may communicate a feeling of release or freedom. Some dance forms use specific

Two directions combined in gesture—up and sideways.

Three directions combined in gesture—up, forward, and sideways.

levels. Classical ballet dancers prefer the high level, seeming to free themselves from the pull of gravity. Some jazz and modern dancers exploit the low level, thus emphasizing our relationship with the earth.

Extensions Gestures made by the arms and/or legs may be near the body or far away from it. Gestures may be small or large in size. These are aspects of extensions in our personal space. In situations where we apply force to project (throw) an object with a hand, we may bring the

Two directions, forward and sideways, combined in gesture.

arm close to the body in preparation. The size of the total arm action (preparation, release, and follow-through) will depend on several factors, including the weight of the object being thrown, the distance, and the speed at which we wish it to travel.

We reach out (far) to catch a high ball. We bring our hands in close (near) to the body center to look at something small. In dance, children enjoy reaching far away from themselves, then bringing legs and/or arms in close to the center of the body.

Air Patterns The concept is similar to that in general space, but is restricted to the patterns we make when gesturing with different body parts in our personal space. We may also wish to focus on the pathway taken by an implement (e.g., baseball bat) as we swing to hit an oncoming ball.

Relationship Concepts

This is the fourth component of Laban's descriptive analysis. It considers our relationship with the environment, which includes people, sounds, and various objects we can touch, hold, hear, see, and smell (figure 2.7). We may pay attention to what is in our immediate environment or we may ignore it. Our past experiences influence our perception of the environment, and each of us interprets and responds to it differently.

In physical education, we are particularly concerned with the differing relationships inherent in the different activities forming the basis of the curriculum (table 2.4).

Figure 2.7 Relationship concepts.

Table 2.4

Some of the Different Relationships in the Three Curriculum Areas—Dance, Games, and Gymnastics

	People in the environment	Objects and sounds in the environment
Dance	Cooperative; ranging from dancing with a partner to being part of a large group	Different kinds of accompaniment, props, and costumes
Games	Cooperative; with a partner or teammates Competitive; playing one versus one, two versus one, two versus two, etc.	Games equipment, referee's whistle, boundaries of the playing area, goals, nets, etc.
Gymnastics	Cooperative; partner work, small groups	Apparatus arrangements

Playing music for a partner to dance.

People in the Environment

Dance, games, and gymnastics all provide opportunities for developing relationships with people, but the nature and purpose of the relationships differ considerably. The pleasure we get from the activities often depends as much on the enjoyment of sharing an experience with others, as on our actual physical skill. Dancing a Scottish reel is great fun; we may enjoy a game of tennis because of being with friends. We need specific skills to be able to relate to other members in the dance group; we need different skills as we try to outplay our tennis opponent. This is discussed more fully in chapters 5, 8, and 11, as we examine dance, games, and gymnastics separately.

Objects and Sounds in the Environment

Dance provides a rich experience in relating to sounds of many kinds. Music often accompanies movement, especially in folk dance and singing games, and music may be the stimulus for the creation of dances (chapter 7). Sounds produced by percussion instruments, voice and body sounds, and nonsense syllables and words can all be important components of dance lessons.

Objects, for example brooms, chairs, newspapers, cloth, and balloons, may be used in dance lessons, either as sources of ideas (i.e., stimuli) or as props.

A very complex environment develops in games playing. Some objects remain stationary, such as boundaries and targets, while others are constantly in motion, such as the ball with which the game is played. We have to understand how to help children cope with both a static and a dynamic environment. You may have read of closed and open skills, the former occurring in a static environment, the latter in a dynamic one. Games activities require mostly open skills; the learning tasks we design

Table 2.5

Some Useful Words for Describing and Developing Relationships

Positional relationships:	Relationships can occur at different times:
I can move across	Successively
under	Alternately
along	In canon
over	and may result in question—answer
toward	action—reaction
away from	leading—following
onto	meeting—parting
off	**Relationships can occur at the same time:**
I can be in front	Together
behind	Simultaneously
at the side	and may result in mirroring
near	matching
far	contrasting

for children must provide experiences and information that will improve the children's ability to play games, rather than do drills in a comparatively static environment (i.e., out of the context of a game).

The environment is mainly static in gymnastics lessons. We design various apparatus arrangements to go over, under, along, across, and around. There are opportunities for developing skill in a dynamic environment—swinging ropes, seesaw benches, and other unstable (yet safe) structures provide exciting challenges enjoyed by many children.

Relationship Words

There are two groups of words that describe relationships: the first tells us *what* the positional relationship is, and the second tells us *when* it is occurring (table 2.5). The merging of these ideas results in a rich and diverse experience in relationships.

Application of the Four Movement Concepts When Designing Learning Experiences (Tasks)

Every movement we make is composed of elements from the four major concepts, but these elements may be unequal in terms of importance or stress. The less experienced and/or less competent learners will initially need challenges that help them understand simple, single movement concepts. As they become more skillful, additional concepts can be added, increasing the complexity of the cognitive, psychomotor, and affective aspects of the learning experience. Examples of tasks in dance, games, and gymnastics are given in figure 2.8.

Notice how in the dance task there are three movement factors stressed, with very little emphasis on the effort content of the task. The

Over and under benches.

Skipping, circular pathway.

prime challenge is to apply the already acquired skills of skipping and galloping in a dynamic environment with a partner.

The games task emphasizes the effort content of the movement (i.e., change of speed). It is complicated further by the spatial focus on changing direction. The environment has static (markers) and dynamic (ball) components.

The gymnastics task is concerned with a change in a relationship with the apparatus, a single bench. Contact with the bench is maintained

Figure 2.8 Using the concepts in dance, games, and gymnastics.

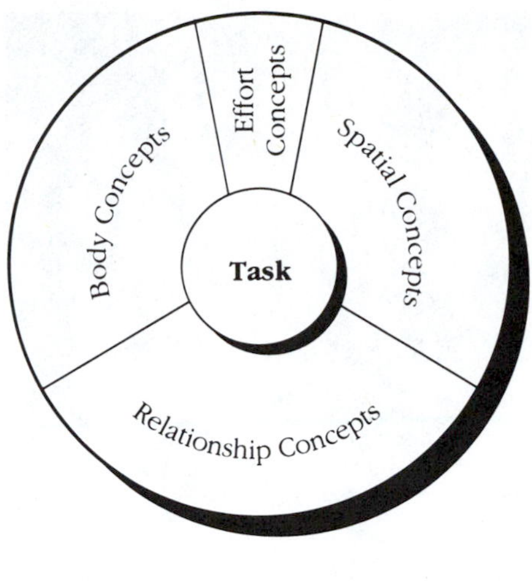

Dance (basic task)
Using a combination of skipping and galloping steps, with your partner design a floor pattern that combines curves and straight lines.

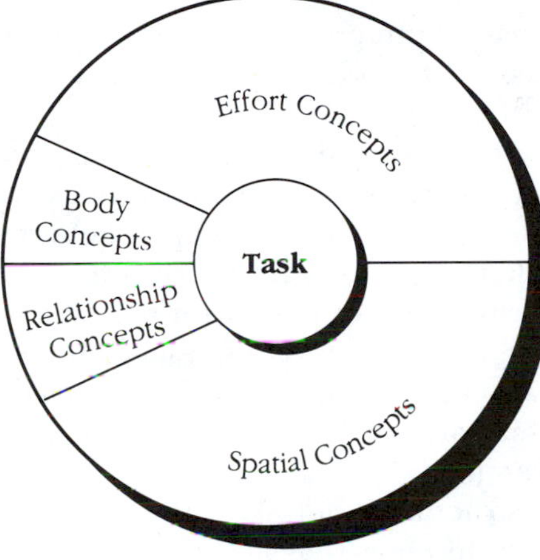

Games (basic task)
Dribble the ball (with hands or feet), changing direction and speed as you go around the markers.

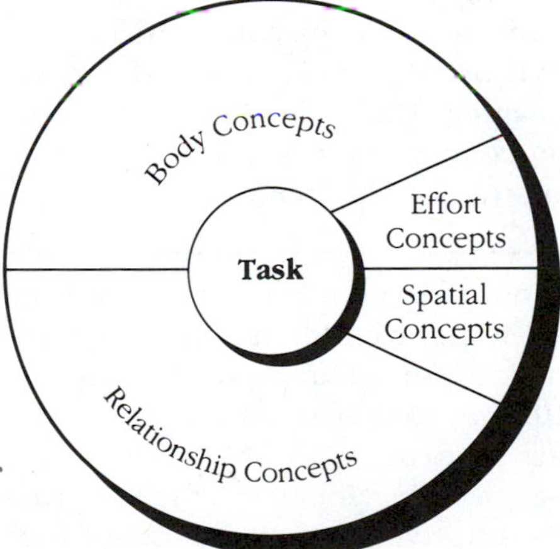

Gymnastics (basic task)
Travel along the bench, alternating being completely on it and being half on the bench and half on the floor.

Acquiring control around markers.

throughout the traveling, thus eliminating jumping. The children must investigate various weightbearing possibilities, and much of their attention will be on exploring what the body can do.

As the children work on one of the tasks, we will observe their ability to apply the specific movement concepts stressed, and we will design refining tasks that focus attention on aspects of the concepts, helping them to improve their performance. In the games example, the children are given the choice of using their hands or feet to control the ball. A refining task, appropriate for everyone, might focus on a spatial concept: "As you approach the marker (relationships), keep your steps small (spatial awareness), so you are better balanced (body awareness) and able to change direction (spatial awareness)."

Chapter 3 discusses in detail the structuring of tasks and the kind of information we need to provide for children as they are in the process of learning new skills or improving already known skills.

The content of all the lessons in the accompanying *Lesson Plan Manual* (Côté-Laurence, Drake, & Wilson, 1990) is based on the movement concepts discussed in this chapter. The manual contains many examples of applying the movement concepts in designed learning sequences in dance, games, and gymnastics for children.

Summary

The *content* of the physical education program is movement, and the long-term educational objective is to help the children become skillful in functional and expressive movement forms. Our aim is to help the children develop a broad base of skills they can use to achieve a product, be it a dance, a game, or a gymnastics sequence.

The concepts on which the program is developed are derived from the work of Rudolf Laban, whose descriptive analysis consists of four

Completely on the bench and partly on the bench.

major concepts: the body, the effort, the space, and the relationships of movement. These concepts have been described and illustrated with examples from everyday activities, as well as from the selected movement forms of dance, games, and gymnastics.

Review Questions

1. Why is it important to distinguish between functional and expressive movements?
2. A physical education program based on Laban's movement concepts has three major long-term objectives. What are they?
3. Laban's descriptive analysis of movement is based on four major concepts; what are they? What does each concept tell us about movement?
4. Three kinds of activities form the core of dance, games, and gymnastics programs; name them and give examples of each.
5. What does Laban mean by *effort*?
6. Name the four motion factors and give the extremes of each.
7. Define (a) personal space, and (b) general space.

8. Discuss some of the different relationships arising in (a) dance, (b) games, and (c) gymnastics.

(Remember that relationships will be discussed more fully in chapters 5, 8, and 11. At this point we hope you understand the introduction to the concept.)

References

Côté-Lawrence P., Drake, V., & Wilson, J. (1990). *Lesson plans: Children and movement.* J. Wall, N. Murray, Dubuque, IA: Wm. C. Brown Publishers.

The Council on Physical Education for Children (COPEC). (1992). *Developmentally appropriate physical education for children: A position statement.* Reston, VA: AAHPERD.

Holbrooke, J. (1973). *Gymnastics: A movement activity.* London: Macdonald and Evans, Ltd.

Laban, R. & Lawrence, F. (1947). *Effort.* London: Macdonald and Evans, Ltd.

Logsdon, B., Barrett, K., Ammons, M., Broer, M., Halverson, L., McGee, R., & Robertson, M. (1984). *Physical education for children: A focus on the learning process* (2d ed.). Philadelphia: Lea & Febiger.

Mauldon, E., & Redfern, B. (1969). *Games teaching.* London: Macdonald and Evans, Ltd.

Russell, J. (1975). *Creative dance in the primary school* (2d ed.). London: Macdonald and Evans, Ltd.

Stanley, S. (1977). *Physical education: A movement approach.* Toronto: McGraw-Hill Ryerson Inc.

Wall, J. (1983). *Beginnings: Movement education for kindergarten and primary children* (2d ed.). Montreal: McGill University.

Related Readings

Barrett, K. (1988). Two views: The subject matter of children's physical education. JOPERD, *59*(2), 42–46.

Bean, D. (1985). Movement education: Potential and reality. *CAHPER Journal, 51*(5), 20–24.

Kerr, K. (1993). Analysis of folk dance with LMA-based tools. *JOPERD, 64*(2), 38–40.

Chapter 3
The Teaching Process

This chapter provides an introduction to some of the factors that contribute to teacher effectiveness and also offers some guidelines for monitoring your own teaching behavior.

Teaching physical education is both rewarding and demanding. Learning to become an effective teacher is somewhat similar to doing a jig-saw puzzle; there are many interlocking pieces, no one piece is more important than another, and different people begin at different places. The similarities end there, as no two teachers are alike. We each take the same pieces of the puzzle and, because we are individuals, end up with our own "picture" or style of teaching. This style is variable, and as we gain experience, or as the situation changes, we become more able to combine the "pieces" in different ways to deal with the changing conditions.

Some Research on Effective Teaching

The study of teaching behavior and the process of teaching physical education have received considerable attention since the early 1970s. Conferences, such as the International Symposium on Research in School Physical Education, Finland 1982, and the International Congress on Teaching Team Games, Rome 1983, provide researchers and teachers with opportunities to discuss issues related to the process of teaching physical education at all levels.

In the United States, the National Association for Sport and Physical Education (AAHPERD) has focused on understanding more about the teaching process, as has the Teacher Education in Physical Education (TEPE Special Interest Group) of the Canadian Association for Health, Physical Education, and Recreation. Refer to their publications for further details.

In physical education lessons, our primary function is to provide learning experiences that lead to achievements in movement skills. To do this, we have to understand the relationship between our teaching behavior, or what we do in lessons, and pupil learning, or the change in children's behavior and/or performance. What do we know about this relationship? The following discussion introduces you to a sampling of the available information.

One study (Grant & Martens, 1982) examined the effectiveness of the teaching skills of elementary education student teachers with physical education student teachers. Both groups were teaching physical education to children. The finding significant for us is that a classroom teacher can be as effective as a specialist. In other words, a good teacher is a good teacher!

The three main findings follow:

1. There were no significant differences in behavioral patterns between the physical education and elementary education teachers.

2. The most effective teachers displayed more versatile behavioral patterns.
3. The most effective teachers provided each child with approximately three times as much purposeful activity, or Academic Learning Time—Physical Education (ALT-PE) as the least effective teachers.

Seidentop (1983) summarized some of the research on teaching behavior and concluded:

> *The effective teacher is one who finds ways to keep students appropriately engaged in the subject matter a high percentage of the time and does so without resorting to coercive, negative or punitive classroom techniques.*

He identified five main components of effective teaching:

1. Children spend a higher percentage of lesson time engaged in learning and practicing their motor skills (ALT-PE).
2. Children have higher rates of on-task behavior. This includes learning experiences, organizational tasks, and watching demonstrations.
3. The teachers match the lesson content to the students' abilities.
4. The learning environment is warm and positive.
5. The teachers develop class structures that allow for high rates of on-task behavior while maintaining warm and positive learning climates.

We also know the following:

1. There appear to be no differences in children's activity when taught by male and female teachers.
2. Experienced teachers appear to give more feedback, and the feedback is more specific than that provided by less experienced teachers. For example, an experienced teacher will say, "Good bend in your knees as you landed," whereas a less experienced teacher is more likely to say, "Good landing."
3. It should not be too surprising to find that enormous differences in ALT-PE appear according to what activity is being taught. For example, gymnastics are often taught in such a way that students have low amounts of ALT-PE. Many tasks are individual in nature, and the children spend time waiting for their turn on a piece of apparatus. A good organizer reduces waiting time by providing several sections of apparatus, so the number per group is small.

Individual sports allow for more ALT-PE, with folk dance and "exercise dancing" having the highest ALT-PE figures (Siedentop, 1992). This finding needs to be considered seriously when selecting activities, a curriculum decision, and planning how to teach each activity, lesson planning (see chapter 4).

> **A Quality Physical Education Program** incorporates knowledge from the areas of research and teaching experience in order to "maximize opportunities for learning and success for all children" (COPEC, 1992).

In general, research in physical education tends to support the findings of earlier classroom studies. Five variables (O'Sullivan, 1985) that consistently discriminate between the more and the less effective classroom teachers follow:

1. Task oriented behavior
2. Opportunities to learn
3. Clarity
4. Variability
5. Enthusiasm

Task-Oriented Behavior

Effective teachers are "achievement oriented," and they develop an environment that encourages children to *learn,* not just "do." Lessons have specific objectives, and the children should know what they are trying to achieve. Feedback provided during lessons is congruent with the task in hand, and children may measure their own success during and after the lesson. This means more than saying, "Oh, we played basketball today." It implies the children can and will discuss knowledgeably the concepts, skills, and other aspects of the lesson.

Opportunities to Learn

Effective teachers are good organizers. Lessons must provide students with the maximum amount of time to be involved in activity. Our organizational skills are employed as we try to minimize time spent waiting for a turn, listening to instructions, and moving and arranging equipment (page 105).

Clarity

This refers to our skill in using language effectively and appropriately for the age, experience, and "know-how" of the students we are teaching. It also refers to our ability to sense whether or not our students are understanding what we are saying. For many children in our multicultural society, the language of instruction may not be in their first language. We need to be able to communicate a message in more than one way.

Blackboards, charts, flash cards, and other interesting, eye-catching visual aids can contribute considerably to lessons. There are some commercially produced aids, but more often than not we need to create our own. Children enjoy creating charts and cards, and it is possible to combine a language arts and/or art lesson with the production of charts and flash cards.

Gestures can help clarify meanings, and we should practice using them, so they become an integral part of our personal "communication system."

Variability

Effective teachers are able to provide a variety of learning challenges. It is a matter of presenting ideas in more than one way, so lessons are nonrepetitive and interesting. The same skills may be the focus of more than one lesson, but the tasks should differ. In lessons, individual children may respond differently to a task; therefore, we need to react differently to them.

A second dimension of variability is our open-mindedness as we are teaching. Effective teachers are able to make changes as the need arises during lessons.

Enthusiasm

Our enthusiasm is communicated to the students by our verbal and nonverbal behavior. Participation in the lessons, the way we move and stand as we observe, and our interaction with the students are indicators of our enthusiasm (Caruso, 1982). We need to be kinesthetically aware of what the children are doing, and we need to be ready to join in with them. This is especially important at the beginning of lessons, as it helps to motivate the group and provides a model of the task. The younger the children, the more you may feel the need to participate. For example, many children love to chase or be chased by the teacher.

It is important to show interest in individual students by learning and using their names during lessons. If you teach children in classes other than your own, it may not be easy to remember the names, other than of the obvious few, usually the very able and the mischievous. The youngest children may not mind wearing large name tags, and some schools have T-shirts with names across the back or front. Taking attendance at the beginning of the first few lessons and adding notes to the class list (e.g., braided hair, freckles, glasses) can be helpful. It takes some determination to learn and use three or four new names in each lesson, but it can be done.

The Basis of Concept Teaching

In addition to developing effective teaching behavior, it is important for teachers to present meaningful content to the children. As a teacher, your presentation must be accurate and effectual. To do this, you must have a thorough understanding of the material with which you are working. The term *movement concept* is an encompassing one and does not necessarily refer to a specific movement. Movement concepts are discussed in chapter 2 and expanded in chapters 5, 8, and 11; they provide the content of dance, games, and gymnastics lessons.

Our primary task is to expand and improve the students' movement responses; therefore, we must be able to select relevant concepts and know how to present, explore, and develop them into skillful dance, games, and gymnastics activities.

Movement vocabulary is a phrase most children seem to understand, especially when it is likened to language vocabulary. Our aim is to encourage versatile movement by increasing the students' movement vocabularies and developing their ability to select appropriate motor responses to the challenges set. We may need to focus on a particular aspect of a movement concept and encourage responses that are not forthcoming from the children. To develop quality movement, we will refine their responses to the tasks, decide whether to restrict or keep the responses open, and work on *consistency* and *accuracy* of response through practice. The long-term objective of the physical education program is for children to be versatile and skillful movers in a variety of movement forms, particularly in dance, games, and gymnastics.

To Do

Balance on the following body parts:

1. Two hands and one foot
2. Your head and two hands
3. Any three body parts

Notice that one of these movements has a specific name and the others do not. Number 2 is called a headstand, while numbers 1 and 3 are called? The concept is weightbearing, and it includes all three tasks.

Dance, games, and gymnastics each has unique content or vocabulary (see chapters 5, 8, and 11, respectively). The idea of expressive (dance) and functional (games and gymnastics) movement helps us define the nature of the movement form. This helps us select the movement concepts appropriately, so the skills (vocabulary) indigenous to that form are developed. The lesson plans in chapters 7, 10, and 13 (combined with the accompanying manual) are examples of learning situations designed to develop skills.

Teaching Skills

A variety of skills is needed, and those common to dance, games, and gymnastics include the following:

- Communicating with the children
- Evaluating teaching
- Observing accurately
- Providing feedback and skill information for children
- Designing learning experiences
- Organizing the children, equipment, and apparatus in large and small spaces
- Planning the curriculum (chapter 4)
- Planning lessons (chapter 4)

For each movement form, our role is multifaceted. We may switch from being the motivator to the organizer, the observer, the comforter, or the participant.

We bring some variables to the teaching situation with which we must learn to live, because we cannot change them. We need to know ourselves, to identify and be objective about our strengths and weaknesses, so we can build on the former and try to compensate for the latter.

We need feedback and practice as much as when learning any motor skill. The help of a videotape, peer, or experienced observer cannot be overestimated. For some, the development of confidence in front of a class is a gradual process, while others seem to be born with it. Initial levels of confidence are not indicators of teaching abilities. There are many excellent teachers who have overcome stage fright.

Less experienced teachers may find it beneficial to spend part of each lesson concentrating on how a personal variable affects our teaching. One example is our height. Tall teachers may have an advantage over shorter teachers. It is easier to observe—and be observed—when we are head and shoulders above the children. If we are less tall we can compensate by being very aware of where we stand when observing the children. For example, we can organize the children into groups and watch half the class at a time. To help the children "find" us, we may choose to wear colors that contrast with our surroundings. To help them focus on us when we wish to speak to the whole class, we may have them sit down. Experimenting with different strategies will help us teach more effectively.

We bring other personal variables to the teaching situation, including our sense of humor, personal preferences, and prejudices about people and the activities we are teaching. The more we are aware of these traits, the more we are able to use them to modify learned teaching behavior.

Communicating with the Children

Before we can really deal with the more technical and applied skills of teaching, we need to be at ease with ourselves in front of other people.

When teaching, we are constantly working in front of an audience, and we have to make the best use of our personal variables so that we communicate with our audience in the most effective way. Teaching is very similar to acting because communication is a combination of the use of voice, posture, and gesture. On paper, we may have an excellent lesson plan, but unless we can feel confident in front of the class, make ourselves heard and seen, communicate our ideas to the children, and interact with them as they are working, it is doubtful whether the lesson will be more than marginally successful, and we may feel very uncomfortable during the process of delivering the lesson.

Communication Skills

Teaching is an interactive process involving the teacher and the learners, a process in which communication skills play a fundamental role. In order to teach effectively, we must have an appreciation of the elements of communication and attempt to develop and practice invitational nonverbal and verbal behavior, because students learn best when invited to learn (Turner & Purkey, 1983).

Nonverbal Behavior

Children receive indications of how we feel about them by our gestures, posture, and facial expressions. If possible, have someone videotape you when teaching and keep the camera focused on you, regardless of what the children are doing. When reviewing the tape, notice how you stand, how you move among the children, and whether you smile as you speak to individuals or groups.

Posture and Movement The way we stand and move among the children indicates our attitude, sense of confidence, competence, interest, and concern. Moving with a sense of purpose, changing the speed at which we move and, when standing still, always exuding energy (albeit "quiet" energy) will have positive effects on the class atmosphere.

The way we move must be appropriate for the movement form we are teaching. This is especially important at the beginning of a lesson when we are establishing the mood. In dance, this means that our movement must be rhythmical and well-phrased; in games, we need a briskness; in gymnastics, our posture and movement should convey controlled energy. Try to be tuned in kinesthetically with the children, "feel" how they are moving, and be ready to move with them. Appropriate, comfortable clothing helps us feel prepared for activity and at ease as we move.

Facial Expression In general, people are very responsive to facial expression. Young children in particular rate a person largely on facial expression. A smile, therefore, is a very important invitational technique, whereas a frown is the opposite. We can consciously increase the amount of time we smile, it just takes a little practice.

Making eye contact is another invitational technique that helps the children to feel included. When we are giving instructions, feedback, asking questions, or generally talking to the class, it is important to make eye contact with as many children as possible. This applies when the group is spread out in the space and when close together.

Gestures These nonverbal cues have already been mentioned when we discussed clarity (page 76). Clear hand and arm gestures animate, amplify, and clarify verbal communication. Some people use gestures quite naturally during conversation, while others do not. Gestures should become part of the collection of communication skills developed by all teachers. In large teaching spaces or areas that have poor acoustics (e.g., outside, indoor swimming pools, etc.), gestures can replace voice commands when combined with established whistle signals.

Positioning Our positioning in relation to the class indicates our concern for control and safety. The aim is to keep all children in sight during a lesson. They should also be able to see us at all times and feel our presence. We must be prepared to change our positioning as the children move around. When our attention is required in one place for an extended period of time (e.g., organizing apparatus or helping an individual), placement must be such that we can give the help needed and still be able to survey the rest of the class. This entails having nobody, or very few people, behind us.

In order to develop and maintain effective nonverbal behavior, we need become more aware of what we are doing. Our behavior must be observed, recorded, and analyzed. This is difficult to do alone, therefore, the use of videotape or a peer observer is recommended. To see ourselves as others see us is a valuable, though sometimes uncomfortable, experience.

Verbal Behavior

Our voices are very important instruments, and we must use them carefully, as well as effectively. We need to know the strengths and weaknesses of our instrument, and learn to use it to its greatest advantage.

To Do

Comment on the teacher's positioning in the following two photographs. Make suggestions for alternative places to stand.

Unfortunately, many of the places and spaces in which we teach do not have good acoustics. Large gymnasia are often equivalent to echo chambers, as are many indoor swimming pools. The activities also have their own inherent noise components, and we are expected to be able to make ourselves heard at all times. A sense of *what, when, how, to whom,* and *why* the teacher speaks can consciously be developed and practiced.

What

1. *Careful choice of words is important.* Become aware of the level of comprehension of the different groups of students; select and phrase your words accordingly.
   a. Being concise will conserve your voice. This means thinking ahead and planning a short statement. Full sentences are often unnecessary as well-chosen key words can be full of information. If more than two or three words have to be said, consider bringing the children to you so you do not have to shout. This will also help them pay attention. A disadvantage, of course, is that it takes time. Children can learn to come in quickly and not dawdle en route.
   b. Word all tasks in nonconfusing ways that motivate, interest, and generally make the children wish to participate.
2. *Develop an extensive vocabulary and be able to give the same information in more than one way.* If a new word is essential in the lesson, write it clearly on a board or make a flash card. Be prepared to spend a little time explaining and discussing the word before using it.
3. *Include color, interest, flavor, and humor whenever suitable.* The more we appeal to the children, the more carefully they will listen.
4. *Our speech should be grammatically correct.* Children are exposed to a considerable amount of poor speech on television, especially if they listen to sporting events.
5. *Avoid repetition and redundancy—the two Rs.*
   a. A common example of *repetition* is the use of O.K., often added to the end of sentences. Once attention is drawn to it, many teachers are surprised to know how many times they say it.
   b. *Redundancy* refers to phrases, such as "What I want you to do is. . . ." Such phrases do not add to the clarity of the message they preface. As with repetition, we should become aware of any tendency to be redundant and try to eliminate it.

All of us have favorite sayings; we should become aware of them and use them sparingly. By listening to ourselves as we speak, monitoring a tape recording of our teaching, and having a friend write down our particular "Two Rs," we can analyze ourselves. It is not that we advocate eliminating a conversational approach as we teach, rather we wish to encourage word efficiency for two specific reasons: clarity and quality.

When

1. Knowing when it is the most appropriate moment to speak is a developed sense. However, it is probably better to say more than is necessary than less. Children left on their own without any input often lose interest in the task, and ALT-PE is lost. When reviewing tape recordings of their teaching, some inexperienced teachers are surprised to hear stretches of silence.
2. Practice talking to the children as they are working, as well as when they have stopped. In both instances, ensure they are listening and preface your information with comments such as
   "Listen as you work."
   "Stop and listen."
   "Come here, look at me, and listen."
   "Stay where you are and listen."

How What we say is inextricably entwined with *how* we say it; it is the combination of the two that results in the message. Our quality of speech is affected by several variables. Our voices must reach all receivers, and the children should not have to concentrate hard to hear what we are saying.

1. *Good breath control is very important;* this includes breathing from the diaphragm and controlling the speed at which we exhale. The louder we speak, the more breath we need to carry the sound.
2. *When speaking loudly, lower the pitch.* This will help reduce the tightness in the throat that often accompanies shouting, which is to be avoided! "Think low" is advice we often give to women who have difficulty making themselves heard in large spaces. At the other extreme, very low voices can be difficult to hear, and some men have to pitch their voices higher.
3. *Speech that is slower than the usual conversational speed is easier to hear.* Emphasize key words and phrases by isolating them from the rest of the sentence—verbally "underline" them.
4. *Vary expressiveness and tone.* It is possible to say "What was that?" in at least two ways, one sounds condemning, and the other genuinely suggests that we wish to know. The two words "Well done!" can be said so that the meaning conveyed is just the opposite. Awareness of tone must be developed, and this is another instance where a tape recorder can be an asset. To hear ourselves as others hear us can be surprising. We may find we do not "mean what we say and say what we mean."

5. *Be articulate;* enunciate words carefully. How often do we say or hear, "I'm gonna . . ." instead of "I'm going to . . ."; "bitta . . ." instead of "bit of . . ."? We have included a few tongue twisters for you to try!

Table 3.1 suggests some ways to help the above develop the "how."

Table 3.1

Voice Skills

Dimension	Skill	Helpful hints
Volume	Able to change according to needs (e.g., large room, poor acoustics, large number of children); against conflicting ambient sounds	Have a peer signal to indicate volume Tape recorder on sideline Converse with peer across empty room
Articulation	Clarity of words Speed of speech Moderate any extreme accent	Practice specific exercises to make tongue and mouth work Listen to own speech on tape recorder Concentrate on delivery
Expression	Able to combine changes in volume, pitch, and speed	Listen to own speech on tape recorder Practice reading stories, poems aloud Think "dramatically" as you speak

To Do

Try the following tongue twisters:

Tongue twisters twist tongues twisted
Trying to untangle twisted tangles
My tang's tungled now!

She is a thistle sifter and she has a sieve of
sifted thistles and a sieve of unsifted thistles
because she is a thistle sifter.

Betty Botta bought some butter to make some batter
but, she said, this butter's bitter.
So she bought a bit of better butter
and it made her batter better.
So 'twas better Betty Botta bought a bit of better butter!

Recorder: ____________________
Teacher Observed: ____________________

In the chart below, place an *X* in the appropriate box when the teacher communicates with the entire class, a group, or an individual. Each column represents three minutes. Summarize your findings and recommend any changes you feel might help improve communication between the teacher and the children.

Class										
Group										
Individual										

Time in minutes
Totals: **C** _____
G _____
I _____
Summary:

Recommendations:

Figure 3.1
Communication—with whom?

To Whom We may speak to (1) the whole class, (2) a group or, (3) an individual.

Often the answer to a question, words of encouragement, and information given to a small group or an individual will be valuable for the rest of the class. In this case, we can take advantage of the **ripple effect** and speak publicly, that is loud enough for everyone to hear. At other times it is more effective, and considerate, to speak privately, especially if for any reason our comments have negative overtones. We may also speak privately if the children addressed are at a different stage in the learning sequence, and the information we are providing is inappropriate for the majority.

Less experienced teachers often give more information privately and find they have to repeat the same information many times. Initially, practice speaking to the whole class more than to groups and individuals. A peer may watch and record to whom you speak during a lesson, so you can find out with whom you communicate most, the class, groups, or individuals. Figure 3.1 is a sample recording sheet you may find useful. You will find another example in chapter 4.

Why We must have a clear reason for everything we say, and our comments should be purposeful and add to the learning climate. We may wish to do the following:

1. Create or develop ambiance and rapport
2. Motivate, encourage, praise
3. Control or discipline student behavior
4. Organize equipment or children
5. Present movement tasks
6. Provide feedback

Evaluating Your Teaching

One of the most useful skills you can develop is the analysis of your own nonverbal and verbal behavior during the teaching process. Besides listening to what you say as you say it, the use of audiotape recordings is recommended. Using systematic coding, verbal behavior can be recorded on paper, analyzed, and evaluated.

You may ask a colleague to evaluate you as you teach, or you may ask your colleague to videotape you, then you can evaluate your own teaching skills. As an example, it is quite easy for someone to watch you and record to whom you provide feedback during the lesson. This evaluation may reveal that you spend more time with the boys than with the girls, or that you provide general feedback to the less-skilled children, and specific feedback to the highly skilled children. This kind of information is most useful if you wish to develop and improve your teaching. As teachers we all form habits over time. All too often, we are unaware of these habits, and we need to take a look at what we are doing. Chapter 4 includes more information on how you may evaluate your teaching.

Observing Accurately

It may seem obvious to say we must be able to observe accurately as we teach. To develop the insight essential for creating appropriate tasks and providing helpful (congruent) feedback, we must become skilled **observers.** We need to play this role constantly if we wish to base our instruction on the current needs of the students. When teaching, we are constantly observing children, and perhaps unconsciously evaluating both the children and our teaching. The aim should be to make a conscious effort to develop the skills necessary to make objective evaluations and informed decisions.

Observation Skills

We are challenged to develop objective and reliable observation skills that are process-oriented and directed towards skill development.

Barrett (1981, 1983) has been responsible for defining observation as a concept and a process involving interpretation and decision making (Logsdon et al., 1984). This means that we must know clearly what we

Table 3.2

The *How, Who,* and *What* of Observation

How do we do what we do?	
Scan	
	Entire class
Focus	
	Small groups Individuals
Who watches whom?	
Teacher	
	Watches the children
Children	
	Watch other children Watch the teacher
What are we looking for?	
Teacher	
	Mood of the class Safety factors Task understanding On-task activity Problems: common and individual
Teacher and children	
	Quality performance Task interpretation Application of concepts

are looking for as we observe; we must be able to understand and explain what we see; and we must be able to take action based on what we have seen.

Table 3.2 summarizes the *how, who,* and *what* of observing.

How

There are two observational techniques: *scanning* and *focusing*. During a lesson, we must learn to switch constantly between the two.

Scanning The first observational technique to use in a lesson is *scanning*. Scanning gives us an overall picture of what is happening. We notice if the spacing is adequate and safe, if all children are on-task, and who is coping well and who is having difficulties. As well as at the beginning of a lesson, scanning is used immediately after a new task has been set and after observing something or someone in particular. It provides us with a general impression of the class and helps us to decide (1) on *whom* we need to focus and (2) on *what* we need to focus.

Focusing Scanning is followed by *focusing.* We may pay attention to one area of the space, a specific individual, a small group, or a particular aspect of the children's responses.

If the children are working in their own space, select an area and observe the children in that area. You can move into the group, still keeping the rest of the class in sight, and give individual and/or small group feedback. You can then move into a new area and repeat the process with a different group of children.

You also may look for a specific aspect of the children's responses. For example, if you set the following open-ended task—"Use upper body parts to keep the ball in the air"—considerable variation of response might be expected. From past experience, we know the chances are high that some children will use their heads. If we wish to develop the skill of heading, we will watch specifically for this response.

Table 3.3 suggests a cyclic sequence of scanning, focusing, and responding.

Who

We should be observing the children at all times during the lesson. In order to do this, we must position ourselves in relation to what is happening. This has already been mentioned briefly [nonverbal behavior (page 81)].

If the children are traveling throughout the general space of the teaching area, it is advantageous to stand still when observing. When the children are scattered or in formations in their own space, the teacher should travel, moving in and out of the class, zigzagging down the length of the teaching area [figure 3.2].

When teachers demonstrate, the children watch the teacher. Teachers may demonstrate to (a) provide a model (b) clarify a concept, or (c) focus attention on a common error and provide the correction. The children must be told what to look for as they watch. The demonstration should be followed by practice or questioning and discussion, followed by practice of the technique or application of the concept observed.

Peer models are very important, and there should be many opportunities for the children to watch and learn from each other. When accustomed to demonstrating their work, most children will work more diligently to select and refine their movement responses and gain approval from the teacher and their peers. This is not meant to imply that only the very skillful are chosen to demonstrate. Because the program is concept oriented and tasks more likely to be open-ended, allowing for variation of response, it should be possible for every child to demonstrate during the school year.

Table 3.3

Observing-Responding Sequence

Step 1	**Basic task is set**
Step 2	**Scan** 1. Safety 2. Spacing 3. Response behavior a. On-task b. Off-task
Step 3	**Respond** 1. Stop and respace 2. Stop and clarify 3. Provide feedback, public and specific, individual and/or group 4. Give refining task
Step 4	**Scan** What you *look* for is determined by your response in Step 3
Step 5	**Respond** What you *say* depends on your response in Step 3
Step 6	**Focus** 1. Group 2. Individual 3. Area of space
Step 7	**Respond** 1. Feedback 2. Refining task(s) 3. Simplifying and extending task(s)
Step 8	**Focus** What to look for depends on your response in Step 7
Step 9	**Respond** What to say depends on your response in Step 7
Step 10	**Scan or focus**
Step 11	The cycle continues. Your response is always determined by what you see. What you look for is determined by your response

In another instance, the teacher may say, "Watch your partner spinning, sinking, and rising. How does the timing of your partner's sequence differ from yours?" In this situation, the children are being asked to discriminate between what they are doing and what they see, which are very different challenges. The continuation may be for the partners to help each other clarify the time element in their sequences.

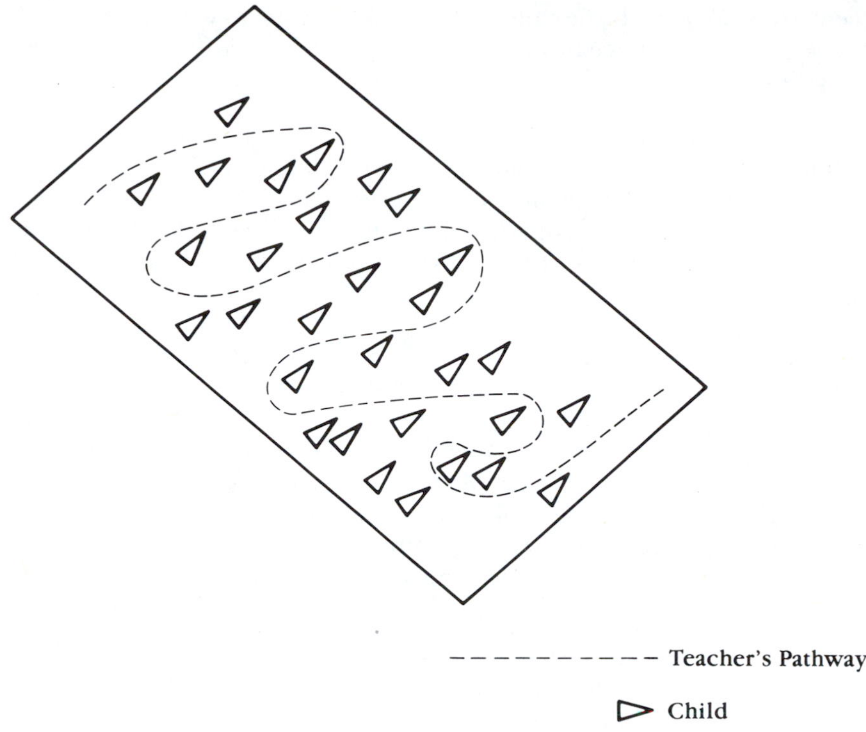

Figure 3.2 Observing children who are working in their own areas.

Children may watch a partner, a small group, half the class, or one child. They should always be told what they are looking for, and time must be spent after the observation to clarify, reinforce, and apply what has been observed.

What

Effective observers decide *what* to look for before they begin observing. This helps them sort out the specific from the general.

The Mood of the Class Each day, we make conclusions regarding the moods of the different groups of students we teach. A class often reflects the general personality of the teacher with whom they spend the most time or the teacher who taught them immediately before coming to the physical education lesson. Some groups are naturally energetic, while others are placid. The time of day, day of the week, season of the year, a change in the weather, or a special event, such as a school play or class outing, will often affect the mood of the class. A wise teacher will attempt to employ an identifiable mood to the advantage of the lesson. A dance lesson which requires sensitivity and slow movements may have to be modified if the class has witnessed some exciting event at recess, such as a fight on the playground. An energetic games lesson may be unsuitable if taught on a Friday at 3:00 P.M., and the children seem tired. We must be flexible and adapt according to what we observe, at the same time safeguarding against the class overruling the planned activities.

Safety Factors We must ensure that the environment is safe as the children participate. Immediate action must be taken if we notice anything that might be hazardous as the children work. Conditions change during lessons as equipment is brought out and put away, and formations change. Therefore, we must try to foresee what hazard might occur and be prepared to interject.

Spacing Continuously scan for good spacing before and during activity. Children need space in order to concentrate on what they are doing, rather than on avoiding others. We must always observe the spacing, changing it if necessary, before beginning a task. Some tasks, particularly those done at speed, need a lot of space, which we may have to create by reducing the number of children on the floor at one time.

We must notice and rearrange gymnastics equipment that is set too close together. We must notice and move dance groups who are so intent on their own creations that they are unaware of crowding other groups.

> **A Quality Physical Education Program** provides children with "an environment in which they have adequate space to move freely and safely" (COPEC, 1992).

Remember That

Children can learn much from observing each other with the following provisions:

1. Children need to be positioned to see the movement pattern being shown.
2. Children need to be given specific elements to observe (e.g., "Watch Billy's stretched feet.") or are asked a question (e.g., "Does Susan travel at the same speed all the time?").
3. Children must immediately apply the concept shown to their own work.

Task Understanding When children begin to respond to a task, we immediately look (scan) for interpretation to ensure everyone understands the challenge. When the task is closed (e.g., "Toss the ball high and catch it after it bounces."), it is comparatively easy to notice if anyone catches it before the bounce or has some other variation. There are several reasons why responses may be different. The intent is not to discover why but to notice who has interpreted the task differently. A quick word to anyone who has misunderstood should suffice. On the other hand, if the majority of the class interprets the task in an unexpected way, then there may be a general misunderstanding. In this case, stop the class and re-explain the task, with a demonstration by the teacher or one or two children who were doing it as expected.

When tasks are open-ended, it is harder to assess the children's interpretation and understanding. Various interpretations may arise because the instructions were unclear or the children may not fully understand the concept(s). Whichever is the case the result is the same: a confused set of responses. When this occurs children need assistance in clarifying, cognitively and kinesthetically, the essence of the task, as in the following example:

Task: "Add changes of direction to the traveling sequence you have created."

Responses: Some children interpret the concept of direction in terms of the general space and produce zigzagging and curved pathways.

Remedies:

1. Children who interpreted directions as traveling right, left, forward, and backward are asked to demonstrate.
2. Half the class watches while the other half demonstrates. The observers are asked to identify children who show clear changes in direction as they travel.
3. Half the class watches the other half travel. The observers are asked to find two different responses. One child is asked to describe the two. Discussion follows, during which the difference between pathways in general space and directions in personal space are clarified. The task is reset and feedback provided.

In all tasks, there are key elements that are included because they are the focus of the learning experience. Refining tasks emphasize those elements and focus the children's attention on these aspects of the task. Before teaching the lesson, we must prepare ourselves to watch for these elements. Notes written on the lesson plan, opposite the task, are helpful. You will find some examples in the sample plans in chapters 7, 10, and 13.

On-Task Activity Some children find it difficult to remain on-task for extended periods of time. Usually, we soon know who they are and can help them by standing close by, separating friends (the last resort!), or giving additional encouragement and/or help. Noticing the general level of on-task activity also gives clues to when the task has been continued long enough, and it is time to change the activity. Sometimes, we may be surprised to find children absorbed in a task, and we might decide to continue with it, forgoing another activity.

Remember That

When observing, you should

1. Decide *what* to observe (safety, use of equipment, response to the task).
2. Decide *whom* to observe (the whole class, a small group, one child, a body part of one child).
3. *Position* yourself to observe (from a corner of the room, from the side of the room, standing on a bench, far from the child).
4. *Look* at the whole response to the task (Was the task answered? How could the movement be improved? Does it need to be simplified or extended?).
5. *Alternate* between *scanning* and *focusing* (Are the children being challenged to produce quality response?).

Source: Adapted from V. J. Wilson, presentation at the Canadian Association for Health, Physical Education and Recreation (CAHPER) 1982, Montreal.

To Do

Remember your own "gym" days, and the importance of the emotional and physical environments and their effects on the children (Koma, 1987).

Individual and Common Problems Because one of our main objectives is to improve the quality of performance, we are always looking for ways to do so. It is not a matter of simply looking for what is wrong, as we are apt to do when we are less experienced. It is more the need to identify and look for problems. Some problems we may be able to anticipate because of the nature of the task. These may be encountered by the majority of the children. We should be able to identify these problems by scanning the class as they work. Other problems will be specific to individuals and will be identified by focusing on each child in turn.

Quality Performance This is always desired. While exploration and discovery are important processes and variety an important product, none should be emphasized at the expense of quality movement. Because the development of physical skill in expressive and functional situations is a major, on-going objective of every physical education program, the children should constantly be directed towards efficient and improved movement. Teacher and peer models are important. When the children know how to observe and relate what they see to their own performance, the quality of movement will be enhanced.

Children readily learn to recognize quality movement. In a game situation, quality may be more easily seen because of the functional nature of the activities. When a goal has been scored, a pass intercepted, or a ball thrown sensitively to a teammate, the movement pattern has been successful and quality is implied. In gymnastics, elements of quality are seen in the appropriate effort content of a skill sequence (e.g., the efficiency with which the child jumped over the box), and in the more aesthetic components, such as change of body shape and continuity during a sequence. In dance, the aesthetic elements, such as the pleasing line within a group or the exciting rhythm emerging, may predominate observation.

"See how tightly Jean curled her body and how smoothly she rolled."

"Was Chris fully stretched during the balance part of the sequence?"

"Watch this group to see how they move into open spaces as they dribble a ball. Who is using the space well?"

"Notice how the dancers arrive at different levels and a strong group focus is developed."

Remember That

You should provide a quality learning experience for *all* your students. This may be easier said than done! The following questions may help you monitor your interaction with your students.

1. Do you smile as frequently at your less-able student as your more-able student or your "least favorite" student as much as your "favorite student"?
2. Do you convey negative nonverbal feedback (e.g., frowns or turning away) to your less-able students?
3. Do you give as much prescriptive feedback on skill performance to your less-able students as your more-able students?
4. Do you praise and respond positively to appropriate behavior and good performance from your less-able students, or do you consider it a fluke and ignore it?

Source: Based on a class handout prepared by J. Wardle (undated), 434–342 Physical Education Methods. Montreal: McGill University, Department of Physical Education.

Task Interpretation Many of the tasks set in a physical education program are open-ended and result in variation of response. This is obviously one of the times the children learn from observing each other's differences or similarities as the movement concepts are applied.

The children who are observing may be helped to see the differences or similarities between two or more performances. The following statements and questions are examples of how they can be helped to focus on the critical features of performance.

"Watch Susan's use of time; sometimes she rolls slowly and then she rolls quickly. Now watch Nancy, how does she use time?"

"Carol, Chris, and José, show us how you each trap the ball as it rebounds off the wall. Which different body parts are they using to stop the ball?"

"This half of the class watch the others as they rise very slowly and collapse very suddenly. Notice how some people come part way up and others all the way up."

Teachers and children gain new ideas from observing other children. A child's unique response may spark new ideas. Children find unusual ways of working with equipment, which may prompt the teacher to challenge the other children, as in "Watch how John keeps his hoop moving as he jumps; now try to keep your hoop moving."

Providing Feedback

Feedback provides us with information on our behavior, information we need in order to learn. It is essential for our development. We need feedback to improve, adapt, and change our teaching behavior; children need it in order to improve their motor skills.

A search of physical education literature reveals that different authors categorize feedback in different ways, and some are quite complex. All researchers agree that feedback is essential for learning to occur, and the ability to provide feedback is one characteristic of a good teacher.

Public and Private Feedback

You may give individual children public feedback as everyone is working on a task, for example, "John, you're keeping your legs together as you jump, that's good," "Chris, straighten up more slowly next time." Public feedback has several advantages:

1. It uses less time.
2. Other children hear and may be able to use the information.
3. Praised children may gain status within the peer group.

It could be a disadvantage if the feedback is interpreted as being negative or critical in nature. Recipients may feel embarrassed or demeaned in front of their peers. In these cases, you will decide to speak privately to an individual.

General and Specific Feedback

These two categories of feedback are easy to understand, use, and monitor when teaching.

General Feedback

This is often our immediate response when watching children begin working on a task; we use it to tell them they are on-task. It can be *verbal* or *nonverbal* (often called body language), and *positive* or *negative.* Table 3.4 gives examples of each type of general feedback.

Positive Feedback Positive feedback provides support and encouragement as the children work. The comments are valuable because they contribute to the learning atmosphere, yet they are limited in usefulness because they neither specify why something is good nor what has been improved.

Table 3.4

General Feedback

	Verbal	Nonverbal
Positive	That's good.	A wink
	Well done!	A smile
	Good try!	A thumbs-up sign
	Great!	A hug
Negative	No good!	Frowning
	That's not right.	Shaking the head
	Poor show!	Pointing a finger
	Oh dear!	Turning away

Negative Feedback Negative feedback should be used sparingly, so the children do not feel incompetent nor threatened. Positive effects will arise only if we follow such feedback with information the children can use to make corrections and improvements to their performance. If the rapport between a child and teacher is "good," occasional negative feedback can be interpreted as friendly and humorous, but we need to be very aware of the signals we send.

Specific Feedback

This is specific information we provide for the children. We can give it to them after they have completed a task (past), or while they are doing a task (during). Specific feedback can be **descriptive** or **prescriptive.** Table 3.5 gives examples of specific feedback.

The amount and kind of feedback we provide affects the learning environment. Siedentop (1983) suggests that "In most skill-learning situations, a rate of 4.0 feedbacks per minute is easily attainable." Research shows that we can significantly increase the amount of feedback we give when teaching (Williamson, O'Sullivan, & Jackson, 1985). To do this, our verbal behavior must be systematically monitored, and we must be prepared to change what we do.

Descriptive Feedback Descriptive feedback is given to the children while they are responding to a task (present), or when they have completed it (past). What they are doing, or have done, may or may not be correct; therefore, we need to qualify the description. For example, we might say, "Good, your hands are shoulder-width apart. Remember where you have them for the next time." This comment reinforces the child's response to the task. It has positive overtones and contributes significantly to the learning atmosphere.

Table 3.5

Specific Feedback

	Descriptive	Prescriptive
Positive	"Your legs were very straight." (past) "You're moving too soon." (during)	"Keep curled." (during) "Push harder next time." (future)
Negative	"You didn't look for the ball." (past) "You're not releasing soon enough." (during or past)	"Don't look at your feet." (during) "Don't hit so hard next time." (future)

Remember That

Specific, positive, descriptive feedback can help you let the children know (1) what you expect and (2) that you appreciate good performance. Comments such as, "I see some beautifully, pointed toes," "There are some good stretches as you jump," "Listen to those quiet landings—they are good," help the children understand that "any old response" does not get public recognition. These public comments contribute to a warm and positive learning environment.

Descriptive feedback may imply the performance needs improving; the child needs to change something. In these cases, the information has a corrective function. "Your base is small, therefore, you are finding it difficult to balance." We may assume the child will make the necessary adjustment(s), or we may have to provide the refining task by telling the child to move his or her hands further apart. This is particularly important when working with younger or less capable children. Siedentop (1983) warns that overuse of feedback focusing on what is incorrect, leads to an "error-centered climate." At all times, the positive message should be emphasized. We can do this by prefacing descriptive and corrective feedback with some evaluative comment, for example, "That is better, but your base is still rather small."

It is most important that we are aware of the nature of what we say to our children and that we tell them what *to* do more often than what *not* to do.

Lesson: ______________________________
Date: ______________________________
Name of Teacher: ______________________________
Name of Observer: ______________________________

Listen to the teacher (or a tape recording); recognize and record with a check mark the different kinds of feedback given during the lesson.

	General	**Specific**
Positive		
Negative		

Totals:

Figure 3.3 Feedback recording sheet.

Prescriptive Feedback We prefer to call this category of feedback **refining tasks,** as information is provided on how to do or how to improve something. A fuller discussion is found in the section on designing tasks (page 102). As with descriptive feedback, we can give this information while the children are working (during) or when they finish (past). In both cases, they need to repeat the task and be given more feedback.

In a dance lesson, we might say, "Open your fingers more as your hands rise." It might be equally appropriate to say this as the children are rising or when they have finished. Your decision will depend on the specific situation.

Remember That

Practice makes perfect—only when we practice the right thing(s). We can just as easily practice a skill incorrectly. Feedback and encouragement are two important factors that help us practice the right thing(s).

When monitoring our teaching, we need to become very aware of how much feedback we provide and the kind of feedback (general, specific, positive, negative, descriptive, prescriptive) we use. Overall, we should aim to score high on providing specific feedback which is both descriptive and prescriptive in nature. We should also be considerably more positive than negative in the content and tone of what we say. By using a simple recording devise, we can discover how much feedback we give and its nature. Figure 3.3 is easy to complete; ask a colleague to use it while observing you teach a lesson, or tape record yourself and complete the chart later.

Designing Tasks

Lesson plans consist of a variety of **tasks,** or things to do. The tasks are designed to meet the objectives of the lesson and, consequently, improve the motor performance of the children. These are called **movement tasks** (Rink, 1979). Another category of tasks, concerned with organizational procedures necessary for the smooth running of the lesson, is discussed later in this chapter.

Movement Tasks

We have stated that the physical education program should consider children's capacities in terms of their cognitive development, as well as their physical skills (see chapter 1). We have also stated teaching implies a "marriage" between movement concepts (content) and what is familiarly termed teaching style. This refers to the amount of freedom the children have to make decisions in a lesson. When selecting and wording the tasks for a lesson, be aware of the kinds of decisions you are making and what decisions will be made by the children. The more "closed" a task, the fewer the decisions for the children.

Closed tasks

1. elicit more uniform responses,
2. remove responsibility from the children,
3. may save time,
4. may focus attention on a specific movement or movement concept.

The more "open" a task, the more decisions for the children to make.

Open tasks

1. elicit individual interpretations of the task,
2. increase the children's responsibility for their own learning,
3. may mean the children spend more time thinking before responding, and encourage exploration and discovery,
4. require a flexible approach to skill development,
5. require good observational skills from teachers.

The kind of decisions that may or may not be left to the children include the following:

1. With whom they will work

   "Make groups of four." (open)
   "Count off in fours." (closed)

2. Where they will work

   "Move into your own space." (open)
   "Stand in your lines." (closed)

3. What apparatus they will use

"Select either a rope or a hoop." (open)
"Everyone take a large ball." (closed)

4. How they respond

"When you hear the music, skip, sometimes going forward, sometimes backward, maybe even try skipping sideways." (open)
"Skip four steps forward, four steps backward." (closed)

To Do

Study the tasks above and decide what choices have been left to the children and what decisions have been made by the teacher.

Change each task. First, try to increase the freedom of choice for the children, then reduce it.

A less experienced teacher, or the teacher meeting a new class, is wise to use more closed tasks, until both teacher and children have become accustomed to each other. Some children balk at being required to make decisions, some may lack the confidence to "try their own thing," still others may not have the movement vocabulary or ability to produce their own response. In all these situations, more closed tasks should initially be provided.

A lesson usually consists of a mixture of open and closed tasks, with the teacher making adjustments as the opportunity and need arise. The sample lesson plans in chapters 7, 10, and 13 include a range of open and closed tasks.

Different Tasks

The concept of tasks is being used more widely in physical education literature (Siedentop, 1983; Logsdon et al., 1984; Siedentop, Herkowitz, & Rink, 1984; and Rink, 1985). In its simplest form, the task concept is a useful method of monitoring the development of a lesson. Five kinds of movement tasks are possible in a learning sequence, each with a specific function (Rink, 1979; Logsdon et al., 1984; and Rink, 1985):

1. Basic tasks
2. Refining tasks
3. Simplifying tasks
4. Extending tasks
5. Applying tasks

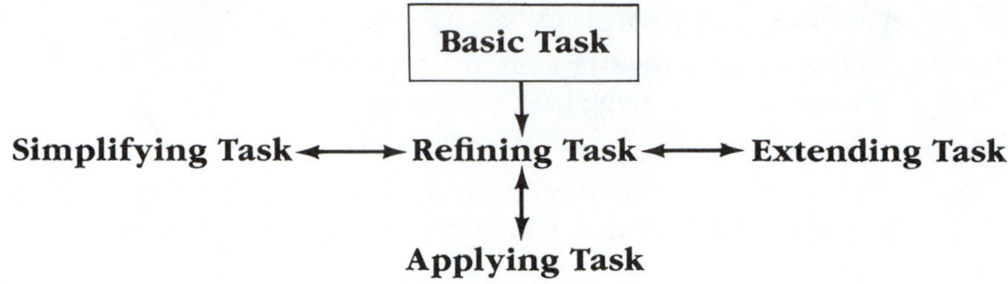

Figure 3.4
Interrelationship between movement tasks.

It is the interrelationship between these movement tasks that allows "a true progression of activities" (Siedentop, Herkowitz, & Rink, 1984) (figure 3.4).

Basic Tasks A basic task is the starting point of each learning sequence in a lesson. A lesson will include a limited number of basic tasks, each relating to one or more of the objectives of the lesson. As a rule of thumb, each basic task is followed by a refining task, as shown in figure 3.4. Basic tasks are the beginning of a learning sequence and cannot stand alone (figure 3.5). Basic tasks can range from being closed to open.

Lessons for young or less-skilled children usually include more basic tasks than do lessons for the older and/or more skillful children. This is because the former need frequent changes of activity to maintain their interest and level of motivation. Skillful children, because they are more successful, are able to spend more time refining and extending their performance.

We receive signals from the children that may indicate when it is time to change to another task. If you notice an increase in off-task behavior, such as an increase in chatter or a drop in skill performance, it is probably time to change the activity. It is better to change too soon rather than wait until the children become tired, bored, and frustrated with what they are doing.

Refining Tasks These tasks tell the children how to improve what they are doing. The information focuses on execution ("I can do a waltz step!") and quality of performance ("My legs are much straighter now when I balance on my hands."). You may recognize them as teaching cues or prescriptive feedback. They are the core of the learning sequence. Our ability to provide appropriate refinement in response to children's movement is dependent on our observational skills, ability to analyze what we see, and knowledge of the components of movement. Refining tasks tend to be more closed because the intent is to focus attention on a specific aspect of a movement concept or pattern.

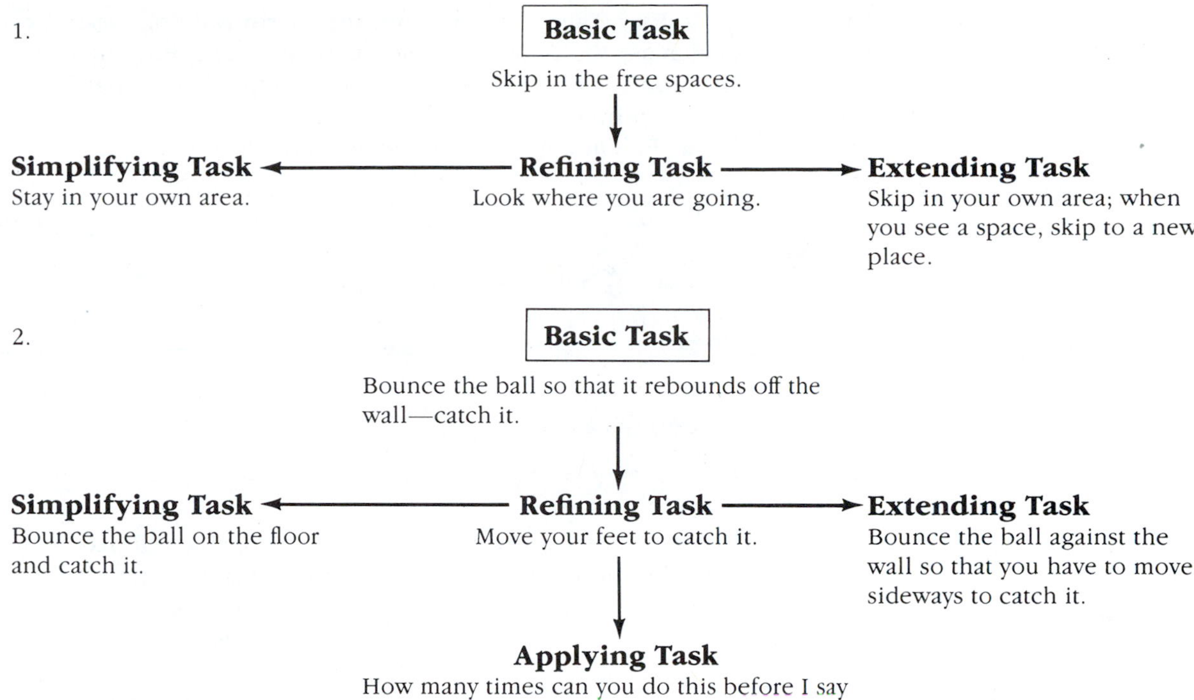
1.
Basic Task
Skip in the free spaces.
Simplifying Task
Stay in your own area.
Refining Task
Look where you are going.
Extending Task
Skip in your own area; when you see a space, skip to a new place.
2.
Basic Task
Bounce the ball so that it rebounds off the wall—catch it.
Simplifying Task
Bounce the ball on the floor and catch it.
Refining Task
Move your feet to catch it.
Extending Task
Bounce the ball against the wall so that you have to move sideways to catch it.
Applying Task
How many times can you do this before I say "Stop"?

Figure 3.5 Sample learning sequences.

Simplifying Tasks The degree of difficulty of a task may need reducing for some children before any improvement or development will occur. Simplification can be done in different ways. The important thing is that we must be able to adjust the task to meet the needs of the moment. Some of the ways we can do this follow:

1. Change the equipment. "We'll take one layer off the box."
2. Alter the environment. "Try it first in this small space."
3. Change one dimension of the previous task. "Instead of running as you bounce the ball, begin by walking."

To Do

Think of different ways of simplifying the following basic tasks:

1. Throw the tennis ball to your partner, so it is caught at different levels.
2. Balance on two body parts.
3. Run quickly and smoothly with small steps, keeping the group close together.

Extending Tasks These are the opposite of simplifying tasks. Extending tasks increase the degree of difficulty to meet the children's new level of competency. It is possible to do this by adjusting similar components, such as equipment, environment, movement concepts, and by combining skills. Extending tasks may range from closed to open.

To Do

Discuss ways of increasing the difficulty of the following tasks:

1. Rise and sink with your partner.
2. Run, jump, and roll.
3. Play three against three Keep Away, using a seven-inch playground ball.

Applying Tasks When a movement concept or specific skill has been explored, expanded, and practiced, it is time to use it, integrate it with other known skills, and enjoy the newfound competency. Applying tasks may come anywhere in a lesson as mini-culminations to learning sequences. They provide the children with a focus and measure of what has been learned. Children lose motivation if they do not have the opportunity to use their skills and knowledge to achieve results. Once a product had evolved, it should be applied in appropriate situations. Applying tasks may range from closed to open.

Relationships between the Tasks

Less experienced teachers tend to provide fewer refining and applying tasks than more experienced teachers. A rule of thumb to remember when planning lessons is to provide at least one refining task after every other task you set. The following is an example of what we mean by this:

Basic task: Toss and catch your beanbag.

Refining task: Put your hands together under the beanbag to catch it.

Extending task: Toss the beanbag a little higher.

Refining task: Let your hand follow the beanbag when you release it. Use a big, smooth arm swing.

A graphic analysis of the information you provide during a lesson gives a clear picture of the interaction between the tasks in the learning sequences you structure. Such an analysis is shown in figure 3.6.

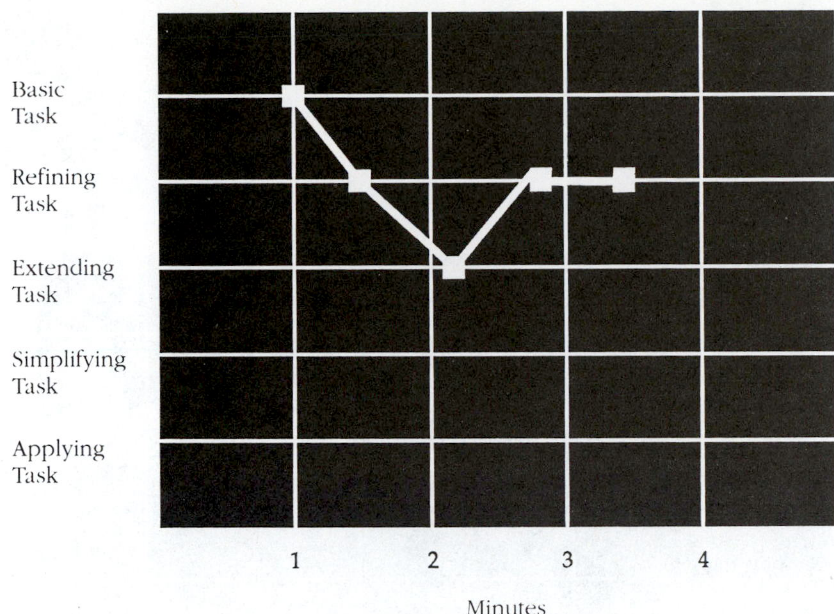

Figure 3.6 Toss and catch learning sequence.

Organizational Skills

These skills are required when we organize the elements of the learning environment and establish and maintain appropriate behavior of students (Luke, 1987). Organizing includes **CATS!**

1. Children
2. Apparatus and equipment
3. Time
4. Space

Good organization results in safety, efficient use of time, and good behavior. Good teachers are good organizers.

Organizing Tasks

You will have to decide on the most effective organizational procedures for your lesson and plan tasks for the children in order to implement this. Such tasks are called **organizing tasks** (Rink, 1979). They tell the children where to go, with whom to work, what equipment or apparatus to get, where to place it, when to put it away, etc. Some typical organizing tasks follow:

"Find a space."

"Find a partner."

"Put the beanbags in the hoop where you found them."

"Your group needs a mat and a bench; remember to lift the apparatus as you move it."

To Do

Discuss the following learning sequences in terms of (1) the interrelationship between the tasks and (2) the amount of information provided in five minutes.

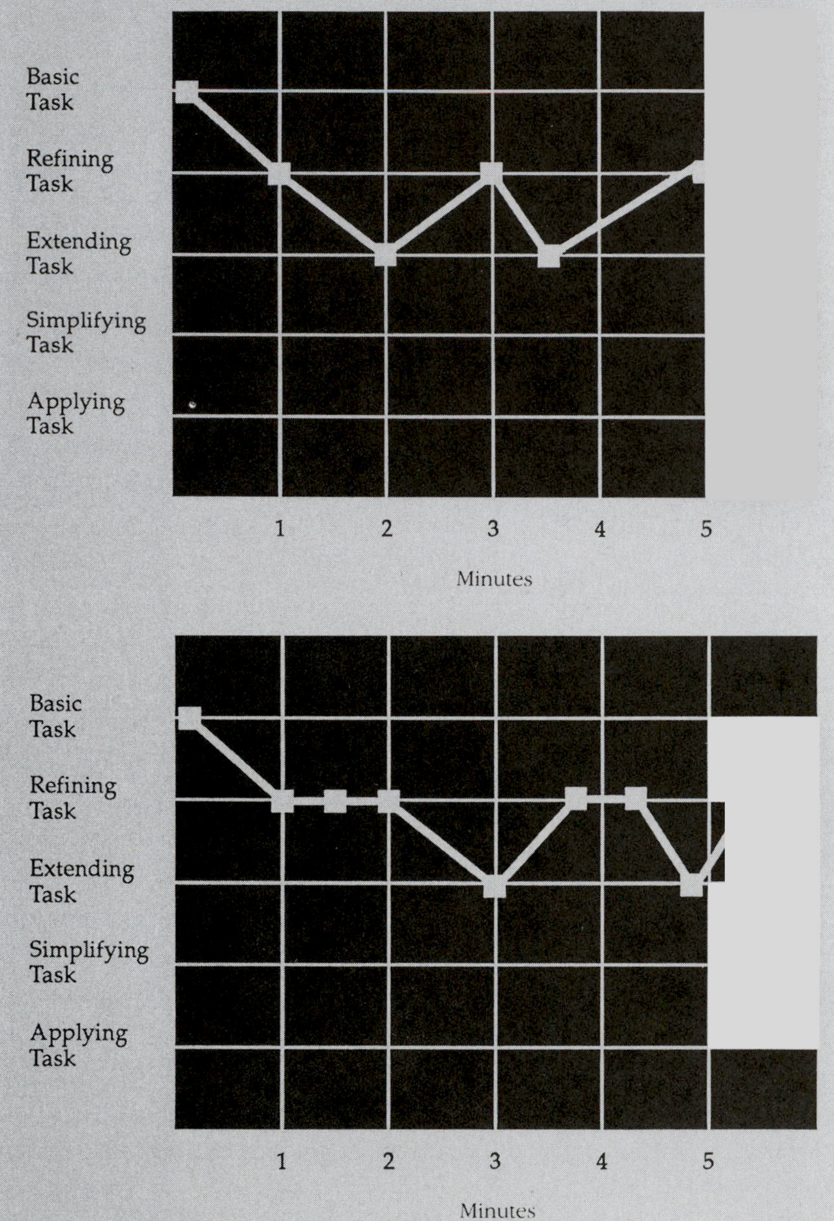

As with basic tasks (page 102), the children may need help to complete organizational tasks successfully. In these instances, simplifying and/or refining tasks are needed. Each "job" should be carefully thought through when planning the lesson, and some tasks will have to be broken down into parts and presented to the children bit by bit. This is particularly important when introducing new apparatus in a gymnastic lesson.

Organizing the Children

Every lesson requires the children to be in specific places and formations. These may be (1) structured, established routines, (2) informal and vary every lesson, or (3) a mixture; this is probably the most usual. Regimented formations, which the children "fall into" at a single command, are used less often these days. Children gradually learn to become responsible for using the space sensibly and safely, forming their own groups and making required formations.

Spacing For safety all children must have adequate space in which to work. The following are examples of organizing tasks related to space:

"Find a large space."

"Stand on your spots."

The second task implies "spots" have been established in a previous lesson.

Formations and Groups Specific formations—circles, lines, squares—are needed in many singing games, folk dances, and many low organization and lead-up games. Children usually work together more effectively when in compatable groups. Depending on the task, this may mean children of similar ability, height and/or weight, or good friends.

Young children in particular need help when getting into groups and making formations, and lesson time must be allowed for this. As a rule of thumb, group size should be small for younger, less experienced children. Formations should also be simple shapes they understand.

When making groups, we prefer to use a variety of systems, with decisions being made sometimes by us, and other times by the children. The following are two ways to facilitate making groups:

1. The children sit or stand in a circle and count off in the number required per group. Each group moves into its own space.
2. The teacher walks among scattered children handing out pinnies. Children form groups according to colors.

When deciding on the number of children per group, consider keeping it low so that participation is increased. There may be a minimum number required for the activity to "work." For example, to experience cooperation and competition simultaneously, a group of four is needed (two versus two). If cooperation is the focus of the task, then two or three may be satisfactory. The larger the group, the more challenging the situation.

> **To Do**
>
> How many different ways of getting into groups can you recall? Make a list and discuss (1) the efficiency of each method and (2) the social implications of each method.

Always think through the groupings needed during the whole lesson. Once a group has been established, avoid breaking it up for the following task. This upsets the children and may mean friends are separated unnecessarily. If you need larger groups, form them by combining existing ones. The following size sequences are suggested as being "socially friendly":

	First group	Second group	Third group	Fourth group
1.	Alone	Two	Four	Eight
2.	Alone	Two	Six	
3.	Alone	Three	Six	Nine (probably only creative dance)

Behavior When communicating with children, you should try to employ preventative discipline. Encourage *good* behavior by doing the following:

1. Be as positive as possible. Look for something good to say to each child every day.
2. Plan to include the children in some decisions, such as music preference, equipment selection.
3. Make few rules, primarily to protect the rights of others. The fewer the number of rules, the fewer there are to break. Whenever possible, include the children in the making and establishment of rules.
4. Respond to a child after misbehavior has occurred; talking things out usually helps.
5. Tell children what *to* do rather than what *not* to do. When misbehavior has occurred, it is better to say, "Put the ball down," rather than, "Don't bounce the ball."
6. Employ preventative planning; construct situations that encourage good behavior.
7. Interfere with misbehavior privately and quietly, so the child does not get the public attention that might have been sought.
8. Expect the same behavior from children of both sexes and discipline them in the same manner when necessary.

Organizing the Equipment

Every subject has its own hardware requirements, and physical education is no exception. A considerable amount and variety of equipment is needed to provide a diverse and complete movement experience for the children. We must know what equipment and apparatus is available for our use. Checking the storage room is a good policy (see chapter 4).

When equipment and/or apparatus has been selected for a lesson, decisions have to be made regarding its placement in the teaching area. This is part of the planning procedure. Occasionally, it may be necessary for you or the children to go to the storage area during a lesson. It is at such a time that a tidy, well-planned storage system is appreciated.

Dance Many dance lessons require a tape recorder or record player, but these are for the teacher's use rather than the children's use. Some folk dances use sticks (e.g., Tinikling from the Philippines and some Morris dances from England), and some have dancers who play percussion instruments (e.g., Tarantella from Italy).

Creative dances may need props, such as masks, costumes, and strips of material that float. However, there will be many lessons in which the children dance without equipment.

Games Most of the equipment for games lessons is not bulky (unless one has to carry goalposts), but there is usually a quantity to cope with. Tasks often require one piece per child (e.g., a tennis ball) or sometimes two pieces (e.g., a ball and bat each). There can be a considerable amount of "taking out and putting away" when children pair up and make larger groups. Before the lesson, or with the help of the children at the beginning of the lesson, the equipment should be placed strategically throughout the teaching area (see chapter 9). ALT-PE is increased if the minimum of time is spent getting equipment and children can do so without colliding with each other. Well-spaced equipment usually results in well-spaced children who are able to begin to work safely without waiting for the teacher to position them.

Gymnastics Gymnastics activities make considerable demands on our organizational skills (see chapter 12). Unlike games equipment, gymnastics apparatus is heavy and large. An on-going objective of gymnastics is that the children should learn how to lift, carry, and place the pieces according to a pre-set plan or to their own design. This is important.

Young children need considerable help with carrying and placing apparatus. If you have four groups working with benches and mats, you will probably need to help one group at a time, even though the apparatus is identical. Children waiting should be told to watch carefully, so they will know what to do when their turn comes.

Organizing for Safety

When children are free to move in open spaces and with equipment, safety becomes increasingly important. Early in the school year, we need to establish some safety skills.

Children must learn to stop correctly.

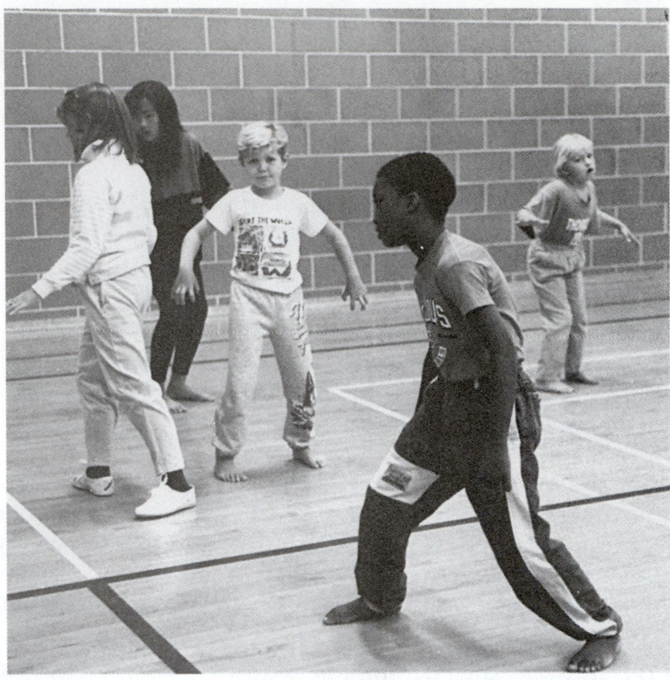

Remember That

- You should establish the command "stop," "freeze," or "rest" (depending on the activity) to gain the children's attention.
- Children should understand they should only attempt skills that are within their capabilities.
- Children should wear appropriate clothing. Baggy sweaters and loose jewelry may get caught on apparatus; too tight pants restrict movement.
- Children should never work in socks; bare feet or sneakers are appropriate and safe.
- Children should stay away from others when they are working on their own.
- Children (and teachers!) should not chew gum—it can choke you.

An important safety skill for the children to learn is how to stop on command. While this may appear exceedingly obvious, few teachers spend time discussing with young children the importance of a wide base of support (feet spread apart), a lowered center of gravity (knees bent), gripping feet (strong legs), and arms out for balance, so they can readily stop.

While a whistle may be appropriately used in some environments (particularly the outdoors) as a "stop" signal, its shrill sound is usually unnecessary indoors. We must find an appropriate command or signal in order to gain the children's attention. A raised hand or the commands "freeze" or "stop" must be used with consistency, and obedience expected from the children.

Children's use of space should be another initial concern in all lessons. When children are working on their own, they should be as far away from others as possible. "Run into the empty spaces" is a good task to promote this skill, whether the class is in the first or sixth grade. After much practice, children will know how important it is to monitor their use of space, paying attention to it automatically when they begin to work.

Organizing Lesson Time

Time should always be used efficiently. A quality program maximizes learning time (ALT-PE) through an effective timetable, established routines, clear-cut behavioral codes, and preventative discipline.

Most children enjoy and feel secure in a well-organized learning environment. Children like to know what is expected of them so that they can follow the rules and work successfully within the guidelines. Many teachers delegate some responsibilities to monitors, leaders or groups of children to ensure that particular duties are carried out. Children will usually be happy to set up and/or put away equipment and apparatus if they are treated as "special workers" for that day or week.

Most children happily anticipate each physical education lesson. Unless safety is of special concern, movement should begin as soon as possible when they enter the space. The first task can be set in the classroom, or as the children change into gym clothes. Having an interesting task to begin a lesson reduces dawdling and control problems. It is when children are unoccupied that they find something to do, and valuable time is wasted regaining their attention. "Get a ball and travel with it," "Practice running and jumping," "Repeat the action phrase you created last week" are the kinds of task that elicit immediate activity in Part 1 of lessons (see chapter 4 for further discussion of the parts of lessons). Task cards or charts suggesting beginning activities can be posted on the gymnasium wall; the children can be told to refer to them and select a task.

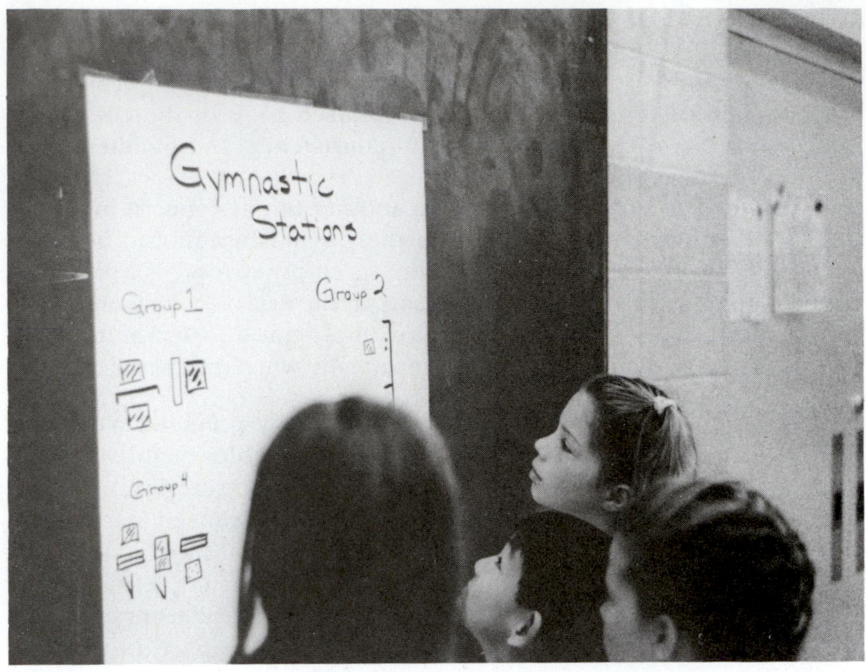

Children may refer to task cards, charts, or diagrams to begin activity.

Summary

Teaching is a cyclic process involving the interaction of many components. Our personal traits, beliefs, and value systems form the foundation of our teaching behavior. In addition, we can learn, develop, and use consistently some very specific, observable, and sometimes measurable, skills. We can practice teaching skills in much the same way we practice other skills. This means we must be willing to monitor our teaching and, based on the information (feedback) generated, make decisions about what changes are needed to improve our teaching behavior. A few suggestions have been made on how you might begin to do this. Readings suggesting other analytical systems will be found at the end of this chapter.

Review Questions

1. What are some of the characteristics of *good* teachers?
2. Six groups of teaching skills are discussed in this chapter. What are they? Which ones do you consider to be your strengths? Which ones do you think you will (or already do) find difficult?
3. Why is specific feedback a critical component of the learning sequence?
4. What are the relative merits of public and private feedback?

5. What different ways do you know of getting children into groups?
6. How can good behavior be encouraged?
7. What kinds of decisions can children be encouraged to make during lessons?
8. What will you look for when observing your students?

References

Barrett, K. (1981). Observation as a teaching behavior. In J. Jackson, & D. Turkington (Eds.), *Quality programming in H.P.E.R.: Vol. II. CAHPER convention papers* (pp. 103–106), Victoria: University of Victoria.

Barrett, K. (1983). A hypothetical model of observing as a teaching skill. *Journal of Teaching in Physical Education, 3*(1), 22–30.

Caruso, V. (1982). Enthusiastic teaching. *JOPERD 53*(3), 47, 48.

The Council on Physical Education for Children (COPEC). (1992). *Developmentally appropriate physical education for children: A position statement.* Reston, VA: AAHPERD.

Grant, B., & Martens, F. (1982). Teacher effectiveness in elementary physical education *CAHPER Journal, 48*(4), 7–10.

Koma, C. (1987). Movement education resource file. Project for 434-324 Movement education for early childhood teachers, Faculty of Education. Montreal: McGill University.

Logsdon, B., Barrett, K., Ammons, M., Broer, M., Halverson, L., McGee, R., & Robertson, M. A. (1984). *Physical education for children: A focus on the teaching process* (2nd ed.). Philadelphia: Lea & Febiger.

Luke, M. (1987). Analysis of class management physical education. *CAHPER Journal, 53*(3), 10–13.

O'Sullivan, M. (1985). A descriptive analytical study of student teacher effectiveness and student behavior in secondary school physical education. In B. Howe, & J. Jackson (Eds.), *Teaching Effectiveness Research.* Victoria, B. C.: University of Victoria.

Rink, J. (1979). *Observation system for content development physical education—Manual.* Columbia, SC: The University of South Carolina.

Rink, J. (1985). *Teaching physical education for learning.* St. Louis: Times Mirror/Mosby.

Siedentop, D. (1983). *Developing teaching skills in physical education* (2nd ed.), Palo Alto, CA: Mayfield Publishing Company.

Siedentop, D. (1992). *Developing teaching skills in physical education* (3rd ed.), Mountain View, CA: Mayfield Publishing Company.

Siedentop, D., Herkowitz, J., & Rink, J. (1984). *Elementary physical education methods*. Englewood Cliffs, NJ: Prentice-Hall Inc.

Williamson, K., O'Sullivan, M., & Jackson, J. (1985). The effects of monitoring on the verbal feedback of student teachers in physical education lessons. *CAHPER Journal, 51*(7), 8–13.

Related Readings

Allison, P. (1988). Strategies of observing during field experiences. *JOPERD, 59*(2), 28–30.

Allison, P., Pissanos, B., & Sakola, S. (1990). Physical education revisited—The institutional biographies of pre-service classroom teachers. *JOPERD, 61*(5), 76–79.

Anderson, A., Vogel, P., & Reuschlein, P. (1991). The implications of teacher expectations: A review of research. *CAHPER Journal, 57*(1), 21–27.

Darst, P., Mancini, V., & Zakrajsek, D. (1983). *Systematic observation instrumentation for physical education*. New York: Leisure Press.

Goldberger, M. (1984). Effective learning through a spectrum of styles. *JOPERD, 55*(8), 17–21.

Grant, B. (1985). The relationship between specialist training and effective P.E. teaching in the elementary school. In B. Howe, & J. Jackson, (Eds.), *Teaching effectiveness research, Physical Education Series #6*. Victoria, B.C.: University of Victoria.

Kovar, S., Ermler, K., & Mehrhof, J. (1992). Helping students to become self-disciplined. *JOPERD, 63*(6), 26–28.

Mercier, R. (1992). Beyond class management—Teaching social skills through physical education. *JOPERD, 63*(6), 83–87.

Radford, K. (1991). For increased teacher effectiveness . . . link observation, feedback and assessment. *CAHPER Journal, 57*(2), 4–9.

Radford, K. (1991). Observational comfort zones. *CAHPER Journal, 57*(1)28–33.

Ratcliffe, T., Ratcliffe, L., & Bie, B. (1991). Creating a learning environment: Class management strategies for elementary physical education teachers. *JOPERD, 62*(9), 24–27.

Williamson, K., O'Sullivan, M., & Jackson, J. (1985). The effects of monitoring on the verbal feedback of student teachers in physical education classes. *CAHPER Journal, 51*(7), 8–13.

Chapter 4
Developing a Quality Program

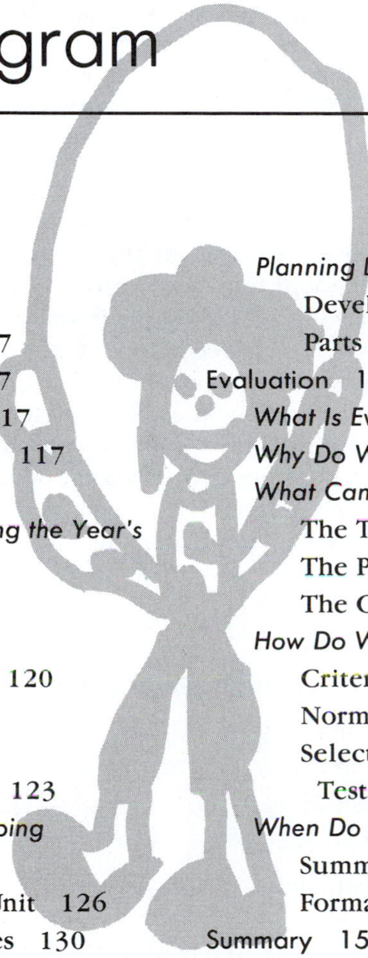

The development of a quality physical education program is dependent upon our knowledge of children and how they most effectively acquire movement skills. A quality program is also dependent upon successful planning and management. Sound planning and organizing practices will promote efficiency, safety, and a positive learning environment in which children's skill development will occur.

Planning and evaluating are important interrelated facets of teaching. How are they related? Very simply, planning comes prior to teaching, and evaluating occurs after teaching. This may be superficially true, but we need to go further. Both planning and evaluating should be continuous and concurrent within the program. That is, planning should be based upon evaluation, and evaluation based upon careful planning.

Planning

The hallmark of an effective teacher is sound planning (Luke, 1987) because it is essential for the development of a quality program. Sound planning will help you create a positive learning environment which is safe, productive, and supportive for the children. Planning benefits children when their needs and interests are considered and all activities are developmentally appropriate for their varying skill levels. Heightened efficiency will occur as you plan for children to participate for the maximum amount of time in each physical education lesson. While at times we may be busy and overcome with new curricula, a child with difficulty, or the feeling that there is not enough time in the day, planning is essential for good teaching.

In order to develop a quality physical education program, you must do the following:

1. Consider children's needs, the community's interests, the local curriculum and your interests and abilities as the teacher.
2. Establish long-term, intermediate and short-term objectives.
3. Plan the year's program.
4. Plan units.
5. Plan lessons.
6. Evaluate.

Planning Considerations

If you are new to teaching physical education, planning a program may seem a monumental task. However, you will be guided by the children's needs (the community's strengths), your local curriculum, scheduling, and facilities, as well as your ideas of what a quality program entails.

The Children's Needs

The children's needs consistently influence our planning. We should consider their differing abilities and interests as we strive to enhance their skills and the pleasure they gain in movement activities. You will teach children who are exceptionally skilled in particular areas, others who seem to have an abundance of energy, others who may have emotional difficulties, and others who are "average." In our planning, we need to consider each individual, as well as the group as a whole.

Every class has a personality, and we should capitalize upon its strengths. Some classes work well in groups; other classes are comprised of children who are more productive working individually. Some classes are noisy; other classes are quiet. While we don't want to label groups, it is wise to take the children's lead and capitalize upon their interests.

Remember That

- Children are not miniature adults.
- Physical education and athletic programs have different purposes.
- Children in school today will not be adults in today's world. (COPEC, 1992).

Community Strengths

The priority of physical education as viewed by your school and school board will also largely influence the type of program you design. The specific athletic interests of the local community may be reflected in the program. Some areas in the United States and Canada are known for their superior programs in gymnastics, swimming, track and field, ice hockey, and other sports. For this reason, the wise teacher will ensure that these activities are given ample time within the program. However, a balanced program is of utmost importance, and no one activity should be taught at the expense of others. For instance, a games unit consisting entirely of basketball or hockey, or a program that does not include dance is totally unacceptable.

Your Local Curriculum

Every school board has curricular guidelines that encourage teachers to employ a collective teaching philosophy through formally established practices. Curriculum guides promote continuity between the grades and within the grades in various subjects. You will find that some curriculum guides are very brief and encourage much freedom for the teacher, while others are more prescriptive and detailed. It is important that you begin with your physical education curriculum guide, and then create a program you believe in and that will benefit the children you teach.

Your Interests and Talents

As the teacher, you are the key figure who will ultimately give shape to your physical education program. It is important that you maximize your strengths and special teaching abilities. What aspects of physical education do you find most exciting? Perhaps you wish to schedule baseball in both the spring and fall because of your exceptional expertise; perhaps you are a music connoisseur and wish to share your enthusiasm and knowledge with children in dance classes. Carefully consider what special talents you may offer your students. Build upon your interests, and you will be enthused about your program!

Establishing Objectives

"An objective describes an intended result of instruction" (Mager, 1975). Writing objectives (or goals) is useful because it helps you to clarify and establish priorities within your physical education program. You may find it helpful to begin with an assortment of considerations, and then ponder each one to establish what you believe is important in a child's program. Ensure that your objectives are attainable; otherwise, you set yourself up—and the children—for failure.

Objectives may be cognitive, affective, or psychomotor. For example, a cognitive objective is "the students will gain an *understanding* of the underlying principles of flight," while a psychomotor objective is "the students will *demonstrate* flight in many different forms."

Sometimes an objective may be expanded to be more inclusive or narrowed to be more specific. Thus, objectives may guide you over a long time period, intermediate time period, or a short time period. If you are planning the entire year's program, then you need to consider your long-term objectives. Long-term objectives are quite general and global, such as the following:

Students will develop an appreciation for various types of music.

Students will experience various forms of flight.

Students will develop an appreciation for their bodies' capabilities.

If you are planning a unit, which is one chunk of your year's program, then you will have objectives that are more specific than long-term goals, called intermediate objectives. The following are examples of intermediate objectives:

Students will be able to discern between European folk dances and American folk dances.

Students will gain proficiency with flight assisting apparatus (ropes, beatboard, springboard, trampette).

Students will develop a sense of expressiveness in the dance unit.

Short-term objectives are useful for a short time, such as for a lesson or for a specific sequence of tasks. Some examples follow:

Students will be able to perform the grapevine step.

Students will be able to demonstrate effective use of the springboard.

Students will demonstrate contrasts in suddenness and stillness in an expressive sequence of stretch-curl-twist.

Table 4.1 outlines the three types of objectives.

Table 4.1

Three Types of Planning Objectives

Long-term objectives →	for the yearly program
Intermediate-term objectives →	for the unit plan
Short-term objectives →	for the lesson plan
→	for learning sequences in single lessons

In **A Quality Physical Education Program,** "children are given the opportunity to participate daily in scheduled, instructional physical education throughout the year, exclusive of recess" (COPEC, 1992).

Long-Term Planning—Developing the Year's Program

At the beginning of the school year, we suggest that you outline when dance, games, gymnastics, and other special units will be taught. Shorter units of activities may also be included, depending on your climate and any special facilities available. These may include swimming, roller-skating, ice skating, or other seasonal activities. You may wish to involve parents or local experts to assist in teaching or supervising these activities.

Your role as a teacher is to facilitate learning by every child in your class. Because children have a diversity of interests and abilities, the program should be well-balanced between the functional and the expressive, the social and solitary, and the competitive and the cooperative. Therefore, we believe in a balanced program that includes equal time spent in dance, games, and gymnastics.

Establishing Long-Term Objectives

Long-term objectives are the goals you want the children to achieve in the school year. (Perhaps you may also wish to establish goals for yourself.) These are usually quite general and are the most global of the objectives you establish. Similar to the other objectives you decide upon, long-term objectives should include *all* aspects of the child's education and be realistic and attainable. The goals for your yearly program should attend to the child's physical, cognitive, and affective development.

The long-term objectives you establish should reflect your philosophy of physical education. Do you believe the most important aspect of physical education is an appreciation of movement, the development of social skills, fitness, or skill development? You may wish to refer to the long-term objectives outlined in chapter 1 and modify them to suit your program.

Planning pays off.

Scheduling and Facilities

Our primary concern is to develop the best possible program for the students as we strive for quality daily physical education. However, the number and size of classes, and the facilities available may influence the schedule because demands for appropriate spaces for activity are usually at a premium.

The length of classes is important. Ideally, younger children should be allotted shorter, and perhaps more frequent, periods for physical education, while older children require longer periods of time to engage in increasingly complex activities.

Once gymnasium time is allotted, check the availability of additional facilities, such as the school's playing fields, a nearby swimming pool, a skating rink, or other special activity area. If these facilities can be reserved for appropriate dates, you can begin to plan a monthly and yearly program.

Sometimes two or even three classes of children will be grouped together for physical education lessons. In this case, a large facility or additional spaces and extra equipment are necessary to accommodate all of them.

Many teachers have successful physical education programs that use the space of a classroom, library, cafeteria, or staff room. If the area is clear, there may be sufficient space available for actviity. In these situations we must exercise our ingenuity and perseverance to cope with a less than desirable situation.

A tidy storage area makes teaching easier.

Remember That

Equipment should be safe. Children should learn to treat equipment with care and report splintered bats, paddles, and other unsafe items. Unstable benches, boxes, and other gymnastic apparatus should also be noted by both teacher and child so that the item is discarded or repaired before causing injury.

Weather

You should consider the climate and weather when planning the physical education program. Most teachers wish to use good weather to the best advantage of the program. For this reason, activities and games are usually played outside during the fall and spring. During the winter, you may have to plan for dance and gymnastic activities indoors.

Equipment

The type and amount of equipment will influence program planning. A sound physical education program may be taught without extensive and expensive equipment, but there should be enough so that each child may actively participate.

> *Maximum participation requires appropriate quantities of equipment. Although one ball or bat may be appropriate for game play, individual dribbling practice requires one ball per student. Teachers should provide for maximum use of equipment within the limits of safety and practicality . . . an attempt should be made to decrease the number of participants interacting with a piece of equipment and to increase the number of pieces of equipment (Harrison, 1984).*

Beanbags, hoops, skipping ropes, paddles, and playground balls of various sizes are some of the essential items for a quality games program. If the largest class in the school has thirty students, then thirty of each

Remember That

Regular quality physical education lessons should be scheduled.
You should adhere to the schedule as much as possible.
Children *need* physical education (don't punish children by taking away their physical education lesson!).
The class prior to the physical education lesson should finish on time.
It is wise to schedule physical education lessons after classes that require a high level of concentration, such as math or language arts, and that don't require clean-up.

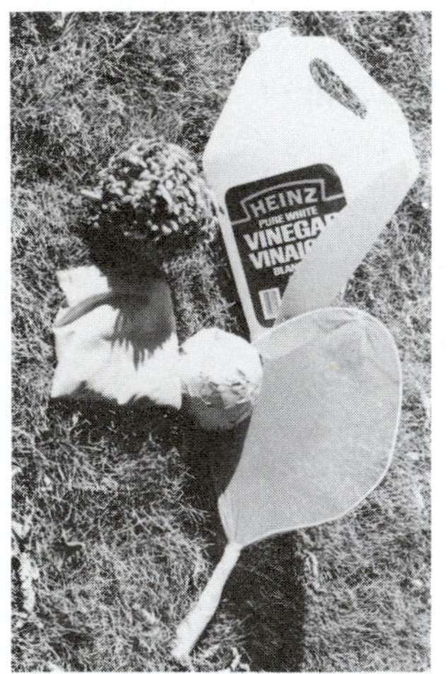

Homemade equipment may be as effective as purchased equipment.

Table 4.2

Suggested Equipment for the Elementary Physical Education Program

Equipment	K	1	2	3	4	5	6
Dance							
Percussion instruments	○	○	○	○	○	○	○
Record, compact disk, or cassette player*	○	○	○	○	○	○	○
Games							
Adjustable basketball hoops (7-feet to 8½-feet)					∘	∘	∘
Adjustable nets (badminton, volleyball, tennis)					∘	∘	∘
Badminton rackets and birds				∘	○	○	○
Beachballs	○	○	∘	∘	∘	∘	∘
Beanbags*	○	○	○	∘	∘	∘	∘
Bowling pins or small blocks	○	○	○	○	○	○	○
Field or floor hockey sticks				∘	○	○	○
Footballs					∘	∘	∘
Frisbees					∘	∘	∘
Hoops*	○	○	○	○	∘	∘	∘
Large utility balls—playground balls (8–10 inch)*	○	○	○	○	∘	∘	∘
Mini basketballs (8–9 inch)					∘	∘	∘
Paddles*				∘	○	○	○
Pinnies (scrimmage vests) or colored team markers					∘	○	○

piece of equipment should be available for use. For dance, a good record, compact disc, or cassette player is necessary, while in gymnastics a sufficient number of mats, benches, and apparatus for climbing will promote maximum participation. See table 4.2 for a comprehensive list of equipment.

As may be seen from table 4.2 an array of equipment is desirable; however, a sound program may be developed with minimal equipment and ingenuity on the part of the teacher. Equipment may be modified or constructed by parents, teachers, students, or other school personnel.

Equipment	K	1	2	3	4	5	6
Pylons or traffic cones	○○○	○○○	○○○	○○○	○○○	○○○	○○○
Scoops and whiffle balls				∘∘∘	○○○	○○○	○○○
Skipping ropes*	○○○	○○○	○○○	○○○	○○○	○○○	○○○
Small utility balls—playground balls (4–6 inch)*	∘∘∘	∘∘∘	∘∘∘	∘∘∘	○○○	○○○	○○○
Soccer balls				∘∘∘	○○○	○○○	○○○
Softball bats, balls (plastic and wood or aluminum)	∘∘∘	○○○	○○○	○○○	○○○	○○○	○○○
Softball "tees"	∘∘∘	○○○	○○○	∘∘∘	∘∘∘		
Sponge balls (Nerf)*	○○○	○○○	○○○	∘∘∘			
Tennis rackets						∘∘∘	○○○
Volleyballs					∘∘∘	○○○	○○○
Gymnastics							
Benches*	○○○	○○○	○○○	○○○	○○○	○○○	○○○
Climbing apparatus*	○○○	○○○	○○○	○○○	○○○	○○○	○○○
Climbing ropes	○○○	○○○	○○○	○○○	○○○	○○○	○○○
Mats*	○○○	○○○	○○○	○○○	○○○	○○○	○○○
Springboard and/or beatboard					∘∘∘	○○○	○○○
Gymnastic stools*	○○○	○○○	○○○	○○○	○○○	○○○	○○○
Trampette or mini-tramp					∘∘∘	○○○	○○○
Trestles	○○○	○○○	○○○	○○○	○○○	○○○	○○○
Vaulting boxes (various heights)	○○○	○○○	○○○	○○○	○○○	○○○	○○○

Used Occasionally ∘∘∘∘∘∘
Used Often ○○○○○
Essential Items *

Remember That

The special needs of some children are more readily apparent and pronounced than others. The enactment of Public Law 94–142 in the United States has made it mandatory for all children regardless of their disability or special circumstances, to receive instruction without discrimination. In Canada, mainstreaming children with special needs means they are scheduled into regular classes of physical education and should participate as fully as possible.

Types of Yearly Programs

When designing your program, you must decide how much overlap or continuity you wish to have between the movement form (dance, gymnastics, or games) and the movement concept. The following four sections outline different ways of scheduling the activities: dovetailing, repeating, monthly, overlapping, yearly, and yearly with little or no overlapping. You will see that each differs in complexity. What we may gain in ease of organization may be lost in the transfer of skills or children's application of the movement concepts (see table 4.6). Conversely, what we may have to grapple with in a more complex organization, the children may gain in their transfer of skills or application of movement concepts, as in table 4.3. Whatever type of program you choose should reflect your priorities, as outlined in your long-term objectives. Samples of program organization are presented for you in tables 4.3 through 4.6.

Table 4.3

A Dovetailing Plan

	Monday	Tuesday	Wednesday	Thursday	Friday
Week 1					
Dance	X			X	
Games		X			X
Gymnastics			X		
Week 2					
Dance		X			X
Games			X		
Gymnastics	X			X	
Week 3					
Dance			X		
Games	X			X	
Gymnastics		X			X

In this program, lessons are taught daily. The movement form is varied, and there is ample opportunity to carry the movement concept from one form to the next.

Dovetailing Plan

If you are fortunate enough to have daily lessons, dovetailing the activities (as illustrated in table 4.3) provides a variety of experiences and reinforces the concept approach to physical education. You are able to plan dance, games, and gymnastics lessons around the same concept. This will help children understand the common basis of movement and how the intention of the movement and the application of the concept results in different movement forms.

Repeating Monthly Plan

Some teachers like to provide continuity through a repeating monthly plan, where the majority of time is spent on one movement form one week, and on another in the next week. While the movement concept remains the same, it is developed through differing activities. For instance, you may work on the concept of body parts in two games lessons and one dance lesson. The next week the concept of body parts is continued with two dance lessons and one gymnastics lesson. The advantage of this plan is that the children are exposed to the same theme through a variety of activities. Its disadvantage is that specific skills are not worked on for a long period of time. Table 4.4 shows a sample repeating monthly plan.

Table 4.4

A Repeating Monthly Plan

	Week 1			Week 2			Week 3			Week 4		
	Mon.	Wed.	Fri.	Mon.	Wed.	Fri.	Mon.	Wed.	Fri.	Mon.	Wed.	Fri.
Dance	X	X							X	X	X	
Games			X	X	X							X
Gymnastics						X	X	X				

In this monthly plan, there are two lessons of one movement form in a week, followed by another movement form in that same week. This provides variety. The next week begins with the previous movement form taught. This plan provides continuity within movement concepts.

Overlapping Yearly Plan

Another type of plan is the overlapping yearly program, illustrated in table 4.5. Here, one month is spent on dance, games, or gymnastics. In the next month, two of the three (dance, games, or gymnastics) are taught. The advantage of this plan is that there is ample time for skill and theme development, while some variety is still employed.

A Yearly Plan with Little or No Overlapping

This plan, illustrated in table 4.6, is designed so that the movement form is taught in lengthy units. This may be appropriate when equipment or facilities are at a premium, and it is a "do it now or never" situation. Here, the children have ample opportunity to develop specific skills, but are not afforded any variety. In this type of program, the primary disadvantage is that once the unit is completed, the children may not pursue the activity for another year and the skill development advantage is lost.

Intermediate Planning—Developing Units

A unit is a sequential progression of lessons unified through one focus. This unifying focus may be one movement form (eg., dance), a movement theme to be developed through three movement forms (eg., theme of body shape may be developed through dance, games, and gymnastics), a behavioral skill (cooperation), or a concept from another subject area (eg., "Australia," "the environment" or "the movies") developed through an array of movement activities. You may wish to capitalize on a special event around which you will plan a unit. In an "Olympic year," this could involve research and movement activities related to the Olympics. You may decide to invite a sport or dance celebrity to your school or take advantage of a local performance by a popular team or dance group and spend a number of lessons preparing for, or following up on, that special occasion. Regardless of the unifying focus, it is important

Table 4.5

An Overlapping Yearly Program

	Sept.	Oct.	Nov.	Dec.	Jan.	Feb.	Mar.	Apr.	May	June
Dance										
Games										
Gymnastics										

Within any given month in the overlapping yearly plan, each movement form is taught for a period of time by itself, and other times it is taught with a different movement form. This provides some continuity within both the movement form and movement concepts being developed.

Table 4.6

A Yearly Plan with Little or No Overlapping

	Sept.	Oct.	Nov.	Dec.	Jan.	Feb.	Mar.	Apr.	May	June
Dance										
Games										
Gymnastics										

This yearly plan has no overlapping, which provides opportunity for much skill development within each movement form. However, the movement concepts will have little obvious correlation from one movement form to another, and the skill development advantage may be lost.

that you establish the movement form, the movement concept, and a progression of developmentally appropriate tasks in order to attain the objectives.

Selecting a Focus for the Unit

Physical education teachers have traditionally structured units around a specific game or sport. For example, teachers plan a three week unit of soccer, then a four week unit of basketball, followed by a three week unit of gymnastics. This type of organization reflects a priority for sport-specific skills and is usually enjoyed primarily by the skilled athletes in the class.

While this type of organization for a unit may be the easiest to teach, we suggest other ways of focusing units. Because of children's various learning styles and their movement preferences, units may be structured around a movement concept; generic skills, such as stretching, curling and twisting; or a concept from another subject. Some of these ideas are outlined for you to consider.

Table 4.7

Unit Outline—Movement Form Focus

Movement form—Games: Grades 3–6

Lesson	**1**	**2**	**3**	**4**	**5**
Movement concept	Pathway of player Relationship to partner	Pathway of ball Levels	Pathway of player Levels	Pathway of players Wide, curled body shapes for defense	Pathways of ball and player
Movement skill*	Projecting into an open space ⟶				
	Passing	Shooting	Passing, Shooting	"Man to/on man" guarding, Passing	Zone defensive positioning
Equipment	Soccer balls, pylons	Soccer balls, goals	Lacrosse sticks and balls or scoops and balls	Floor hockey sticks, balls, pylons	Floor hockey or lacrosse/scoops

*This is the unifying element within the movement form of games.

Movement Form Focus

We suggest a generic or integrated approach, where students experience interelationships within the movement form in a unit. For example, a games unit could focus on striking in the younger grades or spatial strategies in the upper elementary grades. In dance and gymnastics, this plan is quite effective if you wish to focus on gymnastics or folk dance for a period of time. While this may be the least complex way of planning units, we suggest you try the others as well. Table 4.7 outlines how this type of unit may be organized.

Movement Concept Focus

The organization of this type of unit is based on one or two movement concepts which are consistently developed throughout various movement forms. For example, the concept of pathway may be the focus in folk dance, gymnastics sequences in pairs, and in the games of football and baseball. You could choose to study the movement concept of sudden and sustained time in creative dance, in gymnastic sequences on apparatus, in the games skills of "give and go," or in other offensive strategies.

The possibilities inherent in this type of organization may initially appear vague or unclear to you if you are still learning about the movement concepts. However, the more you internalize these concepts, the more you will see the potential for students' true *understanding* of movement when they are used as the focus for lessons. Table 4.8 shows how you could structure a unit with a movement concept focus.

Table 4.8

Unit Outline—Movement Concept Focus

Movement concept—Body shape: Grades 5–6

Lesson	1	2	3	4	5
Movement concept	Body shape →				
	Time	Symmetry with a partner	Relationship to an object (over, behind, under, etc.)	Relationship to others in space	Flight
Movement form	Creative dance	Creative dance	Games	Games	Gymnastics
Movement skills	Stretch, curl, twist Changing shape to a rhythm suddenly	As in lesson #1, with a partner Changing shape with sustained time	Serving, aiming	Defensive positions-block, screen, ready	One and two foot takeoffs and landings, stretch, curl twist in flight
Apparatus/ equipment/ stimuli	Miami Sound Machine "Conga"*	Enya (or other sustained music)	Volleyballs, tennis equipment, badminton equipment, small basketballs	Volleyballs, small basketballs	Mats, benches, trampettes, ropes

*Any Top 40 music with a strong beat would be appropriate.

Integrated Unit

There are many educational developments that have contributed to the integration of various subjects in the child's education. In many schools, specific subjects are no longer treated as isolated, discrete units. Rather, school subjects focus the students' interest on a multitude of aspects of one particular concept or idea. For example, the children may focus on environmental issues. In social studies, they may learn about the native peoples of a particular rain forest; in science, they may study the impact of its destruction upon the flora and fauna; in language arts, the children may write stories about the environment, read newspaper articles and native folk lore or write reactionary letters; in physical education, the children may create dances that celebrate a healthy planet or mourn a troubled planet.

The possibilities for successful, integrated units are endless, provided the focus of study is substantially complex and is of interest to the children. In physical education, integrated units can be very successful with games and dance because we can learn the games of other cultures, dance their dances, and create dances about various subjects. However, integrated units do not lend themselves to incorporation with gymnastics. Table 4.9 provides an example of an integrated unit.

Integrated Unit: A Sample Idea—Australia

Language Arts: reading, and writing about Australia and its people, Australian legends and myths, folk stories, poetry, spelling Australian words.

Social Studies: Australian geography, government, its cities and rural and tourist areas, Australian aboriginal peoples, the Outback.

Science: The Great Barrier Reef, Ayres Rock, flora and fauna, and the physics of the boomerang, sailing, and surfing.

Arts: Australian folk music, Australian aboriginal peoples' music, composers, visual artists, movies, documentaries, playwrights, architecture (e.g., Sydney Opera House).

Physical Education: Dance—using Australian folk music, Australian composed music, learn dances of the native peoples, Australian folk dances. Games—learn about and play Australian football, cricket, and netball. Compare the skills, rules, and strategies involved with their equivalent North American sports.

Table 4.9

Unit Outline—Integrative Focus

Integrating idea—Australia: Grades 2–3

Lesson	**1**	**2**	**3**	**4**	**5**
Developing idea	Abstraction of seashore shapes of sails, water, surfing, shells to create a movement sequence	Occupational rhythms of fishing, surfing, sailing	Tag games	Creating cricket-type games	Creating cricket-type games
Movement form	Creative dance	Creative dance	Games	Games	Games
Movement concept	Body shape, weight	Time, weight	Locomotion	Body parts, weight	Body parts, weight
Movement skill	Stretch, curl, twist	Stretch, curl, twist	Running, dodging,	Running, striking, catching	Running, bowling, catching
Apparatus/ equipment/ stimuli	Pictures "water" music	Pictures of relevant activities	Australian low organizational games*	Cricket bats, balls	Cricket bats, balls

*You may wish to refer to Bowyer (1991) or Kirchner (1991).

Developing Unit Objectives

It is paramount that your objectives for various units should directly reflect the nature of your overall goals of the program. Some teachers feel that a fitness objective should be a part of every unit while for other teachers, affective or behavioral objectives are essential, coupled with skill objectives. Whatever your philosophical orientation to physical education, ensure that your goals are attainable for the children. This implies that you establish a realistic number of objectives- about three or four will help you and the children consciously work towards those goals.

Your objectives should be appropriate for the age level of the children. An objective for a kindergarten unit in gymnastics may be; "Students will learn to respect other children's working space". An objective for a sixth grade class could be; "Students will encourage one another, regardless of skill level."

How To Plan a Unit

It is difficult to provide a step-by-step procedure for planning a unit as we all think differently. Some of us plan from beginning to end in a step-by-step fashion, while others of us begin with assorted ideas and then fill in the gaps as ideas start to flow. However your mind works, you need an initial idea or notion that you wish to develop. You may begin with the idea that you would like the children in your class to get along with one another better, develop a greater understanding of body shape, or watch a particular videotape of a team or athlete. Ponder your idea; take the time to develop it; dream a little! Once you are convinced that your idea has possibilities, refer to other sources. You may research the topic through books, videotapes, or telephoning an authority. The next stages involve the actual planning—establishing objectives, checking facilities and equipment, and outlining specific lessons. The final stage involves planning for evaluation. From there you may wish to repeat the cycle again to further refine your plan. Figure 4.1 outlines a cycle for planning.

Additional Considerations for Unit Planning

There are numerous additional factors for you to consider when you plan a unit. Some may be obvious, such as the booking of special facilities or requesting extra equipment, while others may be more subtle or unpredictable. You may find the following considerations helpful reminders as you plan your units.

Planning Appropriate Activities

The most important thing to remember when planning an activity in physical education is that it must be appropriate for the particular age group. Volleyball is as inappropriate for second-grade children as is the game of "Brownies and Fairies" for sixth-grade children. The teacher must not only consider the children's capabilities in physical skill, but also their cognitive and social levels. We aim, then, to build increasingly complex skills based on what the child can do, rather than "watering down" adult skills.

Start with Some Ideas

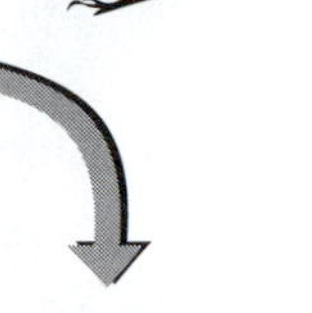

Dream

Consider additional resources/ materials. What else could you include?

Clarify Your Ideas

How many classes in the unit? Where will you begin and end? Will you "touch the peaks "(general) explore a valley (specific)?

Be Realistic

What equipment, resources, funds, and space do you have or want?

Organize

Plan what you know in a schedule including concepts, skills, equipment, and facilities.

Establish Progressions

Write down your ideas, objectives sequentially. Work through your outline; fill in the gaps.

Be Specific

Plan each lesson outline. How will you evaluate yourself? The student?

Figure 4.1 How to plan a unit.

Many lessons may be taught effectively outdoors.

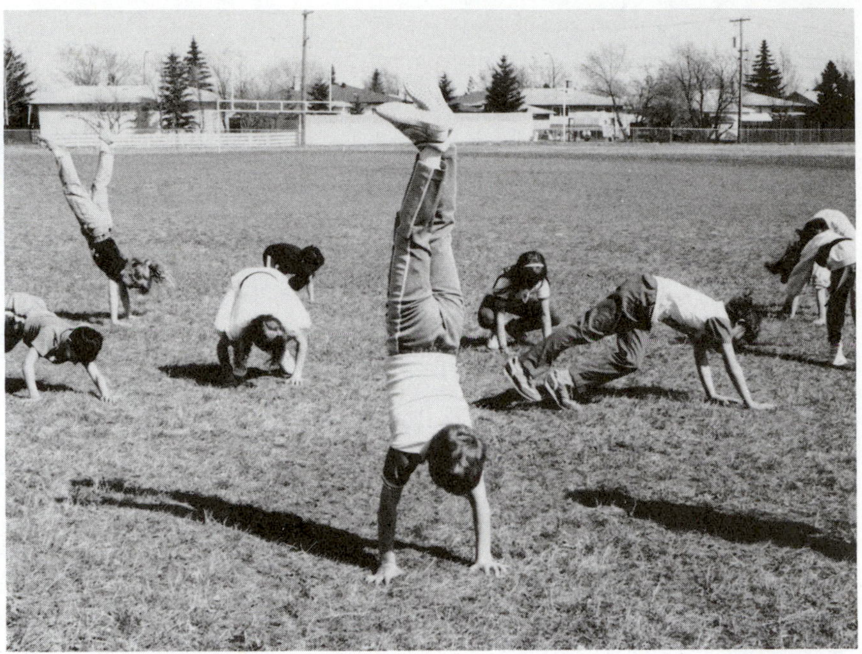

The material in the dance, games, and gymnastics chapters has been developed to assist you in developing age-appropriate activities. You may also refer to table 1.4 for further guidance.

Selecting Equipment

Ensure that equipment is age-appropriate. Games equipment should be designed for children rather than adults. This implies that it is smaller and lighter than the "sport-specific" balls and sticks, for example, that are used in the formal adult game. Much gymnastic apparatus has been designed specifically for children; the Olympic gymnastic apparatus is usually too large and heavy to be easily transported by elementary school children.

In **A Quality Physical Education Program,** "equipment is matched to the size, confidence and skill level of the children so that they are motivated to actively participate" in class (COPEC, 1992).

The Outdoors

In some areas, the outdoors is the only space available for physical education experiences. Under these circumstances weather and alternate facilities will largely govern what activities will be most appropriate.

Often, we do not use the outdoors as fully as possible. On an unexpected nice day, we should be spontaneous and flexible enough to alter the lesson plan and take advantage of the good weather. Some activities are suitable outside despite inclement weather and the snow and rain it may bring. Often it is the teacher who imposes negative feelings about activity in the rain or snow, while the children would tremendously enjoy the fresh air and open space, provided they have appropriate clothing.

Children will delight in a series of dance or gymnastics lessons normally experienced inside. For these activities, a grassy or cement surface needs to be relatively clean and smooth, and the weather warm enough to permit a minimum of restrictive clothing. Often, games are ideally played outside so it is suggested that they be taught outside as often as possible.

Planning for Fitness

The work of the President's Council on Fitness in the United States and of Fitness Canada have served to heighten our awareness of the importance of fitness. A child's level of fitness may be enhanced or maintained through dance, games, and gymnastics. When developing your program, you will need to make decisions regarding what movement form and specifically what skills will benefit the children's level of fitness. If your class is weak in flexibility, for example, you may choose to spend more time on tasks that involve stretching actions in dance or gymnastics.

In May, 1973, at the Child in Sport and Physical Activity Conference held at Queen's University, Kingston, Ontario, it was recommended that there should be thirty minutes of physical education per day (Verabioff, 1986). While a primary goal of physical education is to promote skill development, we believe that the more children are skilled, the greater their fitness levels are challenged. When we are fit and have a positive sense of well-being, it is easier for us to learn new skills. We have more energy and stamina and find it easier to concentrate. Thus, fitness development is one result of quality programming.

Fitness Facts

In order to improve cardiovascular fitness, consider:

F = Frequency: we must exercise at least three or four times a week
I = Intensity: movement activities need to be at an intense level so the heart rate increases
T = Time: the activity should be maintained for at least fifteen minutes to improve our cardiovascular condition
T = Type: the type of exercise will influence how fit we are

In order to improve flexibility, a slow, sustained (twenty-second) stretch is necessary.

In **A Quality Physical Education Program,** "fitness activities are used to help children increase personal fitness levels in a supportive, motivating, and progressive manner, thereby promoting positive lifetime fitness attitudes" (COPEC, 1992).

Planning with Other Teachers

It is wise to consult with other teachers when planning. In this way, specific activities may be coordinated, so common facilities and equipment are available and ready for use.

For example, all dance classes might be programmed for the same day or week so that the floor is kept clean and the record or cassette player remains in the gymnasium. Gymnastic lessons that require heavy mats or large apparatus will benefit from cooperation and joint planning between teachers. One teacher may have the students set up the apparatus, while another teacher has the class put it away. When games lessons are taught on a particular day, week, or in coordinated units, all classes can enjoy the benefits of a net previously set up or all the balls being inflated. Coordination of facilities and equipment between teachers will ensure that the time children spend in the gymnasium is of high quality and maximum quantity.

Planning for Special Occasions

Children love the anticipation of a special day, such as Halloween, Christmas, Valentine's Day, and Easter. Art, music, and social studies often incorporate these special occasions in their subject areas, and physical education can as well. Dance lessons may use Christmas music, Easter poetry, or Halloween stories as stimuli for expressive movement. Games that involve "the witches" competing against "the ghosts" or "the hearts" being tagged by "the cupids" may be played. When you are planning to incorporate special days in other classroom subjects, remember to include physical education as well.

Planning Lessons

The core of our work is the lesson. Everything we learn and practice is to help us function at the highest level possible in the actual teaching situation. Our first task in planning a lesson is to establish our objectives.

Developing Lesson Objectives

Your choice of objectives for a lesson depends on the long-term objectives of the unit. Objectives should be written in terms of what you expect the children to be able to do as a result of the lesson. For this reason, the objectives in the sample lesson plans (chapters 7, 10, and 13) all begin with "the children will be able to. . . ." These objectives are required to ensure the possibility for

1. progressive lesson planning,
2. structuring the tasks,
3. observing accurately,
4. evaluating the children's achievements and the lesson effectively.

If the children know the objectives for a particular lesson, it should help them "organize their own effort toward the accomplishment of those objectives" (Mager, 1975). The decision of whether or not to tell the children the objectives at the beginning of the lesson or ask them to state the objectives at the end of the lesson, is yours to make. The age of the children will be one factor influencing this decision. Lesson objectives may be about emotional reactions, social learning, responsibility, and decision making, as well as skill aquisition as in the following examples:

The children will be able to land with bent knees.

The children will be able to select their own group shapes for their dance.

The children will be able to decide which rules are appropriate for their invented game.

Parts of the Lesson

A good lesson engages all students and progressively leads them from easy and simple skills and concepts to more complex and difficult skills and concepts.

While the lesson is thought of as a whole, we like to think of it in three parts:

Part 1: *The introduction* is composed of mostly basic and refining tasks to review movement skills and warm-up the children.

Part 2: *Concept and skill development* is a mixture of tasks to introduce new concepts and skills and further skill development. This is usually the major portion of the lesson.

Part 3: *Culmination* emphasizes applying and refining tasks as students create or play a game, or develop a dance or gymnastic sequence.

Table 4.10 is a simplified list of the three parts of a lesson plan and the purpose of each part.

Part 1: The Introduction

Part 1 is designed to warm-up the students, introduce the children to the selected movement form, and to establish a movement-centered learning environment. The tasks vary with each movement form and from lesson to lesson, but in general, they are familiar locomotor activities that are comparatively energetic, such as running and jumping.

Dance Lessons These lessons often begin with imitative and rhythmic movements danced to well-known and well-liked music. You may let the children copy you, or the children may be called upon to provide the movement ideas for their peers to copy. In singing games and folk dance lessons, the children may dance freely around the space, recalling and practising a selected dance step; in creative dance lessons, the children may have the choice of responding to the music as they select their own ways of traveling. It is important that a dancelike atmosphere and attitude are established at the beginning of the lesson; the choice of task is made with this goal in mind.

Table 4.10

The Parts of a Lesson Plan

Part 1: The introduction

This should

prepare the body mentally and physically,
be vigorous,
be a review,
stress continuity of action,
include movement both on the spot and throughout the space,
be individual.

Part 2: Concept and skill development

This may

introduce or review concepts,
include discussion to clarify a concept if it is new,
involve application of the concept,
stress continuity of action,
include working with others,
include children observing others.

Part 3: Culmination

This should

stress consolidation of material covered,
include some relaxation,
include children observing others,
include putting equipment or apparatus away.

Dance and gymnastics sequences should stress a beginning, continuity of action, and an ending.

Games lessons should use games skills and concepts, and equipment used in part 2, and include working with others if this was included in part 2.

Games Lessons Introductory tasks for the younger children tend to be gross motor, such as, running, chasing, escaping, and the beginning of guarding skills, as when playing tag games. The emphasis is on good footwork and use of the general space. It is important that all children are very active; therefore, any activities that include "freezing" others and eliminating players are unsuitable. Small equipment, such as ropes and hoops, encourage jumping and skipping skills, both of which are vigorous activities that permit children to work on their own. This saves time. The pace of a lesson can be slowed when children are asked to find partners or form groups.

As an alternative to these kinds of activities, older, more skillful children may begin the lesson by practising manipulative skills, either alone or with a partner. The skills may be of their own choice or selected from the ones included in previous lessons. We can use this time for free activity to help a child who may find difficulty with a particular skill, to watch the children to see if there is a common problem, to join the activity and relate with the children one-on-one. This is particularly useful if you reprimanded someone in the previous lesson, and you feel the need to establish a more positive relationship.

Gymnastics Lessons Again the tasks will tend to focus on familiar gross motor skills—running, rolling, rocking, jumping—all are good activities for the introduction to gymnastics lessons. This can be followed by bending, stretching, and twisting selected areas of the body. You may develop a sequence to teach the children, which they can repeat on their own at the beginning of a series of lessons. During this warm-up period, you can give individual feedback and encouragement in much the same way as the beginning of a games lesson.

Part 2: Concept and Skill Development

Part 2 is the time when new concepts and skills are introduced, known concepts are developed and reinforced, and already acquired skills are practised, extended, and combined.

Dance Lessons In creative dance, the divisions between the lesson parts are often barely discernable. Part 1 may lead imperceptibly to the introduction of the movement concept(s) or stimulus on which the lesson is based. This introduction may be through discussion or improvisation. In singing games and folk dance lessons, the new step(s), figures, and words are learned, gradually integrated, and refined, until the whole dance pattern develops.

Games Lessons There is usually a more definite change of focus in games lessons. New manipulative skills or aspects of known skills are introduced, practised, and combined. Strategies and rules are explained and applied in minigames situations with little or no focus on keeping the score, because the objective is to learn *how* to play, rather than to win.

Gymnastics Lessons As in dance lessons, the children may barely notice a shift in emphasis, as the new movement concept(s) may already have been introduced in Part 1. However, you will now include simplifying and extending tasks to meet individual differences in skill performance.

Repetition of skills or parts of skills occurs as the children strive to gain and increase control over their actions. The environment will be the floor or arrangements of small apparatus, such as mats, hoops, or benches. Skills will be combined into sequences with a focus on transitional actions. The resulting sequence(s) may or may not be applied to the apparatus selected for Part 3.

Part 3: Culmination

Part 3 is the time for the children to use their newly acquired competence and increased movement vocabulary, and to accomplish some specific end, so they leave the lesson with an identifiable product and a feeling of achievement.

Dance Lessons This is the time for dancing—enjoying what has been learned and created in this and previous lessons. Dances can be shared in a miniperformance setting and the performer and spectator roles experienced. (See chapter 5 for more on dance.)

The children's accumulating repertoire can be highlighted and, in singing games and folk dance lessons, the children may be asked which dance(s) they would like to do.

Games Lessons The skills, strategies, and rules are applied within the context of various games. These games may be (a) created by you, (b) created by the children, or (c) selected from one of the numerous resources of children's games. Groups of children may be playing different games (or variations of the same one), which may be very simple, using few skills and rules, or comparatively complex (see chapter 8).

During the playing of the games, you will reinforce the concepts and skills experience during Part 2 of the lesson; do not hesitate, therefore, to stop the game (see chapter 9).

Gymnastics Lessons A different environment is structured in gymnastics lessons due to apparatus arrangements, which may combine large and small pieces. These arrangements provide exciting challenges (see chapter 11). The youngest children will be exploring unfamiliar pieces, while the more experienced and skillful children will be developing sequences they can repeat, refine, and remember.

Lesson Summary Designing good lessons requires considerable planning, and planning means decisions have to be made about the following:

The movement form (dance, games, or gymnastics)

The objectives of the lesson

The tasks

Organization of the students

Organization of the apparatus/equipment

Evaluation

Evaluation is the process of giving meaning to a measurement by judging it against some standard (Baumgartner & Jackson, 1982).

Most of us think of evaluation in terms of tests, exams, grades, and the ominous pressures of striving to perform successfully according to the predetermined standards of teachers and parents. Although formal testing and grading are important facets of evaluation in education, they play only one role in the total teaching and learning process. While you may feel somewhat negative toward evaluation from a student's point of view, as a teacher, evaluation is a most helpful, complex, multifaceted teaching aid.

What is Evaluation?

Evaluation is a form of feedback, where something or someone is measured and compared with an agreed or established standard. It is intended to enhance both teaching and learning, and result in immediate, continuous, and long-range benefits for children and teachers. Evaluation need be neither formal nor threatening to the child. Fowler (1981) states:

> *Evaluation should be a positive process designed to facilitate learning and encourage the development of an awareness of one's own limitations and capabilities.*

Thus, it does not necessarily nor merely imply grading. While formal tests may be used sporadically, informal tests and casual observations (of which children may be unaware) are important tools used extensively by the teacher of a quality physical education program.

Why Do We Evaluate?

Evaluation is used to provide guidance for both the teacher and the student. Through this form of analysis we can determine strengths, weaknesses, and possible means for remediation within our physical education program.

In **A Quality Physical Education Program,** "assessment of children's physical progress and achievement is used to individualize instruction, plan yearly curriculum and weekly lessons, identify children with special needs, communicate with parents and evaluate the program's effectiveness" (COPEC, 1992).

Evaluation may motivate you to improve instruction, or it may motivate the child to improve movement responses. It may be used to clarify the objectives of the program. Because planning is necessary for evaluation, it may encourage you to consider your objectives and indirectly

Table 4.11

Why evaluate?

To improve
To motivate
To clarify objectives
To redefine objectives
To discover strengths and weaknesses
To reward achievement
To provide guidance
To revise
To plan and organize
To report to children, parents, administrators
To be accountable
To provide credibility

clarify the goals for the child. Strengths and weaknesses of both teaching and learning will emerge in almost every type of evaluation. Whether you are employing a formal fitness test or casually observing children's movement sequences, conclusions may be drawn concerning the quality of responses and those that require additional attention.

Evaluation of the program as a whole may reveal that facilities and equipment are insufficient, or that the scheduling of classes needs revision. A questionnaire issued by a teacher to other teachers may reveal that the untidy gymnasium storage area poses a major negative factor affecting the program. Examination of the gymnasium scheduling arrangement may disclose reasons for lack of cooperation between teachers. If teachers' priorities are markedly different because of the interests of their students (i.e., a kindergarten teacher and the school's volleyball coach), then evaluation may be used to revise the timetable.

As parents become increasingly involved in their child's education, they may demand concrete evidence of a quality education. This directly affects you because you may be requested to provide reliable evidence of the credibility of your program. Teachers are usually very aware of the need to be accountable, and it is through evaluation that a positive report may result. Table 4.11 summarizes why we evaluate.

To Do

Focus on interpersonal skills. Ask yourself the following questions or observe another teacher.

Am I warm and friendly?

Do I create situations that will make children feel good about themselves and others in the class?

Do I spend equal time with all children, regardless of their skill level?

Am I open to the children's thoughts?

Do I encourage varied ideas and responses from the class?

Do I allow and encourage the children to make their own decisions for some things?

Do I laugh with the children?

What Can We Evaluate?

Almost every aspect of both our teaching and the children's learning may be evaluated in some manner. This, however, does not imply that formal tests exist for every aspect of the program. It does imply that the totality of all experiences concerning the children and their subsequent learning within physical education is worthy of critical investigation. Thus, we may evaluate by examining the teacher (through self-evaluation or peer evaluation), the child, and the learning experience (e.g., lesson, unit, program).

The Teacher

Self-evaluation is extremely important so that we may develop and mature to become the best teachers we are capable of being. We have all had bad teachers—why didn't they notice we were falling asleep, skipping classes, or talking instead of listening during class? These teachers failed to self-evaluate in order to discover why the students weren't actively involved in their class. We need not be like those teachers, if we take the time for introspection and reflection upon our teaching behaviors.

When students misbehave, fail to understand, or would prefer to sit on the sidelines of the physical education class, self-examination is vitally important. It is our responsibility to analyze the causes for this behavior starting with ourselves. We can examine one of any number of influences we have upon the children. We may wish to focus upon our interpersonal skills, our use of time, or our planning.

Our use of time may also be evaluated in physical education lessons. Minimal time should be used for organization (changing, taking out equipment) and directions, allowing for maximum activity time. While the amount of time you spend on organization and discussion will depend upon the objectives of the lesson and the stage in the unit, movement time should be maximized. In evaluating our planning, we may focus on

Table 4.12

Recording Sheet and Types of Tasks

Task	Basic	Organize	Refine	Extend	Apply
1.		X			
2.	X				
3.			X		
4.			X		
5.				X	
6.			X		

This is the type of task progression we want to see. Try to avoid too many basic tasks, so you also include refining and extending tasks.

a single lesson or the program as a whole. Since we vary in our priorities of what is important in a physical education class, those priorities will be revealed in the questions we ask ourselves in self-evaluation.

When we want feedback on our teaching, it is very helpful for a colleague to gather specific information on what we do, or for us to videotape ourselves to gather information. We suggest that you decide what information you want before you teach, and provide a form or checklist for your observer to use so specific information is collected and observations remain objective. When you design a form or checklist, request facts, not opinions or value judgements. For instance, "Do I talk too much?" is an opinion. Instead, give your observer a stopwatch and recording sheet to note the time and your activity (talking, observing, organizing). "Do I favor the boys?" is also a value laden question. Instead, you may have someone make a drawing of your pathway in the gym and note with whom you spoke. Figure 4.2 is an example of this type of observation. At the conclusion of the lesson, it is best if you self-evaluate based on the information gained.

Some ideas for self evaluation are provided in tables 4.12, 4.13, and figure 4.2.

To Do

Focus on your lesson planning and ask yourself the following questions:

Are all children participating for a maximum period of time?

Are children developing skill?

Are children thinking and learning?

Are positive attitudes toward activity and others being developed?

Table 4.13

Recording Sheet and Teacher's Use of Time

Teacher Mr. Naso
Lesson Grade 6 - projecting skills
Date November 13

Time	Teacher Activity (giving instructions, observing a group, checking equipment, etc.)
3:00	organizing students
3:01	organizing students
3:02	talking - giving instructions
3:03	observing whole class
3:04	observing one child
3:05	talking - giving instructions
3:06	checking Jessie's hockey stick

This type of information is very helpful in detecting imbalances in the teacher's use of time. For example, a teacher should not normally spend five minutes explaining a simple game or talking with one student. However, there are exceptions, and the teacher must be the judge.

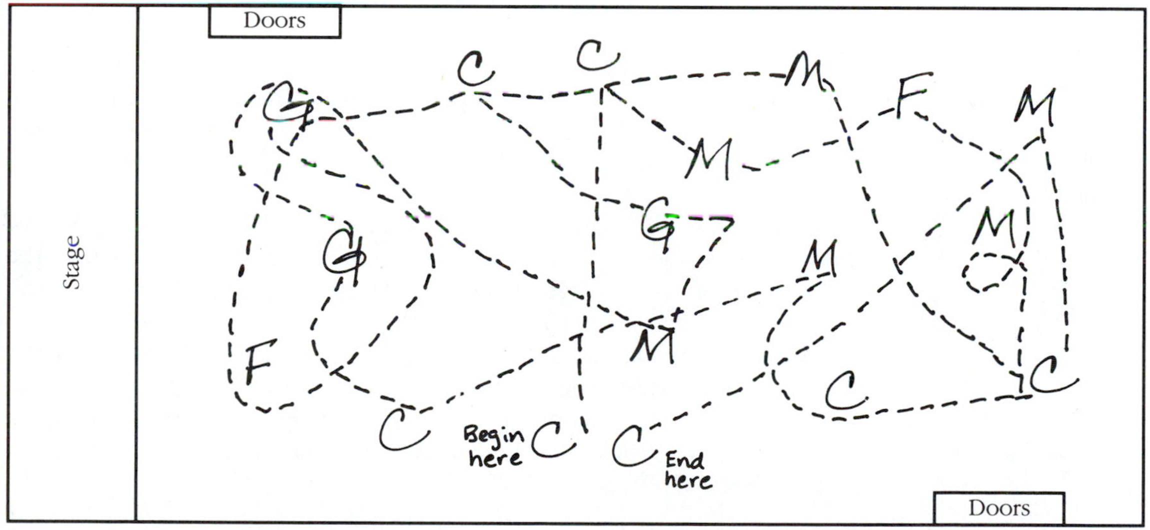

C Teacher Talks to the Class
G Teacher Talks to a Group
M Teacher Talks to a Male
F Teacher Talks to a Female
- - - - - Teacher's Pathway

Figure 4.2 Recording teacher's movement. The teacher may have this information collected to ascertain if he or she is spending too much time with individual males. What do you think?

Table 4.14

Assessing the Program: Sample Questions You May Ask

Is there a balance among dance, games, and gymnastic activities?
Are facilities available when they are supposed to be?
Is the floor clean and free of equipment not needed?
Are children fresh and awake, ready for physical education when it is scheduled?
Are teachers consulted in the scheduling of facilities?
Is there enough equipment for every child?
Is the equipment appropriate for the age and size of the children?
Are girls and boys offered equal activity time?
Is equipment stored properly?
Is unsafe apparatus repaired immediately?
Do children adhere to rules of safety?

We may also be concerned with elements of *physical fitness* and motor abilities, which are basics for success in all activities (see chapter 1). The components of physical fitness may be measured by evaluating muscular strength, muscular endurance, cardiovascular endurance, and flexibility. These components may be evaluated formally or informally.

Motor abilities may be evaluated by examining the child's capabilities in agility, balance, coordination, posture, power, reaction time, and rhythm. While physical fitness tests evaluate whether or not the body is fit, motor ability "takes into account efficiency of basic movements" (Johnson & Nelson, 1969).

A vast number of psychomotor elements may be evaluated within the elementary school physical education program. You will have to decide if you want to formally evaluate the children's fitness. Chapters 6, 9, and 11 will help you make these decisions.

The Program

While frequent self- and child evaluation is essential, other aspects of the programs, such as facilities, equipment and safety, discussed in the first section of this chapter should also be assessed. Some possible questions you may ask are outlined in table 4.14.

Almost every factor that affects your physical education program should be evaluated. You probably will be able to answer many evaluative questions immediately. Since this is not an easy task for every aspect of your program, the following information on when and how to evaluate will be helpful to you.

The Child

Teachers are most commonly concerned with evaluating the child. Formal evaluation has posed problems to most teachers at some point in their careers, for it is a complex and often sensitive issue. However, children should always be evaluated according to our instructional objectives.

We all strive for self-improvement. As we gain experience with children, our teaching methods and skills in selection of appropriate content will be refined and will increasingly benefit the children. When an increased skill level is witnessed, we may deem teaching content and/or method successful. Children also strive for increased mastery in their movement. As they become accustomed to showing their work so others may observe, they will become cognizant both of their own increasing skill and of the skill of others. The children's level of enjoyment may be assessed. While enjoyment is not a prerequisite for learning, it should be an outcome, one that will enhance children's attitudes toward the subject and foster an eagerness for participation.

Evaluating Psychomotor Learning

Within this domain, we may evaluate either the movement *pattern* (how the movement was accomplished) or the movement *skill* (what the movement accomplished). In the nonmanipulative movement forms of dance and gymnastics, we tend to evaluate the movement pattern. Are the children running with full strides, arms in opposition to their legs, and with all action moving forward and backward? Can the children skip with a smooth step-hop pattern? Can they hold a curled shape when rolling? In the manipulative activities found in games, we most commonly evaluate in terms of movement skill. Can the child catch a ball that has been bounced? Can the child strike the ball? These questions refer to the child's skill as seen by the result or product of the movement. To help clarify these differences, additional questions for evaluating psychomotor learning are given in table 4.15.

How Do We Evaluate?

There are probably as many evaluative techniques available in physical education as the total number of tests you have taken in your school career. Evaluating children's knowledge or attitudes in physical education may be accomplished through written tests, such as rating scales, checklists, questionnaires, fill in the blank, short answer, true/false, multiple choice, or essay exams. Their movement skill may be evaluated through standardized fitness tests, skill tests, and motor patterns tests. We can measure or evaluate many things through many and varied means!

However, because we believe children's individual differences are important to note and we do not wish all children to perform the same skill in exactly the same way at the same time, observation will most

Table 4.15

Evaluating Psychomotor Learning

Movement concept	Movement pattern (quality)	Movement skill (quantity)
Locomotion		
Running	With effective strides?	How fast?
Jumping	With feet together?	How high?
Hopping	Using arms?	How many times?
Body parts	How are they being used?	How many?
Directions	Is it forward, backward, or up and down?	How far up?
Levels	Is it high, medium, or low?	How high? How low?
Time	Is it quick or slow?	How fast?

often be employed for conclusions to be made about your program, your teaching, and your students. These observations may be recorded in a variety of ways. You will likely spend the most time evaluating the children through observation of their movement, social development, creativity, and attitudes exhibited toward physical education. Points to remember when observing are outlined for you in chapter 3.

Criterion-Referenced Evaluation

While we believe that norm-referenced standards may be useful at times, a more effective method of evaluating is through criterion-referenced standards. This method is appropriate in assessing all children. In criterion-referenced evaluation, you first establish the criteria, then decide to what degree each child has met the criteria. One of the strengths of this form of evaluation is that it allows you to consider the child's individual progress. Evaluation is based on current and previous performance, not the achievements of a peer.

When evaluating students' progress, we should be prepared to recognize certain factors that can affect performance, such as the child's confidence level, acceptance among the peer group, our own expectations, previous test situations, and the child's preference for certain activities.

> *A child may contribute significantly to a program by being a good observer, an initiator of ideas, an analyzer who poses questions (Wall, 1981).*

Table 4.16

Sample Rating Scale for Evaluating Dance Sequences

	Agree 1	2	Disagree 3
The movement sequence is demanding of the child's skill.	X		
The movement concept developed is obvious.	X		
Body shapes are clear.			X
At least two pathways are incorporated.		X	
At least three directions are used.	X		
At least two levels are incorporated.		X	
The child follows the beat of the music.	X		

Rating Scales

Rating scales are typically used on report cards or progress reports. They are characterized by a quantity that represents the quality of performance. This subjective estimate brings order to the processes of observation and self-appraisal, and provides for degrees of the quality, trait, or factor being examined (Barrow & McGee, 1979).

You may wish to use standardized rating scales, or you may find it helpful to create your own, based on the objectives of the program. When devising a rating scale, you must clearly state the performance objectives to be evaluated. Terms used must be specific verbs, nouns, and adjectives that are attainable and indisputable in their meaning. You may develop a scale based on a rating of 1 to 3, 1 to 5, 1 to 10, or any other number that seems appropriate to you. Rating scales may be used to evaluate almost every aspect of the physical education program. Your teaching behavior, aspects of the program, and the children's movement patterns, skills, fitness levels, attitudes, enjoyment, creativity, and application of movement concepts to movement situations may be observed, evaluated, and translated into a numerical system. A sample rating scale is shown in table 4.16.

Checklists

Checklists (illustrated in tables 4.17 and 4.18) are very similar to rating scales in that they also translate quality into some form of quantity. However, checklists are usually constructed with varying numbers of positive or negative categories, and the appropriate box is checked off. Like rating scales, the value of this tool is that it takes relatively little time to complete, and the results may be readily tabulated. The disadvantage of rating scales and checklists is that the cause for, or remediation of, a problem is not evident. Another problem of checklists having only two categories (i.e., "yes," "no") is that provision is not commonly made for borderline cases, which fall between these categories.

Table 4.17

Sample Checklist for Movement Concepts Developed in the Program

	Not developed	Developed adequately	Developed extensively
Locomotor actions			X
Body shape			X
Body parts			X
Levels		X	
Pathways		X	
Directions	X		
Time	X		
Weight	X		
Relationship to partner		X	
Relationship to objects		X	

Table 4.18

Sample Movement Pattern Checklist

	Child demonstrates clearly	Child demonstrates somewhat/ sometimes	Child does not demonstrate
Throwing			
1. Prepares for throw by bringing throwing hand behind head.	X		
2. Upper body rotates.		X	
3. Takes a step with opposite leg to throwing arm.			X
4. Releases ball at appropriate time.		X	
5. Follows through with throwing arm and upper body.	X		

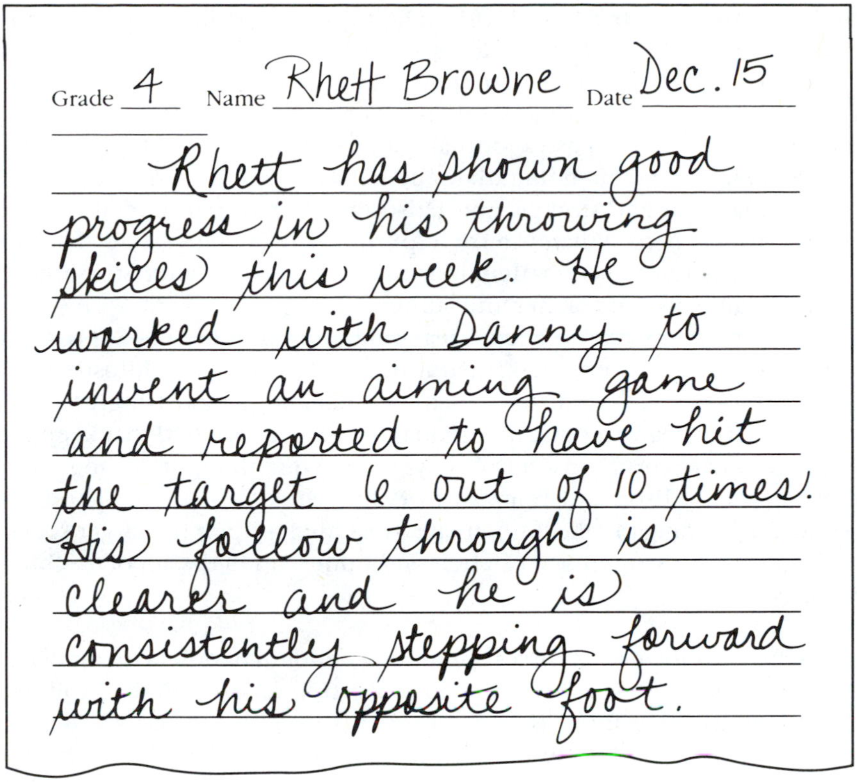

Grade 4 Name Rhett Browne Date Dec. 15

Rhett has shown good progress in his throwing skills this week. He worked with Danny to invent an aiming game and reported to have hit the target 6 out of 10 times. His follow through is clearer and he is consistently stepping forward with his opposite foot.

Figure 4.3 Sample anecdotal record.

Anecdotal Records

Anecdotal records (figure 4.3) may be written by teachers and students as an informal method of evaluation. After a number of records are collected, you may then refer to these notes to gain an understanding of how each child is progressing. Anecdotal records are valuable in that they are candid accounts of useful information. While some teachers find them helpful, others find them time-consuming. These accounts are subjective and are intended to be qualitative accounts.

Writing a Journal

". . . teachers have found that practising diary writing with students may contribute to the learning process as the students are encouraged to continue reflecting on their learning experiences and to try discovering relationships that they might not otherwise see" (Van Manen, 1990).

For both teachers and students, keeping a journal is an effective way to promote contemplation and introspection. Journal writing may be used in a multitude of ways for numerous purposes. Students may write about their experience of working with a new partner to develop a dance sequence, their reactions to a particular physical education class, or how they feel about their fitness levels. The topic of writing may be established by the teacher, left to each student's choice, or may be focused by the students collectively. Students may read their work to others, if they choose to do so, or their work may be treated very privately, for the writer's eyes only. Because a journal usually provides a medium for private and supportive on-going dialogue between teacher and student or between student and student, journals normally are not graded or corrected by teachers. Whatever their purpose, it is imperative that respectful, positive, and challenging discourse is characteristic of the interchange between teacher and student.

Some teachers like to keep a teaching journal, which is a forum to celebrate their joys, vent their frustrations, and ponder the philosophical aspects of teaching. As reflexive teaching is becoming increasingly valued as an essential characteristic of a good teacher, you may find that keeping a professional journal insightful as you see your thoughts change and develop. As Hellison and Templin (1991) write, ". . . there is no substitute for learning to reflect upon one's teaching—upon the larger social and ethical issues, upon one's beliefs and values, upon the act of teaching itself."

Norm-Referenced Evaluation

This type of evaluation involves comparing children to others in our class, school, or country. Norm-referenced evaluation focuses on the product. We might use this form of evaluation to select the fastest runner or the best gymnast. Skill tests and fitness tests are examples of norm-referenced evaluation.

Skill Tests

Skill tests (figure 4.4) rely upon observation but are primarily quantitative, rather than qualitative. These **objective tests** rely minimally upon interpretation by the teacher. Success is most commonly measured in terms of time or distance. Skill tests measure such things as the child's ability to aim at a target, catch a ball from a specified distance, or jump vertically as high as possible. Most of these standardized tests provide the teacher with specific and detailed directions and often include norms or averages for a particular sex and age group. The results are usually easily interpreted.

When you evaluate specific predetermined movement skills, ensure that you have worked with the class on the movement (unless you are testing before the unit begins) and that your test can accommodate even the weakest of children. Very often the child who is the most physically gifted in skill is surpassed by others who are more creative, innovative, or have better "movement intuition"—they are more cooperative or can grasp the movement concepts more readily. We suggest that you praise the children who have these latter talents. You may evaluate each child's progress on these skills.

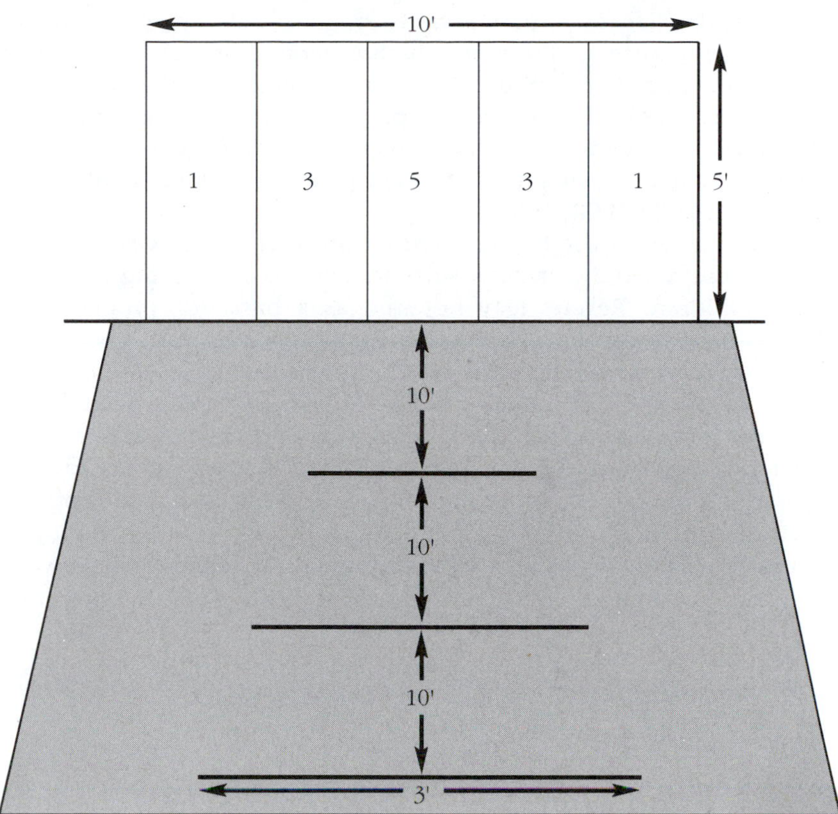

Figure 4.4 Sample test for kicking skills.
This test is designed to measure kicking ability of children in grades one through six. The child tries to hit the center of the target with nine trials. Score by adding the total number of points; when the ball lands on a line, the higher score is awarded. This test could be adapted to assess accuracy in throwing, kicking, or striking skills.
Reprinted by permission of the American Alliance for Health, Physical Education, Recreation and Dance, 1900 Association Drive, Reston, Virginia 22091.

Fitness Tests

Fitness tests are quantitative and objective, because results are measured in terms of time or distance. Fitness tests evaluate such things as running speed and number of sit-ups or push-ups completed in a specific time. Most standardized tests provide you with detailed instructions and often include norms or averages for a particular sex and age group.

> *Fitness Tests must be used judiciously and with care. "For many students, the 'test' approach with an emphasis upon awards has led to feelings of anxiety and failure, negative attitudes toward physical activity and even lowered self-esteem. In other words, it has risked discouraging those individuals that most needed encouragement" (CAHPER, 1992).*

As a result, program revision occurred in both the United States and Canada. In the United States, the President's Challenge and the Physical Best Program were unified to create the President's Youth Fitness Program. This joint program features the Physical Best test items and educational materials, while the President's Challenge award system was adapted to criterion-referenced assessment standards (AAHPERD, 1992).

In Canada, the Canada Fitness Awards Program was replaced with the Active Living Challenge Program which reflects a shift away from performance and awards to supporting a developmental learning process for active living. The objective of the new program is to encourage and enable daily, enjoyable physical activity throughout life and consists of four programs, each aimed at a particular age group and emphasizing a particular theme (CAHPER, 1992).

If you decide to use fitness tests, ensure that you discuss the tests with the children and that the results are used as an ongoing challenge for the children. Results may be used as a basis for programming throughout the year when completed early in the school year. It is strongly suggested that you explain to the children the significance and meaning of one's fitness level, the components of fitness, and the individual's results. This information may spark discussion and be pursued in other subject areas, such as health, science, social studies, arithmetic, and language arts. Some children may enjoy keeping records of their ongoing performance on individual file cards over the duration of the school year (table 4.19). These activities may spur them on to a heightened awareness of the importance of fitness and encourage them to increase their fitness levels.

The Physical Best test items include the following:

One mile run/walk

Sit and reach

Pull-ups

Modified sit-ups (sixty seconds)

Body composition (skin folds with body mass index as alternate)

Further information is available from the American Alliance for Health, Physical Education, Recreation and Dance, 1900 Association Drive, Reston, Virginia 22091. In Canada, further information regarding The Active Living Challenge Program may be requested from Fitness Canada, 365 Laurier Avenue West, Ottawa, Ontario, K1A OX6.

> In **A Quality Physical Education Program,** "children are physically and mentally prepared so that they can safely complete each component of a physical test battery" (COPEC, 1992).

Selecting and Designing Appropriate Tests

Selecting and designing an appropriate test may be an ominous chore if you are vague concerning the intent of the evaluation. However, deciding the basic items you wish to test, what the results will be used for, how many students will complete the test, and how much time you wish to spend on evaluation will assist in the process.

Table 4.19

Sample Index Cards for Fitness Tests

NAME Cara Nielsen AGE 8 TEACHER Mr. McNiven

SIT-UPS (in 1 minute)

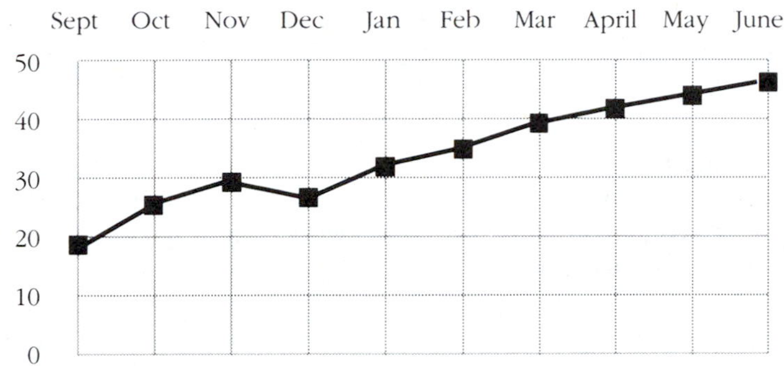

NAME Cara Nielsen AGE 8 TEACHER Mr. McNiven

FLEXED ARM HANG

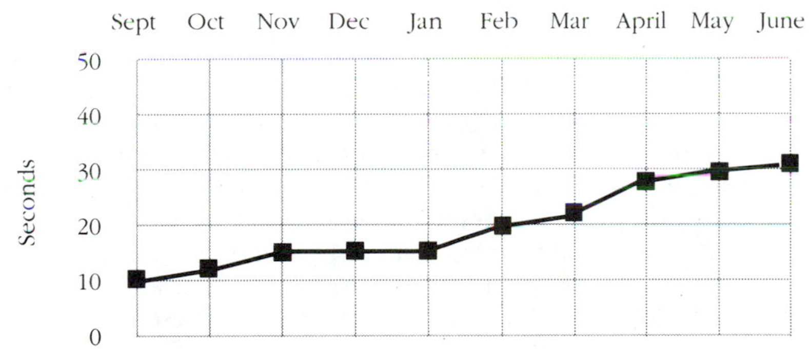

Remember That

Since we believe that individual differences are part of being human, the way in which results are handled is important. Some children may benefit from knowledge of the results. For other children, being told once again of their continued failure could be most destructive. Your sensitivity, as the teacher, is crucial.

Remember That

The amount of time in testing should reflect the amount of time you have spent teaching. Don't spend more time evaluating than teaching! Plan how, what, and when you will test before teaching begins. The test should directly relate to what you've taught, and administration of the test should be relatively simple. Results should be used to motivate and inform, not degrade, children.

Table 4.20

Formative and Summative Evaluation

	When is it used?	Who uses it?	What is evaluated?	Why is it used?
Formative evaluation	Continuously	Teacher, student	Process	To remediate
Summative evaluation	At the end	Teacher	Product	For final evaluation

When Do We Evaluate?

Due to the type of the physical education program we believe in, evaluation should most often occur informally, through your observations and discussion with the children. Evaluation may occur through summative or formative means.

Summative Evaluation

Summative evaluation occurs at the *completion* of a lesson, unit, or program. This term implies the sum or totality of learning that has occurred throughout the unit or school year and may be used to evaluate each child or the class in general. Tests may be norm-referenced or criterion-referenced. Summative evaluation may be used effectively when the same test is given both before and after the lesson, unit, or program. This is termed *pretest/posttest,* and it measures the progress the students have made. While summative evaluation may be valuable at times, it fails to address the process of learning, which we feel is so important.

Formative Evaluation

You should most commonly employ evaluative procedures that occur *during* a lesson, unit, or program. As the term *formative* suggests, your teaching and your student's learning may be formed or changed as a result of this type of evaluation, which is normally criterion-referenced. You may revise your objectives, modify your teaching methods, decide to review previous work, accelerate skills covered, or adapt and modify equipment as a result of your evaluation. Formative evaluation is valued, as it places the focus upon the children's learning and the process of their development. Table 4.20 summarizes these two types of evaluation.

Summary

When you plan the yearly program, you will need to consider the children's needs, your local curriculum, facilities, weather, and equipment, as well as your personal teaching strengths and interests in physical education. Your program should reflect your ideas of a quality program as reflected in the objectives and units you establish and the way you organize the program: weekly, monthly, or yearly, and with much, some, or no overlapping of the movement form.

Evaluation is a vital component of the teaching process. You may employ self-evaluation, peer evaluation, or student evaluation to improve the physical education program. Evaluative techniques exist in rating scales, checklists, anecdotal records, skill tests, and fitness tests, and may be formative and/or summative.

Review Questions

1. How may children's needs be met through careful planning?
2. Discuss why you prefer one particular type of program organization over another.
3. Write three long-term objectives (for a yearly program), three intermediate term objectives (for a unit), and three short-term objectives (for a lesson), and compare their specificity. Are your long-term goals more general than your short-term goals?
4. Using tables 4.6 through 4.8 for guidance, outline a unit of each type. Which was easiest to plan? Which would be the most interesting for the students?
5. What is the difference between formative and summative evaluation?
6. You administer a fitness test to your class in October. Some children do well and others do very poorly. How will you handle the test results?
7. When would you use a skill test?
8. What points would you use as a basis for evaluating children's movement in dance on a rating scale?

References

American Alliance of Health, Physical Education, Recreation and Dance. (AAHPERD). (1992, April). *Update,* p. 1.

Barrow, H. M., & McGee, R. (1979). *A practical approach to measurement in physical education.* (3d ed.). Philadelphia: Lea & Febiger.

Baumgartner, T., & Jackson, A. (1982). *Measurement for evaluation.* Dubuque, IA: Wm. C. Brown Publishers.

Bowyer, G. (1991). Aussie rules football in American physical education. *JOPERD, 62* (7), 24–26, 76–77.

Canadian Association for Health, Physical Education and Recreation (CAHPER). (1992, Summer). *In Touch,* p. 3.

Council on Physical Education for Children (COPEC). (1992). *Developmentally appropriate physical education for children: A position statement.* Reston, VA: AAHPERD.

Fowler, J. S. (1981). *Movement education.* Philadelphia: Saunders College Publishing.

Harrison, J. M. (1984). *Instructional strategies for physical education.* Dubuque, IA: Wm. C. Brown Publishers.

Hellison, D., & Templin, T. (1991). *A reflective approach to teaching physical education.* Champaign, IL: Human Kinetics Books.

Johnson, R. L., & Nelson, J. K. (1969). *Practical measurements for evaluation in physical education.* Minneapolis, MN: Burgess Publishing Co.

Kirchner, G. (1991). *Children's games from around the world.* Dubuque, IA: Wm. C. Brown Publishers.

Luke, M. (1987). Analysis of class management in physical education. *CAHPER Journal, 53* (3), 10–13.

Mager, R. (1975). *Preparing instructional objectives.* (2nd ed.). Belmont, CA: Pitman Learning Inc.

Van Manen, M. (1990). *Researching lived experience.* London, Ontario: Althouse Press.

Verabioff, L. (1986). Can we justify daily physical education? *CAHPER Journal, 52* (2), 8–11.

Wall, J. (1981). *Beginnings.* Montreal: McGill University.

Related Readings

Aicinena, S. (1991). Formal class closure—An effective instructional tool. *JOPERD, 62* (3), 72–73.

Allsbrook, L. (1992). Fitness should fit children. *JOPERD, 63* (6), 47–49.

Byra, M. (1992). Measuring qualitative aspects of teaching physical education. *JOPERD, 63* (3), 83–89.

Chrouser, D. (1990). Variable sequence lesson planning—New flexibility in lesson preparation. *JOPERD, 61* (5), 31–34.

Farley, M. (1984). Program evaluation as a political tool. *JOPERD 55* (4), 64–67.

Fox, K. (1991). Motivating children for physical activity: Toward a healthier future. *JOPERD, 62* (7), 34–38.

Gallant, P. (1991). Expanding your curriculum through cooperatively planned fun days. *CAHPER Journal, 57* (2), 47–49.

Milverstedt, F. (1988, January). Are kids really so out of shape? *Athletic Business,* pp. 24–29.

Pritchard, J. (1987). Programming for quality daily physical education. *CAHPER Journal, 53* (6), 14–19.

Ratcliffe, T. (1986). Infuencing the principal. What the physical educator can do. *JOPERD, 57* (5), 86–87.

Safrit, M. (1986). *Introduction to measurement in physical education and exercise science.* St. Louis: Times Mirror/Mosby.

Verabioff, L. (1986). Can we justify daily physical education? *CAHPER Journal, 52* (2), 8–11.

Virgilio, S. & Krebs, P. (1984). Effective time management tcchniques. *JOPERD, 55* (4), 68–73.

Section 2

Dance

One of the best things to be said about dancing is that like all the arts there is really no end to it. Therefore it is always interesting and no sooner has one learnt one thing than one realizes how much more there is still to know; and with each lesson a little progress only opens up more possibilities. . . .

. . . Dance is language without words, so there is communication and contact among participants through their relationships in lines, circles or groups.

. . . Dance has always been, and always will be, a very basic form of human expression.

Fonteyn, M. 1978. A Dancer's World. *London: W. H. Allen.*

Chapter 5

The Dance Program

Teaching dance is rewarding, exciting, and demanding. Detailed preparation is required so that lessons are times for sharing and developing ideas, as well as becoming more skillful. Dance, probably more than games and gymnastics, offers many opportunities for integrating movement experiences with various aspects of the curriculum. Other art forms, especially music, are quite easily associated with dance, as can be social studies, science, and language arts, especially poetry. Table 5.1 offers examples.

Table 5.1

Integrating Dance and Other Subject Areas

Subject	Dance ideas
Music	
Recorded music	Stimulus for dance
Music played by the teacher	Accompaniment for
Music composed by the teacher	singing games
Music played by the children	folk dance
Music composed by the children	creative dance
Instruments	Make and/or play percussion instruments for creative dance
Language arts	
Poetry and stories	
Published	Stimulus for dance
Written by the teacher	Written after dance experience(s)
Written by the children	
Verbs, adjectives, adverbs	
	Stimulus for dance
	Describing dances
Art	
Adult art	Stimulus for dance
Children's art	Created after dance experience(s)
Pictures, sculptures	
Social studies	
Costumes	Folk dance
Customs	Creating dances
Festivals	
History	
Science	
Natural phenomena: the sea, storms, weather, birth, and death.	Stimulus for dance
Scientific concepts: magnetism, electricity, gravity, crystals	

Dance tends to receive less attention in physical education programs than the objective movement forms of games and gymnastics. This may be partly due to the value society places on dance. "Dance was once an integrated expression of the whole life" (Mettler, 1980). Over the centuries, dance and sport have existed in some form in every culture and society. These two movement forms are so interwoven into human behavioral patterns that, although the forms may change according to the practices and values of the particular society, involvement in them is a hallmark of being human (Hill, 1982).

The inclusion of dance certainly depends on whether teachers consider it important for children to become skillful in and knowledgeable about expressive movement forms. Sometimes there is the question of whether dance is part of the physical education or art education program. On reflection, it probably does not matter where dance is in the curriculum. What is important is that children have learning experiences in the expressive form of movement.

Why Should Dance be Included in School Programs?

This question has been discussed by groups of concerned educators, and several definitive statements and resolutions have been made and published. There is no lack of support for teachers who wish to introduce dance into their schools. The National Dance Association of AAHPERD, the Dance Special Interest Group of CAHPER, and Dance and the Child: International (daCi) are three associations that exist mainly to ensure that all children have the opportunity to dance and to provide help and encouragement for teachers.

The following are statements published by these associations.

National Dance Association of AAHPERD (1976)

Dance education is a medium for enhancing the quality of life for children, youth, and adults. Every human being has the right to move in ways that are primal, expressive, imaginative, and transformational.

Therefore, we urge arts, civics, and educational groups to support dance programs where they exist and to develop programs where they do not exist that:

foster aesthetic-kinesthetic education;
integrate the human capacity to form and transform in and through movement;
celebrate the human ability to move with power and expressiveness;
promote movement skills that explore and extend the artistic, cognitive, and psychomotor potentials of the human being;
articulate and verify a commitment to man's heritage of dance forms from all cultures and all races; and

include sequential dance experiences appropriate to the developmental level of the human beings for whom they are designed.

Reprinted by permission of the Alliance for Health, Physical Education, Recreation and Dance, 1900 Association Drive, Reston, Virginia 22091.

Constitution of Dance and the Child:International (daCi)

Article II (adopted Stockholm, 1982)

Aims and Purposes The aim of Dance and the Child:International is to promote everything that can benefit dance and the child, irrespective of race, colour, sex, religion, national or social origin; and that this aim shall be carried in a spirit of peace and universal friendship.

Its objectives are to:

recognize the right of every child to dance, including those with special needs, the term "child" covering ages 0–18 years.
promote more opportunities for children throughout the world to experience dance as creators, performers and spectators.
reveal and respect the views and dance interests of the child.
preserve a cultural heritage of all forms of dance for children.
promote the inclusion of dance in general education and stimulate the exchange of ideas on dance programs in schools and in communities.

Reproduced by kind permission of Dance and the Child:International, Ontario, Canada.

Dance Special Interest Group of CAHPER, 1983

Statement of Position

It is recommended that:

dance be a part of the school curriculum at the elementary level.
dance be taught at each grade level as a continuous and developmental program.
children be exposed to a variety of dance forms including creative, folk and square as well as suitable current popular dances, singing games and other rhythmic activities.
dance, where appropriate, be integrated with other subject areas such as drama, language arts, music, social studies, art, etc.
dance experiences be taught using appropriate teaching techniques ranging from exploratory to imitative.

opportunities be given for children to improvise and spontaneously create dance works.

a variety of stimuli be used in conjunction with the dance experience; for example music, words, percussion, imaginative ideas and visual stimuli.

dance experiences allow children to develop an aesthetic awareness through the enjoyment of doing and an ability to view attentively and comment knowledgeably on what they see, feel and hear.

The Nature of Dance

Experience in one art form does not compensate for lack of experience in the other arts. In school curricula, the tendency has been for children to have some program in art or music, and possibly some drama included in English lessons, though probably not from the point of view of providing the children with an artistic experience. Dance is a movement form and some people—parents, administrators, and even teachers—may feel that as long as the children have some activity, then it really does not matter whether it is in the form of a game, gymnastics routine, or folk dance. This is not so. It is only when an "arts in education" commitment is made "that the more human purposes of education relating to values and feelings and personal growth and fulfillment of young people" occur (Brinson, 1979). Fortunately, there are concerned parents, administrators, and teachers who are aware of an "essentialist shift which emphasizes that each art form is unique in its own right and cannot be replaced or supplanted by any other art form or movement form" (Boorman, 1980).

Dance is a word which embraces a range of expressive activities and as such

> *has unique and significant contributions to make in the total education of the child. Dance and the arts play a large part in the "humanizing" of man by encouraging creativity, discovery, inquiry and the overall process of flexible cognition, in a changing, challenging environment (Dance Committee of CAHPER, 1983).*

In an educational environment the production of an artistic masterpiece is not the main concern.

> *Whether the dance meets the criteria of being an important art work, whether the dance of the school child is as enjoyable to observe as that of the student of the National Ballet Company is irrelevant to the teaching situation. The priority is not one of judgement, but of providing the artistic experiences (Dewar, 1980).*

Children enjoy simple folk dances.

Source: Royal Bank Junior Olympics.

This is not to say that quality work will not result, but that the reason for the experience is the concomitant learning rather than the products the children create and/or perform.

Dance is varied in nature, and the word may have different meanings for each of us. If you stop people at random on the street and ask them what they think of when you say the word "dance," you may be told the name of the latest craze in the discos, ballet, or jazz. If you then asked these people how many learned to dance, you would probably find very few who had learned to dance as part of their school program. While the majority of people in the Western world have seen dance (as the television has brought dance in some form into the majority of homes), few have had the opportunity to learn about this activity and art form.

We all use expressive movement many times each day, often without being aware of it. We use gestures and postural movements to indicate how we feel about something or to reinforce what we are saying. Watch the politicians and evangelists on television, and notice how much movement is used as they speak. Recognize, too, that we are influenced as much by the movements as by the words. We may feel the speaker is very confident because he or she stands upright, looks directly at the camera, and uses large, definite hand gestures. Conversely, many small, limp hand movements or the repetition of the same gesture, may detract from what is being said by suggesting uncertainty or lack of conviction.

The nature of dance is such that we can develop awareness of our unconscious movement patterns. This enables us to bring our movements under control and to develop our range of expressive movement patterns, so we have a well-developed kinetic mode of communication.

Anthoney (1979) considers the transformation of everyday movement into an artistic experience occurs at three levels. These levels may provide us with a focus when we plan learning experiences for children.

Level 1. Movement for movement's sake, to develop an awareness of enjoyment in moving. Young children and beginners in dance particularly need this kind of focus in their lessons.

Level 2. The concern is with having an aesthetic experience. Our everyday movements are transformed into a form with new meaning. A dance program, such as the one we are proposing, should give the children this level of dance experience.

Level 3. This completes the transition from the "everyday to artistic" movement. The intention is "to give form . . . to create a structured dance . . . to show someone the dance" (Dewar, 1980). An arts program, rather than a physical education program, would aim to reach this level of experience with all of the students.

Each of the three levels is a legitimate dance experience, and more or less emphasis will be placed on each of them at different stages of learning, according to the focus of the learning experience. Reference is made again to these three levels of experience in chapter 6.

Dance Forms

The concept of *functional* and *expressive* movement has already been discussed in chapter 2. A dance program for children in elementary schools should consist of a variety of dancelike experiences, some being more expressive than others. Three dance forms are suggested as a minimum. Each form challenges the children in specific ways, thus the learning objectives vary (table 5.2).

The stage of the children's development will also guide our choice of the form most suitable at a particular time, as suggested in table 5.3.

The choice of form will also be based on the movement concepts considered appropriate for the children's needs and capabilities at that particular moment. For example, you may decide the children need help in working cooperatively in twos. You might, therefore, select a simple partner folk dance that demands coordinating with another, as in a clapping dance, such as the German Clap Dance, or one where the partners

Table 5.2

Expressive = Objective Movement Experience Continuum

Less expressive dance experience		More expressive dance experience
←		→
Singing games	Folk dance	Creative dance

Table 5.3

Suggested Appropriateness of Dance Forms

	K	Grade 1	Grade 2	Grade 3	Grade 4	Grade 5	Grade 6
Singing games	•	•					
Folk dance			•	•	•	•	•
Creative dance	•	•	•	•	•	•	•

have to change hold, such as the Gay Gordons. The main focus of your teaching (refining, simplifying, and extending tasks) will be directed towards the skills and awareness necessary for making the partnership function. Comments, such as "Have your hands ready as you face your partner," and "Keep level with your partner as you travel" will give the children information they can use to improve their relationship.

The following three dance forms are suggested as most appropriate for a school program

1. singing games,
2. folk dance,
3. creative dance.

Each dance form will be discussed separately. Table 5.4 outlines selected characteristics of each, so it is easy to compare them.

Singing Games

Singing games are part of children's oral heritage, and they are closely allied with music and poetry, particularly nursery rhymes. Many singing games are simple coordination exercises, while others are little dramatic experiences, such as The Farmer's in the Dell. Children often know these songs and action sequences before they come to school; therefore, they make a good link between preschool experiences and classroom activities.

Singing games are rhythmic and repetitive in nature. The relationships between the participants are simple, as are the activities. There is little room for individual variations, and the teacher's focus will be more

Table 5.4

Selected Characteristics of the Three Dance Forms

	Singing games	Folk dance	Creative dance
Relationships	Range from individual to group; single and double circles; simple	Partners, groups; lines, squares, circles; range from simple to complex	Range from individual to group; varied formations; range from simple to complex
Rhythm	Metric; preset; simple	Metric; preset; simple to complex	Metric, nonmetric; preset, or created; simple to complex
Stimulus	Song, music	Music	Infinite possibilities
Accompaniment	Music, voice	Music	Silence, music, voice percussion
Activities	Running, skipping, galloping, clapping, stamping	Combinations of step patterns	Combinations of six basic activities (figure 5.1)
Responses	Imitative, predetermined	Imitative, predetermined	Mainly creative

on general participation, keeping in time with the music, and knowing the words, than on improving motor skills. Singing games that require partners and formations, other than scatter and a single circle, are closely related to the beginnings of folk dance.

Folk Dance

This dance form is really "borrowed" from the adult world. Years before the days of radio and commercial entertainment, folk dances were the social dances of the people. When schooling became compulsory and some form of physical activity was considered essential for the children, adult movement activities were scaled down and included in the curriculum. Folk dance was one of these activities. Teachers knew the dances, and they were considered easy to teach.

Over the years, folk dance has become firmly established in many elementary school programs, and it is probably the most common dance form taught.

> *In terms of educational value folk dance is perhaps one of the best examples of integration of subject matter which can be found in the school curriculum. Here it is possible for children to learn about the history and life of people of different ethnic origins: their customs, their music, their celebrations and costumes (Evans, 1980).*

Children can have very happy learning experiences when folk dance is taught by sensitive and confident teachers who are able to select and adapt the predetermined dances to meet the needs of their particular children.

Creative Dance

Creative dance, which offers children a diverse dance experience, demands a disciplined mind and body. The children may dance alone, with a few chosen friends, or with the whole class. In dance lessons, ideas are explored by discussing, analyzing, improvising with or without any accompaniment, synthesizing, and transforming the ideas into concrete, repeatable movement patterns or motifs. These motifs are symbolic representations of the original idea or ideas. It is an opportunity for children both to express themselves and be themselves. This does not mean there is no direction from the teachers or that neither structure nor limitation is set. In fact, the opposite is necessary. A carefully structured environment has to be designed to guide the children (often through the use of problem-solving techniques) to explore, experiment with, and formulate their motifs. Children are helped to evaluate their own work and that of their peers from the point of view of effectiveness. Thus, appreciation and aesthetic judgments are encouraged.

Creators—Performers—Observers

A final comment on the nature of the dance program for children: three very different experiences are possible. As educators we must recognize the importance of each and ensure that the children we teach have opportunities to learn to be *creators, performers,* and *observers* of dance. Each of these roles demands different kinds of knowledge and skill. Table 5.4 gives some indication of which dance form probably provides the best learning experiences in these distinct roles. When observing others dance, try to include dance artists as well as other children. Many dance companies and studios have a special program they bring to the schools. Universities with dance programs sometimes welcome an opportunity for their students to perform. Taking the children to see a performance in a theater is, of course, most valuable, but in days of budget restrictions there often is no money for such expeditions.

Rhythmic Activities

Some programs include general activities to music. The general objectives are to move in time to music, adjust to different tempi, and recognize and move to different rhythmic patterns. Children have these experiences when the program includes singing games, folk dance, and creative dance. The addition of another dimension to the dance program reduces the time available to each one. We feel three dance forms provide in-depth learning and sufficient variety for the children.

The Material of Dance

All dance forms emphasize the expressive, qualitative elements of movement—the ever-changing dynamics which add "color" and meaning to our activities. When put into spatial and relationship contexts, activity becomes a means of communicating and sharing thoughts, ideas, and feelings. Sometimes we are expressing ourselves; at other times, we express other people's ideas and thoughts. In the former situation, we are the creators as well as the performers; in the latter, we learn the dance created by another.

As discussed in chapter 2, all human movement can be categorized into four major concepts: body, effort, space, and relationships. As we develop greater understanding of how these concepts relate specifically to dance and as we become more skilled in producing planned movements at will, our movement vocabulary increases, and we become more able to use our bodies as instruments of expression. We will consider each concept separately as it applies specifically to dance.

> *It goes without saying that teachers of dance, like those of another discipline, should have a total grasp of the basic structure of their subject and the material it contains (Exiner, 1977).*

Body Concepts

Body concepts are concerned with understanding and developing control of our physical selves. An overview of these concepts was introduced in chapter 2. Here, we look at body concepts as they relate to dance for children.

In the dance context, the body is often called the instrument of our expression, with movement being the medium through which we communicate.

> *The body serves the same purpose in dance as, for example, the piano serves in music. The musician uses the piano to create sound. The dancer uses the body to create movement (Mettler, 1980).*

Dance is a **kinetic art** for the dancer and is, therefore, activity oriented. Children "come to dance' through activities, such as skipping, turning, jumping, lifting the arms in reaching gestures, and being "statues." Each of these examples belongs to one of the six general categories of activity (figure 5.1), which can be considered the basic vocabulary of dance:

1. Locomotion
2. Stepping
3. Gesturing
4. Jumping
5. Stillness
6. Turning

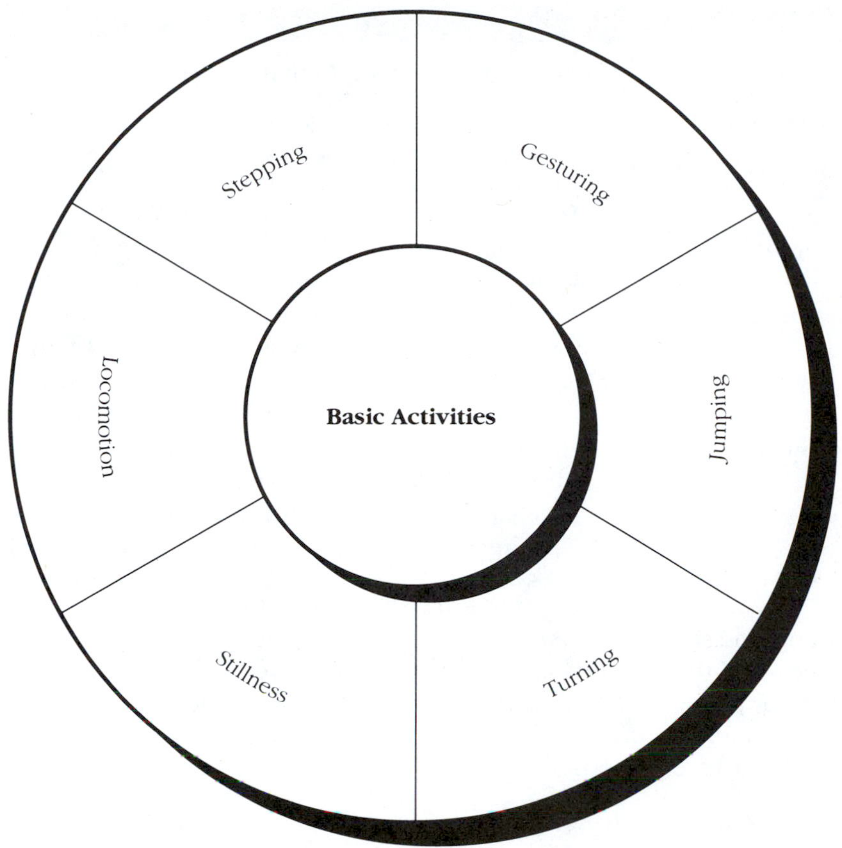

Figure 5.1 Body concepts—the six basic activities of dance.

To Do A Stepping Sequence

Begin with weight on two feet, change to one knee and one foot, one knee alone, and finish on one foot.

Repeat on the other side of the body (i.e., if you put weight on your right knee the first time, use your left knee in the repetition).

Repeat the sequence until you can do it smoothly and seemingly without exertion.

These activities carry the dynamics we select and thus become expressive in nature. There are many variations within each category, and table 5.5 lists examples. These, and other verbs, are very useful when planning lessons (chapter 7).

Locomotion

Locomotion, or traveling, focuses on all the different ways the body can move through the space to new places. The intention of the dancers is to "go somewhere"; therefore, their focus is outward, not on themselves. Examples of simple locomotor activities are walking, running,

Table 5.5

Examples of Verbs from the Basic Activities Vocabulary

Locomotion	Creeping	Galloping	Rushing
	Dashing	Rolling	Skipping
	Fleeing	Running	Sliding
	Walking		
Stepping	Kneeling	Sitting	
	Lying	Standing	
Gesturing	Bending	Reaching	Stretching
	Gathering	Scattering	Twisting
Jumping	Bounding	Leaping	Pouncing
	Hopping	Prancing	Running
Stillness	Freezing	Pausing	
	Hovering	Stopping	
Turning	Pivoting	Revolving	Spinning
	Pirouetting	Rotating	Twirling

rolling, and sliding. An extensive locomotor vocabulary is developed over a period of time, and whole dances can be created based on simple locomotor patterns. Complex patterns, in which stepping and jumping are often combined, include mazurka step, polka step, and skipping. Most folk dances are composed of simple and complex locomotor patterns.

Stepping

Stepping refers to changing the parts of the body supporting your weight. The focus is not on "going somewhere new" but on shifting the weight from one body part to another, an action requiring considerable strength and control. Children often understand this idea if the word *stand* is used in the task, as in "stand on two different body parts, then find how you can change to two new body parts."

Interesting positions of stillness arise; the world can be observed from upside down, and some unusual sensations can be experienced as a result of changing from one base to another. The addition of gestures when the body weight is on different—maybe unusual—bases results in changing visual effects, an important consideration when a dance is to be performed and observed.

Balance and strength are two important factors involved in stepping. Coordination is also involved. This is highlighted in the complex step patterns found in some folk dances.

Gesturing

Movements of the "free" parts of the body, (i.e., those not involved in supporting the weight) are called **gestures.** In our daily lives, our hands and arms are probably involved in gesturing more than any other body parts. In dance, leg gestures and movements of the head and spine all play important roles in clarifying, highlighting, and adding to the aesthetic aspect of the movement.

Moving from standing to kneeling to sitting to lying.

Gesturing with arms and legs.

Table 5.6

The Basic Jumps

The basic jumps	French term	English term
Take off and land on same foot	Temps levé	Hop
Take off on one foot; land on the other foot	Jeté	Leap
Take off on one foot; land on two feet	Assemblé	Jump
Take off on two feet; land on one foot	Sissone	Jump
Take off on two feet; land on two feet	Saut	Jump

Jumping

Jumping is the name given to any action in which the body leaves the floor; the person enjoys for a moment the sensation of being airborne. The focus of attention can be on that moment of freedom from the ground or on the moment of returning to earth.

There are five basic forms of jumping. Each form has a French name because all the jumps are in the classical ballet repertoire. Only two have English names. Table 5.6 lists the five basic jumps.
The variations and combinations possible are numerous, challenging the dancer's stamina, strength, and balance.

Stillness

Stillness is the state achieved when motion is arrested or stopped. It is the activity of stopping and being able to maintain the stillness that is developed. Stillness may be for only a fleeting moment, as in a pause, but the cessation of movement can be as powerful a statement as movement itself. Phrasing and rhythmic patterns are formed as the dancer combines moving and pausing. Stillness in dance is equivalent to silence in music and punctuation in writing.

In photographs, it is just as difficult to give a feeling of stillness, as it is to give the feeling of motion.

Turning

Turning is an activity involving rotation of the body around an axis, so the dancer faces a new direction. The rotation may be small, perhaps a few degrees only; a complete circle (360 degrees), so the dancer ends up facing the starting point; or multiple rotations, which can result in dizziness. Dizziness can be resolved by a sudden action of the head in the direction opposite to the turn, or by moving up and down. Dizziness can also be prevented by the more technical concept of *spotting;* dancers are taught to fix their eyes on one spot on the wall and keep looking at it for as long as possible during the turn, moving the head last and quickly looking again at the same spot. This reduces the eye movement that causes vertigo. Spotting is a technique which is not appropriate or necessary for young children or beginners, but may be introduced when the students are fairly skilled.

Jumping requires strength.

Going and stopping.

Swing your partner!

Table 5.7

Development of the Basic Activities

Body parts		Body shapes
Identification and isolation of parts		Wide
Relationships between parts:	meeting	Long
	parting	
	over	Round
	under	
	around	Twisted
Stressing different parts during activity		Symmetrical
Parts leading the activity:	away from	Asymmetrical
	toward	
	around	
Parts initiating the activity		

In the study of dance the six basic activities are explored and expanded by focusing on different bodily aspects, such as stressing an elbow when turning, making a twisted shape when jumping or stopping (table 5.7). The activities are combined into sequences that can be repeated and clarified.

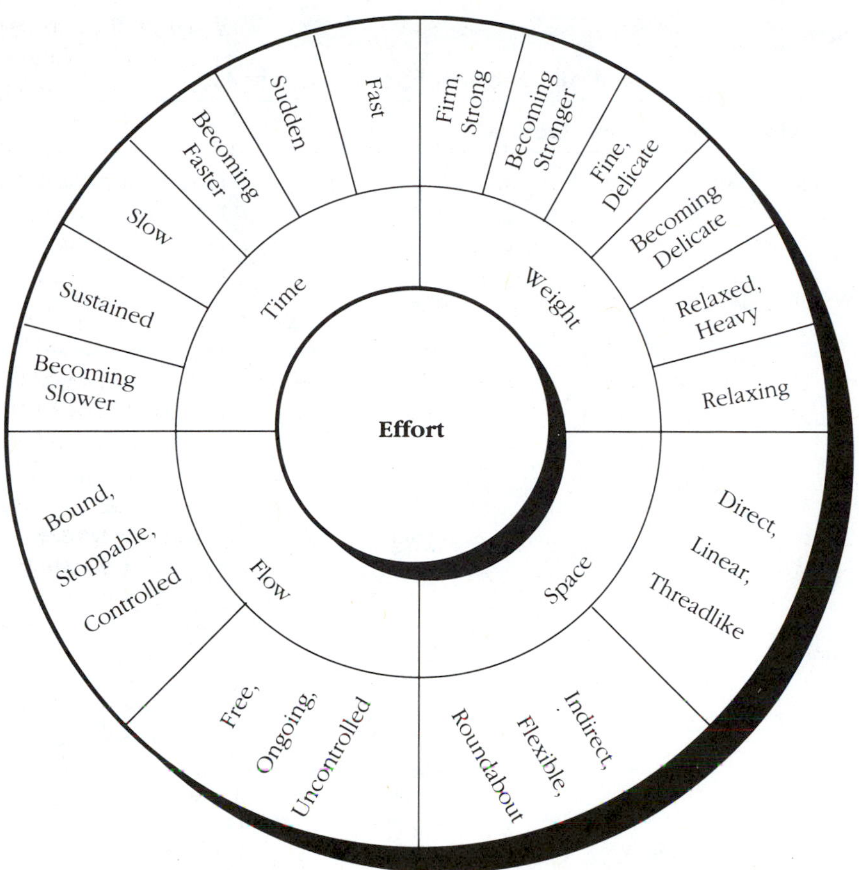

Figure 5.2 Single factor concepts.

Effort Concepts

You may already be familiar with the word *dynamics* in the dance context. The word *effort* has a similar meaning. Both words infer the qualitative dimension of movement, the result of combining aspects of the **motion factors:** time, weight, space, and flow.

These factors may be likened to the primary colors which, when combined in different proportions, produce all the colors known. It is the ability to select, produce, and combine these factors, producing varying shades of effort, which gives the qualitative dimension to activity and results in a rich vocabulary. A jump, for example, can be very strong and explosive, or gentle and appear almost weightless to the observer. Compare the jumps seen in Russian Cossack dances with the jumps in a corps de ballet sequence.

Figure 5.2 expands the basic motion factors to show the range of each. In the early learning experiences, tasks are designed to focus attention on contrasting aspects of one factor at a time. An example is a movement phrase, repeated three times, of a fast run and a slow turn.

Table 5.8

Multiple Motion Factor Concepts

Combining two motion factors			
Weight	+	Time	Firm + Sudden
			Firm + Sustained
			Fine + Sudden
			Fine + Sustained
Weight	+	Space	Firm + Direct
			Firm + Flexible
			Fine + Direct
			Fine + Flexible
Weight	+	Flow	Firm + Bound
			Firm + Free
			Fine + Bound
			Fine + Free
Time	+	Space	Sudden + Direct
			Sudden + Flexible
			Sustained + Direct
			Sustained + Flexible
Time	+	Flow	Sudden + Bound
			Sudden + Free
			Sustained + Bound
			Sustained + Free
Space	+	Flow	Direct + Bound
			Direct + Free
			Flexible + Bound
			Flexible + Free

Combining three motion factors*	
Weight + Time + Space	Firm + Sudden + Direct
Weight + Time + Flow	Fine + Sustained + Free
Time + Space + Flow	Sudden + Flexible + Bound
Space + Flow + Weight	Direct + Free + Firm

*Note: There are eight possible combinations for each set of factors, making a total of 32 combinations!

As the children become more skillful, combinations of the motion factors are explored and dance studies developed, so the children use their widening vocabulary in an artistic way. Table 5.8 shows the combinations possible.

Spatial Concepts

Space is a very important element in dance; the concepts of general and personal space were introduced in chapter 2 (figure 2.6). As we dance in and through the space around us, our gestures make three dimensional

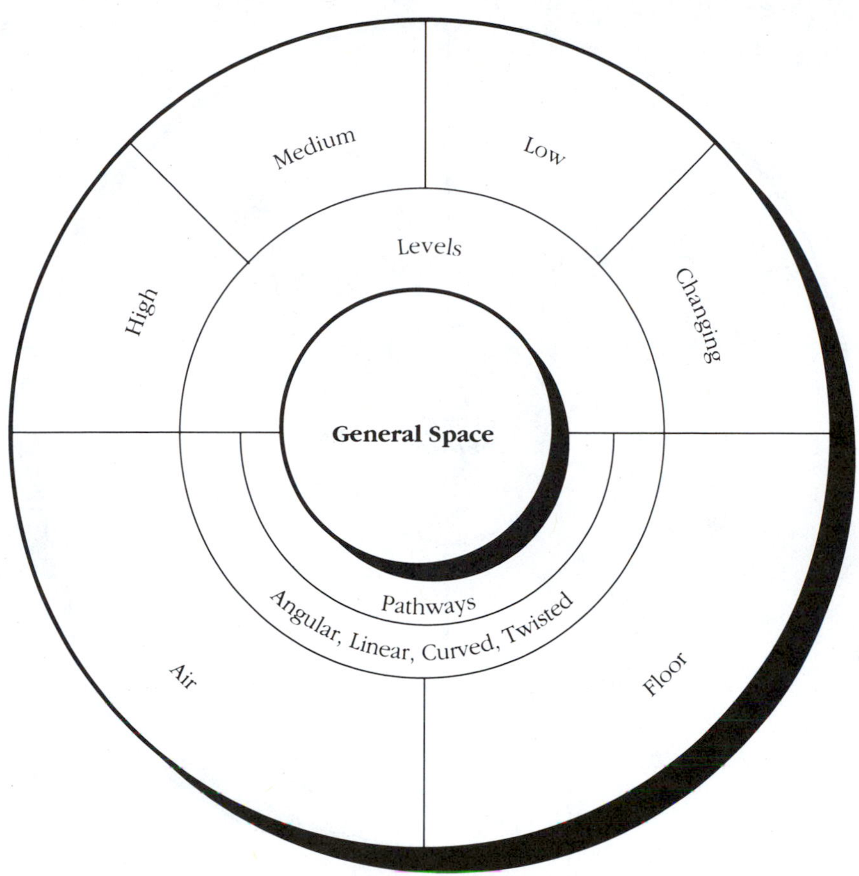

Figure 5.3 Space concepts—dimensions in general space.

shapes in the air and our feet make two dimensional pathways on the floor. An awareness of the shapes and patterns we are creating helps us design and place our dances in the space, in much the same way artists place images on their canvases.

Many folk dances demand a sensitivity to the general space in which the dance is being performed. Remembering the patterns involved in a folk dance is a considerable challenge, and it takes time for children to be able to dance formations without error. Some children become quite frustrated when they feel "lost" in the space in which they are dancing. They are usually easy to identify. If several children give this impression, then it may be that the dance is too complex for them. In this case, either modify the pattern or find another dance. In some dances, it is the patterns made by the group as they travel toward, away from, and around each other that are important. The shapes of the groups may also change from lines to circles to spinning pairs of dancers. The patterns created sometimes need to be seen from above to be appreciated.

Figure 5.3 illustrates general spatial concepts.

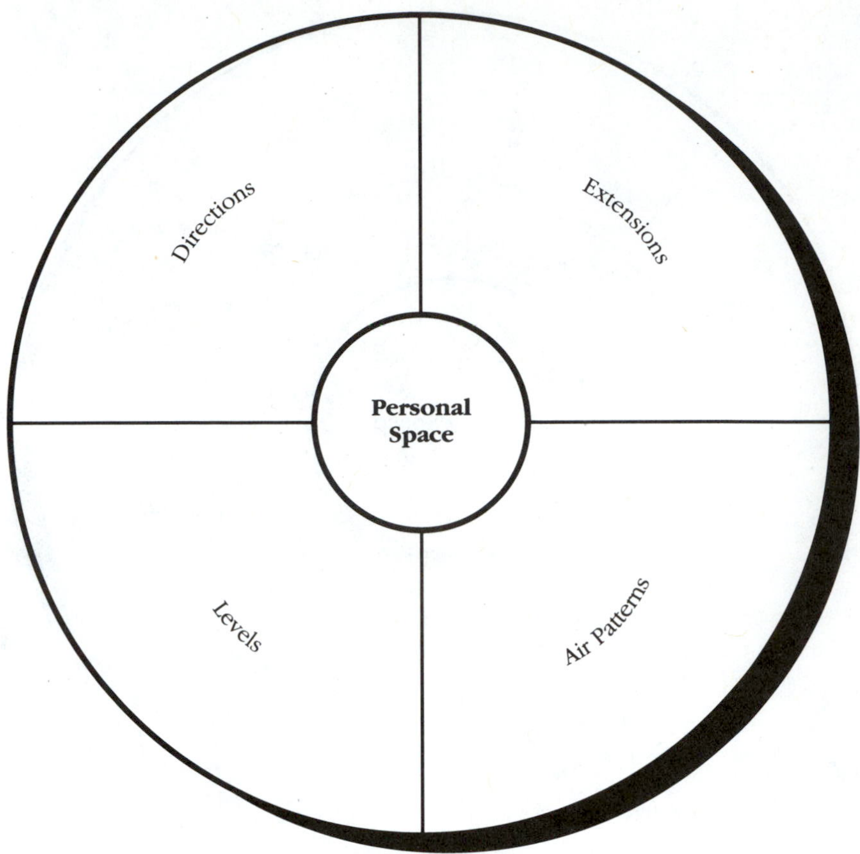

Figure 5.4 Concepts of personal space.

Awareness of space in creative dance is closely connected with expression. The communication resulting from an activity placed at a high level changes when the same activity is placed at a low level. This is seen in the photograph on page 183, in which the children are traveling at different levels.

In personal space, skipping and traveling forward is very different from skipping and traveling backward. There is a feeling of freedom and openness in the former and a closed, more restricted sensation in the latter. Figure 5.4 and table 5.9 illustrate dimensions of personal space.

The reason some creative dances exist is similar to that of abstract sculptures—the enjoyment and appreciation of shapes, sizes, lines, and spaces. Lessons can be developed in which the children transform one art form into the other. Dances can be stimulated by a piece of sculpture and vice versa.

Skillful use of space enriches our dances and adds another dimension to our vocabulary.

Table 5.9

Dimensions of Personal Space

Directions	Extensions
Forward—In Front	Toward—Near to the body
Backward—Behind	Away—Far from the body
Sideways—Left	Small—Smaller
Sideways—Right	Large—Larger
Levels	**Air patterns**
High—Up/above	Straight—Linear
Low—Down/below	Twisted—Convoluted
	Angular—Zigzag
	Curved—Circular

Relationship Concepts

Relationships play a key part in the dance program because much time is spent dancing together, sharing ideas, watching one another, and discussing what has been seen. None of this can develop without an awareness and appreciation of the relationships involved. The attitude we have about the people with whom we are working is always a cooperative one. The dancer's attention shifts from activities to people. The following schema, therefore, have the individual as the core. Figure 5.5 shows basic relationship concepts and table 5.10 develops these ideas.

Much of the enjoyment in dance is obtained from dancing with friends. Both singing games and folk dance provide opportunities for the children to be with chosen partners, to change partners, and to dance in larger groups.

There are times when some children will wish to create and/or dance alone. Creative dance allows for this. In such situations, the children (like painters) are independent of others for their art experience.

Other aspects of the relationship concept include (1) the accompaniment selected for the dance and (2) costumes and/or props that may be used in a dance.

Accompaniment

Music is probably the most obvious form of accompaniment for dance, particularly for singing games and folk dance. Percussion (including sounds made by percussing the body), words, vocalizing, and silence are effective and sometimes more appropriate, especially in creative dance.

Figure 5.5 Basic relationship concepts.

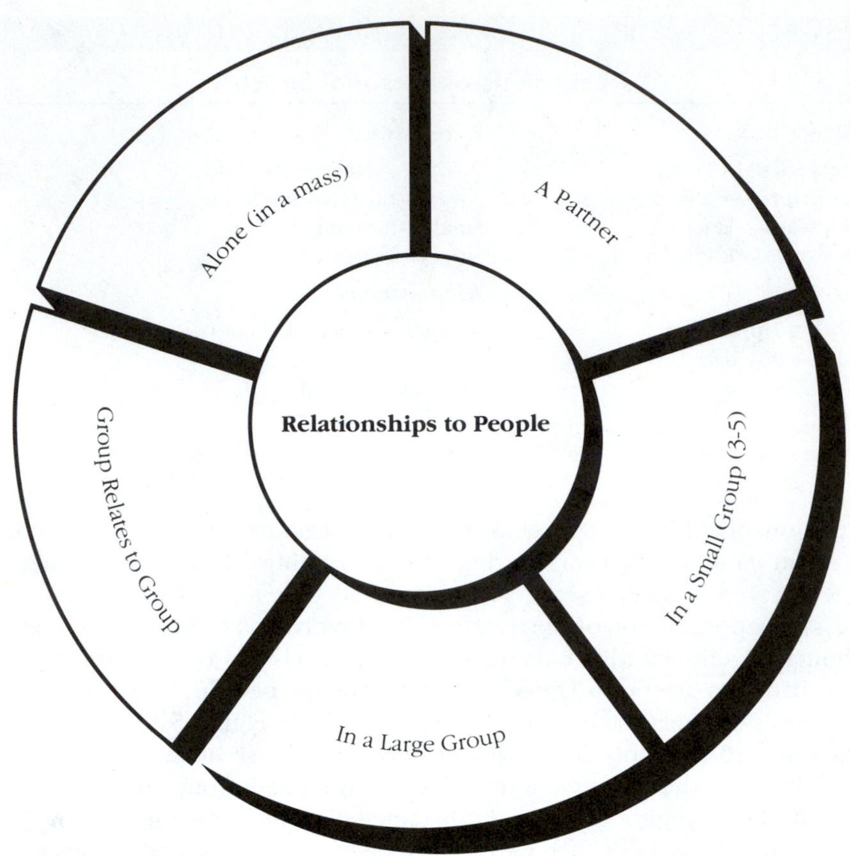

Table 5.10

Developing Individual and Group Relationships

People may
- mingle—separate
- meet—part
- lead—follow
- merge—disperse
- match—contrast
- mirror
- shadow

Spatially, they may move
- toward—away from—around—over—under—between—through

They may be
- close together—far apart—in front—behind—beside—below—above

Temporally, they may move
- in unison—in canon—simultaneously—successively

Traveling high and low.

Whatever sound form you select, the children will probably need to learn how to listen to the accompaniment. Children hear so much music—in supermarkets, at home, on buses—without paying real attention to it. Chapter 7 discusses this more fully.

Costumes and Props

Most children enjoy dressing up, and costumes do not have to be elaborate. Often a piece of draped (and pinned) material is all that is required to identify a particular character or suggest a quality in a dance. Simple masks can be made out of paper bags, or more elaborate ones made from papier-mâché in art classes. What is important is that the children have time to relate to the costume, and that using the material becomes part of the dance, rather than being added as an afterthought.

Props, too, need to be danced with as the dance is developing. For example, a dance based on sweeping actions may include light-weight, oversized brooms that are danced with as partners.

Application of Movement Concepts

Certain concepts discussed in this chapter comprise the content of the dance lesson plans in the accompanying *Lesson Plan Manual.* The Dance Themes Index (table 5.11) lists the concepts of the sample lessons. In these lessons, you will find learning sequences leading to applying tasks in singing games, folk dance, and creative dance lessons.

Table 5.11

Dance Themes Index

Lessons—Kindergarten		Body concepts	Effort concepts	Spatial concepts	Relationship concepts
Singing games	1	Body activities	Rhythmic phrases	Personal-general	
	2	Body activities	Rhythmic phrases	Circular floor pathway	
	3	Body activities	Rhythmic phrases	Personal-general	
Creative dance	4		Slashing and gliding qualities	Personal-general	
	5		Weight: strong-light	Personal-general	
Lessons—Grades 1–2					
Creative dance	6	Basic body actions: bend-stretch-twist			
	7	Body parts—gesture	Time: Fast-slow Weight: changes in tension		
	8	Body shapes	Time: changes in speed	Personal	
	9	Locomotion-gesture	Time: sudden, sustained		
	10	Body activities		Circular floor pathways Big-small pathway	
	11	Body parts leading		Personal-general	Individual in a group
	12		Time-weight qualities	Basic space patterns: straight, rounded, twisted	With props: streamers
	13		Metric meter		Partner: copy

Table 5.11 Continued

Lessons—Grades 1–2		Body concepts	Effort concepts	Spatial concepts	Relationship concepts
Folk dance	14	Body activities		Circular floor pathways	Partner; individual in a group
	15	Body activities	Time: duration (beat, half beat)	Circular floor pathways	Individual in a group; partner, neighbor
Lessons—Grades 3–4					
Creative dance	16	Body shapes	Time: sudden-sustained		Partners
	17	Body activities		Directions	Partners
	18	Weight transference and gesture		Personal-general	Groups of 3
	19			Floor pathways levels	Groups of 3
	20	Symmetry-asymmetry			Partners: simultaneous, successive
	21	Body parts meeting-parting	Time: sudden, sustained		Partners
	22				Groups of 4.
	23				Partners: mirror, copy
Folk dance	24	Body activities		Floor pathways	Partners in a large group
	25	Body activities		Floor pathways Directions	Partners in a group of 8
Lessons—Grades 5–6					
Creative dance	26	Body activities	Time qualities		Partners
	27	Body shapes	Time qualities		Partners

Continued

Table 5.11 Continued

Lessons—Grades 5–6	Body concepts	Effort concepts	Spatial concepts	Relationship concepts
28			Space words: over, under, around, behind	Groups of 4
29	Specific body parts	Time + Weight qualities		Partners: simultaneous, sequential
30		Time: metric meter		Partners: copy; mirror
31	Symmetry-asymmetry			Groups of 4: unison-successive
32			Personal-general	Partners: dancing together
33			Floor pathways	Groups of 8: formations + relationships
Folk dance 34	Body activities		Floor pathways-directions	Partners in large group
35	Body activities		Directions	Partners

Summary

Our dance vocabulary develops as we become familiar with and skilled in controlling our bodies. Our enjoyment in dancing increases, sometimes simply because of the sensations we receive from movement done for its own sake. Laban wrote:

> *A refreshing swim in the sea is a wonderful and health-giving thing, but no human being could live constantly in the water. It is a very similar case with the occasional swim in the flow of movement which we call dance. Such swimming, refreshing in many respects for the body, the mind and for that dreamy part of our being which has been called the soul, is an exceptional pleasure and stimulation. As water is a widespread means to sustain life, so is the flow of movement (Laban, 1948).*

Through planned learning experiences based on Laban's concepts, children's kinaesthetic awareness is heightened as they are helped to focus on the relaying of "muscular, articular, cutaneous, vestibular and auditory cues to the brain" (Preston-Dunlop, 1980). Interpretation of these cues gives the children knowledge of position and movement in space, thus becoming aware of their own artistic instrument.

We have looked at the four major movement concepts as they relate to dance. We can see that two concepts are concerned with self-understanding and the development of conscious control, or skill, over our physical (body concepts) and emotional (effort concepts) selves.

The other two movement concepts relate to our environment; external factors that influence us and to which we react. First, there is the concept of space, general and personal, in which we move and which we can learn to use effectively. In so doing, we develop a different kind of knowledge and skill. Second, we focus on the people around us, learning to adapt, react to, and work with others in groups of varying sizes, always with the purpose of sharing and always in a cooperative manner.

We also learn to attend and respond to other elements in our environment (music, poetry, props, etc.) to supplement and complement our expressive powers (see chapter 7).

Having analyzed some of the multiple strands of human movement, we must weave them into the dynamic fabric of **dance.**

Review Questions

1. What are some reasons for including dance experiences in physical education programs?
2. Which three dance forms are suggested for the program? Discuss the nature of the three dance forms.
3. How should emphasis on the three dance forms change for the different grades?
4. Explain in your own words what Anthoney (1979) means when discussing "the transformation of everyday movement into an artistic experience."
5. Name the six activities considered the basic vocabulary of dance.
6. What are the extremes of the four motion factors?
7. Two of the four major concepts (body, effort, space, relationships) are concerned with developing conscious control of our physical and emotional selves; two are concerned with developing skill in adapting to the environment. Explain.

References

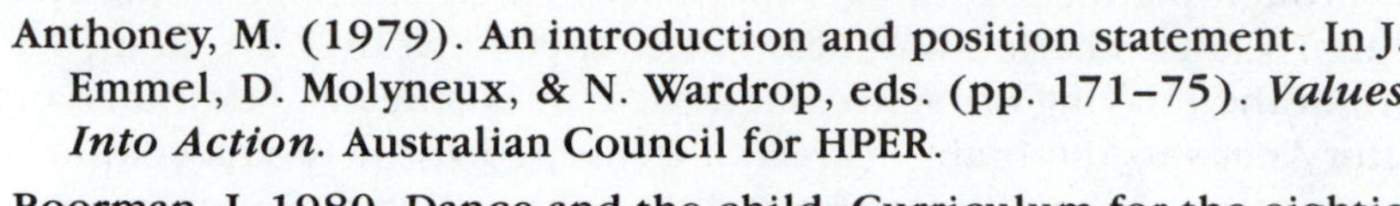

Anthoney, M. (1979). An introduction and position statement. In J. Emmel, D. Molyneux, & N. Wardrop, eds. (pp. 171–75). *Values Into Action.* Australian Council for HPER.

Boorman, J. 1980. Dance and the child: Curriculum for the eighties. *CAHPER Journal 47,* (2), 15–17.

Brinson, P. (1979). Dance in education: An overview. In W. Lett, & S. McKechnie, eds., pp. 18, 28. *Dance in Education Conference Papers.* Melbourne, Australia: A.A.D.E.

Côté-Laurence, P., Drake, V., & Wilson, V. J. (1990). Lesson plans for dance, games and gymnastics to accompany children and movement: Physical education in the elementary school, J. Wall and N. Murray. Dubuque, IA: Wm. C. Brown Communications.

Dance Committee of CAHPER. (1983). *Dance in elementary (K–6) education.* Position Paper. Ottawa: CAHPER.

Dewar, P. (1980). Teaching creative/modern dance in the schools. *CAHPER Journal 46,* (4), 27–29.

Evans, J. (1980). Movement education and folk dance: A rationale (Part 1). *CAHPER Journal 47,* (2), 42–44.

Exinel, J. (1977). Presentation at Dance Education Conference, Melbourne, Australia.

Hill, R. (1982). Let's teach sport and dance. *CAHPER Journal, 48,* (6), 13–16.

Laban, R. (1948). *Modern educational dance.* London: Macdonald and Evans, Ltd.

Mettler, B. (1980). *The nature of dance as a creative art activity.* Tucson, AZ: Mettler Studios Inc.

National Dance Association. (1976). *Dance as education.* Washington, D.C.: AAHPERD.

Preston-Dunlop, V. (1980). *A handbook for dance in education* (2nd ed.). London: Macdonald and Evans, Ltd.

Chapter 6
Teaching Dance

Dance is the art form arising from the expressive use of movement. Because of this, teaching dance differs considerably from teaching games or gymnastics (discussed in chapters 8 and 11) in that we are involved in artistic and aesthetic endeavours. It is comparatively simple to set dance problems/tasks for children; for example, "combine rising, turning, and running into a sequence;" the hard part is to guide its development into dance form. Our teaching behavior must be carefully developed and planned so that we help our children make the "transition from generalized movement into movement as an aesthetic experience" (Anthoney, 1979).

Anthoney (1979) considers this to be a three stage process:

1. *Movement.* Awareness of delight in movement
2. *Aesthetic experience.* Transformation of movement and concurrently a new meaning
3. *Artistic experience.* Intention to give form, to create a structured dance, to show/perform the dance

These three stages are useful guidelines in two ways. First, we can use them to help us become better dance educators by giving us a point of departure as we begin to teach. Once we know we are providing learning experiences in which the children enjoy moving rhythmically just for the sake of it, we are ready to tackle the next hurdle in our development. Likewise, we can assess when we are nearing the third stage in our teaching behavior. At this point, the children will be creating and/or remembering dances which have structure and which they would like to share with others, i.e., to perform.

Second, the stages can help us in relation to curriculum development. Younger children will begin at the first stage. As they become more experienced, they will move through the second stage and then to the third stage. Beginning units in the dance program will, therefore, concentrate more on global concepts related to body management in general space with a strong rhythmic stress. Evaluation of the "products" will be tempered by the stage at which the children are working.

Remember That

For some children, their only chance to learn about dance as an activity and an art form is when they are in elementary school.

Dance lessons should be enjoyable for the teachers and the children. These lessons are times for sharing, selecting and rejecting ideas, participating in the creativity of others, observing dances being developed, and evaluating so we can refine and clarify the product.

Dance Experiences

We need to be creative teachers and become skillful in providing different kinds of learning experiences for our children. These experiences may be **exploratory, improvisational** and **imitative.** Through such experiences, we hope to "enrich, extend and reinforce the child's total dance experience" (CAHPER, 1983).

Exploratory Experiences

Exploratory experiences are learning situations in which teachers must be nonjudgmental, yet provide guidance so the children discover something specific about themselves and dance. It is not an "anything goes" situation; far from it! The learning environment is structured, so the children are secure and know what they are trying to achieve. Open tasks are structured in the form of problems to be solved; for example, "Begin curled up, close to the floor; begin to open and rise. Do this several times, beginning the movement in different parts of your body." The children will find more than one solution to this problem. They may be asked to *select* from the various responses (theirs and/or that of others) and to *develop* a sequence. The result of this repeating and refining is a complete dance. In creative dance lessons, this is probably the most common method of structuring learning sequences and will be used mainly in Part 2 of lesson plans (chapter 4). More examples of learning experiences will be found in the lesson plans in chapter 7.

To Do

Discuss which dance form(s) provides opportunities for

1. Exploration
2. Imitation
3. Improvisation

Improvisational Experiences

Tasks are again open in improvisational experiences, but the objective of the learning sequence differs from exploratory experiences because there is little or no emphasis on reaching a repeatable product. There is more attention to spontaneity of response than analyzing and modifying responses, as in exploratory work.

Lessons may begin with an improvisational task, for example, "Dance freely to this music;" the children should be able to respond immediately to such an open task. Improvisational tasks can also provide a release from concentration. For this reason, they may be used as the culmination of a lesson, especially if there has been considerable attention to detail in skill/concept development (Part 2) of the lesson.

Both exploratory and improvisational learning situations allow for individuality of response, the use of imagination, and acknowledgment of the emotions as a source of ideas.

Imitative Experiences

Tasks for imitative experiences are closed, because the expected response is to reproduce something which already exists. Children greatly enjoy copying and much can be learned by doing so. Much of what children learn is copied, and many ideas come from "internalized copies," which eventually become adapted to meet a new situation. Initially, attention is centered on learning predetermined dance steps, patterns, and sequences. Success is often more immediate than with exploration and improvisation, and many children gain confidence as they master and repeat the step, pattern, or sequence.

Singing games and folk dance lessons usually include more imitative than exploratory and improvisational learning sequences. In these lessons, the initial model is probably the teacher. In creative dance lessons, imitative experiences usually follow exploratory learning, when children may be asked to copy a sequence or dance created by their peers.

Remember That

You are the "significant other" for many children; therefore, you greatly influence their likes and dislikes. If you have an active life-style, enjoying and appreciating expressive and functional movement, there is a greater chance the children will have active life-styles, which include expressive and functional movement experiences.

Teaching Skills

Many of the skills we employ when teaching dance are the same ones we use when teaching games and gymnastics. Discussion of these generalized skills is found in chapter 3. The following skills will be discussed as they apply specifically to the dance situation:

- Posture and movement
- Voice skills
- Organizational skills
- Observation skills
- Evaluating
- Questioning
- Playing percussion instruments

Posture and Movement

Being kinaesthetically aware and ready to dance with the children is important, especially at the beginning of a lesson. It helps set the dance mood, it motivates the children, and your movement provides an instant model of the introductory task, which often demands a degree of uniformity of response. When teaching younger children, you may find you dance more than they! At all times in dance lessons, your posture, gestures, and movements must have a dance quality.

Voice Skills

We depend a great deal on our voices and the spoken word when teaching, and this is especially true in dance lessons. It is a great asset if we can word informing, refining, extending, and applying tasks in clear, concise ways that motivate interest, and invite the children to participate. You may find that some students react more sensitively to comments made during dance lessons than in games or gymnastics lessons. This is understandable as the intention is to "speak from within oneself." The children are emotionally vulnerable, and a misplaced or mistimed comment can be hurtful and have long-term effects on the learners. A poorly expressed comment made during a dance lesson can dampen any spark that may have been there. You must learn how individual children react to praise, criticism, and encouragement, and approach each child accordingly.

To Do

Discuss the following and decide what each means to you:

1. A creative teacher
2. Teaching creatively
3. Teaching for creativity

Voice Sounds

Our voice is a valuable instrument which can be used most effectively as an accompaniment. We probably do not consider and employ our voices enough as an accompaniment in dance lessons. We need to be able to make many different vocal sounds, both rhythmic and expressive, to accompany whole group activity. There are several advantages. We can produce the sound we feel is appropriate for the task; we do not have to explain it to a pianist or other musician; we do not have to seek it on a record. It is ours; wherever we are in the room, it is with us. We can produce it at will as the task is extended; we can produce a portion of it to accompany part of a sequence we wish to repeat and refine.

Practicing humming, lah-lah-ing, zzzzzing, pppppping, and other consonant and vowel sounds, in repetition at different pitches and volumes, is a good exercise. Develop the ability to repeat a phrase of two or three different sounds with changing quality.

Nonsense syllables are useful when a rhythmic pattern is needed. For example, try "dum-di-dum-di-dummmm-di," accenting and drawing out the *m* sound. "Ya-ta-ta, ya-ta-ta, ya-ta-ya" has a different quality and rhythm. It may take a bit of courage to use your voice in this way, but once you begin you will not stop. The voice is a rich source of sound, an instrument that needs developing.

To Do

Have a "nonsense conversation" with a friend, varying the volume and pitch of your voice. Try to convey emotion through the sound, rhythm, and volume of your voice. As you become more confident, add movement to enhance the communication, the movement being secondary to the sound. Gradually, let the relationship between the sound and the movement change, so the movement becomes the main mode of communication and sound the secondary.

Vocabulary

A large vocabulary of descriptive words and phrases is a must for dance teachers. We need to be able to arouse visual, kinesthetic, and auditory images in our students as they respond to the tasks. If, for example, the informing task is "Raise one arm lightly, with sustainment; then lower it strongly and suddenly," what words and/or phrases could we think of as we plan refining tasks that are descriptive? We want to help the children experience the contrasting dynamics and shift from a dreamlike state to a more awake, almost on-guard attitude. Different children will respond to different images, depending on their having (relevant) past experiences to which they can relate this new one.

The English language is rich in descriptive words. We are fortunate to have such a rich resource available, and we should make a conscious effort to extend both our own vocabularies and those of our students. Boorman (1973) indicates that there may be a connection between dance experiences and the development of vocabulary in young children. We should recognize the hidden curriculum components of the dance experience, and if "all teachers are teachers of English" (Russell, 1975), we should use this knowledge as we design the learning sequences and select the words we will use. Table 6.1 suggests some adjectives, adverbs, and verbs relating to specific motion factors. No attempt has been

Table 6.1

Some Descriptive Words

Adjectives	Adverbs	Verbs
Roundabout, plastic, indirect, supple, lithe, pliable, flexible	Wavily, pliantly, convolutingly	Undulate, meander, fluctuate, squirm, writhe
Direct, linear, threadlike, straight	Unerringly, deliberately, smoothly	Drift, glide, slide, soar, press, pull, heave
Strong, firm, forceful, vigorous, powerful, triumphant	Boldly, resistantly, pressingly, tortuously, aggressively	Writhe, beat, stamp, kick, punch, heave, pierce
Delicate, gentle, fine, light, fragile, frail, subtle	Quietly, softly, daintily, sensitively	Stroke, caress, creep, float, drift
Sudden, abrupt, sharp, staccato, flippant	Hastily, excitedly, precipitatingly, joltingly, urgently, lively, unexpectedly	Quiver, jab, stab, twitch, burst, flee, rush, throb, shimmer
Dilatory, sustained, legato, tardy, casual	Calmly, dreamily, slowly, stealthily	Linger, loiter, meander, creep, drift, stroke
Viscous, resistant, stoppable, hesitant, restricted, uncertain, doubtful	Cautiously, reluctantly, unwillingly, fearfully	Ooze, withhold
Continuous, ongoing, free	Abandonly, uncontrollably, willingly	Stream, flow, gush

To Do

Find as many synonyms as possible for strong, light, sudden, and sustained.

1. Use a dictionary or *Roget's Thesaurus*.
2. Ask children of different ages.

made to equalize the number of words in each column, and we hope you will add words. Some of the words are quite complex and more suitable for older, more experienced children. Use your knowledge of the specific children you will be teaching as you plan. Some of the verbs are repeated. For example, ***writhe*** suggests it is pliable and strong, ***drift*** suggests it is threadlike and light.

Organizational Skills

Unlike games and gymnastics, little equipment is needed for most dance lessons. A good tape recorder, record player or compact disc player, a selection of tapes, records, and/or discs, a drum for yourself, and some percussion instruments for the children (see table 6.2) are the basics. It is a bonus if you are able to play an instrument, such as the piano, guitar, or flute, particularly if you can improvise as you accompany the children as they dance.

We recommend taping all music chosen for your dance lessons for the following reasons:

1. A tape recorder is easy to start and stop in a hurry.
2. It is easy to find and play a specific section of the music.
3. A selection of music may be recorded several times, with a pause between each recording, making it possible for you to provide feedback without running to turn off the tape recorder.
4. You can record the music for the entire lesson on one tape.
5. Tapes are small, lightweight, and easy to carry.
6. Tapes are less likely to be damaged than records. If they are damaged, the source of the music is still available.

If the lesson is held in a space other than the gymnasium, you must ensure the floor is clean and free from obstructions. Select the position for the tape recorder so you have a good view of the children. If this means using an extension cord, make sure it is tucked against the wall out of the children's way. Remember that you will need to move to and from the tape recorder as you teach.

If your lesson includes percussion instruments, place them in groups, so they are easily accessible, yet out of the way.

What Is Wrong With This Situation?

A first grade class of thirty children are participating in their first dance experience of the year. Until now, their physical education lessons have been in the gymnasium, but today it is not available. The lesson is being held on the stage, an activity area new to the children. The stage curtains are closed. A tape recorder is situated at the back of the stage with an extension cord running along the back wall. The movement concepts of locomotion and time are the focus of the lesson. Rock music has been chosen as the stimulus. The teacher puts the record on and tells the children to run to the beat of the music. The children respond by running without control, not to the beat of the music, pushing against the curtains, bumping into each other, and giggling as they do so.

In this situation, the following factors contribute to the problems:

1. The space is too small for thirty children to run safely. Activities such as leaping and running need ample space. When children have been used to working in a large area, it is difficult for them to adjust to a more restricted area.
2. Some rules should have been established concerning the potentially dangerous extension cord and the curtains. Young children need time and guidance to adjust to a new space.

3. Moving at a fast speed was not appropriate for this first lesson. The children need help with finding out the size of the new area and adjusting their speed when traveling to that of others. The first task could have been to walk and stop, accompanied by a drum beat played by the teacher. In this way, the teacher could control the speed and spacing.
4. Rock music may have been too exciting in this new environment.
5. The task should be given *before* the music is turned on. We suggest that you let the children listen to the music, then give the task (or vice versa), say, "Begin as you hear the music," then turn it on.
6. When children do not hear the task, they often copy one another. In this situation, wild behavior encouraged more wild behavior!

Safety Tip

Never allow children to dance in socks alone. On a bare floor, there is insufficient friction between the sole of the foot (sock) and the floor.

Observational Skills

Because dance is expressive and difficult to quantify, our ability to observe, understand, and react to the children's dancelike responses to the tasks is crucial. For some tasks, as in singing games and folk dances, we know there should be uniform responses, and we can be prepared with visual and/or kinesthetic image checklists against which we measure the children's movement patterns. In creative dance there will be varied responses, and the amount of variation possible and acceptable will depend on the degree of openness of the task.

There are several strategies we can use to help ourselves improve our ability to observe children as they dance. The following ideas may be helpful. It is an organizational progression which may also be used in games and gymnastics lessons. Two different tasks are chosen, the first is more closed than the second. The expected responses to the first task are uniform; the responses to the second are expected to differ considerably.

Closed Task—Uniform Response

Task: Begin facing your partner; stamp right foot three times, left foot three times, turn to your right taking four steps, finish facing your partner and clap your own hands three times. (Four bars 4/4 may be played on a drum, or a piece of marching music may be played.)

1. With the entire class working, focus on one child. When you have decided whether or not the response is correct, make an appropriate comment to the child. Move to a new place and scan the entire group before focusing on a second child. Mentally note what you have seen; it is no use looking without analyzing.
2. Divide the class into four groups. Have three groups sit down and watch the other group. Tell the children to repeat the pattern twice. Notice and praise the children who are successful; encourage and suggest refinements to the others. Repeat with the other three groups.

On the positive side, this method enables us to observe each child and give appropriate feedback thus improving performance. It is also a good system for improving the children's observational skills. If used after some very energetic activity, it provides children with a rest while keeping them involved. On the negative side, it is a time-consuming method which reduces participation. As we become more skillful observers, this technique may be replaced by the following one.

3. Move around the room as the children repeat the sequence. Focus your attention on a specific small group of children (maybe three pairs) and give appropriate feedback to those who are performing well and those who are having problems. Move to another area, scanning the entire class as you go, providing feedback to everyone if possible. Then, focus on another small group. If you observe a common problem, stop the whole class, give the necessary refining or simplifying task, and let them continue to practice as you move to another small group.
4. When you know your class well, you will probably be able to anticipate who may encounter difficulties with a particular task. Immediately focus your attention on these children, and help them before you observe the remainder.
5. If the children are experienced, used to observing each other, and can work well on their own, you might have three work together in a reciprocal teaching situation (Mosston, 1981), two dancing and one observing. In this case, the observers should have a checklist (such as the one in figure 6.1) to which they can refer. This is one concrete way the children can take responsibility for their own learning, improving their ability to observe, as well as dance. It is successful when the children have some experience in working in small groups without constant supervision. For obvious reasons, this is more appropriate for older children.

   You have two options: you can visit each group, discuss with the observers what they have seen, and offer encouragement and suggestions for refinement as necessary to the individuals; or you can stand "outside" the class, alternately scanning and focusing until everyone has had a turn at observing and being observed. The class can then be brought together. The children can be asked questions about what they saw, whether or not it was successful, and be asked to make suggestions for improvement. This is a demanding challenge for the children because they have to decide what information will improve their own performance. After the discussion, they should try again and notice any changes in their own and peers' performance.

Observer: Melanie
Teacher: Mrs. Roth

Children may observe each other to evaluate progress in specific skills. The observer checks the appropriate box if the student demonstrates the skill.

Name:	John	Susan	Chris
Face partner			
Three steps right			
Three steps left			
Turn right			
Four steps			
Face partner			
Clap three times			

Figure 6.1 Checklist for reciprocal teaching.

6. Eventually, you will be able to scan a whole class accurately and pinpoint who is doing well and who needs extra help. This stage is reached after consciously practicing observing children moving in different settings. In all settings, the mental checklist is a must. For all previously mentioned organizational procedures, the following progression may be helpful:
   a. In the earliest stages, focus specifically on a portion of the pattern, rather than trying to see the whole. For example, ask children for three stamps of the right foot, three stamps of the left foot. Is everyone doing that? During the next repetition, watch the turning activity. Does it begin and end facing the partner? In the third repetition, are four steps taken, beginning with the right foot? On the final repetition, look at the children's hands.
   b. In this kind of sequence, we should also use our sense of hearing, as stamping and clapping are important elements. We need to listen to the rhythm of the stamps and claps, and their relationship to any accompaniment we have provided. Observing, therefore, includes more than seeing.
   c. Feel the movement sequence kinesthetically as you observe. This may help you sense when someone is "out of tune." Go one stage further and dance the pattern with a small group, giving feedback as you participate.

Open Task—Varied Response

Task: Choose either a low- or high-level starting position. Change to the opposite level, showing clearly whether you are more involved with leaving the starting place or arriving at the new level.

Learning to observe open tasks is no more difficult than learning to observe more closed ones, provided you know kinesthetically what the task implies, what experience you wish the children to have, and what new movement concepts are being introduced or what known concepts applied. Suggestions have already been made to help you observe a predetermined pattern, one with no variation in response. What can the teacher do when there may be as many variations as there are children? Even in this case, there will be some commonalities for which we can look.

Options for organizing the children are the same as before (see preceding list), and visual and kinesthetic checklists are just as necessary.

After the children have had a short time to experiment with the idea, you might ask all those who have selected a low starting point to continue to work and have the other children sit down. You now have at least one common factor. The next aspect is the focus of the children. Do they clearly show by focus and use of selected body parts whether they are more involved in leaving or arriving? After watching this group and providing refining tasks, encouragement, and praise, change the two groups.

Evaluating

In dance, we tend to evaluate in terms of the aesthetics of the movement pattern. Since dance is an art form, as well as a physical activity in which equipment is rarely used, we observe how the body moves, and how it is held in stillness. Questions are asked. Was the body shape effective? Was there an appropriate use of tension? Did the children have a clear focus as they traveled? Because dance is a mixture of the physical and the affective, instruments designed to evaluate children's skills need to take into account quantitative (how high? how fast? which body parts?) and the qualitative (how softly? how fluidly?) components. In folk dances and singing games, the stress may be more on the quantitative elements. In creative dance, the qualitative components may be more important. In your dance program, formative techniques are more appropriate than summative ones, and the instruments designed should be criterion referenced.

Lessons

There is considerable potential for variety of content and experience in dance lessons. Preston (1963) suggests the following six points as a guide to whether we exploit and use this variety as we try to cater to individual needs, likes, and dislikes within our classes.

Clear focus when rising or sinking.

1. *Methods of presentation*
   a. Imitation
   b. Exploration
   c. Improvisation
   d. Creation (This is equivalent to applying tasks. The result is a product which can be shared with others.)
   e. Recalling an already-known dance
2. *Movement content.* This refers to which movement concepts have been chosen as the learning focus of the lesson. Over a period of time, we must achieve a balance between body, effort, space, and relationship concepts. As an example, a unit of dance may focus on effort experiences with minimum attention paid to space. This unit should be balanced with one attending to spatial concepts and integrating the children's effort knowledge.

3. *Social aspect.* We can design tasks requiring children to work alone or with others in small or large groups. It is important that we maintain a balance between these possibilities. Over a period of time, we may find that the children have spent more time sharing than developing their own ideas. Their ideas may have been manipulated, changed, and integrated with other ideas. In the final form of the dance, children may recognize very little of their own contribution to it. Their idea is there, but in a different form.
4. *Placement in the working space.* This is an organizational aspect of the lesson. We tell children "Work in your own space," "Use the space freely," "Stay on the spot." Monitoring the amount of a lesson spent in one place and comparing it with the amount for traveling through the space is useful. Young children in particular need to be "off the spot" several times during a lesson. Concentration is assisted by a change of focus and pace; this can partially be achieved by a change in working space.
5. *Accompaniment.* Many people think dance is always accompanied by music. This is far from the case. A balance between accompanied and unaccompanied dance is hoped for. Dancing in silence is challenging and should be part of the overall dance experience.

   The range of possible accompaniment is wide and can vary from voice sounds, words, body sounds to full orchestral sounds; from the latest pop music to the classics. We should take advantage of the wealth of music available and introduce the children to sounds they may not hear on their favorite radio station but may grow to like (figure 6.2).

   One of the great "sound experimenters" of the twentieth century is the composer R. Murray Schafer. He has investigated likes and dislikes in sound and the relationship between sound and visual images. He composes music using a tremendous variety of everyday objects as the instruments. He calls some of his compositions *soundscapes* (Menuhin & Davis, 1979). Children, too, love experimenting with sounds and creating the accompaniment for their own dances. (See section on percussion instruments later in this chapter.)
6. *Link with previous lessons.* After the first lesson in a unit, there will be tasks which relate to already familiar concepts, as well as to new ones. We should avoid introducing too many new concepts in a lesson and monitor how many lessons are spent on each one. Obviously, the first lesson in a unit is more likely to include new concepts, some of which will be to "get the class going," others we will develop over two or more lessons. A balance between the familiar and the unknown is likely to maintain the interest and motivational levels of the children.

I love the music and I love lisning to losts of music.

Heather. Loise. Fagan.

Age 6

Figure 6.2 Child's response to music.
Courtesy of Diane Fagan.

A quick method of monitoring these six aspects of teaching dance, and recording in very general terms the children's responses, is to prepare a page of grids; one grid per lesson in the unit plan. Sample grids are shown in figure 6.3. After reviewing the grids, you will have an overall picture of the concepts taught, the kind of experience, the accompaniment used, and the children's responses to the various tasks. It is a useful means of checking the variety and range of learning experiences provided in a unit (Preston, 1963).

Children's Skills

Children who are good at singing games and folk dances are able to imitate steps, remember combinations of steps and the patterns of the singing game or folk dance, and make the transitions between one sequence and the next. They can anticipate what is coming. These are quantitative elements. "Good" dancers also relate well to their partners or group and produce the particular effort content which gives the singing game or folk dance its particular expression and/or quality. These are qualitative elements.

Simple check lists, such as those seen in figure 6.1, can be employed to evaluate the children's dance skills quantitatively. It is doubtful, though, that you will create checklists for each singing game and folk dance you teach. A more general checklist, including the step and spatial patterns learned in the particular unit, is more likely to be useful. Such a checklist is shown in figure 6.4.

Evaluating creative dance presents us with a quite different (and difficult) problem. Hawkins (1964) provides some guidelines that we have found useful and which have been modified over a period of time to meet the needs of specific situations.

A simple rating scale (figure 6.5) for the younger or less experienced dancers is probably the most useful. It gives an assessment of the children's developing dance vocabulary. This kind of recording sheet may

Figure 6.3 Lesson grids.

Lesson 1

Task	Experience	Concept (s)	Social	Sound	Placing	Link
1	Imitative	Traveling	Alone	Drum	Free	New
2	Explore	Shapes	Partner	Silence	On the spot	New
3	Improvise	Travel, stillness	Alone	Record	Free	New

Comments: Quickly involved task 1; giggled task 2, clearer focus needed, (accompaniment?). Task 3 became imitative—large group unison!

Lesson 2

Task	Experience	Concept (s)	Social	Sound	Placing	Link
1	Recall	Travel, stillness	Alone	Record	Free	New
2	Respond	Shapes, time	Partner	Drum	On the spot	Develop
3	Explore	Pathways	Alone	Record	Free	New
4	Create	Combine tasks 2 and 3	Partner	Silence	Free	Develop

Comments: Danced with them task 1, gradually withdrew; individual response coming. Drum helped task 2, complementary shapes emerging. Class skipped for task 3; poor quality, must work on this. Cue cards for next time. Task 4 surprisingly good.

be filled in during the dance unit, particularly when a child is responding above your expectations. Decisions regarding children responding below your expectations should be left until toward the end of the unit, so they have the maximum chance of improving their performance. A word of caution: we must be objective, accurate observers when using these scales. When using them more than once, we must not allow our objectivity to be influenced by an earlier opinion.

Figure 6.4 Dance unit checklist.

Unit 1—Singing Game

Name: ______________________________ **Grade:** __________

Date: ____________________

Criterion for steps: Dances a complete phrase with correct timing.

Criterion for patterns: Changes direction with the phrases.

Steps:	**Most of the time**	**More than half the time**	**Less than half the time**
Skipping			
Running			
Walking			
Galloping			
Patterns: Circles left and right			
Straight lines			
Turning with a partner			
Other: Transitions			

General comments:

When evaluating the creative work of the older, more experienced children (possibly grade 4, definitely grades 5 and 6) a different format is suggested. The end of a unit might be the sharing of small group dances developed during several lessons. The children may have been working on their own interpretations of a piece of music you selected because it seems to combine the movement concepts that have been the learning focus of the unit, or you may have set them the challenge of selecting their own action words and creating a partner dance based on these words. The checklist seen in figure 6.6 is designed for this latter situation.

The children should be given the evaluation sheet when they are at the refining stage of their creative work. They should be asked to complete Part A. Seeing the criteria in written form helps some children clarify

Figure 6.5 Sample rating scale for dance.

Name: ______________________ **Grade:** ______________
Date: ______________________

Use of Body Parts:	**Below Average**	**Average**	**Above Average**
In isolation			
Integration			
Use of Body Shape:			
Clarity			
Variation			
Use of Space:			
Levels			
Directions			
Pathways			
Use of Effort Changes:			
Time			
Weight			
Rhythm			
Use of Relationships:			
Partner			
Small group			
Large group			
Other:			
Concentration			
Variablilty of response			

Above average: Above that expected for age and experience.
Average: What is expected for age and experience.
Below average: Below that expected for age and experience.

Figure 6.6 Simple checklist for dance sequences.

Date: Nov. 6
Topic: action words - rush, vibrate, spin, rise
Name of students: Chris and Leslie

	Not Used	Used Some	Used Extensively
Changes in body shape			
Body parts stressed			
Changes in level			
Specific pathways			
Changes in direction			
Contrasts in time			
Contrasts in weight			
Changing relationships			
Observer: K. Ottawi	**Not Seen**	**Seen**	**Seen Extensively**
Changes in body shape			
Body parts stressed			
Changes in level			
Specific pathways			
Changes in direction			
Contrasts in time			
Contrasts in weight			
Changing relationships			

Comments:

their dances. Also, as you discuss the checklist with them, you will find those who (a) have a good grasp of the concepts they are including in their dance but have difficulties performing; (b) move well but have little understanding of the concepts; and (c) understand and move well. Enough time must be allowed for this paperwork so the children feel challenged rather than threatened! You will fill in Part B after each pair dances. A comparison can be made between what the children wanted to include and what you saw.

If possible videotape the children dancing so they can see their own creations and you can discuss the completed checklist with them.

Videotape and Evaluation

Watching videotapes can help the children in their creative endeavors when they are past the "Look, there I am!" stage of watching the playback. Videotaping allows the children to try an idea, watch a replay, and make decisions regarding the effectiveness of the developing motifs and the quality of the performance itself. They can see whether lines are straight, toes are pointed, groups are focused in the same direction, where and how a movement spreads throughout the group, etc.

It is important to be able to stand back and view what one is doing. Painters are able to do this because their creations are separate from themselves. The videotape now makes it possible for dancers to stand back and evaluate themselves.

Having someone film the children, thus freeing you to teach, can be very useful, especially when it is time to evaluate the whole class. This will enable the children to spend more lesson time on learning and less on being evaluated. It can be difficult to teach and evaluate performance at the same time.

Questioning

In exploratory and improvisational work, we do not always know what the children intended to happen; therefore, we must find a way of helping them perform what they wanted. Skillful questioning is needed. This point will be illustrated with the following open task: "In threes, begin close together, then move away from each other with strong gallops. Return with slow turns." There are specific challenges of knowing when to begin, of galloping away, turning and meeting again. There are, as well, many aspects of the sequence to be decided by the children, and each threesome will develop different sequences. General questions, such as "When you begin, do you all begin together, or does one dancer move followed by the others?" should help the children clarify their phrase. Some may already have realized there was the possibility of leaving successively or in canon while others may not. Of course, that question must be followed with specific refining tasks for each of the groups; therefore, you need to change your observation from scanning the entire class to focusing on one trio.

Another question, also dealing with the emerging relationships, might be "Where do you look as you move away?" Keeping in mind Anthoney's concern with transforming everyday movement into an art form (Anthoney, 1979), attention to this aspect of the sequence will add meaning to the movements. As the relationships develop in each trio, such states as aggression and fear, equality and unity, or domination and submission may be communicated to the observers. The dancers should be aware of the developing expressive aspect of their sequence and the power of their communication. This, after all, is what creative dance is about.

When the dance activity is more imitative than exploratory or improvisational, feedback will probably be more in the form of statements than questions. For example, if the imitating/informing task is "gallop four steps to the right, stamp left-right-left-right, gallop four steps to the left, stamp right-left-right-left" you may tell the students, "Your line of travel tends to go sideways; try to make it go on the forward diagonal." A demonstration may be useful, after which the children repeat the phrase, refinement given with, it is hoped, immediate improvement.

Playing Percussion Instruments

There are times when the "right" music is just not available—it hasn't been composed or we just haven't heard it—but we know the kind of accompaniment we would select if we could. This is a time when percussion, perhaps integrated with voice and body sounds, may be the answer. One of the great advantages of selecting percussion for a dance is that the music can be composed along with the dance. We do not have to be musicians to play percussion well. What is meant by "well"? It means that we know and can play a range of sounds that can be produced by each instrument, accurately repeat a sound phrase several times, increase and decrease the volume of the sound, change the speed at which the phrase is played, and combine these changes (i.e., play loudly and slowly, quietly and fast). We must also be able to combine playing, dancing, and talking.

Even though percussion instruments have their own particular sound quality, most fit conveniently into one of the three categories in table 6.2.

The rhythmic group is useful for accompanying metrically rhythmic phrases of movement, for example, skipping, galloping, running and leaping. Loud and soft accents can be highlighted with practice, and it is quite easy to increase and decrease the speed at which a phrase is played.

Vibratory sounds elicit small shaking movements; indeed, one uses a shaking action to produce the vibratory sound. Short phrases of vibration are exciting, lively, and surprising in quality, providing a vivid contrast to the rhythmic and resonant sounds.

To Do

Practice producing rhythmic phrases to accompany

1. running
2. skipping
3. walking

For each, know how many steps there are to the phrase so there is "shape" to your playing, e.g., starting in stillness, six running steps, and pause. Repeat.
How will you change the accompaniment if the children are asked to add a change of level as they run?

Table 6.2

Percussion Groups

Rhythmic	Vibratory	Resonant
Drums	Maracas	Cymbals
Tambours	Bells	Chime bars
Claves	Tambourines	Xylophones
Woodblocks		Gongs

The resonant instruments have sounds which begin, continue, and gradually fade, so that an impulsive, flowing quality of movement is suggested. The movement gradually fades to stillness.

We can also produce our own accompaniment or stimulus by using body sounds, for example, finger snapping and hand clapping. An advantage of using body sounds is that we can produce the sound spontaneously at whatever point in the lesson we feel it is appropriate; we do not spend time fetching an instrument.

To Do

1. Select an instrument from each of the three percussion groups.
2. How many different sounds can you produce?
3. Try unusual ways of playing the instrument. For example, if you have a drum, hit it with an open hand, knuckles, cupped hand, wooden stick, or spoon.
4. Create a short composition using (a) at least three different sounds from one instrument, (b) change of speed, and (c) a change of volume.
5. Tape record the composition at least twice. Play it back and listen for variations in sound. Which recording was more pleasing? Can you repeat it accurately?

Sound as Stimulus and Accompaniment

What is the difference between sound as a **stimulus** and as an **accompaniment?** In the former situation, the movement response is elicited by the sound—the sound composition suggests certain activities, spatial ideas, and relationships; it establishes moods that suggest particular qualities of movement. The dance composition develops *because* of the sounds. In the latter situation, the music is composed, or chosen, to fit the movement. Skillful percussion playing and voice sounds, by the teacher and/or the children, can be great fun and advantageous. Tailor-made accompaniments can be modified to meet the needs of the dance composition. The music is secondary to the dance, playing a supportive role instead of an initiating role.

Music is an important aspect of the dance program. Listening to and selecting from various recordings should become an integral part of our lesson planning. Over a period of time you should build up a mini-library of pieces for each aspect of your dance program.

Music for Folk Dance

Whenever possible, choose recordings made of folk dance musicians of the particular country from which the dance originates. The quality of the music, particularly the rhythm and harmony, is usually quite different from that of educational recordings made especially for children's dances. Some countries have their own particular instruments, as well as different combinations of instruments. For example, the Scottish bagpipes are tonally different from Irish bagpipes; French Canadian folk dance bands often include a set of spoons playing exciting rhythms; a Ukranian folk dance ensemble sounds quite different from one from Greece.

If your school is multicultural, you may be able to invite a folk dance band to your school for a special occasion, to accompany dances the children have learned. This could be part of a major social studies project.

Music for Creative Dance

There is a wide variety of music we can use in creative dance lessons. This includes the latest pop, western, traditional jazz, classical, electronic, and film score music (Murray, 1984). Many children know what is broadcast by the local radio station, some children will be influenced by older siblings' likes and dislikes, and children without siblings may hear their parents' choices. One of our objectives should be to broaden the children's musical perspective (incidentally, we may broaden our own as well).

Begin listening for dance music whenever you hear some, which may be in the car or at a party. Begin collecting your own library, remembering that pieces you select must appeal to you as well as the children. You must feel comfortable with the music, and it must elicit a dance response from you.

When listening to a piece, ask yourself if the music suggests activities; for example, does it sound like spinning or rising or jumping? A series of action words may develop, and these might suggest a story or a poem, one already written, or one you or the children write in a language arts lesson. The resulting poem or story could then become the stimulus for the dance.

Clapping hands.

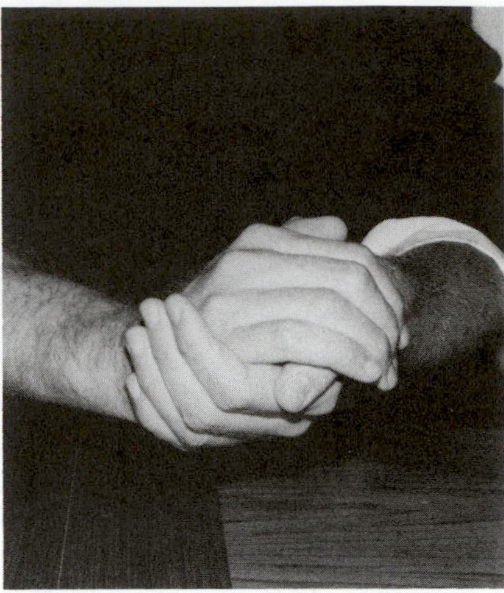

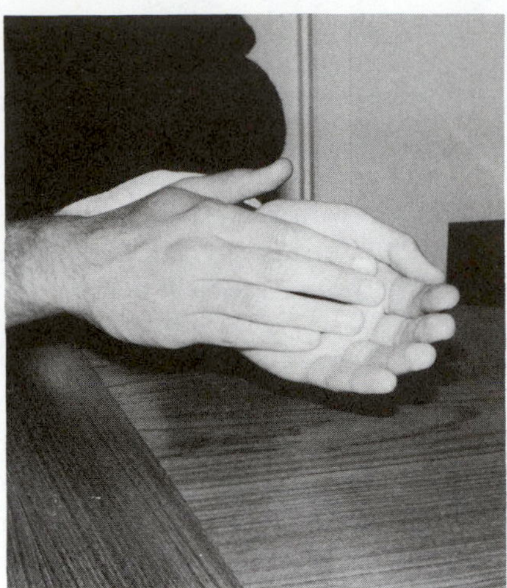

To Do

1. Practice clapping hands, making different sounds by
   a. relaxing hands "soft hands,"
   b. tensing hands "hard hands,"
   c. changing relationship of hands,
   d. rubbing hands, making a continuous sound, (Add accents by changing the speed of rubbing every so often.)
   e. bouncing heels of hands together.
2. Practice snapping fingers loudly, softly, alternating left and right, "running" across several fingers.

Having selected a piece of music, either as the stimulus or the accompaniment for a dance composition, familiarize yourself with it completely, so you "know where you are" in the music. This means listening to it several times and recognizing the musical signposts. This will enable you to help the children learn the music and begin to associate the sounds with specific motifs or dance ideas. You hope that the children will eventually anticipate what happens next, rather than paying attention to what is happening at the moment. When this stage of awareness is reached, the transitions in the dance will be accomplished more easily.

A visual representation of the music is one method of helping everyone become familiar with the composition. An example is seen in figure 6.7. It can also be a useful reference during the lesson. There are several ways of transferring the sound to paper, and each of us may devise our own symbols, adding color to indicate changing dynamics or repetition if we find it aids understanding. The representation can be transferred onto an overhead transparency or a large chart, and the children can refer to it as they compose their dance.

A musical composition is usually divisible into sections, some of which may sound similar, others distinctly different. We need to be able to recognize where one section ends and the next begins and also whether the musical content of the section is the same as or different from the others. Offenbach's famous "Can-Can" from *Orpheus in the Underworld* is used here as an example. It has a short introduction followed by five sections and a conclusion, which is longer than the introduction. Sections 1, 2, and 4 are musically different. Sections 4 and 5 are repeats of 1 and 3. The conclusion, while maintaining the character of what has gone before, is a new idea.

Musical Form A B C A A

2

Figure 6.7 Visual analysis of *Trepak*.

Each section can be analyzed so that the phrase lengths, dynamics, and rhythmic patterns are recognized. The degree of analysis needed will depend on both the nature of the dance composition being created and the nature of your analytical skill. If you feel your musical knowledge is limited, begin by listening to short pieces; for example, R.C.A. Victor's *Listening Series* are very useful because they have notes to help teachers.

To Do

Listen to Offenbach's "Can-Can" from *Orpheus in the Underworld*

1. Find words to describe sections 1, 2, and 3 of the music (e.g., bouncy, energetic, carefree).
2. Do you recognize some of the instruments being played? If not, ask someone to point out the brass, the strings, and the woodwind instruments. Each group is heard separately at some point in the composition.
3. Does the music increase or decrease in energy?
4. Does the music suggest any change in size or flow of movement?

If you have an understanding of basic musical concepts, this will certainly help you. "A teacher with awareness of the elements of both music and movement should be able to enrich and clarify the movement through the music" (Docherty & Churchley, 1982). Of equal importance are the abilities to listen, remember what you have heard, and be persistent in case you are not immediately successful.

Aerobic Dance

Dancers train very hard to maintain the high level of fitness that is required in their profession. Hours are spent developing strong and supple bodies and increasing their levels of cardiovascular fitness. It is acknowledged that professional dancers are fit people.

In the 1980s and 1990s, there has been a big fitness boom, and aerobic dance activities have added a new dimension to the whole business of commercial fitness, a dimension which is appealing to people of all ages and both sexes. However, we must recognize that dancelike activities are being used to improve levels of fitness—the intention is not to teach dance. Because of the general appeal of this dancelike approach to fitness, it may be a useful introduction to the art form of dance, especially when beginning a dance program with older students (grades 5 through 7). At these ages, children may be reluctant to become involved in an expressive movement form. Boys may feel less threatened when asked to repeat a dancelike movement if the focus is on the physiological aspects of the sequence. There will be attendant emotional responses to the movement, but attention will not be drawn to them, nor to any aesthetic components of the sequence, until the children are comfortable with themselves and the teacher. Once this stage has been reached, you can gradually make the transition to the involvement of the aesthetic dimension and the intent of the performer in dance, which "leads to a different kind of end product" (Hodge & Farmer, 1983). It is important that we understand and have clear objectives when setting the tasks in the lesson; we must be aware of when our focus shifts from the very obvious physical aspect of a movement sequence to the emotional, aesthetic aspects. It is at this time that we are concerned with an artistic experience, which is the core of the dance program.

The Influence of Television

It may be helpful to note the influence of television on children's expectations and attitudes towards physical education in general and dance in particular. Children regularly have the opportunity to observe professional and other elite athletes and, as a result, desire to model the behavior of their idols. You will be faced with young children who wish to learn complex skills and rules of specific sports before they are physically, socially, and emotionally ready for them. To compound the problem, dance programming receives much less attention. Many advertisements include dancelike movements, some very poorly performed, but it is rare to find an entire program on dance. Unless they are taken to the theater, children have very little opportunity to see quality dance and dancers, or to discover the variety of dance forms.

Summary

Teaching dance, while demanding many of the same skills we use for all teaching, does have some special requirements. Our approach to the lessons, the model we set, and our interaction with the children must all have a dancelike quality. By this we mean that artistic elements must be stressed, because one of the objectives is to give the children an aesthetic experience. We hope that they acquire movement skills which allow them to be expressive.

The following guidelines may be of some help:

1. Appeal to the interests of the children; use music, poetry, stories, and ideas they enjoy.
2. While considering children's interests, select music you like.
3. Begin with concrete, straightforward action words (examples are given in table 6.1).
4. Avoid asking children to "be" a flower, or to "act out" an idea. Silliness and giggling often ensue as the children feel self conscious. In dance lessons, the children are themselves. Draw their attention to the movement characteristics of the stimulus you or they have selected.
5. Perhaps most important of all is to make sure you feel comfortable and ready to do whatever it is you have planned. Your feeling at ease gives the children a sense of security, in that no one is trying to make them look foolish.

Your choice of words and speech, how you stand and move, and the tools you use for observation and evaluation must all be qualitatively inclined.

The content of dance lessons can be rich and varied, and can provide the children with opportunities to be themselves while performing, creating, and observing. We aim to give them a dance experience—not to make them into dancers (Laban, 1948).

Review Questions

1. Discuss the differences between exploratory, improvisational, and imitative learning experiences for children.
2. It has been suggested that our voices are particularly important when we teach dance. Explain why this may be so.
3. In chapter 3, it was suggested that as you teach, you should move appropriately for the movement form of the lesson. How will this affect your movement in dance lessons? Will it be different for singing games, folk dances, and creative dance?
4. Organizational skills may appear to be used minimally when teaching dance lessons. What safety precautions should we consider?
5. What are some factors influencing the observation of dance?
6. Design a criterion-referenced evaluation form for a dance that you have either taught or performed yourself.
7. Why is percussion so useful in creative dance lessons?
8. What is the purpose of aerobic dance activities?

References

Anthoney, M. (1979). An introduction and position statement. In J. Emmel, D. Molyneux, & N. Wardrop (eds.), *Values into action,* (pp. 171–175). Australian Council for HPER.

Boorman, J. (1973). *Dance and language experiences with children.* Toronto: Longman of Canada, Ltd.

Dance Committee of CAHPER. (1983). *Dance in elementary (K–6) education.* Ottawa: CAHPER Position Paper.

Docherty, D., & Churchley, F. (1982). Making the most of music in teaching movement. *CAHPER Journal, 48* (4), 15–19.

Hawkins, A. (1964). *Creating through dance.* Englewood Cliffs, NJ: Prentice-Hall.

Hodge, L., & Farmer, J. (1983). Dance fitness. *CAHPER Journal, 50* (1), 28.

Laban, R. (1948). *Modern educational dance.* London: Macdonald and Evans, Ltd.

Menuhin, Y., and Davis, C. (1979). *The music of man.* Toronto: Methuen Publications.

Mosston, M. (1981). *Teaching physical education* (2nd ed.). Columbus, Ohio: Charles E. Merrill.

Murray, N. (1984). Selecting music for educational dance. *CAHPER Journal, 50* (3), 34.

Preston, V. (1963). *A handbook for modern educational dance.* London: Macdonald and Evans, Ltd.

Russell, J. (1975). *Creative dance in the primary school* (2nd ed.). London: Macdonald and Evans, Ltd.

Chapter 7 Learning Experiences in Dance

In chapter 5, we suggested that some forms of dance appeal to children at certain ages more than others (see table 5.3). Concurrent with this notion is our concept of **lesson planning** and being concerned with the children's stages of development and experience. At a school where no dance has been taught previously, we would probably plan the first lesson for grades 1, 3, and 5 around similar movement concepts. However, the objectives and design of the learning experiences for the different grades would not be identical because of the varying needs, interests, abilities, and previous experiences of the children. Traveling and stopping with changes in speed might be the content of an initial lesson for grade 1; changes of level or direction might be added for grade 3, and the idea of working with a partner included for grade 5. More is expected from the older children, who should progress more rapidly since their learning rate is faster. They should be able to grasp more complex ideas, motor development is more advanced, and they are more skillful. Our expectations regarding the outcome or product(s) will be very different for each group. Although each group begins at more or less the same place on a hypothetical dance experience continuum, by the end of a unit of ten lessons, for example, considerable divergence will have occurred (figure 7.1).

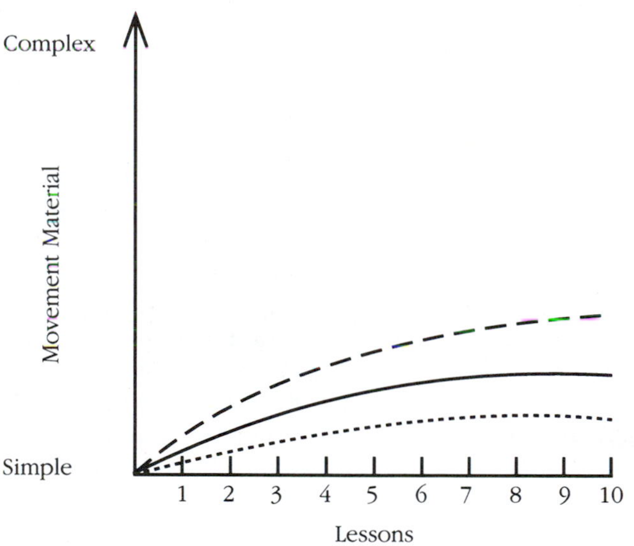

Figure 7.1 Hypothesized differences in progress.

Lesson Design

Laban arranged his movement concepts in a thematic sequence, which progresses from simple to more complex (Preston-Dunlop, 1980). In total there are sixteen themes (Laban 1948 and Preston-Dunlop, 1980) during which the "body, dynamics (effort), space and relationship(s) are gradually studied and trained together. It is impossible to work thoroughly on one aspect irrespective of the other three" (Preston-Dunlop, 1980). Table 7.1 shows the first eight of the sixteen themes that form the basis of the dance program for elementary school children (Russell, 1975 and Logsdon, et al. 1984).

Table 7.1

Laban's Eight Elementary Themes

Theme 1: Body Concepts	Awareness of whole body actions. Emphasis on body parts, especially knees, elbows, hands, feet. Going and stopping.
Theme 2: Effort Concepts	Elements of time and weight. Extremes of each (i.e., fast-slow; strong-light). Getting faster-slower, stronger-lighter. Rhythmic patterns.
Theme 3: Spatial Concepts	Use of general space. Spatial words (e.g., toward, away, big, small, high, low).
Theme 4: Integrating Ideas From Above Three Themes.	Emphasis on flow, linking movements to make sequences; transitions.
Theme 5: Relationship Concepts	Beginning to work with a partner, the development of roles (e.g., leader, follower).
Theme 6: Body Concepts	Isolation and integration of body parts during specific actions; skillful movement is stressed as the body is used as an expressive instrument.
Theme 7: Effort Concepts	Expansion of themes 2 and 4 into eight basic effort actions, combining three motion factors: weight, time, space.
Theme 8: Integrating Ideas From Themes 5, 6, and 7.	Dances created that focus on work rhythms and actions.

Table 7.2

Progression Through the Themes

Theme	Grade K	1	2	3	4	5	6	
1	•	•	•					
2	•	•						
3	•	•	•	•				
4			•	•	•			Integrating themes 1, 2, 3
5		•	•	•	•	•	•	
6				•	•	•	•	
7					•	•	•	
8						•	•	Integrating themes 5, 6, 7

Table 7.2 shows the shift in learning focus over a seven year period. It should help you choose movement material, which provides the ideas and stimuli for your dance program. Notice the overlapping and extending of the movement concepts as the children gain experience and become more skillful, knowledgeable, and independent movers.

In the sample lesson plans that follow, the movement concepts are in diagrammatic form at the beginning of each plan. These concepts are common to each kind of dance experience. The difference is seen in the development and application of the movement skills, which, when combined in the culmination of the lesson, will result in a singing game, a folk dance or a creative dance. Always remember your concern for the "whole child," along with the development of motor competency, in each learning experience. In dance, the unique contribution to education is the aesthetic experience. The lessons should reflect this.

Remember That

Dance involves expression. When you create a dance, it is a sharing experience for all (Koma, 1987).

You will find sample lesson plans in singing games, folk dance, and creative dance. The lessons are not designed for a specific group of children, but are based on our own teaching experience and accumulated knowledge. If you wish to use the sample plans, you will probably have to make some adjustments so they become appropriate for your children. There is no guarantee they will work for you exactly as they are presented here!

For the sake of simplicity, we have decided the first year of the dance program is for kindergarten children aged 5 and 6 years, and the dance program extends over the seven years of elementary school.

Singing Games

Singing games, a minor part of the dance program, are excellent activities to do in a classroom where space is limited. These games include activities familiar to many children. Some have been learned before starting school and, therefore, can be great confidence boosters. They can be learned easily, and the focus is on participation rather than execution. Singing games belong equally in music, language, and dance lessons, with the learning focus shifting from one dimension to another. In dance lessons, singing games are analyzed for the movement content, and the learning objective is on the improvement of motor skills and the development of expression through movement.

In table 5.3, we suggested that singing games are appropriate activities for kindergarten and grade 1 children. More structured singing games may appeal to older children, and they can be an excellent lead-in to simple folk dances. It is sometimes difficult to tell when a singing game becomes a folk dance, as is seen with "Annie Goes to the Cabbage Patch" in Lesson Plan 2.

The general format of a lesson in which the movement material is derived from singing games follows:

Part 1 Vigorous, whole body activities focusing more on being involved, than on quality or standard of performance.

Part 2
a. Specific tasks improving and extending known skills, such as skipping in different directions, "high" skips, introducing new skills, all of which relate to the chosen singing game.
b. Learning the words and tune of the new song. If this has been done during last week's lesson or in the classroom, sit and practice.

Part 3
a. The new singing game.
b. When this is the second or later lesson in the unit, recall and repeat the singing game(s) learned previously.

This format may be varied to be more appropriate and enjoyable for your children. For example, you may wish to begin the lesson with a well-known and fairly vigorous singing game. You may wish to combine stages *a* and *b* in Part 2, perhaps learning the chorus of a singing game and its actions before adding the verses.

The two lesson plans that follow are considered to have fifteen to twenty minutes of content. Each singing game has been analyzed to pinpoint the relevant movement concepts, and the tasks are based on these concepts.

Lesson Plan 2 demands considerably more from the children than does Lesson Plan 1, and it assumes previous knowledge of singing games.

It is not a progression of the first lesson. At the end of each plan there are suggestions of movement concepts that could be included in a following lesson.

Lesson Plan 1

- Dance Form: Singing games
  Grade: Kindergarten
  Time: 15–20 minutes
  Equipment: Drum and beater; flash cards
  Objectives: The children will be able to
    1. travel in the general space without colliding,
    2. sequence travel, stop, collapse, rise,
    3. sing and dance at the same time.
- Movement Concepts: Figure 7.2.

American Version

Ring around the rosey
A pocket full of posies
Ashes, ashes,
We all fall down.

British Version

Ring-a-ring of roses
A pocket full of roses
Atishoo! Atishoo!
We all fall down.

Ring Around the Rosey		
Body Concepts Activities: Walk, skip, collapse, rise, stop, "sneeze"		
Effort Concept	**Spatial Concepts**	**Relationship Concepts**
Phrasing	Moving freely in the general space. Progress to traveling in a circle.	Unison with the teacher. Alone in a group. Progress to holding hands in a circle.

Figure 7.2 Movement concepts—"Ring Around the Rosey."

Figure 7.2 *Continued*

Music:

C
Ring a - round the ro - sey, a
pock - et full of po - sies;
Ash - es, Ash - es we
all fall down.

Tasks	**Teaching Tips**
Part 1	
Basic Follow me around the room, and copy what I do.	Walk, run, skip, weaving throughout the space. Watch the children carefully; adjust your speed to theirs.
Refining Let's have quiet, bouncy feet.	Always stress quality of movement.
Organizing Spread out so that everyone can see me. Look toward me.	The children may need constant reminders to use their own space.
Extending Copy me and when I stop, stop very still.	Begin with equal length phrases of going and stopping, so the stop is predictable, and the children can anticipate the change.

Refining Keep your steps small so you can stop easily.	
Extending Do the same without me. Find your space to travel in. I will play on the drum, so listen very carefully.	Make sure the children are well spaced before they begin. Repeat the same phrasing on the drum.
Refining When you stop, look for a new space to go to. Watch other people. Go on your own "journey." "Grip" the floor when you stop. Strong legs.	If necessary, reposition the children after a stop. Make sure the stop is long enough for the children to feel the position.

Part 2

Basic Kneel in your own space. S-l-o-w-l-y collapse onto the floor.	Do it with the children, stressing slow collapse. Your voice will help.
Refining Let your seat/hips touch the floor, then let your trunk touch the floor. Collapse slowly so there are no bumps.	Move to another place in the room and do it again with the children. You set a model without giving a demonstration.
Extending Collapse to the other side. Collapse and stand up. Now let's try collapsing s-l-o-w-l-y! Stand up.	Children will have a preference and probably will have practiced on one side only.
Refining Bend those knees. Keep your head up.	Control the speed with your voice. Repeat collapse and stand several times.
Extending Put together phrase of skip and stop, collapse and stand.	Remind children of the phrasing previously established. Repeat several times giving refining tasks as necessary.

Part 3

Basic Come and sit down near me, listen to me singing, if you know the words, join in.	Have the words written on the blackboard or flash cards.
Extending Sing again without me.	
Refining Take a big breath before you begin. Sit up tall as you sing.	Gently beat on the drum to keep the children in unison.
Applying Sing, skip and stop. "Ring-a-round-a-rosy, a pocket full of posies." Choose where you go.	Begin children in spaces; eight skips and a stop. Travel freely in the space. Repeat two or three times before adding next part.
Extending Two sneezes, "Ashes! Ashes! We all fall down."	
Refining Travel and find the spaces. Slow, gentle collapse; remember no bumps.	
Extending Now all the way through.	The children should be able to recall the entire sequence without your participation.

Possible Progressions

Skipping was chosen as the form of locomotion in the applying task. An alternative is to give the children the choice of running, walking, or skipping. If this is done, you must ensure equal emphasis is placed on these activities earlier in the lesson, and that the children develop their own sequences of *travel, stop, collapse,* and *rise*.

Another variation is to repeat the singing game three times, the task being "The first time we all walk, the second time we all run and the third time we all skip," or the children could choose their own order.

How much freedom you give the children to make their own decisions will depend on how well you feel they can manage to (a) make their own decisions and (b) remember which activity they have already used and which one(s) to do next.

Relationship concepts can also be developed in a follow-up lesson. Some possibilities follow. Your choice will depend on how well the children relate to each other.

1. Alone in a mass (as in the sample lesson plan).
2. In pairs, follow my leader relationship, no contact. Take turns to lead.
3. In pairs, holding hands for traveling.
4. In fours, linear formation for traveling, no contact.
5. In fours, holding hands.
6. Small circles, four to six children, hold hands and skip, walk, run, around the circle.

Safety Tip

When children are skipping or running, watch for their concentration to decrease, and for them to "cluster" and collide. Develop phrases of "going and stopping" by using a drum or dancing to music that has clear phrasing, so they skip/run for two phrases and pause and clap for two. Being "on the spot" helps young children refocus.

Similar Singing Games

Many singing games stress body awareness, particularly skipping and running, the identification of body parts, turning, rising, and sinking. Some examples of singing games and their country of origin follow: (White & White, 1982).

Singing Game	Movement Concepts
Go Round and Round the Village (England)	Skipping
Garden Game (France)	Walking, different body parts
Bean Porridge Hot (England)	Hands, clapping sequence
Sing a Song of Sixpence (England)	Skipping, arm gestures

Some singing games include role playing and tell a story as in "The Farmer in the Dell" (England, United States), and "Sailboat" (United States). In these games, the actions usually have an effort focus, as in "The Gallant Ship" (England); therefore, the lessons must include learning experiences to help the children produce the appropriate effort.

The singing game in Lesson Plan 2 is beginning to show some folk dance form and "folk quality" (Fleming, 1976). The form (spatial and relationship concepts) has been simplified considerably for this lesson. You may need two lessons to attain the objectives, and an † on page 231 is placed at the point where the lesson might end. An applying task is included for the end of that lesson.

Figure 7.3 Movement concepts—"Annie Goes to the Cabbage Patch."

Song	Action
Annie goes to the cabbage patch	Skipping
Cabbage patch, cabbage patch	
Annie goes to the cabbage patch	
To pick the fresh green leaves	
Johnny sees her	Stand
Ha, Ha, Ha	Clap three times
Now I'll catch you	Stand
Tra, la, la	Stamp three times
No! No! No!	Shake head
Go away	Shake finger
I'll not play with you today.	Skip

Annie Goes to the Cabbage Patch		
Body Concepts Activity: Skipping Body Parts: Feet (stamping) Head (shaking) Hands (clapping, finger shaking)		
Effort Concepts	Spatial Concepts	Relationship Concepts
Rhythmic phrases	Specific pathways to travel 1] 2]	With a partner in a group: 8–12 children

Safety Tip

If you use an extension cord, make sure it is placed very close to the wall and is taped down if possible, so it is well away from feet.

Lesson Plan 2

- Dance Form: Singing games
- Grade: 1
- Time: 20 minutes
- Equipment: Drum and beater
  Stick castanets
  Record or tape of "Annie Goes to the Cabbage Patch."
  Record player or tape recorder.
- Objectives: The children will be able to
  1. skip sixteen steps in sequence,
  2. sequence skip, stop, clap, stop, stamp, stop,
  3. remember the dance sequence well enough to repeat the singing game twice without prompting.
- Movement Concepts: Figures 7.3 and 7.4.

Annie Goes to the Cabbage Patch

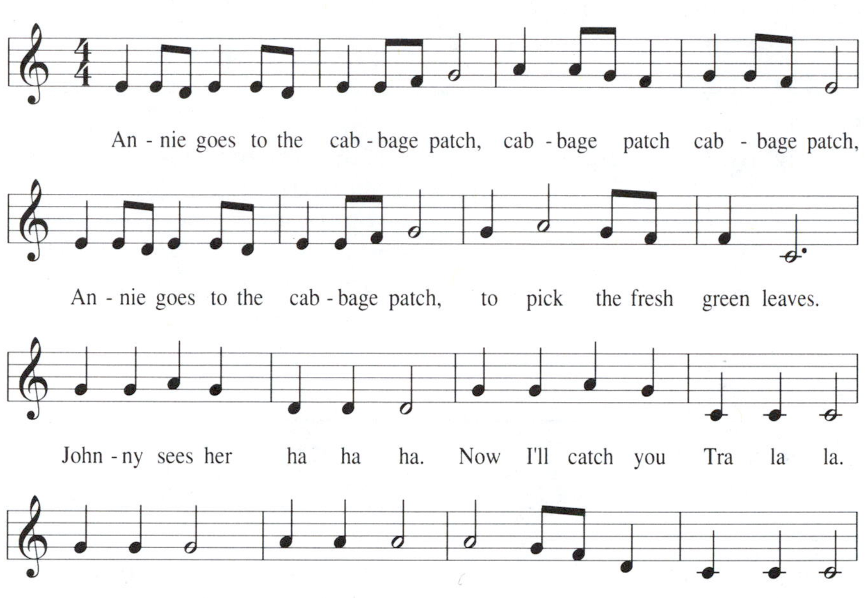
An - nie goes to the cab - bage patch, cab - bage patch cab - bage patch,
An - nie goes to the cab - bage patch, to pick the fresh green leaves.
John - ny sees her ha ha ha. Now I'll catch you Tra la la.
No No No go a - way, I'll not play with you to - day.

Figure 7.4 Music notation for "Annie Goes to the Cabbage Patch."

Tasks	Teaching Aids
Basic Skip freely, on drum beat, freeze!	Make sure the children are spaced apart well before beginning. Double beat on drum for stop, accent second beat.
Refining Keep steps fairly small. Select speed so that you can stop. Push against the floor on hop. Feel "lift" in upper body on hop. Listen carefully for stop signal. Watch for the spaces.	Keep phrases fairly short so excitement of unexpected "stop" is maintained. This also helps with spacing; remember to praise good spacing.
Basic Drum feet on floor, stop.	Use stick castanets to accompany "drumming." Repeat phrase several times. Stress alert stillness and anticipation to begin next phrase.

Refining

Keep body strong when still.
Bend knees to help drumming action.

Extending

Skip lightly, freeze; drum feet, freeze.

Accompany running with quick, light beats on drum, two stronger, abrupt beats for freeze, castanets for feet. When beating drum, hold castanets in same hand as the drum, change to the other hand when playing.

Part 2

Organizing

Sit down near me.

Basic

Shake your hands; stop.
Shake one hand; stop.
Shake the other hand; stop.
Clench your hands, spread your fingers slowly, curl them again.
Shake them again.
Clap your hands in time with me.
Tap your feet on the floor in time with me.
Alternate: claps, pause, floor taps with feet, pause.

Always phrase the actions, shake and freeze! This aids development of hearing and moving to phrases. Begin to introduce the clapping pattern 2/4 clap-clap-clap-pause. Repeat several times to establish rhythm.

Refining

Loose hands!
Watch your hands as you curl and uncurl the fingers.
Watch me as you clap so that you know when to stop.

Continue to participate. Stress slow curling and uncurling so that there is time to feel the difference.

Extending

Three claps—and stop!
Three taps—and stop!

Do this standing so that the children can add skipping. Equal-length phrases as in the dance.

Applying Join together, skip, pause, clap, pause, stamp, pause. Copy me.	Suggested pattern: eight skips, three claps, pause, three stamps, pause. Repeat several times.
Refining Use small steps. Lift free knee in skip. Arms slightly spread will help balance and body lift in hop. Make "up" important in skip. Look for the spaces. Be ready to change direction to avoid others.	Remember, you know the music and are able to structure the sequence accordingly. Gradually withdraw from participating, but continue to give verbal cues; gentle beats on drum may also help. (Note: "Advanced" skippers will swing arms as when walking. Encourage opposition as you see it developing.)†
Basic Sit down and listen to this song. Follow the words on the board.	Sing with the record. Have words on blackboard or flash cards.
Extending Begin to sing. Skip and sing to the first verse.	Repeat first verse ("Annie . . . leaves") alone. Stress the pause at the end of the verse. Repeat two or three times.
Refining Take a breath before beginning. Repeat refining tasks related to skipping.	

Part 3

Organizing Find a partner and stand in a big space.	This presupposes the children are able to find their own partners.

Extending	
Skip and sing, going with your partner, hold inside hands, and travel side-by-side.	If children cannot find their own partners, put them in twos (no attempt to have boy and girl, unless it happens that the two are good friends and wish to be together). If there is an uneven number of children, a threesome will work.
Refining	
Keep level with your partner. Stay fairly close together so there's no pull between you. Remember to keep steps fairly small.	If you find a pair coping well, have them demonstrate and point out what is good.
Basic (performed to the words of the song)	
Stand facing partner. "Johnny sees her." Clap hands three times. "Ha. Ha. Ha." Stand. "Now I'll catch you." Stamp three times. "Tra-la-la." Shake head and forefinger at partner. "No, no, no, go away." Join hands and skip in place. "I'll not play with you today."	Do this sequence with verbal guidance then with the music. Repeat two or three times and give specific help to any pair who is having difficulty.
Applying	
Sit and listen to the complete song. Now begin with skipping then add the clapping and stamping.	This is to refocus attention on the first part of the sequence. It may help if you dance with an imaginary (or real) partner. Dance through once, stop and give feedback. Then dance twice through.

Possible Progressions

You will remember that the formations and relationships in this singing game have been simplified. Figure 7.5 shows the "true" set pattern of "Annie Goes to the Cabbage Patch," which is danced with children in small groups of four to six pairs (eight to twelve children).

Another possible formation is a large double circle, where the couples skip counterclockwise, shown in figure 7.6.

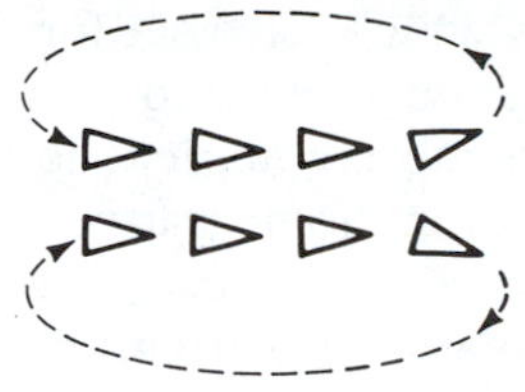

Part 1

Begin facing front. Leaders turn outward. Skip to bottom of set, others follow in line. Meet partners and skip to place. Finish facing partner.

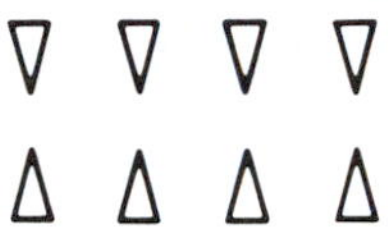

Part 2

Face partner. Begin clapping and stamping in place. Join both hands and skip around in place. Drop hands and finish facing front.

Figure 7.5 Formation of "Annie Goes to the Cabbage Patch."

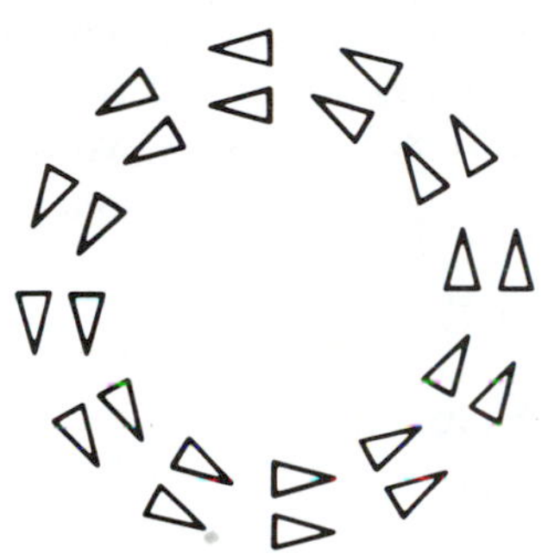

Part 1

Begin facing counterclockwise. Skip alongside partner, holding hands. Finish facing partner.

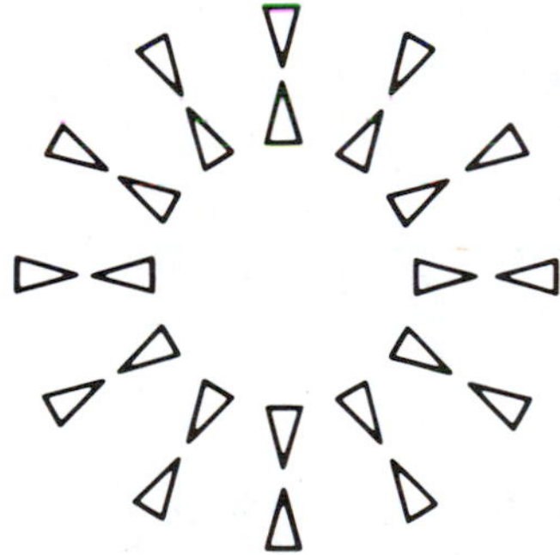

Part 2

Face partner. Begin clapping and stamping in place. Join both hands and skip around in place. Keep holding hands. Finish facing counterclockwise.

Figure 7.6 Alternative formation for "Annie Goes to the Cabbage Patch."

When selecting singing games and folk dances which have set formations, always look for other ways to structure them. Remember, it works both ways—you may either simplify or make more complex, according to the needs and capabilities of your children. Some patterns become firmly established as favorites, and children derive great pleasure from repeating the familiar ones. Other patterns are not particularly interesting but may appeal greatly with some well thought out changes. Be prepared to experiment! Always remember what you wish the children to learn in the lesson (the objectives), and plan with a clear focus of what the children should be able to achieve at the end of the particular lesson. You should be able to tell them at the end what they accomplished; better still, ask them what they accomplished. You may be surprised at their perception of what the lesson was about.

Similar Singing Games

There are a few singing games with a likeness to folk dance, and as has been mentioned in chapter 5, it is sometimes difficult to decide which they are! The distinguishing factors include the relationships (partners) and formations (linear, single, or double circles). The following dances exhibit characteristics of singing games (i.e., all have a song) and of folk dances, dancing with a partner or changing partners.

Song and Origin	Formation
"The German Clap Dance" (Germany)	Double circle
"Skip to my Lou" (United States)	Double circle
"Bingo" (United States)	Single circle

Folk Dance

This form of dance is enjoyed by many children. It provides plenty of opportunity for skipping, running, and jumping combined to form step patterns. It is the patterning and repetition which seem to appeal to all ages, but because of the social nature of folk dance and the more complicated spatial patterns, it is more appropriate for children in grade 3 and above (Evans, 1981).

Fitness Facts

Folk dances that

1. last a minimum of three minutes,
2. include repetitions of galloping, skipping, and running steps,
3. have little "standing-still" time

increase the heart rate (cardiovascular fitness) of the dancers.

The teaching of folk dance closely parallels that of singing games. Each dance is analyzed in terms of the movement concepts, and a lesson plan is developed which provides the relevant learning experiences so the children can dance with enjoyment.

For the folk dance experience to be authentic, the dances should not be modified to meet the needs and abilities of the children. There are plenty of very simple dances from a wide range of countries. Your ability to select appropriately depends on your understanding of the movement content and learning challenge inherent in each dance.

The social dimension (relationships) in folk dancing must be emphasized, and if the children are not ready to work in groups, both with and without partners, then omit folk dance for the time being.

Learning how to select a partner is so much part of a folk dance lesson that it merits special mention. Young children like to work with their friends, and they usually work better when with people they like. We suggest they be allowed to choose their partners. This may be time-consuming, but as social interaction is part of the folk dance experience, then time must be allowed for it. Do not be concerned if initially you have mixed groupings in your class with boys partnering boys, girls with girls, and maybe a few mixed pairs. In many simple partner and line dances, such as The Shoemaker and The Noble Duke of York (CAHPER, 1980), there is no differentiation of roles. In dances where sets are formed and partners are exchanged, complications can arise. Even this situation can be coped with if one partner wears some color identification, so instead of referring to boys and girls, the teacher says, "reds to the right."

Activities challenging the children to find partners, or make groups quickly without being concerned with the "who" element, are useful at the beginning of a lesson. One example is to play a piece of "skipping" music, or music to accompany any step pattern the children know. The children skip freely about the space until the music stops. The teacher says, "Form groups of three and sit." Other groupings ("Find a partner and face each other") are used and the children are praised for completing the challenge quickly. The last challenge can be the formation needed for the dance, for example, circles of six. Of course, there is the perpetual problem of dealing with incomplete numbers, but if we know how many children are present, we can be prepared to deal with it.

While the dances are worth learning for the satisfaction of mastering the various step-patterns, remembering the formations, and dancing with friends, even more pleasure is possible when they are learned in the broader context of social studies. We are suggesting the folk dance unit be closely linked with the classroom study of a particular culture and that, whenever possible, the music used to accompany the dances should be played by folk musicians. The quality of sound produced by an Austrian dance band is very different from that of an Israeli music group.

Fitness Fact

Step-patterns will increase leg strength, especially when they include jumping variations and resiliency is stressed.

Jumping, with clear leg gestures during the flight portion of the jump, requires strong pelvic muscles. Strength is also required when landing.

The combination of instruments is often specific to a country; harmonies and subtle rhythmic patterns differ from country to country, and we should encourage the children to listen with discrimination.

In North America, we are fortunate to have so many cultures forming our national fabric. In most large cities (indeed in many small communities), there are centers where musicians of the various ethnic groups play for dance. It may be possible for them to visit the school and play for the children.

Each country has its own style or quality of movement, and for the dances to be more than exercise, attention must be paid to this. It is important for the children to recognize, understand, and appreciate ethnic characteristics. This is one way respect for differing cultures may develop.

Dances that use already known skills, such as walking, running, skipping, and hopping should be selected for the introductory unit of folk dance. Attention can then be paid to the style and ethnic character of the dance. Formations should be simple, so the children can pay more attention to what they are doing than where they are going. To illustrate this, *Syvspring* (Seven Jumps) from Denmark is chosen as the first dance (CAHPER, 1980 and Evans, 1981).

Syvspring is a cumulative dance in that each figure is a repeat of the previous one with the addition of a new action. Originally danced by young men, it is a dance to show agility, strength, and stamina. The focus is on the awareness of specific body parts, being able to change the base of support and produce vigorous, controlled movement.

Lesson Plan 3

- Dance Form: Folk dance: *Syvspring* (Denmark)
- Grade: 3
- Time: 30 minutes
- Equipment: Tape recorder or record player, and record EMI RLS 720
  European National Dances
- Objectives: The children will be able to
  1. dance with an upright posture,
  2. change direction of the circle on first count of the phrase,
  3. use strong gestures.
- Movement Concepts: Figure 7.7.

Syvspring		
Body Concepts Activities: Walk, step-hop (similar to skip but even rhythm) Body Parts: Elbows, feet, head, knees		
Effort Concepts	**Spatial Concepts**	**Relationship Concepts**
Strong, vibrant quality	Traveling in a circle, first counterclockwise then clockwise	Stage 1: Alone Stage 2: Circle, hands joined at shoulder level

Figure 7.7 Movement concepts—*Syvspring* (Seven Jumps).

Tasks	Teaching Aids
Part 1	
Basic Free skipping.	Use a known skipping tune (e.g., "Pop Goes the Weasel," "Virginia Reel").
Refining Strong upper body, upright posture. Head held high. Look ahead.	
Part 2	
Extending Hold arms shoulder height. Skip eight steps to left, then eight to right.	Have all children face same direction. Count 1–8 then all begin together. This will assist your observation, as well as begin to develop a feeling for group rhythm.
Refining Make last skip small, on the spot. Turn head to face new direction on count of eight. Last hop 1/2 turn to face new direction.	Practice this pattern about three times, with a pause in between so you can give a refining task.

Extending Use even step-hop, eight to left, eight to right as before.	Play the music *Syvspring;* make sure children hear the even beat. Demonstrate the step so they see and listen before they try.
Refining Strong leg lift, on hop. Knee bent, low lift. Ankles should be at right angles.	Reinforce 1/2 turn on last hop. Attention to head position will aid upright posture.
Extending Listen to music. There are thirty-two counts for the chorus. Begin the step-hops with a stamp-hop. Chorus is eight step-hops to left eight step-hops to right eight walks to left eight walks to right	Accentuate first step-hop with a stronger step. Feet are fairly flat throughout the step-hop (i.e., no pointed toes). Show this as you demonstrate. Let them dance the chorus once before forming groups.

Part 3

Organizing Form circles of ten to fifteen. Join hands, keep hands at shoulder level, elbows slightly bent.	
Applying Dance the chorus, finish with left foot forward and a strong gesture.	Repeat two or three times. Use above refining tasks.
Extending Repeat chorus, finish left foot forward, change to right foot.	You can now begin to call the sequence—the cumulative aspect of the dance has begun.

Refining

Make strong leg gestures, place heel on ground somewhat proudly, look across circle, keep hands high. (Note: When the kneeling sequence begins, drop hands; rejoin for chorus.)

The sequence is
figure 1: left foot forward.
figure 2: figure 1 plus right foot.
figure 3: figure 2 plus kneel on left knee.
figure 4: figure 3 plus kneel on right knee.
figure 5: figure 4 plus place left elbow on ground.
figure 6: figure 5 plus place right elbow on ground.
figure 7: figure 6 plus place forehead on ground.

Applying

Repeat entire dance in two circles.

Possible Progressions

The follow-up lesson could begin in different ways. The first task might be to practice the step-hop pattern to a piece of Scandinavian folk music, such as "The Ace of Diamonds" (EMI Records Ltd. RLS 720). If the children learned *Syvspring* very easily and they have good movement memories, they could dance the entire dance. This could be followed by spending some time refining the transitions and repeating the dance before introducing a new dance for them to learn. The selection of a dance can be based on different criteria. You might decide to introduce

1. a new step-pattern,
2. a different formation,
3. partners, keeping the same formation (i.e., circle).

Whichever you decide, there should be enough difference between the dances so the children do not confuse them.

"The Shoemaker" is a very popular Danish partner dance, similar to a singing game in that the actions mimic the work done by a shoemaker. It is very suitable for introducing relationships in folk dance because there is no distinction between male and female roles, and much of the dance takes place on the spot, so children do not get confused. The dance can be in circle or scatter formation. The movement concepts in the dance are shown in figure 7.8, but there is no lesson plan. We hope you will use Lesson Plan 3 as a model. Once you have highlighted the important movement concepts, design the tasks, remembering those directed toward quality performance of the dance.

Figure 7.8 Movement concepts—Shoemaker's Dance.

Shoemaker's Dance		
Body Concepts Activities: Clapping, skipping, gesturing Body Parts: Fists, elbows		
Effort Concepts	**Spatial Concepts**	**Relationship Concepts**
Strong, direct quality with bound flow	Scattered in the general space	Partners

Other Folk Dances

There are many dances appropriate for the elementary school program. The ones you select will depend on whether you integrate them into other subject areas or consider them solely as one aspect of the dance program. When integrating dance into another subject area, you will be choosing dances because of their relevance in this other context. As an example, with a fifth grade class you might be discussing which ethnic groups form the core of the community in which your school is situated. Folk dances from these countries would be selected.

When folk dance is one aspect of the dance program, you may choose the dances because of

1. step-patterns,
2. rhythm,
3. formations.

Because we do not know the rationale behind your selection, the dances are grouped according to each dance's formation. Figure 7.9 shows three general folk dance formations.

Dances that are appropriate for grades 3–6 include the following:

1. Longways

   Virginia Reel (United States)
   The Grand Old Duke of York (England)
   Gigue aux Six (Canada)

2. Square

   Carding the Wool (Canada)
   Cumberland Square Eight (England)
   There are numerous figures that can be combined to make up square dances for your children.

Figure 7.9 Folk dance formations.

1. Longways

Top of Set

Bottom of Set

2. Square

4th Pair

1st and 3d = Head Pairs
2d and 4th = Side Pairs

1st Pair

3d Pair

2d Pair

3. Circles

(a) Single

(b) Double

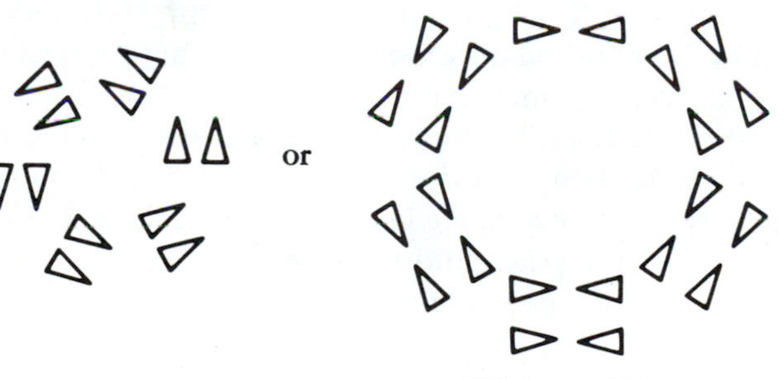

= Child

Safety Tip

Children should be asked to go barefoot only if the floor surface is clean, smooth, and not too cold. If the surface is carpeted, make sure it is vacuumed frequently.

3. Circles

Single
Hokey Pokey (United States)
Peasants' Dance (France)
Dance of Greeting (Denmark)
La Raspa (Mexico)
Double
Lot is Dead (Danish)
Clap Dance (Germany)
Chimes of Dunkirk (Belgium)
Bridge of Avignon (France)

Creative Dance

This dance form is included for children of all ages. There is the potential for a varied range of movement experiences, together with plenty of opportunity for the children to use their own ideas as they create dances. Lessons may center on selected movement concepts which are new to the children, so they will need guidance as the lesson progresses. Such a lesson may end with an improvisation to a piece of music, during which the children use (applying task) their new movement ideas (Lesson Plan 4). In other lessons, the children will develop **motifs,** which are repeatable phrases of movement which can be combined into a dance form. Some of the dances will be very short, lasting less than one minute, while others may last five to ten minutes and consist of several scenes, as can do dance dramas like The Pied Piper (see page 261).

Stimuli

What do we "dance about" in creative dance lessons? When teaching folk dance and singing games, the material and structure are there. We know what should happen at the end of the lesson and, therefore, can plan how to begin and develop the lesson. This is not so in creative dance.

Laban wrote (somewhat esoterically): "The subject matter of dance lies within the verbally almost inaccessible field of vital experiences and qualitative thought." (Russell, 1975). By this he meant that when the "subject matter" of a dance lesson is other than a movement concept, it must be something the children have experienced. They must be able to transpose their images and understanding of the stimulus into movement concepts, which can then be changed into action.

Lessons for young children are often "about" movement, because they need little urging to move. Older children may need the security of a comparatively concrete stimulus. As maturity and experience increase, children are able to return to more abstract ideas. The same applies to us as teachers. When first teaching creative dance, lessons may be more of a creative experience for us than for the children. This is natural.

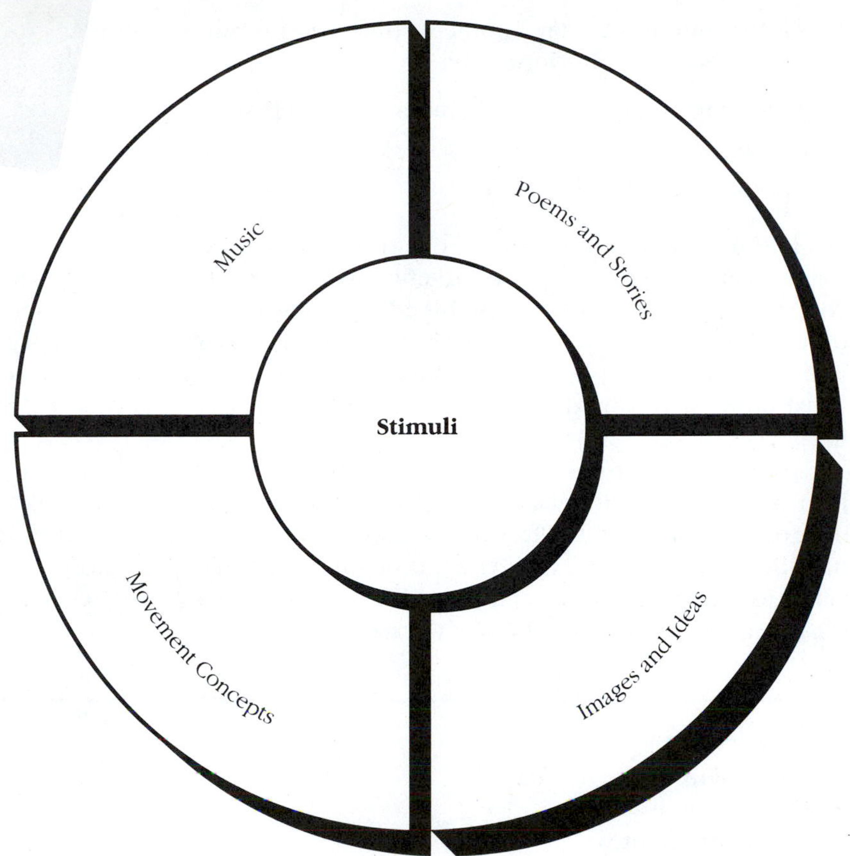

Figure 7.10 Main sources of ideas for creative dance lessons.

Much of the success of a creative dance lesson depends on the stimulus chosen. Stimuli come from various sources (some are listed in figure 7.10) and are often interrelated.

When "searching for ideas that can be worked out in a dance" (Boorman, 1969), be sensitive to whether they will appeal to the children with whom you are working, and that various movement images spring to mind when you and the children think about them. Boorman talks about the "movement potential" of stimuli and poses four questions which are useful guides as we make our selection:

1. What various activities (body concepts) are suggested by the stimulus?
2. How can the stimulus be made "alive" by changing dynamics (effort concepts)?
3. Does the stimulus suggest a varied use of space (spatial concepts)?
4. Does the stimulus suggest we dance alone, with others, or with something (relationship concepts)?

Fitness Fact

Large, slow gestures of the limbs encourage flexibility, especially when the movement is in different spatial areas (planes) around the body.

To illustrate lesson development, there are sample lesson plans for grades 1, 2, 3, 5, and 6. Notice the

1. increasing complexity and number of concepts,
2. abstraction of ideas,
3. length of the final dance.

Movement Concepts

This is the most abstract form of creative dance—the stimulus comes from movement itself. It can be likened to a piece of art in which the artist selects particular colors and blends, contrasts, and highlights them, so the painting is "about" color. The product may evoke emotional responses in some people, while others may look at it from a more analytical point of view and wonder, "What colors did the artist mix to get that shade?"

Lessons may introduce new concepts and skills to the children, ask them to show their understanding of particular concepts, or be a combination of both, as in the following lesson plan. Lesson 4, therefore, is for children with some experience. It begins with fairly vigorous movements, focusing attention on hands and feet. This focus gradually changes to movement of the whole body and changes in level.

Fitness Fact

Curving, stretching, and twisting the trunk, as when exploring different body shapes, encourage flexibility of the spine. Remember, the head is part of the spine; all too often it is left out of the shape.

Lesson Plan 4

- Dance Form: Creative dance
- Grade: 2
- Time: 30 minutes
- Equipment: A variety of rhythmic and vibratory percussion instruments
- Objectives: The children will be able to
  1. improvise with a partner, having a "movement conversation,"
  2. identify the different levels seen as their peers dance,
  3. show clear focus.
- Movement Concepts: Figure 7.11

Figure 7.11 Lesson Plan 4: Movement concepts.

A Movement Conversation		
Body Concepts Activities: Skipping, rising, sinking, stopping		
Effort Concepts	**Spatial Concepts**	**Relationship Concepts**
Children's choice	Contrasting high and low levels	Conversation in twos

Tasks	Teaching Tips
Part 1	
Basic	
Copy me! Shake your hands: up above your head, down by your feet, now in two places. Now shake one hand and stop! Now the other and stop!	Shake hands in different areas around the body. Initially, keep the hands fairly close together, then separate. Begin phrasing the sequence.
Quick runs on the spot—stop! Now hands—now feet.	Establish a pattern.
Refining	
Loose hands. Hold your arms lightly. Little steps, on your toes. "Bright" feet.	
Extending	
Now without me, your own pattern of hands and feet.	Watch for the phrasing chosen. If any children show marked changes in level, select them to demonstrate. Draw attention to these changes
Repeat your pattern and notice if you include changes in level.	Comment on changes seen.
Part 2	
Basic	
Skip, keeping the body as low to the ground as you can.	Accompany the children on a drum.
Refining	
Feet apart may help you keep low. Let your arms swing loosely. Bend your knees and lift them to the side of your body.	The skips may look ungainly due to the unusual posture. Stress resilient footwork.
Extending	
Now skip and keep high.	Tap the metal rim of the drum and produce a "bright" sound.
Refining	
Feel the lift in your body. Push away from the floor.	

Extending Listen to the drum; change the level of your skipping as the sound changes.	Play equal length phrases, the tempo may need to be slightly slower for the low-level skips.
Basic Start close to the floor, look up high. Begin to rise, keeping your eyes on that high point. Stop for a moment, then begin to sink, still looking at the high point.	The focus helps concentration and helps clarify the actions, rather than just "being"low or high.
Refining Push against the floor with your feet. Feel the strength in your legs. Keep moving in a straight line towards your spot.	Watch the tension in the bodies, and encourage an alertness in the action. Some children may need help with their starting position; it should be stable.
Extending Start close to the ground again. This time look at a low spot. It may be quite close to you or a little distance away. Now begin to rise while still looking.	If the spot is too far away the up-down dimension is lost, and a more appropriate action might be to approach it.

Part 3

Organizing Find a partner.	Make sure everyone has a partner before giving the next task. A group of three may be needed.
Choose a percussion instrument different from your partner's.	The instruments should be placed in small groups around the area. Allow the children time to make their choices.

Applying

You are going to have movement conversation with your partner. The conversation is about different levels, getting there and being there.

Discuss with them the ideas already experienced, especially skipping, focusing, rising, and sinking.

Play your instrument as you dance, it is part of your conversation.

The assumption is that the children have experience in playing.

People having a conversation take turns talking, so while one of you dances, the other should be still.

Help them understand the relationship involved.

Let the children try before giving any more guidance.

Refining

Show very clearly which level you are at when still; also where you focus.

They may wish to focus on their partner, or they may decide on an external focus.
Help the children clarify which they prefer.

Your movements may say, "I am skipping at high level, then looking high, sinking low."
Your partner's reply might be, "I'm starting low, focusing low, skipping low, changing my focus to high and stopping low."

The ability to respond to one another with spontaneity is being developed.
There are many variations possible. Some conversations will be longer than others.

Refining

Finish your conversation.

Organizing

Half the class sits at the side, the others spread out in the space.

Set the observers something specific to notice, e.g., do the partners change over quickly? Is one person "saying" a lot more than the other? Did you find a pair who showed the levels very clearly?

Applying	
Show your conversations.	Do people "speak" in short or long sentences? Does one person "say" more than the other? Find a pair who shows the levels very clearly.

The groups then change over so everyone has improvised and observed. Some discussion may end the lesson, reinforcing the movement concepts experienced. The children are then asked to put away their instruments.

Music

A piece of music may elicit comments from the children, indicating they have transposed what they heard into something they have experienced. After listening to unfamiliar music, comments, such as "that sounds like rushing water" or "that was spooky," tell you immediately that the children can relate to the piece you have chosen.

Music associated with a popular film or character will greatly influence the children's interpretations; therefore, be prepared for common reactions. Very thorough preparation is needed to help the children make the experience "theirs" rather than trying to recall what they saw.

If the title of the music is descriptive or narrative (e.g., "Danse Macabre," or "In the Hall of the Mountain King") you may decide not to tell the children until the dance has been finished. Knowing what the composer felt or visualized can affect our perception of the music. Not knowing the title allows the listener's imagination complete freedom. At another time, you may decide selected information will help the children focus on relevant aspects of the music, and therefore, you will tell them something of the composer's ideas or the title of the music.

In some lessons, you may wish to remind the children of a previous dance experience and relate what they did to what they are to hear. For example, figure 7.12 shows the content of a lesson based on contrasting activities that were developed into a short dance.

For the next lesson "Trepak," from the *Nutcracker Suite* by Tchaikovsky, has been chosen as the stimulus for the dance. This music suggests the same activities shown in figure 7.12, though not necessarily in the same order. Figure 7.13 details the movement concepts to be developed into motifs. This is one of the occasions when we do not tell the

Movement Concepts		
Body Concepts Activities: Stopping, jumping, gesturing (pointing), skipping, turning		
Effort Concepts	**Spatial Concepts**	**Relationship Concepts**
Contrasting fast and slow turns Sudden stops ("freezing") Sudden gestures ("pointing")	Skipping forward/ backward Changes of level Clear focus when pointing	In twos, question and answer form

Figure 7.12 Movement Concepts—contrasting activities.

children the title of the piece until after they have created their own dance. Many children have preconceived ideas about ballet, which interfere with the development of their dance.

The lesson is written to give you a feel for the kind of information and guidance necessary. The movement concepts are well within the capabilities of a third grade class. The relationships make it challenging, and therefore the children should be an experienced group. The plan has been presented as one lesson; however, it is more likely that two to three lessons will be needed to complete the dance and before the children can perform it with confidence. It is quite easy to subdivide the plan.

Lesson Plan 5

- Dance Form: Creative dance
- Grade: 3
- Time: 60–90 minutes
- Equipment: Tambourine
  Record player or tape recorder and record/tape of "Trepak," from *The Nutcracker Suite* by Tchaikovsky
- Objectives: At the end of this lesson, the children will be able to
  1. dance in unison in small groups,
  2. dance in canon and unison in a large group,
  3. relate and modify motifs developed in the previous lesson (see figure 7.12) into a group dance.
- Movement Concepts: Figure 7.13.

Figure 7.13 Movement concepts for Lesson Plan 5: "Trepak" from Tchaikovsky's *Nutcracker Suite.*

Movement Concepts		
Body Concepts Activities: Jumping, pointing, running, skipping, stopping, turning Body Shapes: Asymmetric jumps, stops		
Effort Concepts	**Spatial Concepts**	**Relationship Concepts**
Sudden quality Strong quality Contrasting free and bound flow	Curving pathways when running Skipping forward and backward High, middle, and low focus	Four groups merging and separating Canon in small and large group(s)

Tasks	**Teaching Tips**
Part 1	
Organizing Make a loose group in center of space.	
Basic Run lightly in the open spaces. Stop suddenly on loud beat of the tambourine.	Accompany with shaking a tambourine.
Refining Keep weight on your toes. Take small steps so that you can change direction easily. Place feet apart for the stop; stay and look alert.	Watch to see if the group becomes too compact; stop and spread them apart if you see this happening. Vary the length of the phrases so there is a sense of excitement and anticipation.
Extending When you hear a double beat on the tambourine, stop and point strongly in any direction.	Introduce this idea when they can mingle without colliding.
Refining A sudden, strong gesture of the arm. Look intently where you point. Very strong position of legs; wide base.	Encourage complete stillness.

Part 2

Basic Where you are, practice big jumps, landing, and being strong and still.	If necessary, spread the children apart; they need space for this.
Refining Bend your knees before pushing off. Lift in upper body; heads up. Remember, your arms will help your take-off. Bend knees when landing—land quietly. Land one foot after the other, feet apart.	Descriptive words, such as *explode, powerful,* and *surprising,* may help the children understand the strong, sudden quality of the jumps.
Extending Make the jump asymmetrical.	If necessary, clarify the meaning of asymmetry.
Refining Keep your body firm in the air. Hold the shape.	Pay attention to bent/straight arms/legs; tilt of the body will help asymmetry.
Extending Listen to this music. "Feel" the jumps and firm landings, the traveling and mingling, and the sudden stops. This happens four times. We call this *A* music. Now begin as a loose group; decide if you will jump first or second, mingle, stop, and point. This happens four times.	Play "Trepak," finishing after four repeats of the first musical idea. Have a visual representation of the music available and help the children follow it as they listen. The two basic tasks are combined but in reverse order. Verbal cueing may be needed the first time they try. Encourage the children to listen to the music and stop cueing as soon as possible.
Refining Select from the previous ones.	Reminders will be needed as the children focus on remembering the sequence rather than performing.

Organizing Divide into four numbered groups, each in own area of room.	Consider the effect when placing the groups, see the applying task that follows.
Applying Group 1 dances to first section, points at group 2, which begins to dance and points at group 3, etc. Design own starting position.	Repeat this part two or three times so that the sequence becomes firmly established. It is now that attention can shift to quality performance.
Refining Remain very still when waiting to begin and after pointing. Strong arm action so that the pointing toward the next group is very noticeable.	
Basic a) Listen to next part of the music. "Feel" the skipping: large skips then small, quick skips. At the end of this part, be ready to jump. b) Now try it.	Remind children of the skipping sequence done in previous lesson: big skips traveling forward, small skips traveling backward.
Refining Lift arms and free knee for big forward skips. Slight crouch for backward skips. Tuck arms close to side.	
Extending Finish as a loose group ready to jump. There are several, so you decide when to jump.	The group should "pop" at different times so the effect is somewhat unpredictable.
Refining Keep "pops" strong. Be very still when not jumping.	Children should be encouraged to jump to same music each time. Some groups need considerable help to establish the pattern.

Applying

Put the skipping and the "pops" together.
Listen to the music first, then dance.

Begin again from the previous applying task, which ends first part of the dance.

Refining

Watch the other dancers carefully, so that the loose group forms.

Extending

Dance from the beginning.

Help may be needed to link the two parts together. Use refining tasks already listed to help with quality of performance.
Verbal cues should help, remove as soon as possible.

Basic

The group begins to disintegrate; follow a leader out of the group and into the general space.
Run swiftly and make curving pathways.

A music repeated; ignore the jumps.

Part 3

Organizing

Decide whom you will follow.
Lines of three to five dancers.

Depending on number in class, have several lines emerge, with not more than five children per line.

Refining

Smooth running.
Leaders: watch the other lines carefully and avoid them.

Extending

As the music builds to its climax, begin to return to one group, spin, suddenly stop, and make a strong pointing gesture.

The final group must still be fairly loose, yet be a whole. The group must decide on where the focus will be for the final gesture.

Refining	
Listen carefully to final notes so that everyone stops at the same time. Very strong final position. Consider different levels of stopping to clarify group focus.	There are several options: 1. All focus high to same point (this may be above group or outside the group). 2. Some focus high, some medium, some low. 3. All face same direction. 4. All face outward from group and in different directions.
Applying	
Dance from the beginning.	The dance has been built up in three parts; help the children make the transition from one part to the next. Select refining tasks already used as you see the need.

Images

When an image is selected as the "dance idea," the lesson often begins with the children being asked questions about the image. Their answers and ideas can be collected on a board. The children may need some guidance with carefully designed questions in order to elicit information that can be used during the creation of the dance. The image may be strengthened by pictures, poems, films, or maybe even a field trip, to help the child extract the essence of the image.

The image of *snow* is taken to illustrate this stimulus form. The idea is presented for two different levels of experience, beginning with a very simple dance lesson.

The children might be asked questions about what the snow "does" (e.g., it falls, spins, drifts, etc.) and how it does these activities (e.g., softly, slowly, gustily etc.). Two groups of words will result: verbs and adverbs. The lesson is developed around these body and effort concepts. For the culmination of the lesson, some music may be played, for example, Debussy's "Snowflakes Are Dancing" as interpreted by Tomita (The *Newest Sound of Debussy,* RCA ARL 1–0488) and the children set the applying task of improvising, or dancing freely, to the music and incorporating the ideas experienced during the lesson.

Figure 7.14 shows the movement concepts around which a lesson could be developed. The lesson might be twenty minutes long, and would be most appropriate during the winter months, especially if it were taught during or just after a snowstorm.

If the children live in an area without snow, they will need some help understanding what snow is and how it "behaves." Films, photographs, and poems may help. It may be an unsuitable stimulus for your children, and you may wish to replace it with another weather element—sun or rain—that suggests specific movement ideas.

Lesson Plan 6

- Dance Form: Creative dance
- Stimulus: Image of snow
- Grade: 1
- Time: 30 minutes
- Equipment: Cymbal
  Castanets
  Record or tape: "Snowflakes Are Dancing" (Debussy, arranged by Tomita)
  Record player or tape recorder
- Objectives: At the end of this lesson, the children will be able to
  1. change speed of actions,
  2. move with lightness,
  3. relate movement ideas to music and dance freely.
- Movement Concepts: Figure 7.14.

Movement Concepts		
Body Concepts Activities: Drift, fall, spin, sweep* Body Parts: Hands, feet		
Effort Concepts	**Spatial Concepts**	**Relationship Concepts**
Fine touch, light quality Changes in speed	In the general space	Alone (in a group)

*Travel with a horizontal emphasis as if blown by a strong wind.

Figure 7.14 Lesson Plan 6: Movement concepts arising from the stimulus snow.

Tasks	**Teaching Aids**
Part 1	
Basic	
Shake hands and stop suddenly.	Play short phrase on stick castanets. Repeat.

Refining Loose, floppy hands. Strong fingers when stopping.	
Extending Shake hands high, low, around the body.	Encourage children to use all space around their bodies. You might do it with them (i.e., omit percussion and provide ideas visually).
Refining Elbows slightly bent, watch your hands. On "stop" keep whole body still.	

Part 2

Basic Travel with quick, light feet and stop.	Castanet accompaniment, short phrases, maybe uneven lengths to encourage listening skills.
Refining Take small steps. Run on your toes. Look for the spaces. Strong bodies when stopping.	Dance with the children. Provide feedback during the task.
Extending Alternate phrase of 1. shaking hands, stop 2. quick traveling, stop	Verbal cues may be needed, but eliminate as soon as possible.
Refining Hands ready to begin! Keep movements small.	

Bring the children together and sit down with them. Discuss the stimulus (snow). Write their words on a board so they can see them. Select three or four words that will allow for the development of a movement sequence, for example, turning, stopping, traveling, and sinking. Begin working on sequencing two actions, e.g., travel and sink. No tasks are suggested here, because they will depend on the children's responses. The refining task should focus on quality inherent in the actions; the extending tasks should focus on adding another action to a sequence *or* changing the speed and direction of an action.

Tasks	Teaching Aids
Basic Listen to this music.	Play "Snowflakes Are Dancing" and fade at an appropriate moment.
Extending Listen again and imagine dancing your sequences.	Fade the music at the same moment so the children know how much music they have for their dance.
Part 3	
Applying Move into your own big space and show me how you wish to begin; be very still. Ready and. . . .	You may need to provide verbal cues this first time, small reminders of actions, quality, and listening to the music.
Refining Listen carefully to what the music tells you. Watch for the spaces. Light feet as you travel. When still, make it important.	Stillness is very difficult; give plenty of feedback on stillness as an action.
Applying Now you've tried your dance once, think about what you did; keep what you liked, find your space, and dance it once more.	Repetition is important even though this is an improvisation. Only give help if it really is necessary; otherwise, permit the children to focus entirely on their movement and the music.

A more complex idea for the upper elementary grades, possibly grade 4, still based on the stimulus of snow, is suggested in figure 7.15. In this instance, the dance has four distinct parts—*A, B, C, D*—which are patterned according to the wishes of the class; for example, *A-B-C-B-D-C-B.* This may be too long, in which case A-B-D-C-B has good potential. Notice that both dance forms finish with group shapes and stillness. This is very important. Dances where everyone finishes in a relaxed, shapeless heap on the floor—which could happen with the idea *melt*—are visually boring.

Figure 7.15 Development of a "snow dance."

A. Falling Snow		
Body Concepts Activities: Sinking, rising, spinning, hovering Body Parts: Upper body parts leading activities		
Effort Concepts	**Spatial Concepts**	**Relationship Concepts**
Changes in speed Sustainment Light quality	Changes in level, stressing high and low Air pattern	Alone (in a group)

B. Snowflakes Falling on the Ground		
Body Concepts Activities: Jumping, rolling, stopping Body Parts: Different body parts taking weight Body Shapes: Different body shapes		
Effort Concepts	**Spatial Concepts**	**Relationship Concepts**
Contrasting strong and light qualities Sudden and slow "arrivals"		Small groups forming and dispersing

C. Snowflakes Drifting and Freezing into Shapes		
Body Concepts Activities: Travelling, turning, stopping Body Shapes: Shaping of the body in groups		
Effort Concepts	**Spatial Concepts**	**Relationship Concepts**
Contrasting free and bound flow Firm body shapes Fine touch when travelling Sustained quality		Small groups, 3's 5's Group shapes

Figure 7.15 *Continued*

D. Melting Snow		
Body Concepts Activities: Gesturing Body Parts: Isolation of parts Body Shapes: Asymmetric shapes		
Effort Concepts	**Spatial Concepts**	**Relationship Concepts**
Fine touch, changing to heavy (relaxation) Contrasting slow and sudden (dripping) qualities		Alone or in small groups

The accompaniment to the dance could be voice sounds, appropriate words, percussion instruments, or any combination of the three. Much experimenting will be done to find the "right sound" the children want as they create their "music." They may wish to tape record their composition, or they may prefer to have live music, playing and dancing at the same time. This is one of the many situations when roles can be found for the children who, for various reasons, are not able to take part in the dance itself. They can be part of the "orchestra" and thereby share totally in the creation of the dance.

Poems and Stories

Boorman (1973) writes of the close links between our verbal and motor languages, and there are several publications which help with the development of lessons which use words as stimuli (Shreeves, 1979 and Wall, 1983).

When selecting a poem or a story as a stimulus for a dance, the most important element is its movement potential. The following characteristics can be used as criteria. Two or more should be present in order for there to be sufficient movement content for the development of a dance:

1. A clearly defined story line
2. Plenty of activity
3. Well-developed characters
4. A series of events so that the poem or story can be divided into scenes or acts
5. Contrasting moods and characters
6. Strong imagery
7. Onomatopoeia
8. Words and/or phrases with strong rhythmic content

The kind of dance developed will depend on the combination of the characteristics listed. The dance could be completely nonliteral, its ideas abstracted for their own worth and the story or poem almost disregarded. Other dances will have closer alignment with the original source of the movement ideas. The resulting dance may be one of the following:

1. *Dramatic dance, developed around effort and relationship concepts.* The dance is an abstraction of moods and does not tell any story. If told the original idea, observers may see no connection between it and the finished dance.
2. *Lyrical dance, developed around space and effort concepts.* This dance is also an abstraction, but of shapes and sensations of flow rather than specific moods. This kind of dance is often accompanied by music with a strong melodic line.
3. *Rhythmic dance, developed around body awareness and effort concepts.* This is also abstraction; the interest and excitement come from the ability to "play" with different rhythms. Children may create their dance around words taken from a poem or story. The words make no verbal sense on their own, but the resulting dance is totally logical. Nonsense poems, such as *The Jumblies* by Edward Lear and *The Jabberwocky* by Lewis Carroll, are wonderful for both rhythm and onomatopoeia.
4. *Dance drama, developed around body, effort, and relationship concepts.* This is the most concrete dance form because it includes characterization and a fairly clear story line.

When selecting a poem or story do not feel you have to follow it word for word. If two or three dance ideas are suggested by parts of the poem or story, and these ideas make sense on their own, then discard the remainder. Remember, it is a dance that is being created, and the focus is on conveying the essence of the stimulus rather than its literal translation into another medium.

The poem chosen for a series of lessons is the *The Pied Piper of Hamelin* by Robert Browning. This is a long narrative poem that has elements of both stories and poems. The resulting dance is a dance drama, which means the movement ideas are developed into motifs and mimetic action is minimized. This is very important to remember, otherwise the result is neither dance nor drama.

In this example, the characters of the poem are the main source of ideas, the story line being hinted at by the order in which the characters appear and what they do. The characteristics of each character are discussed with the children and the ideas noted on a board, as they must be kept in mind as the motifs are developed. Some suggestions are shown in table 7.3. Your children may have other thoughts, and those are the ones that should be kept.

Table 7.3

Ideas on which the Dance Drama *The Pied Piper of Hamelin* is based

The rats	Mischievousness "Popping" out of spaces Highlighting long tails, which can be used to hang onto, jump over, etc.
Mayor and corporation	Ceremonial in style Pompous "Thinking" motifs Posing Procession and grand entry before council meeting
The Pied Piper	Playing of pipe, wooden stick about 30 cm long and held either as a flute or a recorder Dancing through the space and around people
The children	Playing games of tag, leap-frog, hide and seek, jumping rope, throw and catch, on a seesaw and other activities that can be developed into motifs

A dance drama unit of fourteen lessons is probably required; three lessons per scene, plus another two to put the dance drama together. If it is not possible to spend fourteen or so lessons with one group of children, scenes can be given to different classes to work on separately. Time then has to be made available to bring the different groups together to share their dances and rehearse putting the scenes together. Because this is a major unit with a very definite product orientation, it follows that a performance with an audience is appropriate.

A synopsis of each scene follows with task ideas. We hope this model will help you plan similar dance experiences for your children.

Dance Drama: The Pied Piper of Hamelin

Scene 1 If possible, structure an environment that provides holes to creep into and pop out of; objects to hide behind, peer over, jump off, and scurry around (figure 7.16)

Synopsis	Task Ideas
1. Groups of "rats," some hiding, others peering, listening intently. Dancers have tails consisting of ropes tied around their waists.	Mingle freely, then freeze. Select interesting positions that result and practice them.
2. Rats scurry, stop, appear, disappear, listen, always "on guard."	Short phrases of quick, small running steps and stops at different levels; appearing and disappearing behind and into; jumping on and off obstacles. Stress stillness at different levels with hands, heads; alert bodies are important.

Figure 7.16 Scene 1: The Rats.

The Rats		
Body Concepts Activities: Hiding, peering, scurrying, jumping, stopping Body Parts: Emphasis on hands, heads, tails (skipping ropes)		
Effort Concepts	**Spatial Concepts**	**Relationship Concepts**
Sudden and light Fast and light Free flow	Changing from high to low	Pairs Groups 5-7

Music: "The Fossils," from *The Carnival of Animals* by Saint Saens

Figure 7.17 Scene 2: The Mayor and Corporation.

Mayor and Corporation		
Body Concepts Activities: Walking, sitting, gesturing, stopping Body Parts: Stressing trunk, arms, head		
Effort Concepts	**Spatial Concepts**	**Relationship Concepts**
Strong, direct Sustained Bound flow		Unison walking Two groups alternating sitting and walking

Music: March from *The Love of Three Oranges* by Prokofiev

3. Rats play with tails: use as skipping ropes; hold onto as in a line dance; wrap and unwrap each other, etc.

   Practice rhythmic swinging of tails, dancers in small groups of 3–5. Each group develops its own motifs based on play actions.

4. "On guard" motifs repeated. Finish dance with scurrying, hiding, and peering.

   Traveling in small groups, stopping, hiding behind each other, peering out from behind another, etc.

Scene 2 Chairs or a platform of different levels to represent steps to a council house (figure 7.17).

Synopsis	Task Ideas
1. Procession appears very stately, slow march, unison action.	Develop a step pattern with very definite leg gestures. Arms carried pompously. Group processes in unison.
2. Procession approaches the steps or chairs; half of the group sits and other half stands. Everyone is thinking. Groups change over, (the number of times this happens will depend on the counting of beats).	Develop "thinking" poses, stress posture and gesture of upper body, especially arms and heads. Change over must be counted so there is either action or stillness. Suggest four counts for each idea.

The Piper		
Body Concepts Activities: Skipping, turning, various step patterns Body Parts: Stressing feet, arms, hands (holding the pipe)		
Effort Concepts	**Spatial Concepts**	**Relationship Concepts**
Light touch Rhythmic Free flow	Pathways	Alone (in a group)

Music: *Tambourin*, by Hasse, arranged by James Galway

Figure 7.18 Scene 3: The Pied Piper.

3. Grand entry of Mayor. If children are strong enough the Mayor can be carried on a chair; if not, the Mayor walks ahead of a small procession acknowledging the onlookers. Mayor sits or stands in a highly visible place.	A new step pattern is needed for the Mayor. If the Mayor is carried, much practice of slow, unison lifting, carrying, and lowering is needed.
4. Angry citizens surround the Mayor, who is protected by the councilors.	Action-reaction motifs developed in pairs, one councilor and one citizen.
5. Everyone becomes aware of a strange sound from far off. The group becomes less hostile, more fearful, and gradually retreats.	Change of focus, from one-on-one to outside the group. Actions are more flexible, hesitant; gestures are protective.

Scene 3 The Piper's Dance is a dance for many pipers, depending on the number of students in the class. Dancers create their own step patterns and style of playing a pipe, which may be a piece of dowling 30–40 cm (12–14 inches) long (figure 7.18).

Synopsis	Task Ideas
1. The pipers enter and dance in general space.	Individual or small groups (2–3), unison step patterns, hands and arms important as they hold pipes.
2. Half the group poses on steps used in scene 2 and play their pipes, other half dances. Change over.	Dancers: line dances, circles, unison step patterns. Players: accentuate upper body gestures and fingers on pipes.
3. Whole group dances and exits (a line dance).	

Scene 4
Figure 7.19

Synopsis	Task Ideas
1. Four groups of children enter, one group at a time, and pose.	Traveling motifs developed with skipping, hopping, and galloping steps.
2. Each group plays its own game(s).	Enlarge mimetic actions, stress rhythm, shape, and variety.

Figure 7.19 Scene 4: The Children.

The Children		
Body Concepts Activities: Skipping, jumping, running, dodging, throwing		
Effort Concepts	**Spatial Concepts**	**Relationship Concepts**
Working activities with appropriate effort content	Large movements Each group in its own space	Small groups Unison for conclusion

Music: *Ruralia Hungarica Suite*, by Dohnany

3. Piper enters, children stop playing and watch, as each group is visited by the Piper. — Develop interesting group shapes for stillness; heads and eyes follow Piper everywhere.
4. Piper sits on steps and watches the children, who begin to play again. — Repetition or development of motifs previously created.
5. The children gradually form circles around the Piper, as if mesmerized by his/her presence. — Unison advancing and retreating (wavelike) motif develops with two circles, (inner and outer) changing places.
6. The Piper dances down from the steps, and the children follow him/her from the dance area. — The Piper selects one of the step-patterns used previously. Children skip, gallop, etc., after him, with no attempt at unison.

An Important Difference

How do **dance** and **drama** differ? In the former, the focus is on developing motifs that are representational of a situation or character. The essence of a situation or character is abstracted and transformed into a new form—dance form. In the latter, a more literal reproduction of the stimulus is sought. It may be in the realm of fantasy rather than our concrete world, but the children, for that moment, enter into that world and become some one or thing other than they are.

In dance, the children are not asked to "be" anything other than themselves; neither are they asked to act out a story. Both suggest a somewhat literal interpretation of the stimulus. The process of abstraction is less obvious.

If animals are used as stimuli, the children's attention is drawn to the qualities of the stimuli; their own movements are modified so that these qualities are highlighted. Phrases, such as "ponderous as an elephant" or "hovering like a humming bird," help clarify the quality of the movement being developed.

Summary

Three dance forms are suggested as being appropriate for the dance program: singing games, folk dance, and creative dance. Each dance form provides different learning opportunities and challenges for the seven-year span of the elementary school. The ideas presented in this chapter have been chosen to give a feeling for the diversity of the dance program, which can be as exciting for the teacher planning it as it is for the children who will share it.

Overall, the dance program should provide rich and varied experiences for your children, reinforcing their innate impulse to move expressively and helping them to enjoy the worlds of imagination and fantasy with a disciplined and artistic communicative focus. Laban's words (1948) concisely state the objective of such a program:

> *It is not the creation of sensational dances which is aimed at, but the beneficial effect of the creative activity of dancing upon the personality of the pupil.*

Review Questions

1. Why is it important to consider both age and experience when beginning a dance program with children? How will these factors influence your (a) planning and (b) expectations?
2. Why are singing games considered to be an important, yet minor, part of the program?
3. Discuss possible lesson formats for singing games and folk dances. Why may they be considered together?
4. Select a singing game and extract the movement concepts. Design tasks that could be used in a lesson.
5. Discuss different ways of finding partners for folk dancing. Why is it important to understand the difficulties children sometimes have when selecting partners?
6. Select a stimulus from nature and analyze it so that the movement concepts could be translated into tasks for an age group of your choice.
7. Discuss how creative dance differs from drama.

References

Boorman, J. (1969). *Creative dance in the first three grades.* Toronto: Longmans of Canada, Ltd.

Boorman, J. (1973). *Creative dance and language experiences for children.* Toronto: Longmans of Canada, Ltd.

CAHPER (1980). *Folk dance in the elementary school.* Ottawa: Canadian Association for Health, Physical Education and Recreation.

Evans, J. (1981). *Let's dance.* Toronto: Can-Ed Media Ltd.

Fleming, G. (1976). *Creative rhythmic movement: Boys and girls dancing.* Englewood Cliffs, NJ: Prentice-Hall Inc.

Koma, C. (1987). *Movement education resource file.* Montreal: Project for 434–324 Movement Education for Early Childhood Teachers, Faculty of Education, McGill University.

Laban, R. (1948). *Modern educational dance.* London: Macdonald and Evans, Ltd.

Logsdon, B., Barrett, K., Ammons, M., Broer, M., Halverson, L., McGee, R., & Roberton, M. (1984). *Physical education for children: A focus on the teaching process* (2nd ed.). Philadelphia: Lea & Febiger.

Preston-Dunlop, V. (1980) *A handbook for dance in education* (2nd ed.). London: Macdonald and Evans, Ltd.

Russell, J. (1975). *Creative dance in the primary school* (2nd ed.). London: Macdonald and Evans, Ltd.

Shreeves, R. (1979). *Children dancing.* London: Ward Lock Educational Books.

Wall, J. (1983). *Beginnings: Movement education for kindergarten to grades three* (2nd ed.). Montreal: McGill University.

Recording

White, R., & White, D. (1982). Singing games. Los Angeles: Rhythm Productions; Tom Thumb Music (ASCAP) T321.

Related Readings

Baloche, L., & Blaska, J. (1992). Learning together—A new twist. *JOPERD, 63*(3), 26–28.

Côté-Laurence, P. (1987). Dance and music: A look at an old alliance. *CAHPER Journal, 53*(4), 16–20.

Frosch-Schroder, J. (1991). A global view. Dance appreciation for the 21st century *JOPERD, 62*(3), 61–66.

Hankin, T. (1992). Presenting creative dance activities to children: Guidelines for the nondancer. *JOPERD, 63*(2), 22–24.

Hill, R. (1986). Tribute to Lisa Ullman: A shining star in the dance world. *CAHPER Journal, 52*(6), 13–15.

Jensen, M. (1983). Composing and guiding creative movement. *JOPERD, 54*(1), 85–87.

Macdonald, C. (1986). Yes, you can teach creative dance. *CAHPER Journal, 52*(3), 17–22.

Riley, A. (1987). Can dance break the sex barrier? *CAHPER Journal, 53*(3), 14–18.

Werner, P., Sweeting, T., Woods, A., & Jones L. (1992). Developmentally appropriate dance for children. *JOPERD, 63*(6), 40–43, 53.

Van Gyn, G., & Docherty, D. (1985). Skill acquisition and creative dance: A conflict in goals? *CAHPER Journal, 51*(6)9–12.

Sources for dance ideas:

CAHPER. (1988). *Creative dance; basic skills series.* Ottawa: CAHPER.

Shreeves, R. (1985). *Children dancing.* New York; Ward Lock Educational Books.

Stinson, S. (1988). *Dance for young children.* Reston, VA: AAHPERD.

Section 3

Games

Games are fun, challenging, meaningful and uniquely satisfying to everyone. People like to play games whether they are skilled, unskilled, adults or children.

Schurr, E. 1980. Movement Experiences for Children, *3d ed. Englewood Cliffs, N.J.: Prentice-Hall Inc.*

Chapter 8
The Games Program

Probably more has been written on games for children than on other aspects of the physical education program. Playing and watching games are important aspects of North American and many other societies around the world. Concern has arisen because, in many instances, the intrinsic value of *playing* has been lost. Scores, standings, medals, and other awards have become more important, the playing becoming the means of achieving an end, rather than being an end in itself.

> *Ideally the objective of the game is non-productive in that the value of the game is intrinsic, not dependent on external award. When this equilibrium is disturbed, through infusion of rewards external to the game, play loses its character and takes on the character of work. (Saunders, 1969)*

Why Should Games be Included in the School Program?

> *People of all ages play games—many of us play games our entire lives while others of us feel that games are played only by the young. (Morris, 1980)*

Children begin to play games at a very early age. Many of the activities, in their unsophisticated stages of development, quite naturally become part of the children's movement vocabulary. How many of us have played "peek-a-boo" with a baby? Probably all of us have. Preschool children play games of hide-and-seek and enjoy the excitement of being chased by a friendly older sibling or parent. Here are the beginnings of role playing and offensive and defensive strategies, which are important aspects of conventional games of our society.

Objects fascinate children. They pick them up, shake them, and often drop them. Initially, the children are exploring the nature of the object, but soon their attention transfers to controlling the object and dropping becomes a deliberate action. Adults' reactions reinforce these activities, and so manipulative skills are developed. Many toys are designed to develop manipulative skills, and fortunate children are given balls, skipping ropes, hoops, bats—the paraphernalia of games playing.

Games provide children with opportunities to be in control of themselves and the environment. When allowed to design their own play, they often surprise adults with their ability to create situations which are self-testing, have structure and rules to be followed. They sensibly adapt the game to meet their own needs as they play. If the game doesn't work, is too easy, too difficult, or not interesting, they change it!

As our life-styles change, playing spaces diminish, and children are bused considerable distances to school, their chances to indulge in play are reduced. It becomes more important for the school program to provide children with games experiences. We must ensure that the *children's* perspective of "playing a game" is fostered, and the adult achievement-oriented attitude is avoided.

The Nature of Games

Sports and *games* are familiar words that we may use interchangeably. In this book, however, they are considered to be different. **Sports** is a generic term meaning any formal activity in which there is an element of competition, either direct or indirect. Gymnastics, swimming, cross-country skiing, track and field (indirect competition), and such games as football, tennis, and softball (direct competition) are sports. This chapter examines **games** and games playing along a broad spectrum from the simple chasing games so enjoyed by five-year-olds to the complex, formal games played by adults.

Games are competitive activities in which the individual or group objective is to win, while using strategies and skills to prevent the opposing individual or group from winning (Saunders, 1969 and Stanley, 1977). **Cooperative games,** a different concept of games, are discussed in the section on relationships, later in the chapter.

If you recall your own games experiences in elementary and secondary school, you may remember lessons in which the focus was on the development of individual skills (e.g., the basketball chest pass) eventually used to play a game. Unfortunately, games playing is not that simple. Games are unpredictable and the context in which the skills are used varies each time the game is played. Skills used in these conditions are called **open skills.** Children who are taught skills out of the context of a game environment have little understanding of *why* or *when* to use them. Too much time has been spent on specific motor responses or techniques, and insufficient time has been spent understanding "the contextual nature of games" (Bunker & Thorpe, 1982). As "much of the pleasure involved in games playing lies in making correct decisions in the light of tactical awareness" (Bunker & Thorpe, 1982), lessons must help children understand the nature of games playing, so they can make decisions and use their specific skills appropriately.

We suggest the games program should focus on developing general games knowledge and appreciation through games playing (figure 8.1). Common to all games is the concept of **fundamental games knowledge,** and we wish to underscore that this is what should be stressed in games teaching. The belief is that knowledge and appreciation are transferable from one games situation to another (Piggott, 1982). Our responsibility is to help children develop an understanding and appreciation of the interrelatedness of rules, strategies, players' roles, and specific skills or techniques. In other words, children should have the opportunity to learn to play and to enjoy playing.

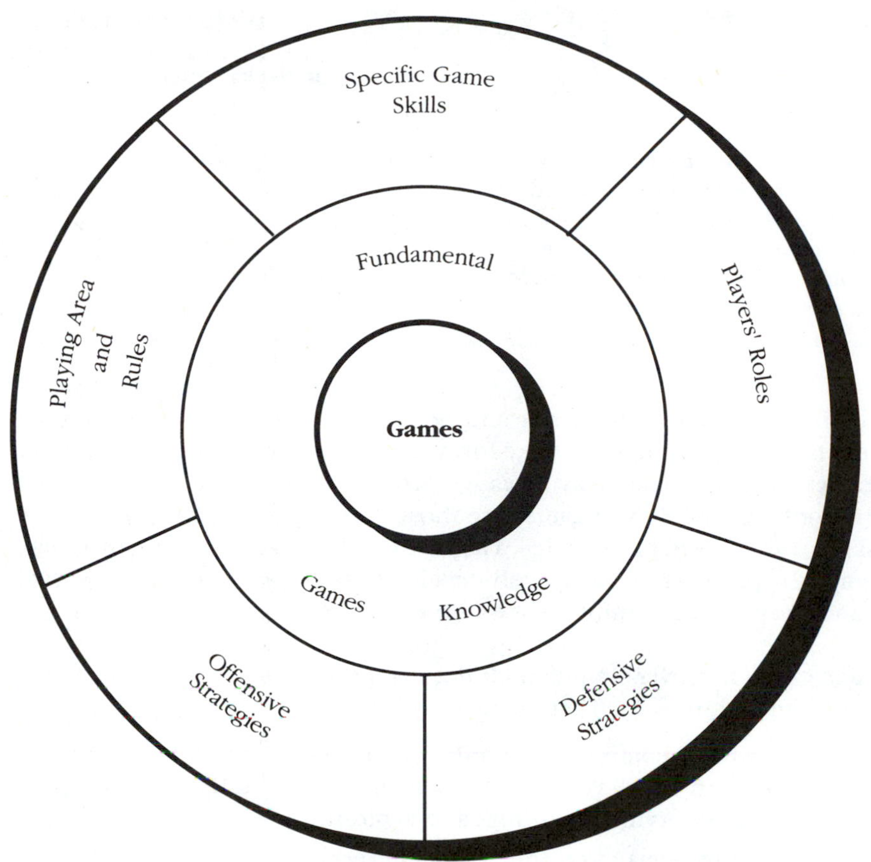

Figure 8.1 Games understanding.

Hierarchy of Games

It may be useful to group games according to their complexities. Three such groups are

1. low-organization games,
2. lead-up games,
3. formal games.

It is helpful to understand this hierarchy, because it provides a continuum of experiences. There is a progression from low-organization games to formal games, and the overall objective of the games program is for the children to learn the fundamental skills of games playing, as well as the skills of specific games (table 8.1).

Table 8.1

A Comparison of Low-Organization, Lead-Up, and Formal Games

Simple elements found in many games; no game form specified	——→	Low-organization games
Combination of elements found in a selected formal games form	——→	Lead-up games
Combination of elements found in a specific formal game	——→	Formal games

Because low-organization and lead-up games focus on the fundamentals of games playing, they form the core of the elementary school games program. They may already exist or be created by the children and/or teachers. Formal games are those with established rules, specific skills, and defined player roles. They are exciting and challenging to play when the players have fairly well-developed skills. For this reason, formal games have a very limited place in the elementary school program.

Low-Organization Games

Each game, however simple, includes components of fundamental games skills (see figure 8.1). These games

1. emphasize locomotor and nonlocomotor skills; provide plenty of opportunity for developing body management skills of running, dodging, swerving, guarding, and avoiding;
2. make little demand on the players in terms of roles, strategy, and rules;
3. bear little resemblance to formal games (see table 8.1).

All low-organization games include introductory elements of competition, such as chasing and being chased in a group (What's the time, Mr. Wolf?) or in pairs (one-on-one tag), or comparing scores, as in Danish Rounders, a game in which running is "matched" against accurate throwing and catching. The game is described in table 8.2.

Lead-up Games

These games are more complex, and a greater resemblance to formal games is apparent. The games are designed to

1. combine selected nonmanipulative and manipulative skills in a game structure;
2. include role playing, i.e., introduce the concept of offensive (attacking) players, defensive (guarding and goalkeeping) players;
3. require an understanding of strategy fundamental to the related formal game form.

Table 8.2

Danish Rounders

Two groups of players, 8–12 players per group.
Objectives:
Group *A* passes a ball around the circle and keeps account of how many times the ball is successfully caught. If the ball is dropped, return to zero.
Group *B* runs around the circle ("follow the leader") as the ball is being passed. On crossing a designated mark, the last runner calls "Stop!"
Groups *A* and *B* change over. Group *B* tries for more passes than *A;* group *A* tries to run the circuit faster than *B.*

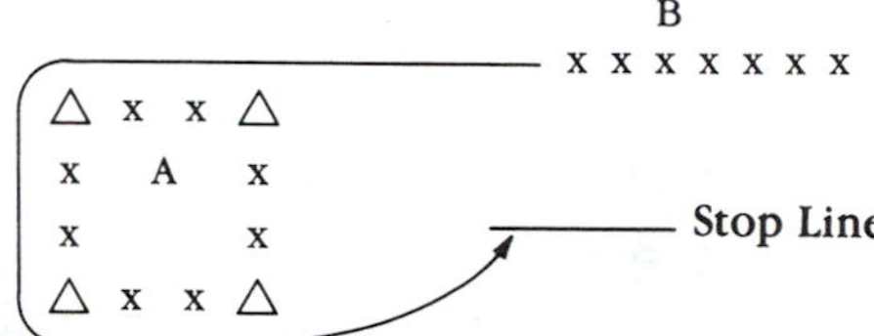

△ Pylons to Establish Size of Circle
x Players
——→ Running Track

To Do

Observe children playing in their school yard. If possible, do this at a school where you are teaching and you know some of the children.
Notice:

1. What games activities they use in their play.
2. The size of group preferred by children of different ages.
3. Any children who appear to be excluded from playing. What do you know about their skill level?

At times gamelike tasks will be set with the objective of developing cooperative play, for example, "keep the pot boiling" or "how many can we do?" when alternating with a partner to bat a ball against a wall. In such a situation, the players strive to send the ball so their partners can also bat it. Other cooperative relationships important in team play, such as "where do I go when I don't have the ball?" can be addressed in situations involving three players, in either a cooperative or a 2 versus 1 situation.

Both low-organization and lead-up games can be adapted, simplified, or complicated to meet the skills of the children and relate to the learning objectives of the lesson. There are numerous games from which to select, and often children and/or teachers can make them up (see the related readings at the end of chapter 10 for sources of games).

Formal Games

These games are "grown into" gradually as children's locomotor, nonlocomotor, and manipulative skills develop along with their knowledge of game concepts. A considerable amount of games learning precedes the playing of formal games with any degree of satisfaction. The structure of each game is such that

1. the players have to adapt to the demands of that game;
2. there are specific skills to be learned;
3. the rules are established and have to be understood;
4. the number of players is predetermined;
5. the equipment and playing area are standardized. Each time the game is played, the structure remains the same.

As players become more skillful, they tend to select and concentrate on one game. Their enjoyment increases as their competency increases. To play formal games with any degree of satisfaction, the players, teammates, and opposition, need levels of competency that are roughly equal. Unequal skills result in some players dominating play, while others are almost left out.

Categorization of Formal Games

In 1969, a book on games in education was published in England. The book, *Games Teaching: A New Approach for the Primary School,* by E. Mauldon and B. Redfern has had a considerable influence on the way games are understood and taught. Many of the concepts presented in this chapter were developed around their ideas.

Formal games can be categorized according to

1. specific games skills,
2. the playing area,
3. players' roles,
4. offensive strategies,
5. defensive strategies.

Table 8.3

Target Games

Common aspects		Variations
Sending-away category.	**Specific game skills**	Great variation in skills (e.g., drive, release, deliver).
Playing area shared; players take turns.	**Playing areas**	Great variation, ranging from eighteen-hole golf courses to sheets of ice, as for curling.
Same skill for all players; no interaction.	**Players' roles**	In team games, role differentiation is strategic rather skill oriented (e.g., skip in curling).
To hit a target.	**Offensive strategies**	Hole—golf Button—curling Gold—archery Jack—lawn bowling
To put up obstacles to prevent opponents from hitting target.	**Defensive strategies**	No defensive strategies in individual games i.e., archery, ten-pin bowling, golf.

Examples: Bowling (ten-pin, lawn), curling, golf

This may help us understand "the factors common to a number of games rather than view each game as an isolated unit" (Mauldon & Redfern, 1981). The categories of formal games are

1. target games,
2. net games,
3. batting games,
4. running games.

Target Games These are either small team games, four players per team as in lawn bowling and curling, or individual games where one plays against oneself and the environment, as in golf and ten-pin bowling. In these games, the scores of different players are compared, and it may be the one with the lowest score (golf) or the highest score (bowling) who wins. Table 8.3 lists some factors common to target games

Target games are often enjoyed as recreational pursuits and are played by a wide age group. Many seniors enjoy and are able to continue to play them for many years. Curlers and lawnbowlers in their seventies and eighties are not unusual.

The following are the fundamental skills and movement concepts of target games:

1. Sending away an object, ranging from an arrow approximately 55 inches (141.4 cm) long that weighs a few grams, to a curling stone, 36 inches (91.44 cm) in circumference, 4.5 inches (11.43 cm) high, and weighing a maximum of 44 pounds (19.96 kg) (according to the Curling Rule Book, Canadian Curling Association, 1979).
2. Aiming at a specific, stationary target.
3. Small range of body management skills. Stability and good balance at moment of delivery. Ten-pin bowling and curling are the only target games in which the player delivers the object on the move.

Most of these games need special facilities and are too expensive to be part of the regular school program, although some secondary schools do include them as lifetime sports for their more senior students.

Low-organization games based on target game concepts are very appropriate when developing the fundamental skills of sending away. Young children gain much enjoyment and satisfaction from hitting a target, especially if it is one that falls over on impact.

Net Games These games also include sending away skills, and all are various striking skills. The main intention in all the games is to return the object, ball, or badminton bird, to the opponent or opponents. The only time the object is held is when being put into play or served. Table 8.4 lists aspects of net games.

The following are the fundamental skills and movement concepts of net games:

1. Hitting an object to a space (body and spatial concepts).
2. Covering the playing area and anticipate where the opponent(s) will send the object (relationship concept).
3. Moving quickly in all directions (effort and spatial concepts).
4. Changing direction suddenly (effort and spatial concepts).
5. Striking the object at a variety of levels. In games such as tennis and squash, the ball may bounce before it is struck. In such games as badminton and volleyball, the object is counted out of play when it touches the ground (spatial concept).

Table 8.4

Net Games

Common aspects		Variations
Sending-away category; striking with an implement.	**Specific games skills**	No implement used in volleyball.
Area divided by a net; opposing players separated.	**Playing areas**	Squash and racquetball where area is shared; ball rebounds off wall.
All players require same skills as they rotate positions.	**Players' roles**	In volley ball, some specialization at elitist level of play (e.g., spikers).
Place object so that opponents are unable to return it.	**Offensive strategies**	The size, weight, and shape of the object varies from badminton bird to volleyball.
Return object and keep it "in bounds."	**Defensive strategies**	In squash and racquetball, return ball above designated line on front wall.

Examples: Badminton, racquetball, squash, tennis, volleyball

6. Sending the object over a net or, in the case of squash and racquetball, make the object hit a wall above a designated line (spatial concept).
7. Striking the object when close to and far away from the body (spatial concept).

Sometimes there is confusion because of the use of the term *receiver* in net games. A player or team may be designated the receiver, indicating the need to be mentally prepared and in a position to strike the ball as soon as it comes into the playing area. At no time is the ball stopped or controlled by catching or trapping.

Children of all ages enjoy striking a ball, with or without an implement, alone or with a partner. Large, light balls, even balloons, are ideal for the youngest children. Considerable fun and satisfaction result from volleying a balloon or beachball. In these playlike situations are the beginnings of net games.

Table 8.5

Batting Games

Common aspects		Variations
Sending-away (throwing, striking) Receiving (catching, collecting).	**Specific game skills**	Special gloves/mitts used to receive ball in baseball and softball. In cricket, the wicketkeeper wears gloves. Implements for striking vary in shape and size.
Area shared; offensive team has designated track to run.	**Playing area**	Shape of running track differs.
Variation in roles for defensive team (e.g., pitcher, catcher).	**Players' roles**	
Related to scoring runs, therefore, batting oriented. Each team stays on offense-defense until designated number of batters have a turn.	**Offensive strategies**	
Fielding team tries to prevent runs from being scored. Emphasis on receiving and sending-away quickly and accurately.	**Defensive strategies**	

Examples: Baseball, cricket, softball

Batting Games These games use sending-away and receiving skills. The sending-away skills are different methods of throwing and striking. The receiving skills are catching and trapping, often in combination, as players intercept the ball by placing their bodies to stop it. They then pick it up and throw. Table 8.5 lists common aspects and variations of batting games.

The games are characterized by each team having two distinct roles to play. Team A bats and team B fields; after so many players have been at bat, the teams change over. Only the batting team can score; the fielding team tries to prevent scoring.

> In **A Quality Physical Education Program,** "teams are formed in ways that preserve the dignity and respect of every child" (COPEC, 1992).

The following are the fundamental skills and movement concepts of batting games:

1. Players at bat
   a. striking the ball a considerable distance and to specific areas (body, effort, and spatial concepts),
   b. sprinting a specific pathway (body and effort concepts).
2. Players in the field
   a. receiving the ball at various levels (body and spatial concept),
   b. throwing accurately (body, effort, and spatial concepts),
   c. covering a designated area (body and spatial concepts).

Role differentiation occurs when players are fielding. The catchers (baseball) and wicketkeepers (cricket) develop specialized receiving skills, while pitchers (baseball) and bowlers (cricket) develop specialized throwing skills. (Note: When bowling, the wrist action is restricted, and the action is not considered a throw. In the categorization system used here, it is considered a throw because the bowler has possession of the ball.) All other players use the same skills, even though there are specific positions when fielding.

Batting games are usually played outdoors, and all need comparatively large areas. Boundaries may vary according to the space available, but the running track for the batters is standardized.

As soon as the baseball or cricket season arrives, children will enjoy playing modified versions of batting games. When designing or selecting lead-up games for lessons, make sure the players spend a short time at each role. When children are learning to bat, fielders may spend considerable time with nothing to do! Games in which the pitcher/bowler cooperates with the batter are often more satisfying than when the pitcher/batter is an opponent.

Running Games These are the most numerous and complex of all formal games. They include all three categories of manipulative skills: (1) sending-away, (2) receiving, and (3) retaining and traveling. Historically, all except basketball were played outside but now there are indoor versions of several of these games. Table 8.6 lists common aspects and variations of running games.

Table 8.6

Running Games

Common aspects		Variations
Sending-away (throwing, striking) Receiving (catching, collecting) Traveling (carrying, propelling).	**Specific games skills**	In hockey, the "running" is skating.
Rectangular, mostly outdoors, with standardized boundaries. Area shared by all players.	**Playing areas**	Great variation in size of area; shape, size, and position of goals; shape of implements; and shape and size of ball. Field lacrosse has no designated boundaries.
Designated goalkeeper, other players need same skills; gradual emergence of offensive and defensive players.	**Players' roles**	Football has many specific roles requiring specialized skills.
To hit, carry, throw ball to a specified area, goal, basket, or end zone. Rapid and frequent changes from offensive to defensive.	**Offensive strategies**	Game stops for change of players when offense becomes defense.
Intercept ball/puck before it goes into goal or over line.	**Defensive strategies**	

Examples: Basketball, field/ice hockey, lacrosse, soccer

The following are the fundamental skills and movement concepts of running games:

1. Running a considerable distance at speed with and without the games object (body and effort concepts).
2. Swerving, dodging, and faking to avoid opposing players (body, effort, and relationship concepts).

3. Guarding an opposing player (relationship concept).
4. Guarding/protecting a space (body and spatial concepts).
5. Changing swiftly from offensive to defensive play (relationship concept).
6. Intercepting the game object (body, space, and relationship concepts).

Most of these games need a large number of players, the exception being basketball which has ten players. In contrast, there are thirty rugger players on a field at one time. Players, therefore, need considerable skill and understanding of their cooperative and competitive roles.

Strategy can become very complicated, and the players have to be able to pay attention to numerous simultaneous happenings, sift out the relevant from the irrelevant, and make split second decisions. The players' intellects and memories are involved when practiced patterns and sequences are put into play. For these reasons alone, formal running games are more suitable for the more mature students.

Children in elementary school play their own versions of running games and are adept at modifying the demands of the formal game to meet their own capabilities. Regardless of how many players there are, there is always a goalkeeper. Children see that as a very important role. Goalkeeping skills should be developed alongside the other fundamental skills of games playing, and all children should have a turn playing that role.

The Material of Games

The games program differs considerably from dance and gymnastics programs in that a major focus is on developing a variety of manipulative skills. However these can be used successfully only if the players have control over their general body management skills (locomotor and nonlocomotor). Figure 8.2 shows the fundamental skills.

The movement concepts (body awareness, effort awareness, spatial awareness and relationships) are discussed in the games context; first applied to locomotor and nonlocomotor skills and then to manipulative skills.

Locomotor and Nonlocomotor Skills

These skills include jumping, running, stopping, and turning. Observation of skilled games players reveals they have excellent locomotor and nonlocomotor skills. They can dodge out of another player's way, turn quickly and run in a different direction, run fast into open spaces, and stop suddenly. Games playing involves the successful integration of locomotor and nonlocomotor skills with the manipulative skills (e.g., jumping to catch a ball, dribbling a ball in the playing area, or turning to throw the ball).

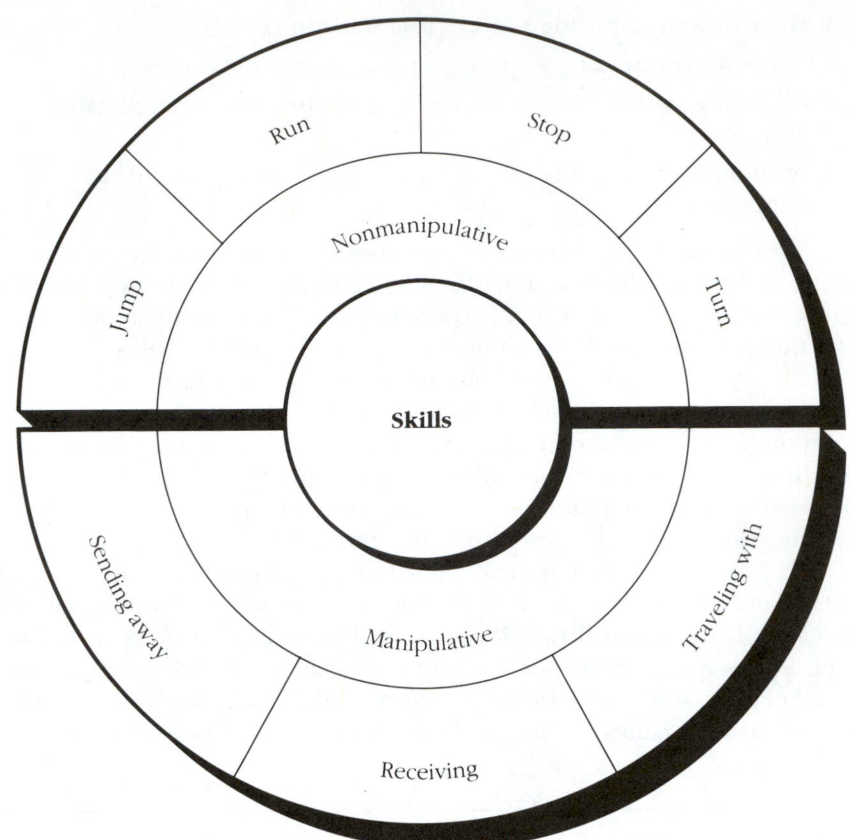

Figure 8.2 Fundamental games skills.

Body Concepts

The fundamental vocabulary of body concepts is small (listed in table 8.7). As selected effort, space, and relationship concepts are added, the vocabulary becomes diverse and yet more specialized (e.g., run becomes swerve, break, dodge).

Activities

All games players need to be able to run, jump, turn, and stop. Sequences, such as running–jumping with a turn, and running–stopping–turning, help develop skillful body management, especially when a "surprise" element is introduced, perhaps by the teacher signaling with a whistle to indicate a change of activity.

Shape

Players need to be able to change their body shape according to the role they are playing. On the offense, players may need to travel through small spaces and, thus, may need to narrow the body (elongated shape). In contrast, defensive players broaden the body to block an opponent (wide shape). When jumping to receive a ball, the player with the most elongated shape is often the one who reaches it first. In games that involve a

Table 8.7

Locomotor and Nonlocomotor Skills

Body concepts	Actions—bending, stretching, twisting Activities—run, jump, turn, stop Shapes—changing from stretched to curled, to wide to twisted Parts—recognition of the roles played by different parts during activity
Effort concepts	Time—changes of speed, suddenness, fast Weight—resiliency Space—direct and flexible Flow—control, continuity, go and stop
Spatial concepts	Changes in direction, extension Traveling different pathways
Relationship concepts	To team members, opposition, boundaries, goals

To Do

List the locomotor and nonlocomotor skills needed for the following games:

a. Baseball

b. Tennis

c. Hockey

lot of running, such as basketball, lacrosse, and soccer, players may have to twist as they run and avoid (dodge) other players. They may also twist as they prepare to receive or throw the ball.

Body Parts

The hands and arms become very important when facing and shadowing an oncoming opponent. The head is important when faking and dodging. The shift of weight from one foot to the other is facilitated by movement initiated by the upper body. When all parts work harmoniously, efficiency and control result.

Effort Concepts

All functional movements involve very complicated effort changes, and it is the ability to combine the appropriate effort elements that produces efficiency. The children need to be able to produce the right amount of each element at the right moment. What follows is a simplified analysis of the effort content of locomotor and nonlocomotor skills.

Weight

Most games activities require firmness rather than fine touch. It is the interplay between increasing and decreasing tension (muscle power) that produces the power and resiliency for running, jumping, stopping, and turning.

Time

Different games have different time elements. Some games are played at a constant pace (basketball, hockey); others have bursts of speed followed by a rest (badminton, squash, tennis, volleyball) or fluctuations of speed (soccer, softball). Fundamental to all games is the ability to move suddenly, to change speed, and to maintain a certain speed.

Space

Flexible movements assist all activities requiring a change of direction, so turning and twisting are assisted by the flexibility of the body parts initiating the action. Other skills are helped by a more direct movement quality, such as when planting a foot in preparation for a jump.

Flow

Functional movement tends towards bound flow, and efficient movement is often called *controlled,* which means it is predictable. Free flow activities tend to be unpredictable because they are ongoing and "unstoppable." Players who collide with others, fall over, and generally appear uncontrolled in their actions may require help with binding the flow of their activities.

Flow may also refer to continuity of activity. In order to produce continuity, the activity must be under control or bound to a degree. It is the interplay between withholding and freeing the movement that results in control.

Spatial Concepts

Considerable emphasis should be placed on this concept because all strategic decisions require spatial knowledge and skill. An understanding of space is fundamental to games playing.

General Space

The general space is usually defined by boundaries. The players have to be able to move efficiently within this restricted area, finding and creating spaces.

To Do

Play tag in pairs and gradually reduce the space in which you run. How does your running change? Does anything else change?

Pathways Many different pathways are traveled as players move around the playing area. In games such as softball and football, some pathways are predetermined, and time is spent running and rerunning precise patterns. In other games, the pathways are determined by where the other player(s) are in the designated area.

Children should learn to run zigzag, hairpin, curving, right-angled, and other pathways. It may help to have markers for the children to run around. As proficiency increases, remove the markers.

Extensions The pathways will vary in size. A small zigzag pattern may result in swerving around a defender; an uneven hairpin (one long arm and one short) may create a space and free the player to receive a pass. Being able to decide what size pathway to run is one of the fundamental skills.

Personal Space

Skillful use of personal space is demonstrated magnificently by the Harlem Globetrotters. As they play basketball, the players turn in their own space, run backward as well as forward and sideways, and change direction at a moment's notice without the opposition realizing what is happening. The members of the opposing team are teased and often seem to end up running chaotically in the playing area.

Directions All games players need to be able to run in different directions. In the personal space this means being able to run forward, backward, and sideways and changing from one direction to another. If you hear the phrase "good footwork" used to describe a player, it implies the ability to run and change direction swiftly. Each game has its own specific footwork demands, and you must be able to determine what they are. Compare, for example, the footwork required when playing games in small areas (badminton), with those in large spaces (soccer). Compare games requiring the players' feet to be in bounds when receiving a ball (football and basketball) with games not requiring a player's feet to be in bounds when receiving a ball (tennis and volleyball).

Remember That

Direction is related to the body (personal space). *Pathways* are related to where you travel (general space). Therefore, you can travel sideways, backward, and forward in circular, straight, zigzag, or angular pathways.

Extensions Good footwork is also being able to change the size of your running steps. It is only when the feet are in contact with the floor that the force can be produced for stopping and changing direction. Small steps are required when increasing and decreasing speed, and changing direction and stopping. When running at a constant speed, steps are usually larger.

Relationships

Table 2.4 introduced the concept of relationships in games playing. The games environment consists of people and objects that are both moving and static. It is the interaction between the objects and players that makes each game, and all strategic decisions are made in relation to these objects and people.

Objects

Nonmanipulated objects are the boundaries, zones, and targets needed for whatever game is being played. Many chasing games, such as What's the time, Mr. Wolf? and Crusts and Crumbs have zones designated as being "safe." It is by playing such games that children begin to learn about boundaries.

Boundaries may also indicate certain zones of the playing space are reserved for particular aspects of a game, such as the service zone in tennis or badminton. There is a close connection between boundaries, rules, and the beginnings of strategy.

Targets are part of the games environment, but because they are so closely allied with manipulative skills, they will be discussed in that part of the chapter.

People

Two different relationships arise with people when playing games, *cooperative* and *competitive.*

Staying "in bounds."

Cooperative Relationships These are relationships in which a group (a minimum of two people) works together to achieve a common objective. To do this the group members may play similar or very different roles. Words used when referring to cooperative relationships are *with, partner,* or *team.*

Each member of the group/team has to be aware of all the others all the time. The more participants there are in the group/team, the more complex the situation and the greater the demand on each member. To make the group/team *work* means having to watch carefully, adjust speed, change direction, anticipate, modify decisions, sometimes lead, and sometimes follow. Cooperative games, sometimes called **new games,** are designed to develop these group skills and reduce the emphasis on competition that has prevailed in many physical education programs. They are situations in which every child can be successful.

Challenging tasks can be set to help children understand how to make a group work. Two examples follow:

1. *Groups of three to five holding hands to form a line.* One end of the line (head) is the leader who runs with the group around the space in such a way that the chain remains intact. This sounds very easy, but children who are still mostly egocentric find it difficult to lead and be sensitive to the speed at which the others can run. The more curvy the pathway chosen the harder it becomes to remain intact as a whiplike effect arises for the "tail" (end).
2. *Short lines (three to five) run in the space.* On a given signal the tail of the line becomes the leader. Group focus shifts from one end of the line to the other. This demands a major group adjustment if the line is to remain intact!

Competitive Relationships In a competitive relationship, the participants try to achieve opposing objectives; therefore, they play different roles. In a simple situation such as one-on-one tag, participant *A* tries to avoid being touched by *B,* and simultaneously, participant *B* is trying to touch *A.* The running skills each employs are similar, but they are used to achieve different results. Words used when referring to competitive relationships are *against, opponent,* and *opposition.*

There are many group chasing games which provide plenty of practice for the beginnings of offensive and defensive strategy. These skills can be developed only if the players assume the roles which arise from competition, as in "you against me."

Examples of group chasing games are What's the time, Mr. Wolf? and Crusts and Crumbs. In these games, the groups are not teams, as the players are independent of each other. They do have to be able to keep out of each others way when trying to escape the taggers, but that is the only cooperative skill needed.

Games which begin to combine a degree of cooperation are the tag and release variety. The "free" players have to judge when it is a good moment to release a team member and have to be able to assess where the taggers are and act accordingly. Elementary strategy is employed, both offensive and defensive, and the children should be helped to understand these fundamental elements of games playing. These games can be played by children with differing levels of skill, and many find them challenging and great fun. It is important to change the roles often, especially if someone finds it difficult to tag.

Table 8.8 suggests progressions for developing cooperative and competitive skills. As soon as stage 4 has been reached, cooperative and competitive skills are always present and the playing situations become more similar to formal games. At the same time, gradually increase the group size so the players have the challenge of relating to more team members and more opponents. By the time the children have reached grade 6, they may be playing in groups of ten (five versus five).

Manipulative Skills

Manipulative skills fall into categories determined by our intentions as we relate to the game object, which is usually a ball of some kind (Mauldon & Redfern, 1981):

1. Get rid of the object—**sending-away skills.**
2. Gain control of the object—**receiving skills.**
3. Retain and take it with us—**traveling** and **propelling skills.**

Attention to specific movement concepts increases skill efficiency and versatility (table 8.9). For each group, there are fundamental components which must be the focus of the earliest learning experiences. It is through a variety of tasks, and the use of different implements (bats, sticks) and objects (beanbags, balls, frisbees) that efficient, fundamental manipulative skills are developed. The development of this kind of generalized games vocabulary equips the children for specialization in the upper elementary grades and in the secondary school.

Body Concepts

In all manipulative skills, the body is used as a tool to control an object in a variety of ways. The object may become "part" of the body for a short period of time or it may remain separate from the body.

Table 8.8

Progressions for Developing Cooperative and Competitive Skills

Grade level	Relationship	Example
	Stage 1: Alone	
K, 1	Alone	Running and stopping on signal
	Alone in a group	Avoiding being caught in a group tag game
	1 vs. group	Being the catcher in a group tag game
	Stage 2: In pairs	
K–6	With a partner (cooperation)	Holding hands, running, and changing the leader on signal Throwing and catching
	1 vs. 1 (competition)	Tag Child *A* kicks ball at designated target (e.g., a pylon); child *B* defends target, using any body part to stop the ball
	Stage 3: In threes	
2–4	Group (cooperation)	Keep the ball in the air (volley) using hands
	2 vs. 1 (cooperation and competition)	"Monkey in the middle"
	Stage 4: In fours	
3–6	3 vs. 1 (cooperation and competition)	Child *A* defends a designated goal; other players pass and shoot
	2 vs. 2 (cooperation and competition)	Keep-away-type games, tennis-like games
	Stage 5: In sixes	
5–6	3 vs. 3 (cooperation and competition)	Keep-away games Volleyball-like games
	Stage 6: In eights	
5–6	4 vs. 4	
	Stage 7: In tens	
5–6	5 vs. 5	

Table 8.9

Manipulative Skills

Body concepts	Activities—sending away an object receiving an object retaining and traveling with an object Shapes—awareness of shape during the activity Parts—awareness of different parts used during the activity
Effort concepts	Weight—variations in strength required to send, receive, retain, and propel the object Time—timing of contact/release of object; speed of arm/leg swing Space—direct/flexible use of arm/leg during activity Flow—change from going to stopping; continuity; control
Spatial concepts	Judgment of distances; height and size of targets, sending/receiving objects from different directions; retaining and traveling different pathways; sending/receiving at different levels
Relationship concepts	To other players, team members, and opposition To implements and/or balls To targets

Activities

Each category of manipulative skills has its own vocabulary. Children soon learn the terms for the skills found in the games related to their culture. During the baseball season in North America, children talk about pitching. The comparable game in Australia and England is cricket, and the children talk about bowling.

Shape

Changes in body shape occur when catching an object and absorbing the impact. The body curves as the limbs move towards the center of the body. Rounding of the body also happens when trying to protect the object from other players.

Goalkeepers have to be able to make very quick changes of body shape to block off the space they are defending. When goal spaces are comparatively small, as in hockey and European handball, wide and rounded shapes are most often used. Defending a soccer goal also requires elongated shapes as the goalkeeper strives to catch or tip the ball over the top of the goal.

To Do

For each category of manipulative skills, list verbs that are variations of the same skill (e.g., throwing, pitching, and bowling are forms of throwing).

Wide shapes are often used in defensive situations.
© *James Shaffer*

Body Parts

The most obvious body parts used to manipulate objects are the hands and feet. Other parts may block or stop oncoming objects; the feet or hands are then used to kick it away or pick up the object and throw. Soccer players, for example, may block the pathway of a ball with any part of their body, except their hands, and then kick the ball to another player. Only goalkeepers may use their hands to stop the ball.

Lessons should include tasks which give experience in using different parts of the hands and feet to control objects when sending, receiving, and traveling with them.

The addition of implements, bats and sticks, increases the complexity of the skill. The implements become extensions of the hands, and attention has to be paid to how to grip these implements. It is essential that the implements are the right size for the children.

Effort Concepts

Weight

Variations in strength are needed when controlling objects. Tasks which challenge the children to throw different distances, receive fast-moving objects, and run at different speeds while keeping an object close enough to the body, all demand adjustment to the amount of force produced.

Time

Timing is important; knowing when to release the ball, swing the bat, and "give" with the hands. A second aspect of time, perhaps the more obvious one, is the *speed* of action. How fast should the arm move when throwing, or the bat swing when hitting? Efficient movement has a rhythm of execution, which can be observed when watching good players. Inwardly, respond (empathize) with what you see and try to repeat the pattern. The rhythms will be nonmetric, and no two players will move with the same rhythm or tempo.

Coordination problems include mistiming actions. Children can be helped develop a sense of "when" by beginning with slow movements, which allow more time for them to react to what they see. When trying to kick a ball, for example, begin with the ball stationary, so the chances of success are high. Then, roll the ball slowly towards the child. Gradually increase the speed at which the ball travels, all the time reinforcing the idea of the "feel" of the pattern.

Space

Flexible use of different body parts is required during throwing actions; direct or linear qualities are required when striking and receiving objects. As with all the effort factors, it is the interplay between flexible and linear qualities that results in efficient skills. It is important to observe for effort changes, and to be able to provide congruent refinement which focuses on effort changes, so the childrens' manipulative skills become more efficient. It is sometimes easy to know when a skill needs more strength or is performed too slowly. It may be less easy to know, for example, when less flexibility will improve a skill.

Flow

One aspect of efficient action is being able to combine several skills, or repeat the same skill in fluid succession. This can only be done when movement is controlled and the players anticipate the sequence of events.

The following are examples of tasks demanding flow and anticipation:

1. Striking the ball continuously against the wall (use a paddle bat and 4 in. plastic ball).
2. Rolling the ball against the wall so that it rebounds to a partner, who collects it and throws it back.

The end of one action becomes the preparation for the following action.

Spatial Concepts

Considerable spatial judgment, both general and personal, is required when playing games. Many spatial words are used when tactics are discussed, which happens as soon as the children begin playing in groups. The learning focus is now on *games playing* rather than isolated skills. Questions, such as "Who is in a free space and ready to receive the ball?" "Who is closer to you?" and "Which way do you think the opponent will go?" help the children understand what factors have to be considered when making strategic decisions.

General Space

The following spatial concepts relate to specific manipulative skills, not games playing. As soon as the children use these manipulative skills in a games playing situation, the tactical aspects have to be added.

To Do

Observe a skilled outfielder in a baseball game and a receiver in football. Notice the continuity of action as the players

1. prepare to receive the ball,
2. receive it, then either
   a. throw it to a base player, or
   b. run across the goal line.

Floor Pathways Carrying and propelling skills imply that the players are traveling, combining running, turning, and stopping. Being able to travel different pathways with and without an object is a fundamental skill of games playing. It has been introduced in the section on locomotor and nonlocomotor skills (page 286).

Air Pathways Objects that are thrown or struck make pathways as they travel through the air. Objects thrown or hit with equal amounts of force will travel along different pathways according to the position of the hand when the object is released or struck. The pathway also affects the distance an object will travel. Children need to experiment with early and late moments of release and discover what happens to the object. Some young children seem to generate considerable power when "winding up" to throw . . . only to have the ball land at their feet! This is because they hold on to the ball too long and the angle of release is wrong. When striking a ball, it is the angle of contact between the object and the implement that determines the pathway.

Personal Space

In some games, the players have to be able to receive objects coming to them from the front, the side, and sometimes from behind the body. The body may have to twist so that hands, feet, or implement are placed in direct line with the approaching object. The player to whom an object is being sent may be in front, at the side of, or even behind the sender; again, the body may have to twist. Tasks with such challenges have to be included in lessons.

Extensions This concept is about how near to or far from the body the object is. We sometimes have to reach out to receive a ball. Watch basketball and football players reach up to intercept balls intended for another player. Notice, too, how quickly they bring the ball close to the body to protect it from other players. When practicing soccer or basketball dribbling, the closeness to the body will change as the speed changes.

"Throw the ball so that your partner has to reach to the side to catch it" and "in threes, *A* throws to *B, C* tries to intercept" are examples of tasks related to the concept of extensions.

Levels Players have to be ready and able to receive objects at different levels. Even in games where the object, usually a puck or ball, is played on the ground (low level) for most of the time, the players may be required to deal with a rising object. In baseball and basketball-type games, considerable versatility in coping with balls at different levels is required.

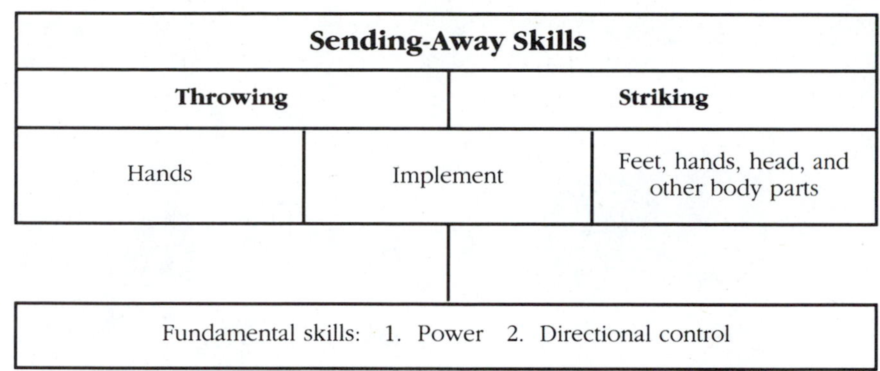

Figure 8.3 Sending-away skills.

Categories of Manipulative Skills

Within each category there are two subdivisions as follows:

1. Sending-away skills
    a. Throwing
    b. Striking
2. Receiving skills
    a. Catching
    b. Collecting
3. Traveling skills
    a. Carrying
    b. Propelling

In subdivision *a,* the object is held in some way; it becomes part of the player. In subdivision *b,* the object remains separate from the player, who has to be able to "find" it in the space.

Sending-Away Skills

This is the first group of skills children learn. The beginning stages are seen at an early age as the grasp reflex becomes inhibited. (Everyone has probably been with a child who persistently drops a toy!) There is little "sending" in the action, that comes later.

There are two ways to send away objects:

1. **Throw** the object using hands or an implement, such as a scoop.
2. **Strike** the object with hands, feet, head, or an implement.

Design tasks for your lessons which help the children develop the fundamental skills of (1) producing the right amount of force to send the object the required distance and (2) positioning to send it to the desired place (figure 8.3).

Targets of some kind are essential. There is no game situation where the object is intentionally thrown haphazardly! Targets may be markings on a wall, wastepaper baskets, hoops, or partners; they may be still or

Target practice.

moving, high or low, horizontal or vertical. Children can monitor their own achievements because there is instant feedback. The object either hits or misses the target. This may help them modify their actions, as well as set their own challenges. In a game, targets may be other players, the space for a player to move into, or the goal.

Table 8.10 suggests the components of a learning program from which tasks can be developed with specific objectives. Variety is stressed so that the child develop versatility and an understanding of the fundamental skills related to all sending-away skills. Through this generalized approach, we also hope they maintain open minds toward games playing.

Variety also allows greater chances of success, and it is important to give the children opportunities to select their own equipment. Some will choose equipment with which they have previously been successful, while others will experiment with new combinations. Both situations are important aspects of the learning process.

There are many different kinds of implements (bats and sticks) available in toy shops, as well as through sports manufacturers and suppliers, some of whom have specialized in producing good equipment that is

Table 8.10

Sending-Away Skills

Throwing	Striking
Hands	Specified body parts (hands, head, feet)
Implements:* Scoops Lacrosse sticks	Bats: long, short, flat, rounded (table tennis) Sticks: broom handles, hockey sticks, field hockey sticks, small golf clubs Racquets: badminton, racquetball, squash, tennis
Objects:* Whiffle balls Frisbees Rubber rings Beanbags Playground balls Nerf balls Fluff balls	Fluff balls Nerf balls Whiffle balls Shuttlecocks Playground balls Tennis balls Beach balls
Setting: Air—self receive partner receive small group activity Against wall—self receive partner receive small group cooperative activity To specific targets—unguarded guarded	
Hit off batting tee or other support.	

*Vary size, weight, shape, texture, and color.

appropriate in weight and size for children. At no time should seven-year-olds be struggling with a regulation baseball bat when a plastic, possibly somewhat fatter one, would provide them with success and enjoyment.

Receiving Skills

These skills are soon linked with sending-away skills, and the two become inseparable. Children begin to play Toss and Catch alone or in small groups, and we should recognize the importance of combining the two skills early in the program.

There are two ways to receive an object:

1. **Catch** the ball as it travels through the air, either before or after it rebounds off the ground or wall, or even off another player as happens in basketball and football.
2. **Trap, collect,** or **block** the ball as it travels along the ground (toward and away from the body) or through the air.

Children need bats to suit their size.

The fundamental aspects of receiving skills are

1. being in the right place at the right time,
2. being able to absorb or cushion the impact of the object as it arrives (figure 8.4).

Design tasks which develop a sense of positioning in relation to objects moving in the air and on the floor. Initially, the children send and receive on their own by tossing the object (such as beanbag or ball), into the air or against a wall, and then moving to catch it. When they do this, their success depends on themselves, rather than on the throwing expertise of a friend. As with sending-away skills, there is instant feedback which helps maintain motivation. However, if any children are unsuccessful more often than successful, intervene quickly and change the conditions (e.g., increase the size of the object). It is most important that the children wish to remain on task and do not become discouraged.

Table 8.11 suggests the components of a receiving skills learning program. Again, variety is stressed when designing tasks, so the children become versatile and understand the fundamental skills.

When children show some competency at catching and using different parts of the body to block oncoming objects, the tasks should require the children to travel to meet the ball. The use of sticks to receive the object increases the difficulty, so it is important that the size and weight of these implements are suitable for the children.

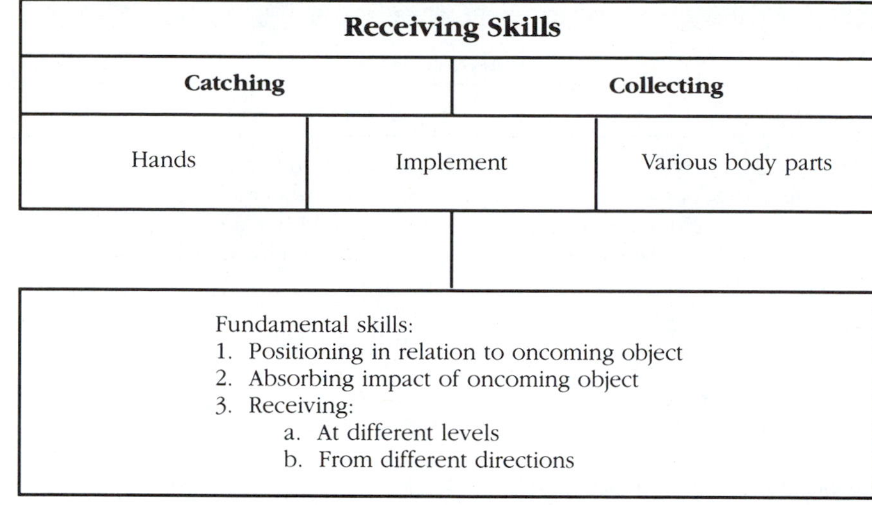

Figure 8.4 Receiving skills.

Retaining and Traveling Skills

These skills are often the link between receiving and sending skills. In some games, the sequence of events is receive–travel–send. In others, the sequence is receive–travel, as in football, because one way of scoring is to carry the object over a line.

The two ways to travel with an object follow:

1. **Carry** the object with hands or an implement.
2. **Propel** the object.

Carrying an object requires being able to hold it firmly, and shift it from one side of the body to thc other according to where the opponent is. Tag situations, in which the player with the object tries to avoid being caught by swerving or passing the object to another player, are examples of learning experiences.

Considerable time is spent on propelling skills because games requiring these skills are popular in our society.

The fundamental skill components of propelling balls, whether with hands, feet, or an implement, are being able to do the following:

1. Produce the appropriate amount of force and speed to propel the ball, yet keep it reasonably close to the body (under control).
2. Travel various pathways.
3. Change direction when traveling at different speeds (figure 8.5).

Beginning tasks should focus on adjusting to the implement and/or object being used. Pay little attention to where the children are going beyond reminding them to avoid other people. When watching less-skilled children, notice how they either overrun the ball or send it too

Table 8.11

Receiving Skills

Catching		Collecting	
Hands		Specified body parts	
Implements:*	Scoops	Sticks:	Ice hockey
	Fielder's mitts		Field hockey
	Lacrosse sticks		Broom handles
Objects:*	Frisbees	Beanbags	
	Rubber rings	Rubber rings	
	Beanbags	Playground balls	
	Playground balls	Whiffle balls	
	Nerf balls	Tennis balls	
	Fluff balls	Solid rubber balls	
		Pucks	

Setting: Air—Self send and receive
- Partner send and receive
- Small group activity sending and receiving

Rebounding off wall, ground—self
- partner
- small group activity

Skill variations:
- Use dominant/nondominant side of body when
  - standing
  - kneeling
  - running
  - jumping
  - diving/sliding
- Receive at different levels from different directions
  - in front
  - behind
  - the side
- Receive when object travels toward/away from, with varying extensions:
  - near to the body
  - far from the body
- Receive fast/slow oncoming object; judge speed
- Add obstruction (e.g., opponent)
- Change implement and/or object
- Receive objects traveling different trajectories (straight, curved)
- Receive thrown/struck object
- Intercept an object sent to another player

*Vary size, weight, shape, texture, and color of objects and implements.

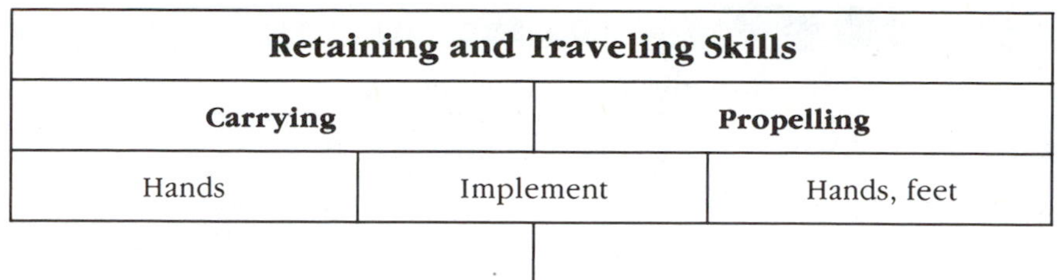

Retaining and Traveling Skills
Carrying
Propelling
Hands
Implement
Hands, feet
Fundamental Skills:
1. Adjustment of speed and force when propelling
2. Traveling various pathways
3. Changing direction

Figure 8.5 Retaining and traveling skills.

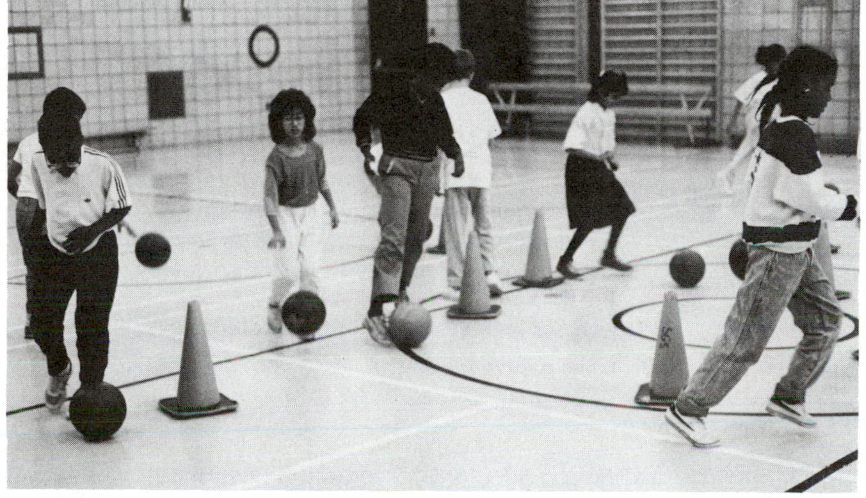

Negotiating uneven spaces.

far ahead, temporarily losing the ball. The secret is to be able to keep the ball close enough to the body so that no one else can get it and still be able to travel at various speeds throughout the playing area.

Attention to changing direction and traveling different pathways entails taking the eyes off the object, lifting the head, and looking around the space. As skill increases, the children should be able to look where they are going more, and look at the object less. "Heads up as you travel" is a useful refining task to include in learning sequences. As skill increases, children can be helped to use peripheral vision to monitor the object, other players, and the general space simultaneously—no mean achievement!

Remember That

Children need plenty of opportunity to practice manipulative skills. Whenever possible, make balls, bats, sticks, and other game equipment available for use during recess.

Table 8.12

Retaining and Traveling Skills

Retaining	Traveling
Hands, feet	Hands, feet
Implements:* Broom handles	Scoops
Hockey sticks	Lacrosse sticks
Field hockey sticks	
Objects:* Hoops	Nerf balls
Nerf balls	Tennis balls
Tennis balls	Solid rubber balls
Solid rubber balls	Plastic footballs
Playground balls	Whiffle balls
Plastic soccer balls	
Mini-basket balls	
Setting: In open space	
Around, between obstacles	
Stationary: pylons	
beanbags	
hoops	
Moving: people	
Skill Variations: Use dominant/nondominant hand/foot	
Alternate between dominant/nondominant feet/hands	
Change grip on implement when walking/running/being chased	
Add a "chaser" who tries to touch the object	

*Vary size, weight, texture, and color of objects.

Various pathways to travel can be designed by using pylons to show the route; spaces may be even or uneven.

Table 8.12 lists other aspects of a learning program designed to develop the fundamentals of and versatility in retaining and traveling skills.

It is possible to devise many interesting traveling and propelling tasks which encourage the development of the fundamental skills leading to manipulative control.

Some tag games, used in the development of locomotor skills and the introduction of roles in games playing, can be adapted to include traveling and propelling skills. These tasks give children gamelike experiences which encourage good footwork, an essential aspect of this group of skills.

Application of the Movement Concepts

The lesson plans in the accompanying *Lesson Plan Manual* (Côté-Laurence et al., 1990) provide numerous examples of tasks and learning sequences based on the movement concepts discussed in this chapter. Table 8.13 lists the specific concepts around which the individual lessons are developed.

Table 8.13

Games Theme Index

Lesson—Kindergarten	Body concepts	Effort concepts	Spatial concepts	Relationship concepts
1	Stretched shapes Curled shapes		Directions	
2	Locomotion Body parts			
3	Locomotion Body parts			
4	Locomotion Body parts			
5	Locomotion Hands	Force		
Lessons—Grades 1–2				
6			Pathways	Partners
7	Feet		Directions	
8	Hands		Directions	
9			Levels	Small groups
10	Body parts		Levels	
11		Fast Slow		Equipment
12				Objects Space
13	Body parts		Levels	
14	Stretched shapes		Directions	
15				Objects People
Lessons—Grades 3–4				
16			Straight pathways Curved pathways	Small groups
17	Locomotion		Directions	
18	Hands		Directions	Space
19			Levels	Implements Partners

Table 8.13—*Continued*

Lessons—3–4	Body concepts	Effort concepts	Spatial concepts	Relationship concepts
20			Levels Directions	People
21	Extension Contraction	Force		
22		Force	Zigzag pathways	
23		Time	Straight pathways	
24	Twisting	Force		Equipment
25				Space
Lessons—Grades 5–6				
26	Body parts	Time	Directions	
27	Body parts			Cooperation
28	Body parts	Fine/Firm Time	Pathways Directions	
29	Twisting	Time Force		Offense Defense
30	Twisting Turning		Levels	
31	Wall shape Pin shape Transfer of weight		Levels	Copying
32	Fingers Forearms		Levels Directions	
33	Transfer of weight			Space Players
34		Force Time	Directions	Equipment
35		Force	Directions	Space Players

Summary

Games are exciting, complex activities. A wide range of skills is required by all children so they can make informed choices about which games they wish to play in a recreational setting. We advocate teaching variety to children from the beginning of the educational experience with games. Remember, it is games knowledge and competency in its widest sense which is the basis of an educational program.

> *The playing of games requires that the players be able to make motor adjustments as they interact with other players, game conditions and games equipment (Morris, 1980).*

Locomotor, nonlocomotor, and manipulative skills can be practiced separately in the early stages of learning, but should be integrated as soon as a reasonable degree of competency is achieved. Lessons may begin with practicing individual or combined locomotor skills, followed by integrating them with manipulative skills.

Children may choose to attend an afterschool program that focuses on a specific game. The community and sports associations may also provide training opportunities for a child interested in becoming, for example, a tennis player. The desire to become involved in such a program, which may make great demands on a young child's free time, should be a result of an enjoyable educational experience in school.

Review Questions

1. Differentiate between sport and games.
2. What is the relationship between low-organization, lead-up, and formal games? How does the emphasis on these games change throughout the school years?
3. What is meant by "fundamental games knowledge"?
4. Name the three categories of manipulative skills that form the basic vocabulary for games playing.
5. What are the four categories of formal games? What factors determine these categories?
6. What games situations can you think of that require considerable change(s) in body shape?

References

Bunker, D. & Thorpe, R. (1982). A model for the teaching of games in Secondary schools. *Bulletin of Physical Education, 18,* (1) 5–8.

Côté-Laurence, P., Drake, V., & Wilson, V. J. (1990). *Lesson plans for dance, games, and gymnastics to accompany* Children and movement: Physical education in the elementary school, J. Wall and N. Murray. Dubuque, Iowa: Wm. C. Brown Communications.

The Council on Physical Education for Children (COPEC) (1992). Developmentally appropriate physical education for children: A position statement. Reston, VA: AAHPERD.

Mauldon, E. & Redfern, B. (1981). *Games teaching* (2nd. ed.). London: Macdonald and Evans, Ltd.

Morris, G. (1980). *How to change the games children play* (2nd ed.). Minneapolis: Burgess Publishing Co.

Piggott, B. (1982). A psychological basis for new trends in games teaching. *Bulletin of Physical Education, 18*(1) 17–22.

Saunders, E. (1969). Some sociological aspects of rugby union football. *Physical Education Journal, 61,* 182.

Stanley, S. (1977). *Physical education: A movement orientation* (2nd ed.). Toronto: McGraw-Hill Ryerson Ltd.

Chapter 9
Teaching Games

Playing games is an important aspect of the North American life-style. Skillful games players are valued in our society, as can be seen by the high salaries paid to professional athletes and the correspondingly high prices we pay to watch baseball, football, hockey, tennis, and other sporting events. At an early age, many children have a favorite team game and are familiar with the skills and rules. These children are often "hungry" for games skills and opportunities to play.

School programs often place a greater emphasis on games than on dance and gymnastics. If our backgrounds are richer in the games area, we may feel more confident when teaching. The material of games is concrete; most games have specific forms; the products are easy to understand; and there is comparatively little freedom for individual variation of response. These factors can also contribute to our feeling more confident.

Some teachers feel games lessons are comparatively easy to teach, since "unlike dance and gymnastics, games are self-propelling. Once students grasp the basic concepts of a game, they require little intervention" (Graham et al., 1980).

Learning to play games well requires more than having the opportunity to play. Our task is no different from when we teach dance and gymnastics. We still have the responsibilities of designing the appropriate learning sequences, observing individual progress, and providing feedback so that all children "reach their full potential as skillful games players" (Logsdon et al., 1984). As for other movement forms, this is a large mandate. It means meeting the needs of everyone who comes to our lessons, "the gifted and talented, the slow learner, the less mature, the handicapped, the motivated, the disinterested and the average" (Logsdon et al., 1984). The big advantage when teaching games lessons is that many children come with more knowledge and personal experience.

To Do

In small groups, recall your own experiences in elementary school. List the kinds of activities you did, and then find out what percentage of your learning experience has been games oriented.

As an educator, what do you feel about an imbalance between the three movement forms?

Myths About Games Experiences

Games have been taught for many years because of their educational values: ideas of sportsmanship, honesty, conformity, loyalty, and learning to cope with defeat, as well as graciously and humbly accepting the laurels of success. Experience has led us to examine some of these tenets and to question the hidden curriculum which accompanies the teaching of games in school programs.

> *What the relationship is between rules in games and moral rules and principles of everyday life is a complex aspect of what is itself a highly controversial matter, namely how morality—and hence moral education—is to be characterised (Maulden & Redfern, 1981).*

The implied transfer of training does not occur. Because we may obey a referee, it does not follow that we will obey the law of the land. Notice how some professional players respond to referees. Willingly? Courteously?

Teaching Skills

A variety of skills is needed to teach games and many of these skills have been discussed in chapters 3 and 6. Here we wish to emphasize some skills that relate more specifically to the teaching of games:

Movement and positioning
Voice skills
Using whistles and gestures
Organizing children and equipment
Observing games playing
Evaluating
Participating

Movement and Positioning

Games are often taught in large spaces. We must be able to move swiftly from one area to another in order to visit the various groups of students as they practice and play. When children are spread out—and one of the joys of being outside is using the large space—walk briskly or even jog between groups (the exercise will be beneficial, too!).

When teaching outside, we can help the whole class attend to what we are saying and /or demonstrating by positioning ourselves so we face the sun. We want the children to see us clearly as we talk to them and demonstrate an aspect of the task.

Young children are easily distracted. When playing in an area shared with other children or with a street running alongside, they may be more interested in attending to other children or passing cars than the task. Whenever possible, place children with their backs to any distraction as they work. Make sure that when you speak to them, you face the distraction. If something exciting happens on the street (a fire engine races by), it is better to allow the children to look and talk about it rather than attempt to ignore it. The children's curiosity will be satisfied, and they will be more willing to return to the lesson.

Voice Skills

Teaching games demands much from our voices. Many of the activities are inherently noisy (e.g., balls bouncing on a hard floor), while others are played in spaces with poor acoustics (e.g., large gymnasia or the outdoors). Some of us have a hard time making ourselves heard.

Remember to be concise; think ahead and plan short statements. Moving to the middle of the teaching area reduces the distance the children have to travel if you decide to bring them close to you when you speak.

Take a deep breath before speaking, speak more slowly than usual, breathe out slowly as you speak and let the expired air "carry" the words. If there is a wind blowing, stand with your back to it, and use it to help carry the sound of your voice.

Vocabulary

There is a specific vocabulary related to games playing. We should know and use the correct terminology. For example, there are many words that mean to hit a ball: bat, bunt, kick, punt, putt, tap, volley. Variations in meaning may be subtle, and children need help to discriminate between them.

To Do

1. Discuss with a friend what you learned from playing games in school.
2. Has acquiring games skills and learning games influenced your behavior as a member of society as a whole?
3. Read chapters 1 and 2 in Mauldon and Redfern's book, and compare your discussion with their ideas.

To Do

The following situation may illustrate the kind of confusion that can result from being nonspecific:

Third grade children were playing in twos, each pair with a 7-inch playground ball. The task was to use their feet to send the ball to their partner. The children were fairly close together so strength was not a factor. The teacher told the children, "Pass the ball to your partner." All the children kicked the ball, and some used too much strength, and the ball went far beyond their partners. The teacher stopped the class and said, "Pass the ball, don't kick it." This had little effect on performance.

1. What did the teacher wish to change?
2. Reword the refining task so the children know how to modify their responses.

When we wish to refine the children's skills, we must be able to state the specific modification clearly and specifically, so the children know what is expected from them. If there is a choice of response involved, "pass the ball" may be correct. The children then have the freedom to kick, bounce, throw, or employ any other sending-away skill. We must decide very carefully how open the task is and what responses are acceptable, and then word the task so the children recognize the amount of freedom they have.

Using Whistles and Gestures

We can supplement our voices, and clarify our communication, by the sensible use of whistles and gestures.

Remember That

Children involved in playing together may take more time to be aware of your stop signal; make sure that it is obvious enough to attract their attention.

A good whistle is an essential piece of equipment, and skillful use of it is a great asset when teaching games. Learn to use it sparingly and appropriately. Like any instrument, there is a technique involved, and this means practice is needed. Always take a deep breath before blowing and control the expiration by using the tip of your tongue against the roof of your mouth.

Of course, a whistle is usually required when games are refereed; indeed, we will need several whistles when the children are learning to play the role of referee. Our discussion here is centered on using a whistle to help us communicate, rather than arbitrate.

Figure 9.1 Equipment arrangement for a sixth-grade class of 30 children.

Establish a system of signals gradually, beginning the first time you teach games activities to a class. A single short, sharp blast usually means "stop immediately"—this is probably the most important signal to establish. Two or three quick, short blasts may mean "come here." You can play "how quickly can you run to me" with kindergarten and first grade children, praising those who respond immediately to the sound. With older children use the same signal several times in a lesson, praising the children when they respond quickly.

It is important not to overuse the whistle and yet have distinct signals for different responses. Children become confused when the same signal means "stop" and "go."

Gestures and mimetic actions can be used very effectively to communicate ideas when outside or in a large gymnasium. If, for example, you wish the children to change from tossing and catching a ball to bouncing it at a low level, attract their attention (whistle) and mime or demonstrate the action. No words are needed. If you wish them to run to you, use large beckoning gestures and run in place. You will soon develop your own system, and the children may be able to help you create your gesture vocabulary.

To Do

How many synonyms can you find for the following games skills?

- Running
- Jumping
- Avoiding an opponent
- Sending-away ball
- Receiving a ball
- Traveling with a ball

Organizational Skills

Games lessons differ from dance lessons in that the majority of tasks in a lesson involve the use of some equipment. Because of this, considerable attention must be paid to organizing tasks when you plan your lessons.

Equipment

Storing balls, beanbags, ropes, etc. in portable boxes facilitates the carrying of equipment from one area to another.

Figure 9.2 Specified pathways for a running task.

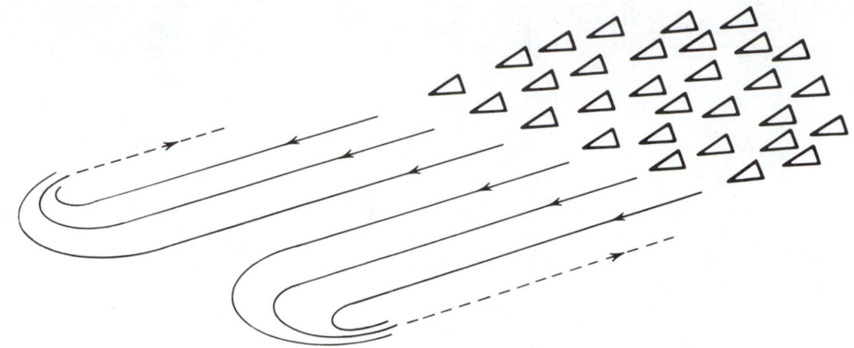

Once in the area where the lesson is to be held, have the children place the equipment in dispersed groups, so that when given an organizing task, such as "get a bat and ball," the class spreads out in the area. In figure 9.1, for example, the lesson includes using floor hockey sticks, plastic pucks, and ropes. The children begin the lesson working on their own, then they form groups of three. These groups of three combine for Part 3, the culmination of the lesson. Behind each bench (turned on its side) there are six sticks, six ropes, and six pucks.

When children finish using equipment, they should learn to replace it where they found it. In this way, unused balls will not roll across the playing area, and ropes left on the floor will not trip unsuspecting feet. Time is saved at the end of lessons because the children know where to find everything when putting the equipment away in the permanent storage area.

Using the Space

When the lesson is outside, it may be necessary to establish boundaries, especially if there is more than one class sharing the space. With older children, the boundaries can be described; younger children will need visible reminders, such as pylons, of their designated area.

Pathways in the general space may need specifying for safety reasons. The following two examples illustrate this:

1. The basic task is to roll a hoop and run around it. All children run in the same direction (figure 9.2).
2. The organizing task has the children in groups of three, each with a pylon, batting tee, plastic softball bat, and nerf ball. The applying task is for child *A* to hit the ball off the tee, and children *B* and *C* to field it and return it to the tee before child *A* runs around the pylon (figure 9.3). All groups are placed so that the batters hit away from the center of the space.

Remember That

In large spaces,

1. the combination of a whistle and clear gestures can be very effective.
2. there will be more occasions to bring the children in close to you when you wish to provide public feedback and/or give a new task.

Figure 9.3 Placement of batting tees.

Indoors

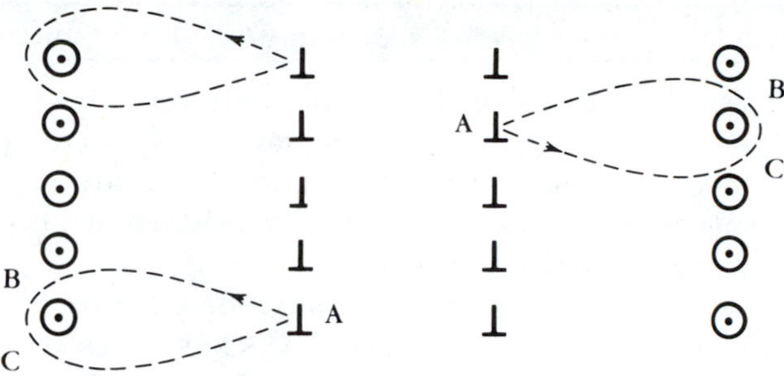

Outdoors

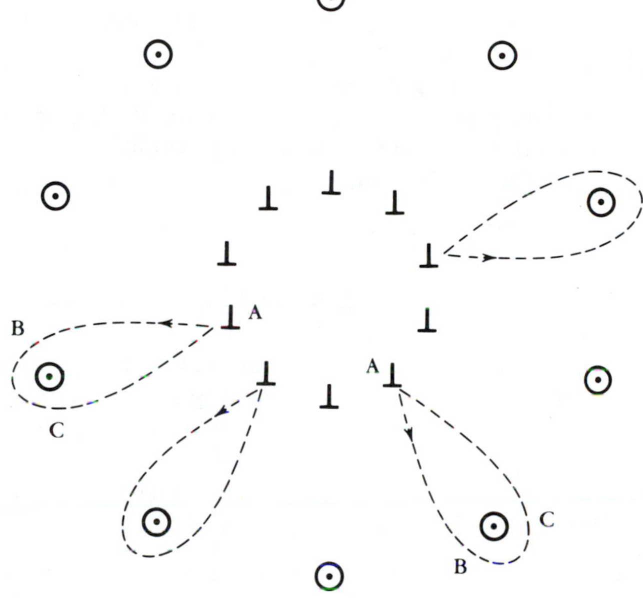

⊥ Batting Tee

⊙ Pylon

- - ➤- Pathway

Safety Tip

Children learning to control an object are less able to pay attention to where they are in space. It may, therefore, be necessary to designate the specific pathways or areas for them.

What Is Wrong With This Situation?

In a sixth grade games lesson, the children form groups of six to play floor hockey, with no goals. The task is to pass the puck between team members and prevent the opposition from intercepting it. The number of successful passes is to be counted. When five is reached, the other team begins with the puck.

Some children are in socks only, some are barefoot, and the remainder are wearing sneakers. Hockey sticks and pucks are stacked in one corner of the room. The teacher tells them to collect their equipment and begin their games.

What is wrong?

1. Children must wear sneakers for games activities. They are needed for protection from being stepped on, to cushion any kind of impact, and to provide a grip on the floor.
2. The equipment should be placed around the area for easy access, preferably one set for each group. Doing so is safer, increases the children's playing time, and spaces the children in the playing area.
3. The teacher should tell the children to keep their games within their own area.

Grouping the Children

Find a variety of ways to group the children, especially for tasks where the children perceive scores to be important. At no time should children be put into situations where they feel unhappy, as when captains are designated to choose teams. The less able or popular children are made to feel unwanted by being chosen last. Some ways to divide the class into groups include the following:

1. Count off in the number of groups needed; for example, a class of thirty children playing three against three floor hockey means there will be five games. Give each child a number one to five, and have all children of the same number collect in a designated space. You now have five groups of six children. Have pinnies for three children, so each subgroup of three is identified.
2. Divide the class according to alphabetical order, first or last names. This can be done before the lesson begins.
3. Group according to ability or height.

It is important to use a variety of methods, so the children expect to play with different people and, we hope, learn to accept players of differing abilities.

In many lesson plans, groups for Part 3 (Culmination) will evolve gradually during the lesson, as in the following sequence:

1. Children work individually.
2. They find partners or form groups of three.
3. The pairs or trios combine and play two versus two or three versus three.

Once children have formed their groups, avoid splitting them, (e.g., change from working with a partner to groups of three), because friction often arises.

Observing

We have already stressed that the first observational skill to use is scanning, followed by focusing (see chapter 3). If the children are working in their own space, select an area and observe the children working in that area. You can move "into" the group, still keeping the rest of the class in sight, and give individual and/or group feedback. The process is repeated by moving to a new area and observing a different group of children.

Observing Individual Skills

When the children are traveling, remember to stand "outside" the class and observe one or two children for a short time. Public feedback may be given as they continue the task, such as "John, you're keeping the ball close to you, that's good" and "Chris, go more slowly until you can keep the ball in front of you all the time." Alternatively, you may decide to stop individuals and speak privately to them.

Whatever games skill you are observing, watch the children's feet. Give plenty of refinement directed towards improving footwork because all games skills depend on the players being in the right place at the right time. Begin encouraging "moving feet" with your kindergarten children and continue to stress its importance at all levels of performance. In every lesson, some time should probably be spent on improving footwork by itself, as well as in combination with selected manipulative skills. Tag games, enjoyed by children of different ages, are excellent practice, but simply participating in such games is insufficient. It is possible to practice poor footwork!

Table 9.1 has been developed to help you observe the children as they practice games skills (Stanley, 1977). The table has two components, questions to ask yourself about the movement concepts/demands of the task and questions to ask about the children's responses. All the movement concepts will not apply to every task or game; therefore, you must select what is relevant.

Table 9.1

Observing Game Skills

Skills	Questions to ask yourself before you observe (*A*) and as you observe (*B*)	
Body management	**A** What are the *game demands* on the player's ability to 1. Shift weight? 2. Balance? 3. Use different activities? 4. Use specific body parts? 5. Bend, stretch, twist? 6. Change body shape?	**B** Responses observed
Effort	**A** What are the *game demands* on the player's ability to 1. a. Change speed? b. Move at constant speed? 2. a. Use force? b. Change the degree of force? 3. a. Move with flexibility? b. Move in a direct manner? 4. a. Move continuously? (free flow) b. Stop and start? (bound flow)	**B**
Spatial	**A** What are the *game demands* on the player's ability to 1. Change direction a. alone? b. with the ball? 2. Change level? 3. Travel in specific pathways a. alone? b. with a ball? c. with someone else? 4. Send ball along a specific pathway? 5. Receive a ball from different directions?	**B**
Relationship	**A** What are the *game demands* on the player's ability to 1. Relate to the playing area? 2. Relate to the equipment? 3. Relate to team members? 4. Relate to the opposition? 5. Relate to the referee?	**B**

Observing Games Playing

It is comparatively difficult to observe children playing complex games, to decide what is needed—at this moment—to improve the playing, and what action to take if you decide to stop the game. Since we are suggesting the children spend more of their lesson time playing games, it follows that more of our teaching must be done in the context of the game. This means we must be able to identify a skill or strategy that needs improving, stop the game, devise a practice or simplified game, give the players information in the form of refining tasks, provide descriptive feedback, and when we feel the children are ready, return them to the original more complex situation. This sequence of observation is shown in figure 9.4.

Teaching open skills demands a lot from us. The situation changes so quickly, and it is sometimes difficult to recall exactly what happened. Try to reconstruct the situation, so the children can examine what they did, and make suggestions about what changes are necessary.

Evaluating

Games are functional activities. Efficiency, or the quantitative aspects of movement, are important. In addition, however, games involve the understanding, development, and implementation of various strategies; the understanding and following of rules; and in the majority of games played, the ability to be a member of a team. Our methods of evaluation should reflect these components.

Because games are so functional, it may be easier to evaluate them rather than dance and gymnastics. It is, for example, comparatively easy to evaluate individual games skills from the quantitative point of view. The number of successful attempts at hitting a prescribed target or the speed at which a child can dribble a ball around markers is easily tallied. A team is often evaluated on its win-loss record. However, this may give an inaccurate and/or incomplete picture of the individuals making up the team. It is, therefore, an inappropriate evaluation technique in an educational program. When designing tools for evaluation, we should consider the means (movement patterns) of achieving functional results (movement skills). We need to attend to activity with and without equipment, and with and without other players.

Individual Skills

Young children will be evaluated on the performance of individual skills, with more attention paid to the movement pattern, (the qualitative aspects of the skill) than to the movement skill or result (the quantitative aspect of the skill). As the children mature, more attention is paid to the relationship between the movement pattern and the movement skill. Gentile (1972) produced a model which helps us understand the relationship between movement pattern and movement skill (figure 9.5).

This model has been translated into a form that may be used for evaluating children's performance, illustrated in figure 9.6. A simple tallying system will give you a percentage score.

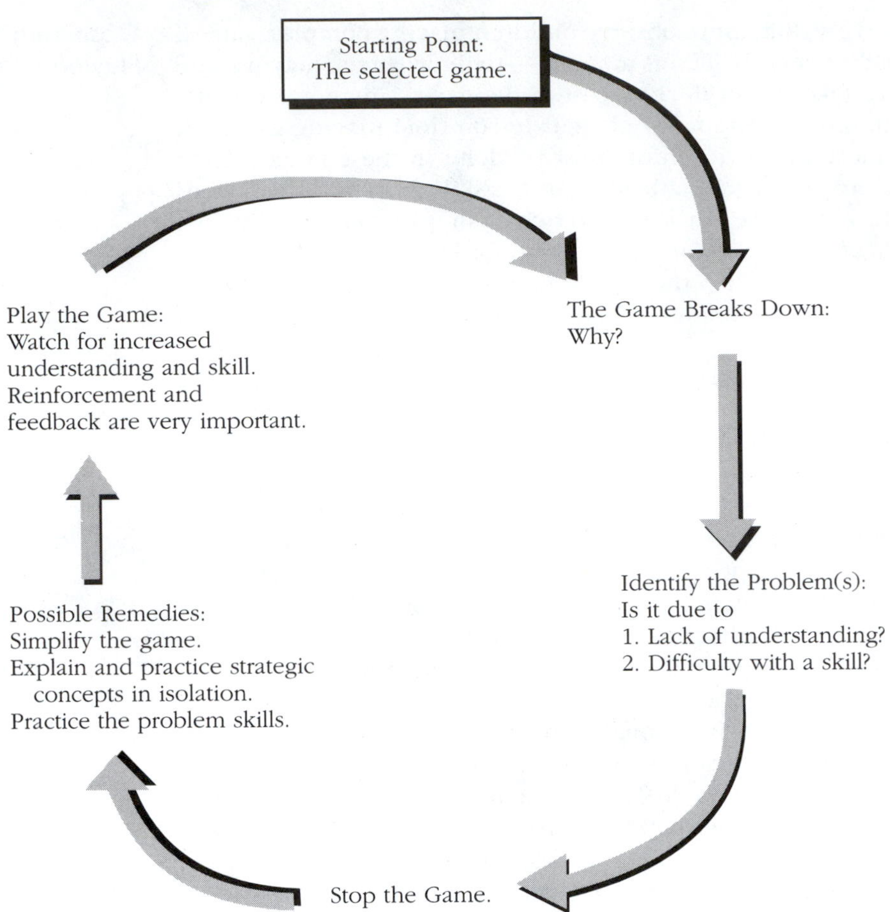
Starting Point:
The selected game.
The Game Breaks Down:
Why?
Identify the Problem(s):
Is it due to
1. Lack of understanding?
2. Difficulty with a skill?
Stop the Game.
Possible Remedies:
Simplify the game.
Explain and practice strategic concepts in isolation.
Practice the problem skills.
Play the Game:
Watch for increased understanding and skill.
Reinforcement and feedback are very important.

Figure 9.4 The observation cycle.
Modified from D. Jones, "Teaching for Understanding in Tennis" in Bulletin of Physical Education *18:1, 29–31, 1982. Used by permission.*

In this example, the child shows "skilled responses" only 25 percent of the time, i.e., the movement pattern and movement skill coincide, yet the movement pattern is consistent 68.75 percent of the time (sum of boxes 1 and 3). Careful observation will be needed to make the necessary adjustments to this child's performance. This kind of detailed evaluation may be appropriate once a year or if a particular child is having difficulty and you need specific information in order to provide specific help.

It is possible to evaluate several children at the same time, and figure 9.7 shows a tool developed to evaluate the aiming skills of a class of first graders. Lines are set at four, six, and nine feet (1.5, 2.0, and 3.0 meters) from the wall, on which there are clearly marked targets. Groups of four or five children work at this task, while the other children are set different challenges, working on a rotational system at stations.

		Movement Pattern Was the movement executed as planned?	
Movement Skill		**Yes**	**No**
	Yes	Everything's right!	Surprise!
Was the result the expected one?	**No**	What's wrong?	Everything's wrong!

Figure 9.5 Relationship between movement pattern and movement skill.
Adapted from A. Gentile, "A Working Model of Skill Acquisition with Application to Teaching," Quest *Monograph 17.3–23,* Learning Models and the Acquisition of Motor Skills. *Copyright © 1972 Human Kinetics Publishers, Champaign, IL. Used by permission.*

Grade: 3

Skill Observed: Aiming at target; paddle bat & ball

Name: Chris Martin

Date: Feb. 6 1990

Movement Skill	**Movement Pattern** Expected	**Movement Pattern** Unexpected
	Box 1	**Box 2**
Expected Result	XXXX 4	XXX 3
	Box 3	**Box 4**
Unexpected Result	XXXXXXX 7	XX 2
% Scores	Box 1: 4/16 (25%) Box 3: 7/16 (43.75%)	Box 2: 3/16 (18.75%) Box 4: 2/16 (12.5%)

Comments: Chris' movement pattern is consistent and has improved during the unit on net games. Attention needed on consistency of result.

Movement Pattern Consistency = 68.75% (Boxes 1 and 3)

Movement Skill = 43.75% (Boxes 1 and 2)

Figure 9.6 Evaluation of games skills.
Adapted from A. Gentile, "A Working Model of Skill Acquisition with Application to Teaching," Quest *Monograph 17.3–23,* Learning Models and the Acquisition of Motor Skills. *Copyright © 1972 Human Kinetics Publishers, Champaign, IL. Used by permission.*

Grade: ________ **Date:** ______________________________
Skill: ____

Names	**Movement Skill: Hits the Target**			**Movement Pattern**			**Comments**
	1.5m	**2.0m**	**3.0m**	**1**	**2**	**3**	
1.							
2.							
3.							
4.							
5.							
6.							
7.							
8.							
9.							
10.							

1—below what is expected for age and experience.

2—what is expected for age and experience.

3—above what is expected for age and experience.

Figure 9.7 Group evaluation.

When watching the children, you might first notice the children who stand close to the wall in order to be successful. Others may begin too far away and will miss the target every time. You will need to help everyone make a wise decision regarding where to stand. It is important that each child hits a target several times, so the motor pattern can be observed first in a "successful" situation. The children can then be encouraged to have several tries at a greater distance.

Games Playing Knowledge

Strategy and rules can be evaluated by asking questions. Some teachers decide to test the children's knowledge by giving tests at the end of a unit. Children's understanding of rules can also be determined by having them referee situations within class or in the intramural program. Some children thoroughly enjoy being involved in games while not actually playing the game. Children who have difficulties with ball handling skills may find great satisfaction in refereeing. You may establish a unit on selected refereeing skills, and the children can be evaluated on their ability to apply the rules and control a game. This is appropriate for children in the fifth and sixth grades. Because they may find it difficult to take charge of a game played by their peers, it is suggested that they begin helping with games played by children in grades 3 and 4.

Participating

Participating in children's games is a useful and enjoyable teaching technique. When doing so, remember to adapt to the skill level of the children with whom you are playing. This means you should still show good performance of the skills involved while being careful not to dominate the game. Our aim is to act as a *catalyst,* not to demonstrate our prowess.

When playing with the children, you can help distribute the play. You can provide encouragement for all players and stretch the children beyond their normal standard of play. Even when not playing all the time, by being part of the game you can redistribute the flow and involve some of the less-able players. Do not hesitate to stop the game, reposition the players, give a tactical task, ask a player to repeat a skill (and improve it!) and then continue the game as is suggested in figure 9.4.

Responsibilities

The score is an important part of any game; indeed it is the reason for the activity. However, the actual score achieved is relatively unimportant. What is important is the combination of skills culminating in the *act* of scoring. Concurrent with that is the combination of skills which may *prevent* the act of scoring. One of our roles in teaching games is to help the children appreciate skillful plays, both offensive and defensive, and help them derive satisfaction and pleasure from their participation in the game itself, rather than in the outcome.

We have a responsibility to "help children understand philosophical differences between the games they play and professional games shown on television. The professional is an entertainer and a wage earner whose play often reflects these facts" (National Task Force on Children's Play, 1979). Other responsibilities include

1. teaching a variety of basic skills;
2. changing the positional roles children play in a game, thus avoiding specialization;

Remember That

1. It is easier to catch a ball you have bounced off the wall or floor than one thrown by a peer.
2. A small object that you can grip firmly is easier to throw than a large object.
3. Young children find it difficult to track a green ball on grass; it is camouflaged!

3. praising skill improvement and reflecting this in our grading system (anecdotal reporting may be appropriate here);
4. emphasizing *learning* skills and *playing* games rather than the final result;
5. preparing the children for competition at intramural and interscholastic levels by providing good learning experiences, so they have the necessary skills and appropriate attitudes which will permit them to enjoy the competition (National Task Force on Children's Play, 1979).

These five "nutshell statements" may help us to focus on the children, so the play aspect of games remains important. The inherent competition should extend the children as they use their skills; it should not be used as a measure of their performance. We hope that children's enthusiasm for active participation in games activities remains with them throughout their lives.

Summary

Games playing is a complex movement form which demands quality teaching if the children are to become skillful and knowledgeable. One must be able to analyze the intricacies of strategy, as well as help the children acquire efficient movement patterns.

The teaching environment is not always sympathetic, and teachers have to be able to communicate well when outdoors, sometimes under very windy conditions when voices are truly tested. Develop and use a variety of skills that differ from those employed when teaching dance and gymnastics.

The quantitative aspect of games playing sometimes takes precedence over those less easily quantified. The evaluation system developed should reflect the multifaceted nature of the program.

Review Questions

1. Discuss organizational skills specific to the teaching of games.
2. When teaching outdoors, how can you attract the children's attention?
3. Why is it important to observe children's feet when they are playing games?
4. Why do we evaluate movement pattern rather than skill (result) when working with young children?
5. When we participate in children's games, it is to act as a catalyst. What is meant by this?

References

Gentile, A. (1972). A working model of skill acquisition with application to teaching. *Quest,* (27), 3–23.

Graham, G., Holt-Hale, S., McEwen, T., & Parker, M. (1980). *Children moving: A reflective approach to teaching physical education.* Palo Alto, Calif.: Mayfield Publishing Co.

Logsdon, B., Barrett, K., Ammons, M., Broer, M., Halverson, L., McGee, R., & Roberton, M. (1984). *Physical education for children: A focus on the teaching process* (2nd. ed.). Philadelphia: Lea & Febiger.

Mauldon, E., & Redfern, B. (1981). *Games teaching* (2nd. ed.). London: Macdonald and Evans, Ltd.

National Task Force on Children's Play. (1979). *Fair play codes for children in sports.* Ottawa: Canadian Council on Children and Youth.

Stanley, S. (1977). *Physical education; A movement orientation* (2nd. ed.). Toronto: McGraw-Hill Ryerson Ltd.

Chapter 10 Learning Experiences in Games

Considerable attention has recently been paid to the teaching of games in both school and community settings (Piggott, 1982, Bunker & Thorpe, 1982, and Riley, 1977). There has been concern about games being presented to children "as more or less complete discrete entities" (Piggott, 1982) and a generalized games sense being ignored, or unrecognized, and therefore undeveloped.

We have already indicated we consider the development of this general games sense to be the major objective of games teaching (see figure 8.1). It is through the playing of different games, related or not, that children learn about and understand the nature of *games playing*. This means that when new games are introduced, the players quickly perceive the strategies and players' roles. The acquisition of the specific manipulative skills (techniques) and knowing the rules of the selected game are the missing links (table 10.1).

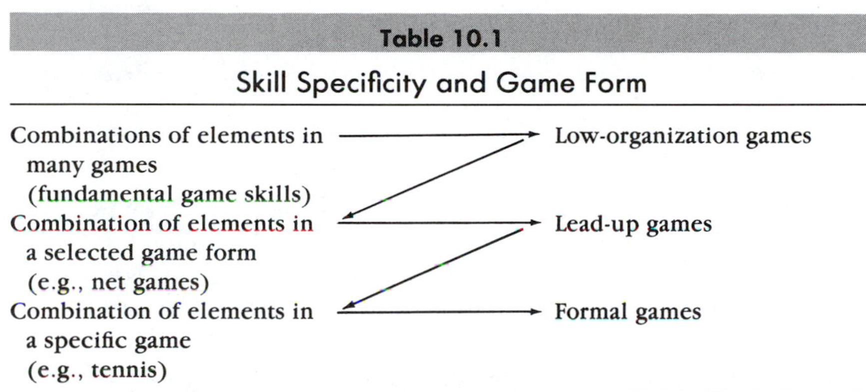

Table 10.1

Skill Specificity and Game Form

Skill specificity	Game form
Combinations of elements in many games (fundamental game skills)	→ Low-organization games
Combination of elements in a selected game form (e.g., net games)	→ Lead-up games
Combination of elements in a specific game (e.g., tennis)	→ Formal games

Progressive Learning

To develop the concept of games playing, we propose a departure from the usual games pattern established in many elementary and secondary schools. We suggest the following programming be used throughout the school years (table 10.2):

K–grade 2. Games and activities which focus on (1) the fundamental skills of games playing and (2) generalized knowledge of manipulative and nonmanipulative skills. This is achieved by learning and playing a wide variety of low-organization games, which include simple offensive and defensive strategies.

Grades 2–4. This is a transition period during which skill learning becomes more specific. Simple lead-up games, which require the application of combined games concepts, are introduced.

Fitness Fact

Tag games increase the heart rate, as does continuous rope jumping. To affect cardiovascular fitness, the activity should last for a minimum of three minutes.

Table 10.2

Game Type Selection for the Elementary School Program and the Link with the Secondary School Program

Grade	Emphasis on low-organization games	Emphasis on lead-up games	Emphasis on formal games
K	Major		
1	Major		
2	Major	Minor	
3	Equal	Equal	
4	Minor	Major	
5	*	Major	Minor
6	*	Equal	Equal
7	*	*	Major
8	*	*	Major
9	*	*	Major

**Denotes the game type is used to practice and reinforce specific game concepts related to the formal game selected.*

Grades 4–6. The sense of games playing is further developed by playing lead-up games related to the three most common kinds of formal games: net, batting, and running (see chapter 8). Equal emphasis on the three game forms is needed to develop an all-round playing sense.

Grades 6–8. We recommend selecting and focusing on *one* formal game from *each* game category, with the possible exclusion of target games for the reasons stated in chapter 8. This programming allows enough time for the children to develop competency in the selected games and to develop understanding and appreciation of the parameters of each game form. Which three games are selected will depend on your own experience and knowledge, the facilities and equipment available, and the interests of the community.

If possible, program parallel learning so that reference can be made to each game form. The focus of learning shifts from the general parameters of the lead-up games to the specifics of the selected formal game. Children in this age group are able to deal with the formal equipment, but the rules, sizes of playing areas, number of players, and length of the games will probably need modifying.

> *Experience has shown that a modified game promotes more efficient learning of skills, allows a more fluent pattern of play and, perhaps more important of all, provides more involvement and enjoyment for children of all abilities (Sleap, 1985).*

Grade 9 and up. Increase the students' repertoire by introducing additional games. A focus on lifetime games is recommended; target games may now be possible. Attention to individual talents and interests is paramount at this stage and, whenever possible, the children should be encouraged to select games they have a chance of playing after leaving school.

Many children are introduced to formal games too soon, well before they have the necessary physical, cognitive, and social maturity to be successful and have enjoyment. When there is little attempt to highlight the elements common to games playing, the specificity of focus minimizes the children's perception of games playing.

Lesson Planning

For lessons to be progressive and related to the needs of the particular children for whom you are planning, there must be realistic expectations based on your observation of the children in the games situation. As with the other areas of the program, it is unlikely that the same plan will be appropriate for any two classes or grade levels. We have already indicated a sequence for the selection of game type in table 10.2. Now we will examine some of the other factors which should be considered when designing learning sequences and selecting games for your lessons.

Relationships and Roles

The complexity of the relationships and roles must be appropriate for the developmental and experiential stages of the children. Remember, children gradually learn the skills required for cooperating and competing; therefore, we must structure tasks accordingly. Table 10.3 shows increasing complexity of relationships and how the environment changes from being more closed to more open as the number of players increases and both cooperation and competition are involved.

Table 10.3

Games-Playing Progression

Group size	Relationship(s)	Environment (More closed ↔ More open)
Alone	—	←
In pairs	a. Cooperative	←
	b. Competitive: One versus one	→
In threes	a. Cooperative	←
Two versus one	b. Cooperative and competitive: Two versus one	→
In fours	Cooperative and competitive: Two versus two	→
In sixes	Cooperative and competitive: Three versus three	→

Remember That

Games lessons provide plenty of opportunities for the children to make their own decisions regarding task and equipment. The following list shows the range from the teacher deciding on the equipment and task to the children making their own decisions.

Equipment		Task
1. Teacher selects (e.g., a rope)	and	Teacher specifies (e.g., "jump rope staying in your own area")
2. Teacher selects (e.g., a ball)	and	Children decide (e.g., free play with the ball)
3. Children select (e.g., choose either a stick and ball, or ball alone)	and	Teacher specifies (e.g., "Dribble the ball")
4. Children select (e.g., ropes, bats, sticks, balls, hoops available)	and	Children decide

To Do

Discuss other decisions that can be made by the children in their games lessons.

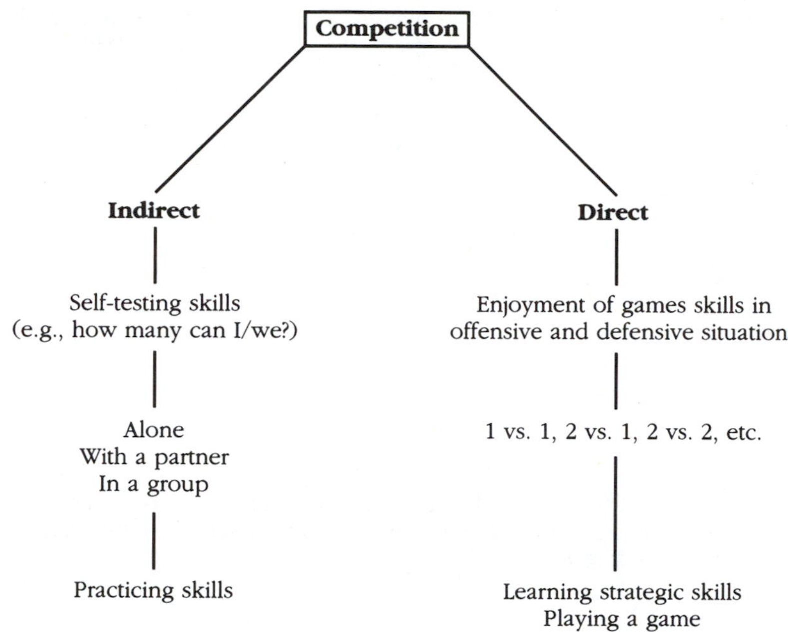

Figure 10.1 Direct and indirect competition.

Competition

Understand the kind of competitive challenges you are setting. There are two kinds of competition possible during games lessons (figure 10.1).

Direct competition is part of the activity and implies the use of offensive and defensive strategies. All net, batting, and running games are directly competitive, and also a few target games, such as curling and lawn bowling.

Indirect competition is a form of self-testing, because individuals really play against themselves and the physical environment. Most target games are indirectly competitive—examples are archery and golf. The scores are usually compared with those of others; at other times, they are compared with the player's own previous scores, as when handicapping in golf.

Many learning sequences designed for skill improvement include indirect competition. An example is the "how many can I or we?" kind of tasks. Indirect competition may be introduced to add a challenge, provide the children with some knowledge of their skill level, and encourage a little risk taking and add excitement.

Any direct competitive element should be added with discretion because, when introduced too early, the children become too concerned about the result, and the execution of the skills deteriorates and learning stalls.

Figure 10.2 Indirect competition—running task.

Needed: one ball, three pylons, four players (*A, B, C, D*). Players *A, B,* and *C* stand by a pylon, placed as in the diagram. Player *D* stands near player *A*.

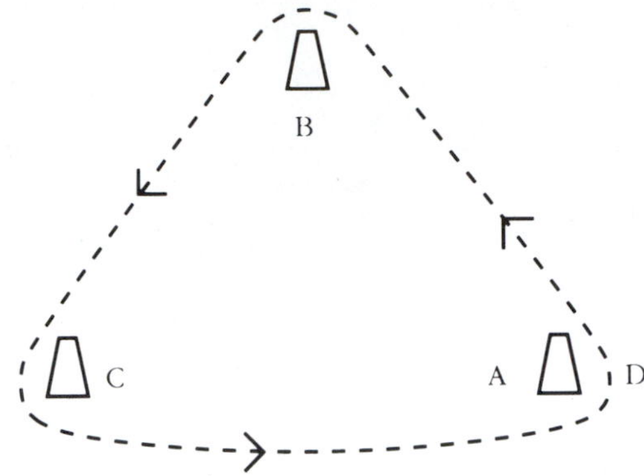

When player *A* calls "go!" the ball is thrown from *A* to *B* to *C* to *A*. Player *D* runs around the pylons from *A* to *B* to *C* to *A*, trying to reach "home" before the ball gets back to *A*. Players should rotate so that everyone has a turn running.

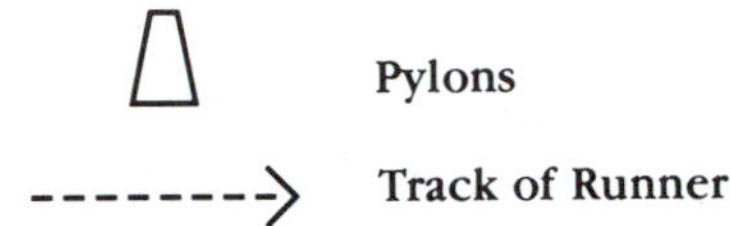

Fitness Fact

Throwing overarm requires flexibility in the upper body.

The following examples underline the fact that a degree of efficiency must be present before indirect competition is added, or the tasks will not be possible or enjoyable. Applying tasks, such as "Can you keep the ball in the air until I count to ten?" include indirect competition between the students and the teacher. A basic task designed to practice running around a designated track (as in batting games) challenges the children to outrun the ball as it is thrown around the bases (figure 10.2). The fielders are also challenged to throw accurately and catch well. The inclusion of indirect competition makes the learning situation more gamelike.

Movement Content

There are three points to remember when selecting the movement content for your lessons:

1. The movement content of all lessons must contribute to the objectives selected.
2. The movement content of the game(s) you select for the lesson must use the skills taught in the lesson. This suggests that you decide on specific aspects of games playing as the focus of your lesson and then find or create a game which uses them. This form

Table 10.4

Game Analysis

Game: Juggle a Number	Simplify	Extend
Game Focus: Keep balls in play		
Skill Objectives: a. Receive from and send to different players b. Speedy reactions c. Remember numerical sequence		
Skill Focus: Throwing and catching		Add traveling
Number of Players: Five	Reduce to three	
Organizational Pattern: Circle; players numbered at random 1 4 3 2 5	Numbered in sequence 1 5 2 4 3	Random formation
Equipment: Two seven-inch playground balls	Reduce to one ball	Smaller balls; increase group size by one
Rules/Limitations: If ball is dropped, continue with the one(s) in play. Game over when all are dropped.		

Source: Data from E. Schurr, *Movement Experiences of Children*, 3d ed. Copyright © 1980 Prentice-Hall Inc., Englewood Cliffs, NJ.

of planning is most appropriate with low-organization and lead-up games and when children are learning the fundamentals of games playing.

3. The skills taught in a lesson must relate to the game selected for Part 3 of the lesson (see chapter 4). When children are reaching the transition between lead-up and formal games, it is the game itself that directs the selection of content for Parts 1 and 2 of the lesson.

You will need to analyze the game you select for Part 3 of the lesson, in order to determine whether it is appropriate for that lesson. This may be done in different ways; one example is shown in table 10.4, where some headings are suggested and used to analyze the game Juggle a Number (Kirchner, 1985), a challenging low-organization game requiring quick reactions for throwing and catching, and a memory for a sequence.

Participation

Select games which allow maximum participation for all. Children should not be spectators during lessons. Ask yourself if all participants have an equal opportunity to play. In order to achieve this, there are some situations when you may wish to group the children according to ability or height. Participation can be increased by good organizational planning. Four ideas follow:

1. Have several small groups/teams instead of one large group.
2. Use maximum equipment, improvising if necessary, so children do not have to wait for a turn. Also use maximum space.
3. Avoid eliminating games; many games can be modified by counting negative points and playing to a predetermined score or time limit. At this point the game begins again.
4. Plan stations, each one with different equipment. The children rotate and use each station either in one lesson or over several. This organizational system is often used in gymnastics lessons.

Complexity

Select games which are easily explained and organized. Ask yourself how long it will take to get the game or activity started. If a lengthy explanation is needed, the game or activity is probably not appropriate. When the game is new to the children, you may be able to simplify it when introducing it, adding a complication or two as the children become familiar with its structure.

Indoors or Outdoors?

Teach games lessons outdoors whenever possible. Historically, most games have been played outside, and it is in comparatively recent times that indoor facilities have been available for the majority of games.

Key factors influencing your decision to play outdoors include

1. the size of the outside space available,
2. the kind of surface (grass, concrete, loose gravel),
3. the cleanliness of the area (free from litter, especially broken glass),
4. the grade of the area and if it is without potholes or other obstructions,
5. the fencing of the area to prevent equipment from "escaping" onto any nearby road.

The amount of distraction from pedestrians, dogs, and traffic may make you decide to teach indoors, although you may be more affected by the distractions than the children.

The weather, of course, is a major factor in your decision making. There are many sunny, cooler days in the fall when outside lessons would be very enjoyable if the children have warm clothing to put on. The lesson content may have to be adjusted as catching balls can be difficult when small hands are hidden in gloves, but striking is possible and balls can be controlled by feet. Plenty of vigorous activity for everyone and short rests should be included, with minimal time spent giving instructions. The lesson could even be cut short if any children appear cold.

Remember That

Young children sometimes feel "lost" in large spaces. Physical boundaries (e.g., benches, pylons) that identify the playing area help them "know where they are."

Extra care is needed to organize the carrying and collecting of the equipment. Specific children can be responsible for helping you do this. When taking kindergarten and first grade children outside, it is a great help to have an older child assist. Some schools have leadership groups for grades 5 and 6, and one of their learning experiences could be to help with the physical education lessons for the lower grades.

The game form may also dictate whether the lesson is indoors or outdoors. Some schools have fixed basketball hoops in the playground, others may have portable hoops. Few schools have portable fixtures for nets needed in net games (badminton, tennis, volley ball); therefore, the use of improvised equipment is needed whether teaching indoors or outdoors. Do not, therefore, be restricted by the existing conditions or what has been done before. If you wish to have your lesson outdoors and there is a suitable area, you will find the means of doing so.

Sometimes a lesson plan is appropriate for either an indoor or an outdoor setting. If it is not and your plan is designed for outdoors, it is advisable to have an alternative plan in case the weather is unsuitable. A minor adjustment may be all that is needed, but it is better to have it thought out beforehand. The sample lessons in this chapter state whether they are designed for indoors or outdoors. It is mainly the organizational procedures that will have to be changed; the tasks should need very little adaptation.

Safety Tip

Outdoor playing areas often have two or more different surfaces. Place your lesson away from the junction of different surfaces.

Created Games

Children should be given the opportunity to create their own games or to modify a game they already know. Created games allow the children to select which skills they wish to practice and also develop strategies and rules required for enjoyable games playing.

Children may be given almost free choice or some limitations and a problem to solve, for example, the number of players, the equipment to use, the skills to include, and the space in which to play. In both situations, the children may need help in clarifying their intentions and pinpointing problems which arise as they play. The complexity of the problem set, of course, depends on the capabilities of the children.

Table 10.5 is an example of a problem set a fourth grade class which has an understanding of running games. Schurr (1980) points out that it is when children have an understanding of games playing and "experience in variations of each component, and opportunities to make variations of known games" that they are able to create new games.

Safety Tip

Keep boundaries for games well away from walls and other objects in the teaching space.

Fitness Fact

Games played in small areas and needing quick footwork, many changes in direction, and the ability to stop and start suddenly, require leg strength, and muscle endurance.

Table 10.5

Creating a Game

Game form:	Running games soccer hockey (ice or field)
Skill objectives:	To send the ball ahead of the receiver Players to be on the move
Skill focus:	Running Striking Your choice
Number of players:	Three
Organizational pattern:	Your choice
Equipment:	Either: a. Seven-inch playground ball or b. Three plastic hockey sticks and a three-inch plastic ball
Rules/Limitations:	Your choice

Source: Data from E. Schurr, *Movement Experiences of Children, 3d ed. Copyright © 1980 Prentice-Hall Inc., Englewood Cliffs, NJ.*

Progressions

Long-term plans are needed to ensure the kind of progressive teaching that leads to competency in games playing. You must recognize the children's past learning. To do this, you need to know the content of the games lessons in the previous year. If there are several teachers responsible for physical education in your school, it will be helpful for you—and beneficial for the children—to coordinate your long-term planning. Table 10.6 is an example of a plan developed for a seven-year program leading to selected formal games that the children will begin in grade 5 and continue in the first years in the secondary school. It should be comparatively easy to make adjustments to the plan and substitute other formal games.

Enjoyment

Finally, and just as important as the previous factors, the tasks and games should be enjoyable for the children. Remember, not all children enjoy the same game, and it may be possible to select two or three games with similar skill objectives and skill focuses and allow the children to choose which game they play. An alternative is to ask the children to design their own game(s).

Table 10.6

Progression to Formal Games: A Seven-Year Plan

K–Grade 2	
Net games:	Generalized nonmanipulative skills. Variations in striking with no differentiation of game form (i.e., use hands, feet, implements). When striking with hands, use fairly large, lightweight balls such as balloons, beach balls, bladders of volleyballs. Bright colors are enjoyed by children. Cooperative play and low-organization games in twos and threes.
Batting games:	Generalized nonmanipulative skills. Striking, throwing, and catching skills using a variety of implements and objects. Use hands, or an implement to strike stationary ball off a support or tee. Low-organization games in groups of three: one batter, two fielders. Change places after a predetermined number of turns; individual or no scoring.
Running games:	Generalized nonmanipulative skills. Use of feet and implement to strike, stop, travel with, and propel a ball. Use targets for aiming and obstacle courses for propelling. Sending and receiving in groups of two or three. Taglike games that include balls. Develop the ability to run with the ball, stop, change direction and speed, and make floor patterns.
Grades 2–4	
Net games: Volleyball	Low-organization and lead-up games, which emphasize striking objects with hands; still use lightweight balls. Introduce indirect competition, e.g., "How many times can you 1. hit the ball against the wall, 2. keep the ball going over a net to your partner?"

Continued

Table 10.6 Continued

Progression to Formal Games: A Seven-Year Plan

Grades 2–4	
Net games: Volleyball Continued	Develop 1. fundamental skills of run, jump, hit up, hit down. 2. basic strategies of a. hitting to a space b. positioning in relation to the ball. Games of two versus two and three versus three, to maximize participation and teach cooperative and competitive skills.
Batting games: Softball	Low-organization and lead-up games, which include running, striking, throwing, and catching skills. When introducing pitching in a game, begin with cooperative pitching; i.e., have a member of the batting team pitch. Include batting off a tee when you wish to focus on running and fielding skills.
Running games: Soccer	Low-organization and lead-up games, which require skilled footwork and controlling a ball with feet. Aim ball at both undefended and defended targets/ spaces. Begin goalkeeping skills in one versus one and two versus one situations. Use playground and large plastic balls that "run" easily on the playing surface.
Grades 4–6	
Net games: Volleyball	Lead-up and modified formal games with boundaries, scoring, and selected rules of volleyball. Increase the size of the playing group as the skills develop. Be prepared to decrease if the game breaks down or you introduce a new element. Slightly underinflated volleyballs can be introduced as the hands (particularly the fingers) become larger and stronger.

Table 10.6 Continued

Progression to Formal Games: A Seven-Year Plan

Grades 4–6	
Batting games: Softball	Play lead-up games that include running around a diamond, which is considerably reduced in size. Introduce selected softball rules and team scoring. Groups of eight or ten (four vs. four, five vs. five) are probably the maximum for participation to remain high. If batting skills are weak, a. hit off tee b. change the bat c. have fungo batting—the players toss the ball for themselves to hit. d. continue with cooperative pitching.
Running games: Soccer	Groups of six-ten players (three versus three, four versus four, five versus five). Lead-up and modified versions of soccer. Games with boundaries, reduced playing area, small goals, selected soccer rules. Introduce regulation soccer balls when strength and skill level warrant it. Until then, give children a choice of balls when playing.

Lesson Plans

The lesson plans that follow are designed to show the changing expectations and skill progressions as the children become more experienced. To do this, the net games form has been selected, and three lessons are planned, one for each stage of the games program. You will notice how the tasks in the lessons gradually become more volleyball-like. The lesson plan book that accompanies this text has many other examples of lessons.

The first lesson is for grade 1 children who have minimal experience in striking a ball with their hands; consequently, the children work alone. Cooperative tasks in pairs should be introduced as soon as ball control is such that pair work is appropriate. In the early learning stages, joining with a partner is an extending task. As ball control increases, basic tasks in pairs are appropriate. This will be seen in the Lesson Plan 2.

Fitness Fact

Throwing for distance requires strength and flexibility. Children may be given a choice of ball size and weight as their strength increases.

Lesson Plan 1

- Topic: Games
- Skill Focus: Striking skills, running, jumping
- Grade: 1
- Time: 20 minutes
- Equipment: One rope per child
  Eight-inch ball per child (plastic or foam)
  Ten hoops
- Place hoops around edge of area, three ropes and three balls in each hoop.
- Lesson held outdoors
- Objectives: The children will be able to
  1. strike ball using different body parts,
  2. position themselves in relation to returning ball.
- Movement Concepts: Figure 10.3.

Figure 10.3 Movement concepts—Lesson Plan 1.

A.

Manipulative Skills: Striking		
Body Concepts Body Parts: Hands and feet to strike the ball		
Effort Concepts	**Spatial Concepts**	**Relationship Concepts**
Changing amount of force	Up	Alone

B.

Nonmanipulative Skills: Running, Jumping		
Body Concepts Activities: Running, jumping		
Effort Concepts	**Spatial Concepts**	**Relationship Concepts**
Resiliency	Change of direction	Alone Large group

Tasks	**Teaching Tips**
Part 1	
Organizing Get a rope and find a space.	Praise quickness and good spacing.
Basic Free activity with the rope.	Look for three different jumps: both feet; one foot to same (hop); one foot to other. Describe the variations.
Refining If traveling, look for the spaces. Bouncy jumps. Strong push off from feet. Keep arms away from body when turning rope.	Select one for demonstration and lead into extending task.
Extending (Having watched a child who was hopping.) Hop three times on one foot and three on the other.	The children may tire quickly. Give them a rest, feedback (encouragement, praise); you may do the activity with the children.
Simplifying Without your rope, hop three times on one foot, then the other.	Use if some children have difficulty.
Refining Hold free leg bent. Make it a "strong" leg. "Big" turn of rope.	
Extending Travel through the space.	Concentration shifts from self to the general space; this is relaxing.
Refining Run on toes. Springy run.	Stop and respace children if they crowd together.

Organizing Fold rope in half, and place it on the floor; sit at one end.	Ensure ropes are spaced far apart.
Basic On "go," run around rope and sit down.	Comment on those "home" quickly. Notice (without comment) who is last, watch to see if he or she is faster next time; if so give praise.
Refining Small running steps. Keep close to rope. Strong "brake" leg when changing direction.	Repeat the task three or four times before changing the task.

Part 2

Organizing Put your rope way in a hoop and take a ball; sit in your own space.	The equipment should be arranged around the space. The children exchange the rope for a ball.
Basic Use hands to hit ball into the air; catch it.	Good spacing is essential because the children will be watching the ball, not each other.
Refining Be ready to run to the ball. Watch it and move under it as it drops. Have your hands ready to catch ball.	If the balls are hit with abandon restrict the height. As control increases, move to extending tasks.
Extending Use a different body part to strike the ball.	Name body parts used successfully (e.g., elbows, head, thighs, wrist).
Refining Gentle hits, especially if balance is difficult.	Provide more individual feedback.

Extending Try several hits before catching.	Watch the spacing.
Refining Be ready to move under the ball. Watch ball as it comes down.	
Applying Choose two parts, hit alternately.	Comment on successes and improvement, especially if a child has chosen a difficult combination.
Refining Small, gentle hits. Move to the ball.	Task requires control of force.

Part 3

Organizing Put the balls away in the hoops. Fetch a rope; make a circle on the floor. This is your rabbit hole.	Return balls to same hoops. Good spacing necessary.
Basic Running game—Rabbits and Holes. On "Go" run around other "holes;" On "Rabbits" return to your own hole and sit.	
Refining Look for others as you run. Slow down if you think you are going to bump into someone.	Speed is not important, but awareness of space is. Repeat two/three times before extending.
Extending On "Foxes" sit in nearest hole.	Name two/three children who quickly find a circle and sit.

Refining

Zigzag among the circles so you are close to one all the time.
Use small steps so you can stop quickly.

Name different children who quickly find a rope.
Repeat several times.

Organizing

Fold ropes and put them away where you found them.

Possible Progressions

Safety Tip

1. Check that all shoelaces are tied tightly.
2. Children who wear glasses should be encouraged to have safety straps. If you wear glasses, help by wearing a safety strap when you teach games and gymnastics.

The skill level achieved at the end of this lesson will determine the content of the next lesson. You may decide to repeat it in almost the same form, perhaps finishing with a low-organization game which uses some of the ball skills practiced. Or you may decide to challenge the children a little more by designing basic tasks from the extending tasks. An alternative is to design new basic tasks by changing the equipment, adding a partner, or changing the conditions, such as striking the ball against a wall.

In your long-term plan, you may have decided to rotate the three games forms, in which case the next lesson will include completely different content. Whichever plan you select, make sure that all the fundamental skills and each game form receive equal emphasis over the period of time allotted to games lessons. To help you do this, a record chart might be a useful addition to your plan book. If you teach more than one grade, it becomes a necessity. Figures 10.4 and 10.5 are two such charts; however, design whatever meets your needs.

The content of Lesson Plan 2 is designed for a third grade class. Again, the lesson is designed for outdoors, but it can easily be transferred to an indoor setting. The one outdoor requirement is a wall against which balls can be hit. Many gymnasia have uncluttered wall space, but it may be difficult if your lesson is held in another area of the school. In this case, a substitute task will be needed.

All the tasks require the children to work with others. Initially, they will work with partners, then two pairs join and small groups of four are formed. Usually, children choose with whom they will work; however, in this lesson, height is a factor in the second basic task. When the children pick their partners, you may wish to explain the nature of the second task and suggest they choose someone who is of similar height. An alternative is to ask the children to line up in order of height and pair them yourself.

Grade: 2
Teacher: Mr. Chen

Date: Sept. - Dec. 1993

Skills	Net Games	Batting Games	Running Games
Striking			
Throwing			
Trapping			
Catching			
Propelling			
Carrying			

Comments:

Figure 10.4 Record chart 1 —Manipulative skills.

Grade: 1
Teacher: Mrs. Aguirre

Date: Sept. - Dec. 1993

	Sending-Away			Receiving		Traveling
Lesson	**Net**	**Batting**	**Running**	**Batting**	**Running**	**Running**
1	Volleying with hands					Bounce ball and walk
2	Paddle bats	✓		✓		
3		Throw at wall		Toss and catch in twos		
4			Kick ball at wall		Kick ball and run after it; trap it with feet	
5						

Figure 10.5 Record chart 2 —Manipulative skills.

Lesson Plan 2

- Topic: Games
- Skill Focus: Striking, quick footwork
- Grade: 3
- Time: 40 minutes
- Equipment: Seven-inch plastic ball for each pair of children
- Objectives: The children will be able to
    1. volley continuously with a partner; in groups of four,
    2. bounce ball so it rebounds high,
    3. jump for a ball; move to a ball.
- Movement Concepts: Figure 10.6

Figure 10.6 Movement concepts—Lesson Plan 2.

A.

Manipulative Skills: Striking		
Body Concepts Activities: Volleying, bouncing Body Parts: Hands, fingers		
Effort Concepts	**Spatial Concepts**	**Relationship Concepts**
Strong actions Sudden accent when striking	Up Down Forward	Over/under the ball

B.

Nonmanipulative Skills: Running, Jumping		
Body Concepts Body Parts: Feet, legs Actions: Bending/stretching when jumping		
Effort Concepts	**Spatial Concepts**	**Relationship Concepts**
Explosive action	Small steps Change of direction in personal space; i.e., forward, backward, sideways	Cooperation in twos, fours Taking turns/rotating

Tasks	**Teaching Tips**
Part 1	
Organizing Find a partner; stand in a good space.	
Basic *A* runs and tries to lose *B,* who is the "shadow." On signal, stop.	Encourage the children to stay in a small area. Have short bursts of activity; stop and give some refinement. Change roles after two to three turns.
Refining *A:* Swerve, change pathway often. Quick feet, small steps. Use upper body when swerving. *B:* Use arms to help you balance. Watch *A* and try to anticipate changes. Quick feet, small steps.	Refinement is needed for both players.
Basic Face each other; *A* jumps and tries to see over *B*'s head.	Encourage the children to pair with someone of similar height. Some may need to change partners. Children should not touch each other; help adjust distance between them.
Refining Bend knees before take off. Upward arm swing will help jump. Take off from both feet. Firm, straight body in air.	Bent arms, which thrust upward at moment of take off, will add "lift" to body.

Part 2

Organizing One player gets a ball; other finds a good space.	Balls are distributed around the area for easy access.
Basic *A* tosses ball and volleys it high for *B* to catch overhead.	Encourage the children to hit the ball when it is above the head, palms up, fingers pointing backwards. Some children will be ready for this before others.
Refining Toss ball straight up before volleying. Hands under ball to strike. Keep under ball. Watch it carefully.	
Extending Volley twice before partner catches.	When children are able to volley straight up, eliminate catching.
Refining "Lively" feet. Move away when you have volleyed, so your partner can move under the ball.	
Applying How many times can you volley? Try to repeat the same number or try to increase.	The focus is on consistency of response. You may find a pair achieving five volleys; set that as the challenge for the class.
Refining Select from previous tasks.	It is important to recognize consistency and improvement publically.
Organizing Find your own space along the wall.	Space pairs apart. If space is limited, have half the class bounce in hoops (figure 10.7).

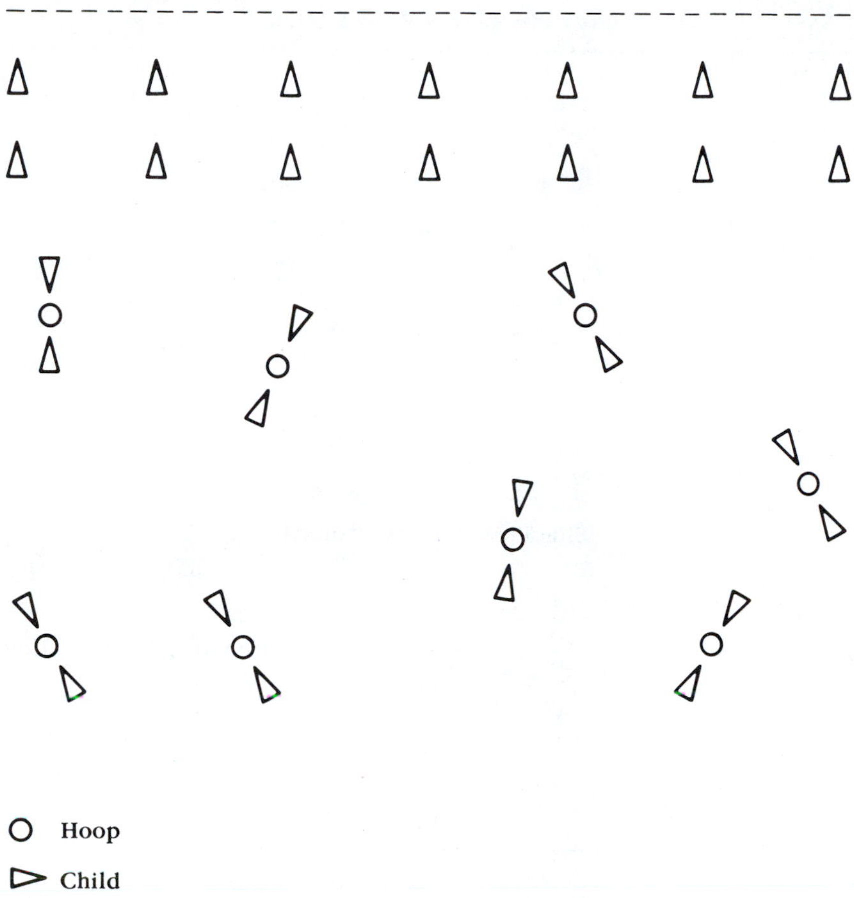

Figure 10.7 Organization of a class of 30 children.

Basic

A bounces ball so that it rebounds off the wall for *B* to bounce ball so that it rebounds.	Try to keep the ball in the same place, so children are in front of each other rather than side by side (figure 10.8).

Refining

Use fingers to push ball down.
"Bouncy" arms as you push.
Aim ball firmly toward area at foot of wall.
Move away after bouncing; be ready to move into place for turn.
Jump for ball if it is high.

Figure 10.8 Relationships of players.

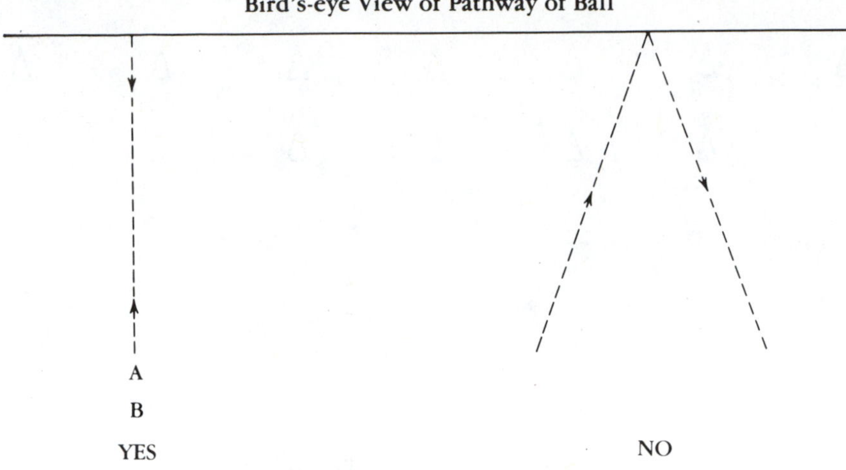

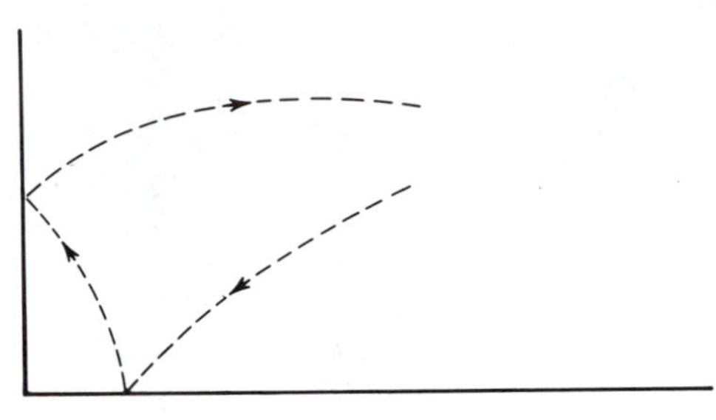

---➤— Pathway of Ball

Part 3

Organizing
Join with another pair.
Put one ball away.

Extending
Continuous bounce-rebound;
"Keep the kettle boiling."

Refining
Select from previous tasks. Emphasize moving toward/away from ball.

Praise jumping and bouncing ball from a height. (This is the beginning of spiking.)

Applying	
In your groups, either (1) see how many times you can bounce-rebound or (2) volley ball high and see how many times your group can pass the ball.	Observe agility; praise good footwork (i.e., moving to/from the ball). If any group is unable to cope, split into pairs. Ask scores as you visit each group; help children monitor their performance. Avoid comparisons with other groups.
Organizing	
Collect the balls.	This is a time when you can provide individual feedback or discuss the tasks with the whole class before putting the equipment away.

Possible Progressions

The follow-up lesson for these children might include the addition of a net of some kind, so the volleying is over a barrier separating the partners. The barrier could be a lowered volleyball net, badminton nets, or ropes hung between jumping standards. Some objects must be hung from a single rope, so it is easily visible.

When the children can volley continuously, they are ready for an element of competition. The task "volley 4 times and then make your partner run for the ball" shifts from indirect to direct competition. This is repeated several times with little or no attention paid to a score, just the successful completion of the task. Making the partner run may involve placing the ball well to one side or hitting it higher and harder, so it goes behind the player.

As skill level increases, all tasks become more gamelike, as several skills are combined and simple rules are introduced. More time will be spent on applying tasks. This is shown in Lesson Plan 3.

The formal game of volleyball is easily identifiable in Lesson Plan 3. The organization involved is considerable because it includes the erection of a volleyball or badminton net and jumping standards and ropes. If the playing space is large enough, it may be possible to do some of the preparation before the lesson begins (figure 10.9). Having the volleyball/badminton net in place is a great help. Remember to adjust the height of the net to suit the height of the children. The net must be high enough to encourage an upward, rather than a forward, flight of the ball. A rough measure is the finger tips when the arms are fully extended.

Remember That

Once children have formed groups, they will be reluctant to split and reform groups with different people. Keep this in mind when planning your organization. We recommend grouping in multiples of two or three as follows: alone, with a partner, then in fours or sixes; alone, in threes, then sixes.

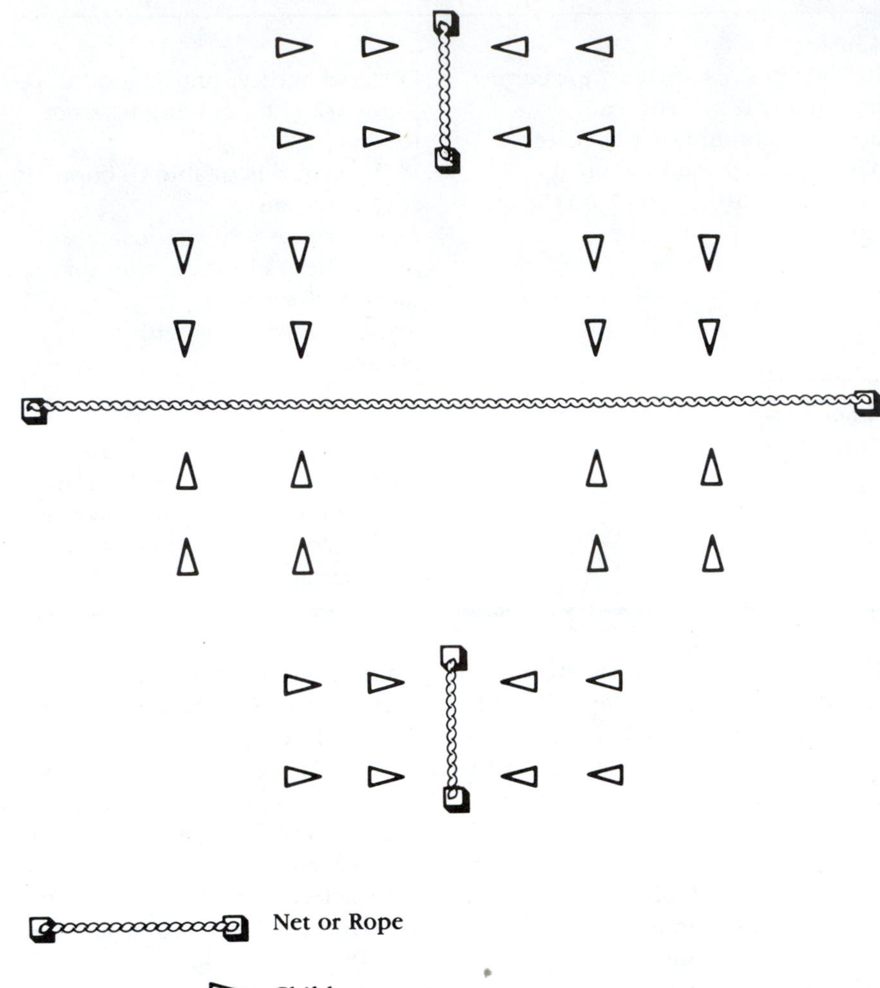

Figure 10.9 Organization of equipment for 32 children.

As in the previous two lessons, the focus is on skill development and cooperation in small groups. The tasks themselves are sufficiently challenging, and any added competitive factor might detract from skilled performance. The children are set tasks in which they use their skills and can monitor success though indirect competition ("How many can I/we. . . ?" situations). Satisfaction, a sense of achievement, and enjoyment are some of the feelings that should result. Direct competition can be added in the follow up lesson by using the same skills in different applying tasks.

In this 40 minute lesson a minimum of twenty minutes should be spent on the final applying task. This should increase in subsequent lessons which focus on the same formal game.

Lesson Plan 3

- Topic: Net games (indoors)
- Skill Focus: Striking, positioning, cooperation
- Grade: 5
- Time: 40 minutes
- Equipment: One volleyball (or similar) for each student
  Volleyball/badminton net, four jumping standards, two long ropes
- Objectives: The children will be able to
  1. volley and bump continuously, both alone and in small groups,
  2. position themselves in relation to the oncoming ball,
  3. rotate the playing sequence in a group of four players.
- Movement Concepts: Figure 10.10

Figure 10.10 Movement concepts—Lesson Plan 3.

A.

Manipulative Skills: Striking		
Body Concepts Activities: Volleying, bumping Body Parts: Forearms, fingers		
Effort Concepts	**Spatial Concepts**	**Relationship Concepts**
Strong actions Continuity	Up Down	Under the ball Over the ball

B.

Nonmanipulative Skills: Running		
Body Concepts Actions: Crouching, extending Body Parts: Awareness of feet (footwork)		
Effort Concepts	**Spatial Concepts**	**Relationship Concepts**
Strong take-off Fast running	Specific pathways	Cooperation Partners Groups of four Rotation within the group

Tasks	Teaching Tips
Part 1	
Organizing Find a partner; one gets a ball and the other finds a space.	
Basic Run and bounce the ball to each other. Only one bounce is allowed.	A demonstration may be needed. One student will probably be using left hand and the other uses the right hand.
Refining Adjust your speed so you keep level with each other. Keep fairly close together. Use fingers to push ball. Slight twist in upper body to face ball. Bounce ball slightly ahead of partner.	Stress that this is not a race; the challenge is to keep ball under control. Some "traffic control" may be necessary (e.g., pairs traveling in same direction the length of the area) (see figure 9.2).
Extending Change sides and use the other hand. Increase speed when you feel ready.	
Refining Select from previous tasks.	
Part 2	
Organizing Fetch another ball Find a good space and face each other.	
Basic Bounce your own ball; change places and catch your partner's ball.	Children must make it possible for their partners to catch; the bounce must be of reasonable height.

Refining Bounce ball vertically. Begin fairly close together. As the distance increases, prepare feet for a sudden start.	
Extending Increase the distance between you.	
Refining Watch your partner to know when to bounce. Reach for bouncing ball.	One player may need to say "Go"; suggest this only if there is a problem with timing.
Organizing Move into your own space.	
Basic Toss ball into air, volley ball once, twice with both hands, then catch.	You may wish to use volleyball terminology (i.e., two-hand overhand pass or set shot).
Refining Position yourself under the dropping ball. Bend knees before striking. Feet astride. Hands ready above face.	
Extending Volley several times before catching. Toss to the side or in front, so you have to move your feet and reposition.	
Refining Hands together, fingers flexed and spread.	
Applying How many volleys can you do?	Have three or four turns and encourage the children to "beat their own records." Recognize achievement and improvement.

Organizing Find some wall space.	If wall space is limited, half the class continues to volley, other half begins new basic task; then change over.
Basic Toss ball against wall so that it rebounds; hit it off your forearms.	
Refining Hit ball when it is about waist level. Crouch and get arms underneath the ball so it bumps off your arms. Keep arms straight and strong. If using both arms, clasp one hand in the other.	

Part 3

Organizing Make groups of four; put three balls away.	
Extending Forearm volley around the group.	This may be random, or the children may decide on a specific sequence. If the ball is dropped, the player begins by tossing and volleying.
Refining Anticipate the ball's movement. Move to the ball as it comes. Crouch and get forearms under ball. Follow through in an upward direction.	Encourage high flight of ball.
Organizing Join another group; put one ball away. One group each side of net (shown in figure 10.9).	A diagram on the board or a large card will help clarify the organization. One group may also demonstrate.

Applying	
Volley or bump ball across the net and try to keep it going. After a few turns begin rotating places.	Select one rotation pattern for this lesson. The pattern may change in the next lesson. See figure 10.11 for rotation variations.
Refining	
Anticipate when and where to move. Keep knees slightly bent, so you can easily move in any direction. Hit under the ball and follow through in an upward direction. Watch the ball right onto fingers or forearms.	
Extending	
If rotations *B* or *C* is chosen, reverse the route. (This may be too much for first lesson.) Add a second ball.	Help the players understand what happens to the feet when direction is changed; for example, the push-off foot becomes the "brake," the body weight shifts, etc.
Organizing	
Put away the net and ball you have used.	

Possible Progressions

Some variations in basic tasks might be introduced together with another skill, such as serving, or another dimension to setting and bumping, such as hitting a specific target or sending the ball so that the receiver has difficulty either in catching the ball or volleying.

A different lead up game can be chosen for the final applying task. Newcomb, with four players per team, or volleyball Keep Away (Kirchner, 1985) both use the movement concepts around which Lesson Plan 3 is developed. Scoring can be introduced into this lesson's final applying task, the simplest way probably being to score a point if the opposite player fails to return the ball. Decisions have to be made about restarting the game. If two balls are used, toss the balls from opposite sides of the net (figure 10.12). This initial toss must be cooperative, so the balls can be played; placing the ball in nonplayable areas comes next.

Figure 10.11 Rotation variations and the pathway of the ball.

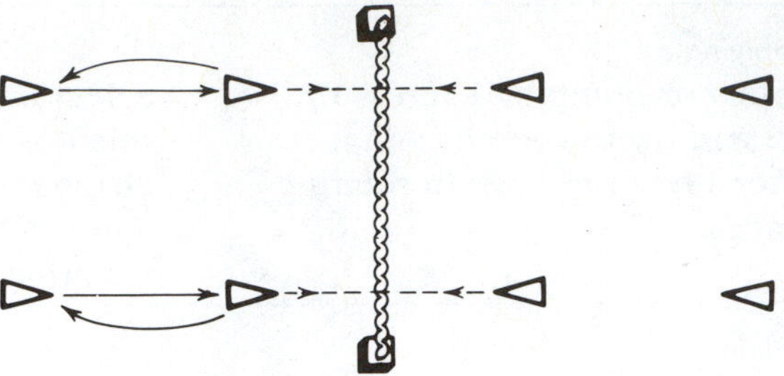

a.

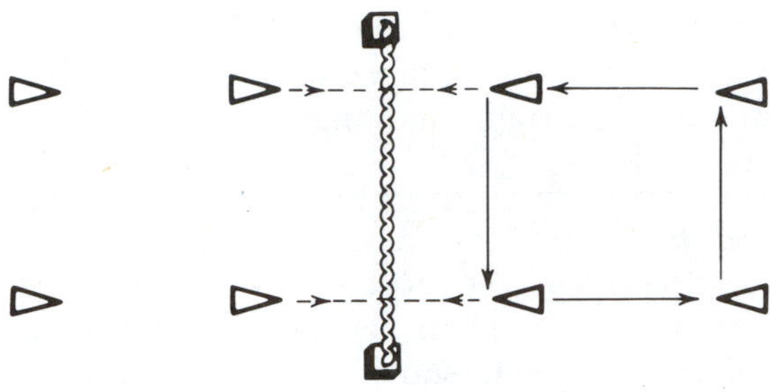

b.

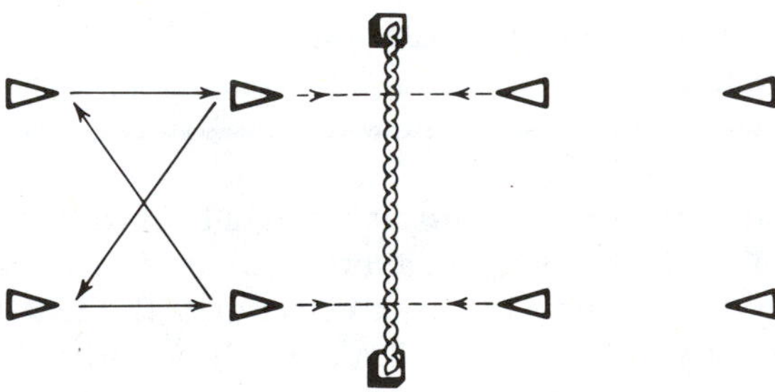

c.

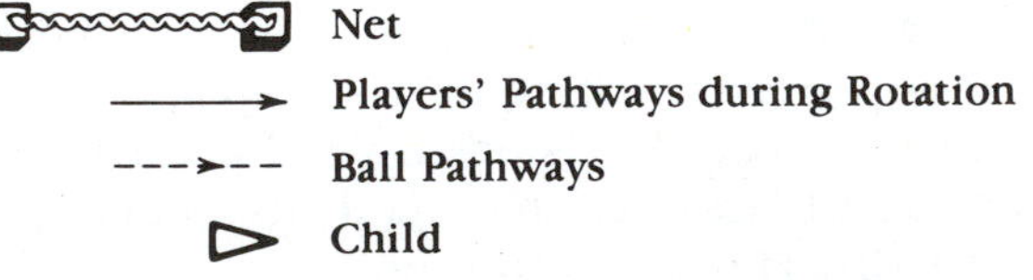

Safety Tip

Make sure all unused balls are contained at the side of the playing area, perhaps in a hoop or cardboard box. It is dangerous to have loose balls rolling across the floor.

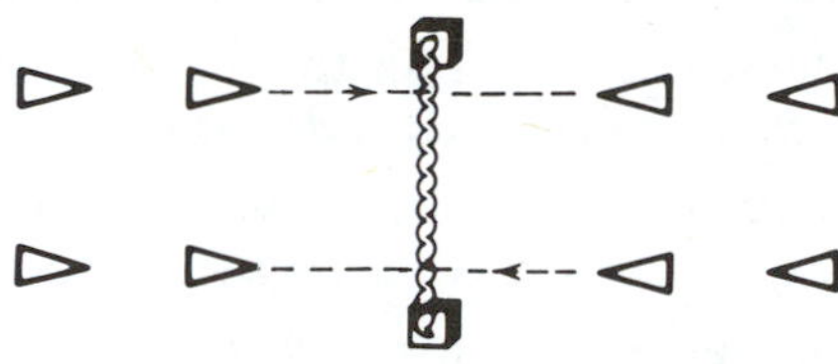

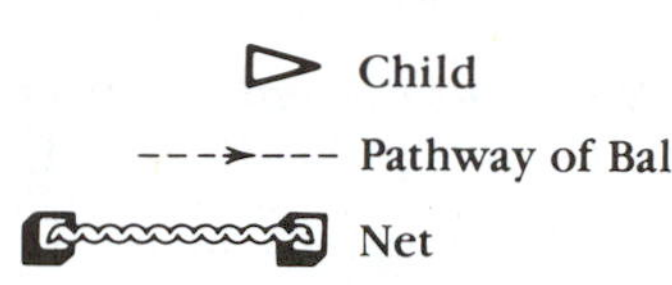

Figure 10.12 Restarting head-up games.

Whenever a game breaks down, employ the observation cycle (see figure 9.4). Your decision may be for the children to return to cooperative play in which continuity is stressed. You may remove one ball and maintain scoring. Whatever decision you make, provide the children with encouragement and the information they need as they strive to improve their skills.

Summary

Planning games lessons demands a very clear focus of intent. Your understanding of the nature of games playing, the different game types and forms, the categories of skills, and indirect and direct competition are some of the prerequisites for developing plans which meet individual needs and provide progressive learning experiences for your children.

Because of the diversity of the content, a careful record of the concepts and skills taught should become part of your plan book. It is exciting to observe the children's increase in competency over the seven years. We hope both they and you will have enjoyment when playing and that many of the children will develop a lifelong interest in games playing, both as participants and spectators.

Review Questions

1. Differentiate between direct and indirect competition.
2. What factors will help you decide to hold your games lesson outdoors? Give some of the advantages of playing outdoors.
3. What progression/programming of games throughout the school years is suggested?
4. How does adding players affect a game?
5. Four ideas are provided to help maximize participation in games playing. What are they?
6. What factors influence the selection of a game or design of an applying task for Part 3 of a games lesson?

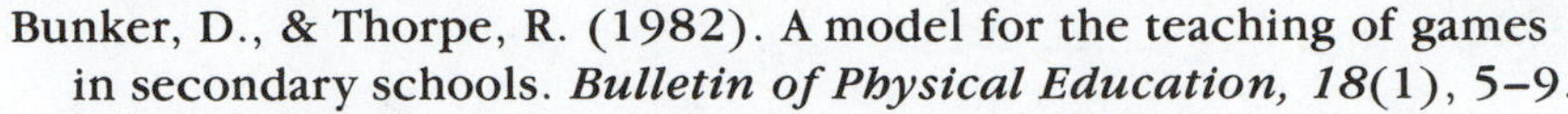

References

Bunker, D., & Thorpe, R. (1982). A model for the teaching of games in secondary schools. *Bulletin of Physical Education, 18*(1), 5–9.

Kirchner, G. (1985). *Physical education for elementary school children* (6th ed.). Dubuque, IA: Wm. C. Brown Publishers.

Piggott, R. (1982). A psychological basis for new trends in games teaching. *Bulletin of Physical Education, 18*(1), 17–22.

Riley, M. (Ed.). (1977). Games teaching. *JOPER, 48*(7), 17–35.

Schurr, E. (1980). *Movement experiences for children* (3rd ed.), Englewood Cliffs, NJ: Prentice-Hall, Inc.

Sleap, M. (1985). Mini-sport; State of the art. *British Journal of Physical Education, 16*(2), 68–69.

Related Readings

Brown, L., & Grineski, S. (1992). Competition in physical education: An educational contradiction? *JOPERD, 63*(1), 17–19, 77.

CAHPER (1980). *Basic skill series.* Ottawa: CAHPER.

Docherty, D., & Turkington, D. (1986). A model for the sequential development of sports skills. *CAHPER Journal, 52*(2), 16–19.

Doolittle, S., & Girard, K. (1991). A dynamic approach to teaching games in elementary school physical education. *JOPERD, 62*(4), 57–63.

Evans, J. (1986). A look at the team selection process. *CAHPER Journal, 52*(5), 5–9.

Galkas, B. (1991). Teaching cooperative skills through games. *JOPERD, 62*(5), 28–30.

Johns, D. (1987). Persistent problems related to adult intervention on children's sport. *CAHPER Journal, 53*(1), 19–24.

Peterson, S. (1992). The sequence of instruction in games: Implications for developmental appropriateness. *JOPERD, 63*(6), 36–39.

Schwagger, S. (1992). Relay races—Are they appropriate for elementary physical education? *JOPERD, 63*(6), 54–56.

Sources of low-organization and lead-up games:

Kirchner G. (1992). *Physical education for elementary school children* (8th ed.). Dubuque, IA: Wm. C. Brown Co. Publishers.

Nichols, B. (1990). *Moving and learning: The elementary school physical education experience* (2nd ed.). St. Louis, MO: Times Mirror/Mosby College Publishing.

Pengrazi R., & Dauer, V. (1992). *Dynamic physical education for elementary school children* (10th ed.). New York: Macmillan Publishing Company.

Section 4

Gymnastics

Within most of us lies a sense of adventure and a strong desire to defy the laws of gravity. We are all enthralled with flight and the unique sensation of being suspended in air. Mary Poppins captured this magical sense for children when she slowly descended, umbrella in hand. The myth and wonder of superhumans who defy gravity in comic strips and television shows has been evidenced in the popularity of "Superman," "Wonder Woman," and "Batman." We have a strong desire to control our environment, to find reassurance that we are kings and queens of our castle.

Gymnastic movement is unique in that the focus is upon the body and how and where it moves in relation to the floor or apparatus. Whereas dance is expressive, gymnastic movement is functional, like games, but is not performed to manipulate equipment. Stanley (1969) describes gymnastics as

> Activities which arise when the performer strives to test his ability to control his body movements in relation to the force of gravity in deliberately selected circumstances of difficulty.

The acquisition of (gymnastic) skill is not an end in itself, but the means by which children can experience and understand movement in a variety of situations *(Williams, 1974)*.

Chapter 11
The Gymnastics Program

Because children naturally delight in running, jumping, rolling, and climbing, the gymnastic experience should be a positive one for all, where movement exploration and refinement result in gymnastic skill. It is our responsibility to foster children's love of gymnastics and channel it into worthwhile learning experiences.

Why Should Gymnastics Be Included in School Programs?

Gymnastic movement is worthy of equal emphasis within the physical education program due to the physical demands it requires. Muscles of the arms, legs, and trunk are taxed as children balance, spring, climb, and hang. Experience with large climbing apparatus provides excitement and challenge. Gymnastics also contributes to the development of fundamental movements necessary for other physical activities. Controlling the body effectively and efficiently is extremely desirable whether one is rushing down a crowded street, throwing a Frisbee, or competing in the Olympics. Since the skills of running, jumping, and rolling are used in every sport, they may be developed in gymnastics and applied to all activities. If the child gains effective body control early in life, this is sound preparation for whatever movement activities will be pursued later.

Body control is the major objective of gymnastics; efficient movement is necessary in a variety of situations, both on the floor and on apparatus. Body awareness is heightened through a focus on the body's shape in jumping, landing, rolling, balancing, hanging, swinging, and climbing. Children learn to control body parts and use them effectively to receive and support their weight as they perform various activities. They will discover that sudden, forceful movement is necessary at times, while energy must be harnessed to create an effective movement at other times. They will grow to realize the importance of timing and rhythm, so movements may progress smoothly through a sequence of activities. Spatial dimensions will be explored so that height and distance are judged accurately in relation to the body's activities.

The Nature of Gymnastics

For many people, the term *gymnastics* elicits images of thin and muscular adolescents whirling through the air, twisting and turning with great speed and strength, or delicately balancing in contorted positions upon the smallest of surfaces. These images are those of the elite few who choose to compete in gymnastics at the highest level.

Let us look at the other side of the coin at those of us who are "average." If you can, recall your childhood and a carefree summer day with nothing in particular to do. A grassy surface and a clear blue sky may create images and sensations of rolling down a hill, climbing a tree, or gleefully viewing the world upside down. Children find tremendous joy in climbing, swinging, hanging, rolling, and lifting their feet to the sky!

Gymnastics is physically demanding.

The infant's first gymnastic skill is that of rolling. Standing, balancing, walking, climbing, hanging, and jumping follow later in the hierarchy of skill acquisition. These fundamental movements, which develop so naturally in the healthy child, form the basis of gymnastics.

Parents who have the luxury of a backyard may purchase swing sets for their children. The neighborhood park and school playgrounds sometimes provide children with larger apparatus for gymnastic play. While these structures seem a natural part of the landscape to most of us, they are designed to promote children's innate urge to test their skills in new and challenging ways.

Children delight in testing their physical abilities. The thrill of climbing a tree, walking along a skinny fence, and jumping from a high place are movement sensations most of us can recall.

> *Climbing seems to satisfy a desire to be high up, a vivid experience in itself, and little children will often climb to the top of a piece of apparatus for the satisfaction of sitting high up and looking at the familiar environment from a new angle (Jordan, 1970).*

Playgrounds offer a gymnastic challenge.

Children enjoy the sense of vertigo, produced by swinging as high as possible or watching the world speed by when on a merry-go-round. The speed and motion is a delightful kinesthetic sensation. The "Tarzan" exists in each one of us. It is gymnastics that employs this delight and fosters a love for movement in relation to a challenging and exciting environment.

Gymnastics is concerned with movement itself, the focus being how and where the body moves in relation to the floor and obstacles. What the action is and how it is performed is the essence of gymnastics, not the result of the action, nor the effect of the action. At all times you are trying to prove that you can defy gravity in a variety of specially constructed situations. Finding out what your body can do and bringing it under conscious control when interacting with the special gymnastics environment is the challenge of gymnastics.

Table 11.1

Variations in Gymnastic Forms

Educational gymnastics	Artistic/Gymnastics	Modern rhythmic gymnastics
Functional	Functional, minimally expressive	Functional and minimally expressive
Educational	Educational but performance-oriented	May be educational but performance-oriented
Noncompetitive	Usually competitive	Usually competitive
Process-oriented	Product-oriented	Product-oriented
Movement skills are predetermined by teacher and student	Movement skills are predetermined by teacher or coach	Movement skills are predetermined by teacher or coach
Performed alone or in small groups	Performed individually	Performed alone, in small or large groups
Appropriate for both males and females	Females have four events; males have six events in competition	Only females may take part in competition
Small equipment is used	No small equipment is used	Small equipment is used
Apparatus is not standardized	Apparatus is standardized	No apparatus is used

Gymnastic Forms

The challenge of controlling the body in new and efficient ways has long lured humans.

> *We can deduce that the term gymnastics has for 2000 years been synonymous with physical exercise and indeed was the embryo of our contemporary physical education (Russell, 1980).*

Through the centuries, many variations in gymnastic forms have evolved. The three most common forms of gymnastics taught in schools today are modern rhythmic gymnastics, artistic gymnastics, and educational gymnastics. The basic similarities and differences between these forms are outlined in table 11.1.

Modern Rhythmic Gymnastics

Modern rhythmic gymnastics originated in Europe and has spread in popularity primarily in the private gymnastic clubs and studios of North America. A dancelike movement form, modern rhythmic gymnastics was first included in the Olympic Games in 1984. In this form of gymnastics, elements from dance and games are used to create a floor routine in which a ball, rope, hoop, ribbon, or club is manipulated in time to the music.

A dancelike quality pervades all movements as rhythm, flow, dynamic contrasts, and aesthetic appeal are essential elements in a quality performance.

Elementary school children greatly enjoy the rhythmic elements of movement, and when they can catch, bounce, and throw balls with a high degree of skill they will react positively to the challenge of doing these skills to music. They will also enjoy the challenge of composing a simple gymnastic routine to popular music. Challenges such as these may be included in the games and gymnastic lessons at appropriate times. However, due to the complexity of rhythmic gymnastics per se, we do not consider it an appropriate movement form to include in the elementary school program.

Artistic Gymnastics

Artistic gymnastics (Olympic) is the form in which a high degree of proficiency in established movement skills is developed. While movements may be simplified for the beginner, the ultimate goal is to perfect predetermined routines on set pieces of apparatus. These routines are then judged. Because the focus of this gymnastic form is upon the movement product rather than the process (how we learn to move), we suggest it is inappropriate in elementary physical education.

> *Formal or traditional gymnastics . . . consists of learning numerous, though often unrelated, skills on the various apparatuses of artistic gymnastics. These skills can be very difficult and sometimes risky. Thus, little thought is normally given as to whether the student is receiving well-rounded physical development or is merely performing set gymnastic skills because they are supposed to be "good" for the student (Russell, 1980).*

Educational Gymnastics

Educational gymnastics is aptly termed, and its major goal is education. This implies that the child is most important, as opposed to the activity or movement skill. This is the form we believe should be included in elementary school physical education programs.

In educational gymnastics, children work at their own level on tasks structured to develop understanding and skill in applying selected movement concepts. While each child is responding to the same task, the theoretical framework allows for skill progression appropriate for every child. Your role as the teacher is to encourage the child to think and solve movement problems through gymnastic activity. When competitive gymnastics was taught in schools, the premise was that each child was to learn a specific skill on a specific day. In contrast, educational gymnastics is founded upon the premise that children learn at different rates, and the discovery of how and why a movement is appropriate is valuable during the process of skill acquisition (see table 11.2).

Table 11.2

Teaching Styles of Gymnastic Forms

Competitive gymnastic forms	**Result**	**Movement product**
Teacher: "Do a cartwheel." (Children practice) →	Some succeed, some fail →	Range from poor to excellent cartwheels
Educational gymnastics		
Teacher: "Transfer your weight onto your hands." (Children practice) →	All succeed →	With variation in body shape, result is handstands, headstands, frog stand, cartwheels, back arch
"Take weight on your hands and stretch your feet to the ceiling." (Children practice) →	All succeed →	With variation in degree of stretch, result is handstands, headstands, cartwheels
"Take weight on one hand at a time and place your feet in a different spot from where they began." (Children practice) →	All succeed →	Variations of the cartwheel

You will rarely need to demonstrate specific skills or products. Instead, you will pose tasks, such as "Find different ways of taking weight on your hands," "Find a way to take weight on your hands only, stretching your feet to the ceiling," or "Take weight on your hands only with a wide body shape and place your feet in a different spot from where they began." A cartwheel may result with students showing variation in degree of stretch and control. You would progress to refining the responses so that more stretch, control, and effective body alignment develops. The educational aspect of this gymnastic form is that all children may succeed and acquire movement skills as they discover their levels of competence.

New movements may also be discovered, as the children are required to use movement knowledge as well as ingenuity and creativity to seek an appropriate response. A task that requires the students to alternate stretching and curling while traveling may result in a simple jump, a front walkover, or a dive roll.

Unlike other forms of gymnastics which require precise actions to be done for specific activity or stunt, educational gymnastics uses the dynamics of movement to create new activities and

Educational gymnastics should be included in elementary physical education programs.

> *movement sequences. Many variations of known stunts and vaults are produced, as well as activities and sequences which have no known names (Wilson, 1979).*

Even though each child within the class may respond to a task in a different manner, skill development will result if the teacher provides simplifying, extending, and refining tasks that encourage children to challenge themselves. Students need time to explore, discover, consolidate, and refine new movement as each movement concept is studied.

The concepts of what the body is doing, where the body is moving, and how the body is moving in relation to the floor or apparatus are constantly being explored. Small apparatus, such as small mats and hoops, as well as large apparatus are additional stimuli for the child.

When children work together, challenge is also increased. A partner may contribute to the movement sequence as an obstacle, a leader or follower, one who matches the movements, or as one who assists a partner's movement.

To summarize, educational gymnastics holds tremendous value in the elementary physical education program for numerous reasons. Morrison (1969) reinforces this by stating:

> *The functional, objective side of movement can best be served by educational gymnastics which can be freely adapted to the skill, spirit and needs of any group.*

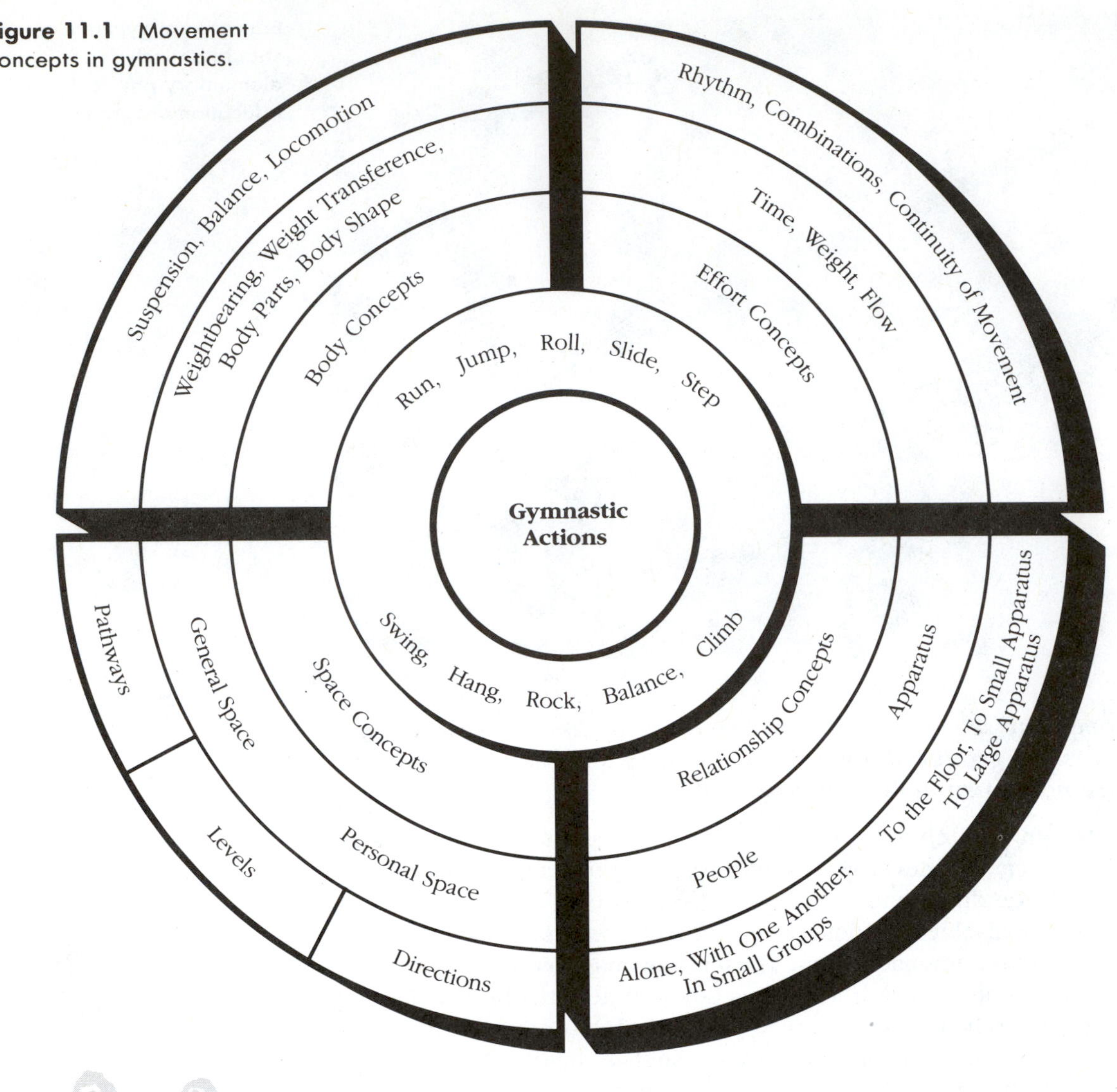

Figure 11.1 Movement concepts in gymnastics.

The Material of Gymnastics

In chapter 2, movement concepts are presented in a general way to provide the foundation for the elementary school physical education program. While chapters 5 and 8 present the material of dance and games, respectively, this section concentrates on the material of gymnastics. You may already be familiar with some of the terminology of gymnastics, as presented in figure 11.1.

Movement concepts are developed through a number of specific gymnastic activities. These are presented for reference in table 11.3.

Table 11.3

Gymnastic Actions

Weight transference		**Weightbearing**	
On the floor	***With apparatus***	***Balance***	***Suspend***
Run Jump Roll Slide Step	Climb Jump Roll Slide Step Swing	Balance (static) Rock	Balance Rock Hang Swing
Each of the above may be developed through focus on:			
Body concepts	***Space concepts***	***Effort concepts***	***Relationship concepts***
Stressing specific body parts Stretching, curling and twisting Changing or maintaining a body shape Flight	Direction Level Pathway	Time Weight	Partner work In small groups

Body Concepts

Body concepts fall into two groups, each with a specific antigravity challenge, on the floor and on the apparatus (see figure 11.2).

1. Weightbearing, in which various skills of balance and suspension are developed
2. Transference of weight, in which locomotor skills are developed. These include jumping, rolling, and stepping activities

Weightbearing

Weightbearing is one of the most simple body concepts because it only deals with *how* we are supporting our weight. When you introduce this concept, focus on which body parts may take the body's weight (points of support). Children will find that in combination, almost all body parts may take weight in some way. We may bear weight on our stomachs, holding our ankles with our hands and arching backwards, or we may take weight on our back by tucking into a ball shape. We may take weight on the shoulders by placing the feet behind our head or supporting our body on our shoulders only. Weight may be taken in totally inverted positions where the hands solely bear weight, hands and head only, or forearms only. Combinations of body parts and numbers of body parts make

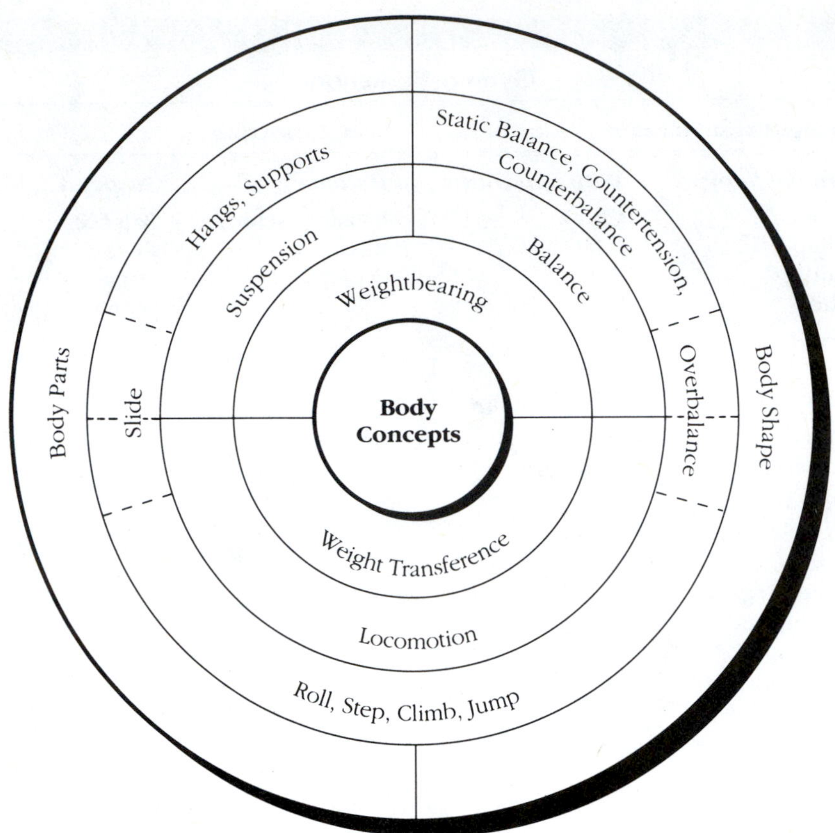

Figure 11.2 Body concepts in gymnastics.

this work challenging for children as they learn how to support their weight. They will find that the fewer the number of body parts, the smaller the surface of the body parts, or the smaller the base makes it difficult to maintain the balance and shape being held.

Large apparatus introduced in the theme of weightbearing provides a world of new possibilities. When a child is offered the potential of hanging, gripping, or holding onto ropes, bars, rings, and ladders, suspension is possible. The hips, backs of knees, crooks of elbows, hands, ankles, and neck in isolation or combination may provide sufficient support to take the body's weight.

Balance

Balance requires muscular control—a sense of equilibrium, as well as a sound kinesthetic sense (table 11.4). Balance includes static or stationary shapes when the center of gravity is above the base of support and is held for a period of time. Examples of static balance include standing on the ball of one foot, balancing on the hands only, or sitting with legs and arms outstretched off the floor (V-sit).

Table 11.4

Factors that Influence Balance

Principle	Interpretation	Gymnastic implication
Base of support	Some body parts make better bases than others. The wider the base of support, the more stable the balance.	It is easier to balance on your bottom than your knees. In a headstand, the head and hands should form a triangle to create a wide base of support. Palms and fingers should be placed flat on floor to increase the size of the base of support.
Center of gravity	The center of gravity must be above the base of support. If it is not, the person will fall over. The lower the center of gravity, the more stable the balance.	Hips should be above the hands in a handstand. Begin teaching balance with curled shapes; progress to stretched shapes.
Law of inertia	An object continues in a state of rest (or uniform motion) unless it is compelled by some external force to change that state.	"Tight" muscles will hold a balance. Relaxing the muscles will cause the body to fall.
Segmented body	Stability is greatest when each segment of the body is vertically above the center of gravity of the segment below.	In a handstand or headstand, the body should be as straight as possible.
Supporting surface area	The more stable the supporting surface area, the more stable the balance.	A firm, flat, and slightly textured surface is easier to balance on than a bar, mat, or slippery floor.
Absorption of force	Force needs to be absorbed in order to balance.	If jumping and balancing, the force first needs to be absorbed by bending the knees and then balancing.

We may bear weight on various body parts.

Static Balance Static balance involves balancing on specific body parts. Common static balances include the headstand, handstand, frog stand (where the hands provide the base of support and the body is in a curled shape, knees resting on elbows), and back arch.

Children will initially practice balancing on various body parts and then may be guided to create various shapes on selected body parts. The teacher may provide such tasks as "Balance on one foot creating a wide shape," "Find a twisted shape and balance on shoulders only," or "Create a sequence of balance in a stretched shape; roll and balance in another stretched shape." A difficult task that children enjoy is "Run, leap, and balance on the foot you landed on."

Developing the concept of balance may also be accomplished through partner work. Partial and total weightbearing may be studied both in dance and gymnastics. However, in gymnastics the movements will be functional rather than expressive and will occur as an outgrowth of partner work sequences and exploration of shape and balance. Children in grade 4 will likely be mature enough to take each other's weight as they balance together. They will enjoy some of the typical ways of taking the weight of another; for example, child *A* crouching in a ball shape to provide partial support for child *B* in a back arch; child *A* on all fours while child *B* puts his arms around *A*'s stomach to balance vertically; or child *A* lying on her back, supporting the weight of *B* by extending her arms and feet to contact *B*'s hips and hands.

Overbalance Balance with overbalance is an enjoyable concept to explore with older children. It is not physically difficult, but the basic mechanics of balance must be applied. Overbalance involves balancing and then slightly shifting the weight (center of gravity) outside of the

Counterbalance involves pushing in order to achieve stability.

base of support in order for a transference of weight to occur. A common example of overbalance is a handstand or headstand into a forward roll. However, the balances created to explore overbalance need not be this difficult or established. Children will enjoy simply balancing in shapes they have created, adjusting their center of gravity (usually the hips), and allowing gravity to pull them into a transfer of weight, usually a rolling action. In rolling, the teacher must stress that the soft body parts should receive the weight, and a round body shape is necessary to prevent injury.

Counterbalance Counterbalance and countertension are also challenging concepts appropriate for older children who work well with partners. Counterbalance involves two people pushing against one another in order to achieve stability. A typical example of this is two people leaning into each other, shoulders contacting to create an inverted V.

Countertension Countertension involves pulling away from the partner to achieve balance. A typical example of this is two people locking hands and leaning backward, creating the shape of a V. Initial attempts at both counterbalance and countertension will probably involve contact with hands, while feet provide the base of support. Symmetrical shapes will be attempted first but children should be encouraged to progress to asymmetrical shapes and contact made with different body parts. An ankle may pull away from a partner's bent knee, one person's head may push against the hips of a partner, and the base of support may be hips, shoulders or feet, and hands. In both countertension and counterbalance, children will need guidance to ensure that one child is not carrying the weight of another but both are actually pushing or pulling so that balance is maintained.

Counter tension involves pulling to achieve stability.

Suspension

Balance on apparatus takes the form of supports or hangs. In supports, the head is above the base of support (e.g., gripping on a horizontal bar, hips resting on the bar). In hangs, the head is below the base of support (e.g., hanging inverted by the knees on a horizontal bar). Such apparatus as ropes, ladders, bars, hanging rings, and vertical poles encourage suspension.

Weight Transference

Weight transference implies a change in base of support, whether it is on the spot or is intended to take the body to a new place. Whether the concept is studied with or without apparatus, it will be of value for children to explore the range of ways in which their weight may be transferred. In this theme, the focus is on the action—what the movement is—rather than which body parts are taking the weight, or the body shape employed.

Much gymnastic sequence work will involve some transference of weight with the exception of a series of shapes being consistently supported by a few body parts (balance, suspension). For instance, if a child creates a pin shape, supported by the feet, and then curls to create a ball shape, still supported by the feet, weight transference has not occurred. In this case, the movement may become quite expressive, tending toward dancelike movement rather than gymnasticlike movement. (The only exception to this is work on the hanging rings when the hands always support the body as it rotates or holds various body shapes.) In skill development of weight transference, the children's movement responses will be similar to those found in other themes, but their concentration will be directed toward the *action* of the movement rather than where, how, or with whom it travels.

Weight transference may be accomplished in various ways. The body may stay on the spot and merely change shape as new body parts take the weight. Examples include the headstand, handstand, and shoulder stand. Here, the base of support changes and a transference of weight results.

Weight may be transferred from one body part to the same body part, not traveling to a new spot but employing flight. In jumping actions, there is no change in parts bearing weight. However, the weight is taken off the feet and then returns to the feet, implying weight transference.

Weight transference may also take the body to a new space, or it may take it away and back again. One may use stepping actions, rolling actions, or jumping actions to initiate momentum for transference of weight. We may transfer weight to and from the feet while jumping on, off, or over apparatus.

When apparatus is used, there is even greater potential for weight transference because new body parts may support weight. The child may hang from knees and elbows while other body parts, such as the head, neck, shoulders, back, hips, legs, ankles, and hands may assist in taking weight or allow for a smooth transference of weight.

Sample tasks for weight transference follow:

"Transfer your weight onto your hands in different ways."

"Take your weight on your shoulders and transfer it onto your feet."

"Travel over the bench, transferring your weight from one body part to another."

"Transfer your weight from feet to hands to feet suddenly."

"With your weight on your stomach, transfer your weight onto your hips."

Locomotion

Locomotion implies traveling to a new place. Common types of locomotion used in gymnastics activities focus upon the feet (e.g., running and jumping), feet and hands (e.g., cartwheeling), and rolling.

Rolling Most children can roll in some way. Rolling provides for the child's safety upon landing while forming the basis for rotation in gymnastic movement. When a program involves children climbing heights, traveling in unconventional ways, springing off apparatus into the air, or traveling backward, the teacher must provide a safety mechanism to prevent injury. The ability to tuck the body in a curled shape and continue moving until the momentum is dissipated prevents injury. If a child happens to fall either from a balance on the floor or off apparatus, injury may be prevented by rolling rather than extending the arms to "catch" the fall or slamming an isolated body part (such as the back) against the floor. Because of this, the sequence of ***run, jump, land, and roll*** must be learned early in the gymnastic program.

Safety Tip

Teaching points at this stage should stress the importance of bony body parts being tucked in and the more muscular body parts taking the weight. Body parts that may take weight include the side of the leg (rather than knees), the shoulders (rather than the elbows), and the lower back, hips, or upper back (rather than the head).

In initial gymnastic lessons, rocking, which leads to various types of rolling, will establish a sound movement basis. Rolling has tremendous value for the child, not only as a form of safety but also because it necessitates focus on the use of body parts, body shape, weightbearing, and transference of weight. Unlimited potential exists in rolling movements because the child may be encouraged to perform symmetrical and asymmetrical rolls; backward, forward, sideways, and diagonal rolls; shoulder rolls; chest rolls; rolls with straight legs; rolls with no use of arms; and rolls that link other movements. Rolling may also be performed in relation to apparatus, as well as other children. Children may work on their own, rolling along, over, under, around, and through various pieces of apparatus, such as hoops, ropes, benches, boxes, and beams. They will enjoy the challenge of mirroring, matching, leading, following, or meeting and parting with a friend as they refine sequences that involve rolling. Partners may also be used as stationary obstacles to be rolled over, under, or through (separated legs). Great challenge is provided when the partner moves, and timing is essential in the rolling actions.

Rolling should be taught in the early stages by having children create curled shapes to rock back and forth. Because children are so flexible, many curled shapes, including ones where the back is arched, are possible. The next step in this sequence is to rock and roll in all directions. Teaching points at this stage should include keeping the head, elbows, knees, and feet tucked in, and allowing the body to be taken in whatever direction momentum will take it.

Once children are adept at rocking and rolling, you may ask them to create a sequence of a stretched shape and a curled shape that will roll. These shapes should be joined together in a continuous fashion so that movement is not jerky and the rolling appears to grow naturally out of the curled shape. Stretched shapes may then be required to be vertical—or mostly vertical—so the child must tuck and roll, taking downward momentum into sideways, forward, or backward movement. This stage provides the basis for the absorption of downward force.

When children can perform these actions with relative ease, they may progress to tasks such as the following:

"Begin with your weight on your knees, tuck and roll sideways and take your weight on your knees again."

"From a standing position, tuck and roll in any way you like."

"Jump very lightly, landing on your feet and roll forward, backward, or sideways."

At this point in children's skill development, you may urge students to explore different ways of jumping, landing, and rolling. While jumping on the spot will be explored and refined initially, jumping in different directions should soon be attempted, so the children not only learn to deal with movement down, but also with movement down and forward, down and backward, or sideways.

Once children have mastered rolling in these round shapes and can precede them with jumping and landing, they are ready to provide further momentum with running. Then, the sequence of *run, jump, land, and roll* should be attempted. When children have practiced this sequence sufficiently and are adept at handling the momentum of their body weight as it travels in various directions, they have acquired the basic safety skills necessary for work with apparatus.

Stepping Stepping actions are a form of locomotion involving either the feet, hands, or both feet and hands to travel. Walking on both hands, traveling along a bar while hanging, cartwheeling, and scampering with feet and hands all involve stepping.

Climbing Traveling up hanging ropes, vertical ladders or poles, and climbing frames promote climbing. These actions promote upper body strength and require gripping with hands, ankles, and/or feet. Children will enjoy the sense of accomplishment that climbing activities bring, especially when significant heights are achieved.

Jumping Jumping may take the form of a transfer of weight from two feet to two feet, one foot to two feet, two feet to one foot, one foot to the other (leaping), and one foot to the same foot (hopping).

Jumping is first experienced by the preschooler in stepping down from a minimal height. As the preschooler matures, jumping will be gained in such activities as running and jumping. Later, the skill of jumping onto a height will be mastered. For this reason, the progression of jumping down, then up, over, and later onto apparatus should be employed.

Jumping is normally initiated by a spring action, which is essentially a curling and sudden stretching action. To gain as much spring as possible, all force must be projected in the desired direction of the spring. In the take-off, joints compress for the greatest extension of trunk, legs, and arms to occur in flight. While the body is in the air, muscles must be firm and the body "tight," especially in the lower trunk area.

Flight Flight is produced when we are without support, totally off the ground. Flight is a product of jumping but may also be achieved by releasing our base of support from large apparatus. Children may experience flight by letting go of swinging ropes or hanging rings, by jumping off a high box, or by springing off a springboard.

When children enter grade 4, they should have sufficient physical and mental maturity to experience the joy of flight. It is at this stage that the teacher may introduce flight-assisting apparatus, such as springboards, beatboards (reuther boards), and trampettes. These pieces of apparatus require good bodily control, strength, balance, and the ability to land correctly. When flight-assisting apparatus is used initially, it must

Flight requires much control.

Safety Tip

Apparatus that assists in flight or is used with flight-assisting apparatus demands much bodily control and a sound sense of balance. For this very reason it is suggested that springboards, trampettes, beatboards, and trampolines not be used with children under age 8, because they don't possess the dynamic balance required to safely use them without assistance.

be used in isolation, without boxes or horses adjacent. In this way, children will be free to explore various types of take-offs, create shapes in the air, or attempt to rotate in flight, as well as land in various ways. Only when children are adept at using flight-assisting apparatus should it be used as a means for getting onto or over other apparatus.

Flight may also be developed as a minor concept with older children through partner work. This requires physical skill and cooperation between children. Flight may be gained as child *A* supports the weight of *B* as he gains flight, *A* may push off *B* to gain flight, or *A* may prolong the flight of *B* by establishing contact while *B* is in the air.

> *If this type of partner work is to be of value the child who is in some way assisted in flight must himself be able to take-off effectively, land safely and control his body in the air (Mauldon & Layson, 1965).*

Remember That

The following suggestions may be of value in helping students maintain the necessary round shape when rolling forward or backward:

1. Bring into a class a box (a shoe box is fine) and a ball. Discuss the shape of each object; push the box and then the ball. Which one rolls? Stress that round shapes roll, square ones do not. Therefore, we need to maintain a round shape to roll.
2. Students should start a rolling action with their hips off the ground.
3. When rolling backward, students should start with the palms of their hands facing forward near their ears. (We call this "Mickey Mouse Ears" with young children.)
4. Place a beanbag in between the student's chin and chest to ensure that the head is tucked in as much as possible during rolling. (The forehead should not contact the ground during rolling forward. Rather, it is the back of the head that should contact the ground in the forward roll.)
5. Ensure that children roll in the direction that their momentum is carrying them. For instance, if a child jumps up and forward, the roll should continue to travel forward. Children should also be able to twist and roll sideways because it is sometimes difficult to control forward momentum (see figure 11.3). Many children have difficulty with this concept as they attempt to change the direction of the force.

Because flight is difficult and potentially dangerous, some elementary school children may never acquire the skill necessary for this concept.

Sliding Sliding is unique in that it is a form of locomotion but does not involve a transference of weight. Sliding requires tension as the body shape is held while traveling. We may slide along the floor or bench, slide up or down an inclined bench on body parts, such as our bottom, stomach, or back.

Body Parts

Body parts may be used in numerous ways. As stated in chapter 2, body parts may lead or initiate action, as well as support or receive weight. You or the children may point out which body parts are being used in locomotor and nonlocomotor actions. In stillness and motion, parts may lead or initiate an action as do the hands in a cartwheel or handstand, the head and shoulders in a forward roll, the hips in a swinging action, the hands in rope climbing, or the stomach facing upward in a back arch. When children are developing and refining newly acquired movements, you will inevitably provide guidance with reference to specific body parts. Comments, such as "Place your hands further part," "Kick your feet higher," and "Tuck your head in as you roll," illustrate the importance of specific body parts. In most gymnastic movements, the feet and knees, as well as hands and elbows, are of particular significance in rotating actions, and their positioning and role will be stressed to achieve quality.

Young children will enjoy discovering new movements through exploration of leading with different body parts. Leading tasks include, "Travel, leading with your knees," "Lead with your head as you find a twisted shape," and "Transfer your weight with hips leading the action and then roll." When children are working on such movements, the body parts will need emphasis for skill development and sound kinesthetic awareness to ensue.

Use of Hands

Because our hands are used so extensively in gymnastics, children should learn to always place their *whole palm* on the floor when taking weight on their hands. Some children will tend to place only their fingers on the floor, lifting the palm, while others may contact the floor only with the fingertips. When we are using a base of support as small as the hands, we want to make them as big as possible. Fingers should be spread apart so that we have "big hands."

Use of Feet, Ankles, and Knees

Feet, ankles, and knees are the body parts that not only provide tremendous force when they are suddenly stretched, but they also effectively absorb force when they bend. Dancers, divers, and gymnasts are the few athletes who use their lower legs effectively to jump or spring. Most other athletes rely more heavily on the quadriceps (thigh muscles) to produce force. The teacher may find it worthwhile to stress full extension of the feet, ankles, and knees in springing actions. When landing on the feet, the toes, balls of the feet, then heels should strike the ground to absorb force effectively and without injury.

Use of Arms and Shoulders

At some point in the children's skill development, springing actions with weight on the hands will be covered. The teacher may pose the task, "Transfer your weight from feet to hands to feet with a springing action." This task may be answered in an array of ways. One child may attempt a type of bear-walk, where hands and feet spring from one to the other. Another child may attempt a handstand and attempt to spring back onto his feet. A truly skilled child may attempt a back handspring or a cartwheel with flight (called a round-off).

To Do

Stand with your palms touching a wall, arms outstretched. Push your body away from the wall without bending your arms. It is possible to produce momentum in this manner without bending your arms because of the mobility in the shoulder girdle.

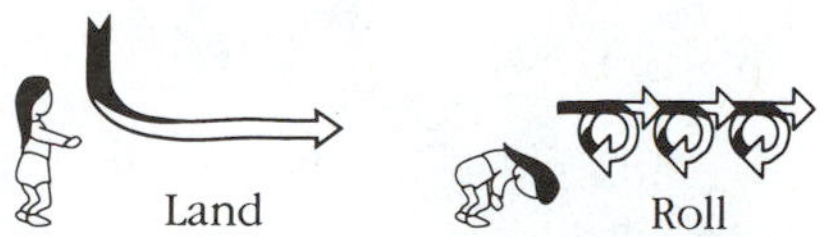

Figure 11.3 Children should roll in the direction of the force.

We know that spring is produced by bending or curling a joint and then suddenly extending it. In the case of arms producing spring, the arms bend, then stretch to create force. The shoulders can also produce spring because of the structure of the joints in the shoulder girdle. Thus, one may produce spring from a handstand without bending the arms.

The Head

Head placement is extremely important in games activities because it provides us with the direction of our vision. In dance and gymnastic activities, the head serves this function as well, but it may also provide an aesthetic appeal due to the focus on the body shape. In a leap, for instance, the eyes should focus upward to provide the appearance of greater height and lightness. Head placement is also important for continuity of line in body shape. The head sometimes serves a functional purpose in dance and gymnastics because it can initiate a turning action.

Body Shapes

Body shape refers to the lines or forms the body creates in motion and in stillness (figure 11.3). This is a direct result of the bending, curling, stretching, and twisting actions of the body.

Round Shapes

When the joints of the elbows, knees, hips, and spine are primarily bent or curled, the result is a curled or ball shape, where the extremities give the impression of meeting at the body's center. Round shapes may also be achieved by curling sideways or backward (as in a back arch). These shapes rotate most efficiently, because this tucked position provides a curved surface on which to rock and roll. In preparation for take-off and in landing, the body tucks and assumes this round shape as well. Round shapes are easier to hold in balancing activities, because the center of gravity tends to be lower due to the compactness of the extremities.

Stretched Shapes

When the body is stretched, the direction of the reach may either be vertical or horizonal. A *long* shape is achieved when the hands and head are as far away from the feet as possible. The body may be lying prone on the floor or on a piece of equipment, such as a box, horse, bench, or beam. The shape may be supported by one leg as in a "scale," creating a T shape. The long shape is used in diving actions where the body stretches in flight as much as possible to achieve height and/or distance. The headstand and handstand are examples of long shapes in balance.

Figure 11.4 Body shapes in gymnastics.

A *wide* shape is also a stretched shape but the body is stretched sideways rather than up. The wide shape in its extreme form takes the shape of an X. The most common example of the wide shape is the cartwheel, where the motion is sideways in a foot-hand-hand-foot sequence. Static and dynamic wide shapes are easily balanced on two feet due to the wide base of support. However, when other bases are used, balance is difficult, due to the raised center of gravity caused by the stretched extremities. Wide shapes are most commonly employed with other shapes in gymnastic movement. A straddle jump in which the feet meet the hands in flight is a combination of a round and wide shape. A static balance on the hands or head and hands where the legs form a V will combine a long and wide shape. Many wide shapes may also be twisted and a roll or new balance may result.

Twisted Shapes

The twisted shape involves rotation of the trunk with the hips and shoulders facing different directions. Twisted shapes are always asymmetrical, usually facilitate change in direction, and most commonly join movements together. Like wide shapes, twisted shapes are often created in combination with other shapes. Figure 11.4 illustrates various body shapes.

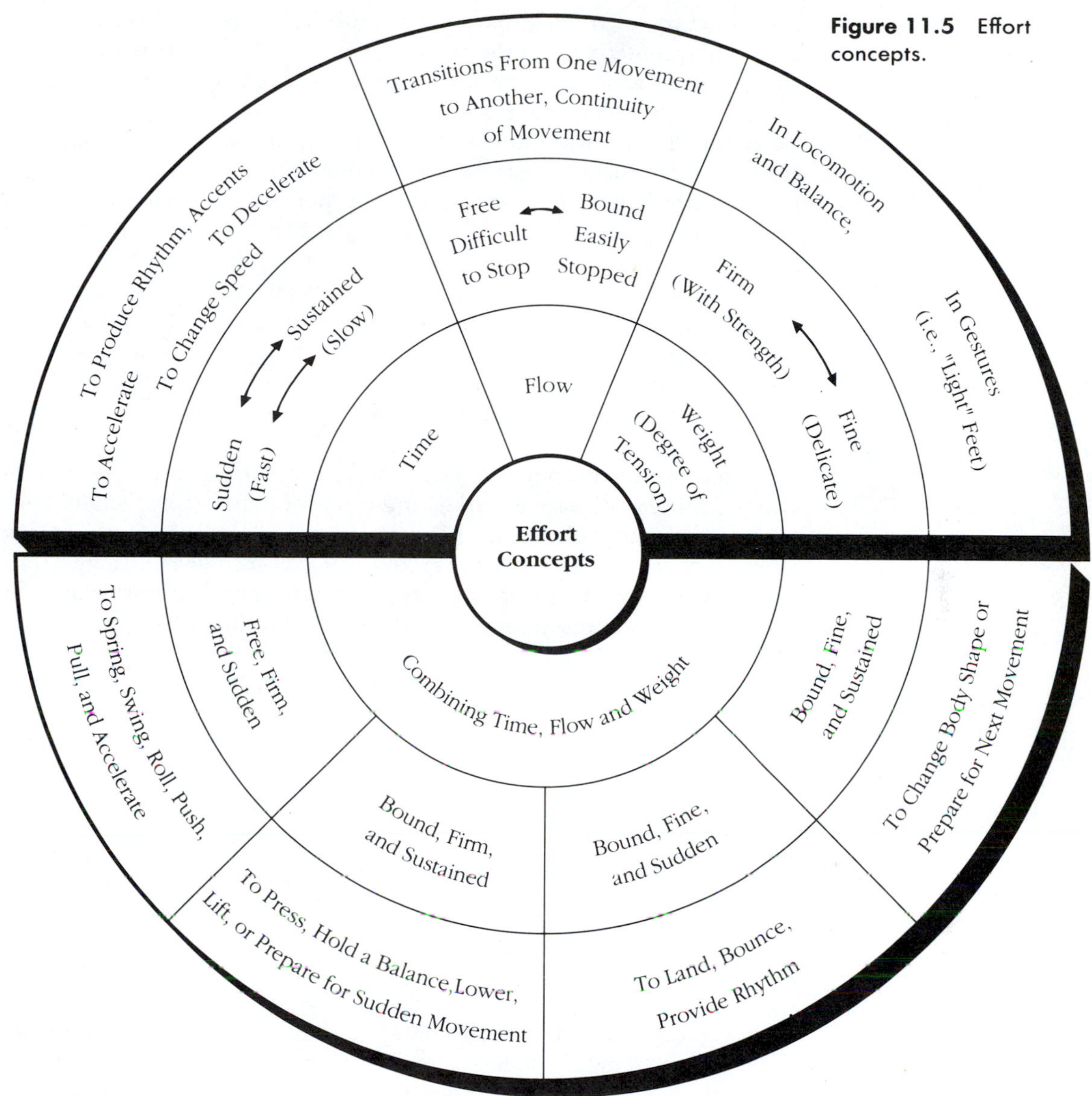

Figure 11.5 Effort concepts.

Effort Concepts

The proportions of time, weight, and flow are the factors that directly influence bodily control in gymnastics (figure 11.5).

> *. . . skill is acquired through the gradual refinement of the feel of the movement and any training has indeed to promote this feel which, in its essence in the awakening of the sense for the proportions of motion factors (Laban & Lawrence, 1948).*

The concepts of time and weight should be introduced separately, so children become aware of the range of movements possible within sudden and sustained time, and firm and fine weight. Young children are capable of rather superficial movement exploration of the effort concepts, because they tend toward firm and sudden actions in their everyday lives. However, familiar locomotor movements of running, skipping, galloping, jumping, and hopping may be performed with emphasis on "light" or "strong" feet. Balancing activities that focus on changing shape in a slow, sustained manner are within the capabilities of young children. Because their muscular control is limited and they are only beginning to appreciate time and flow, movements will tend to go and stop, go and stop. Continuity of movement, which is so necessary for quality sequence work, will develop as the child matures both physically and cognitively.

Time

Sudden movement is necessary to achieve force for springing, swinging, sliding, and many rotating actions and forms of transferring weight. Older elementary school children will enjoy "playing" with the factor of time. Once they are adept at rolling, taking weight on their hands, and transferring their weight in various ways, the teacher may introduce performing these actions in a sustained way. Rolls, handstands, headstands, cartwheels, and variations of all of these will provide tremendous challenge when attempted slowly with unexpected changes in time, or sequenced rhythmically.

Weight

Firm movement is required in almost all gymnastic activities and children must learn to gauge how strong the action needs to be in order not to provide too much force for the action. However,

> ***If adequate tension is not retained, heaviness will result and the body will become inert and unready for action. Overtension is a waste of energy, cramps the body and causes it to be unprepared to move readily (Stanley, 1969).***

Flow

Flow relates to the degree of control one has over the action. In most sustained movements, such as slowly lifting or lowering the legs or arms in hanging or balancing activities, the flow will be bound. In actions that involve flight, the flow will be primarily free; that is, the movement will be difficult to stop, as in springing, leaping, and jumping. It is the interplay between releasing and binding flow that results in control. While we often discuss flow with respect only to the extremes of bound and free flow, the child will experience and use varying degrees of flow within particular movements.

Once children have focused their action on weight and time, combinations of time and weight may be attempted. Phrasing, rhythm, and accents will provide the "final touch" to gymnastic sequence work.

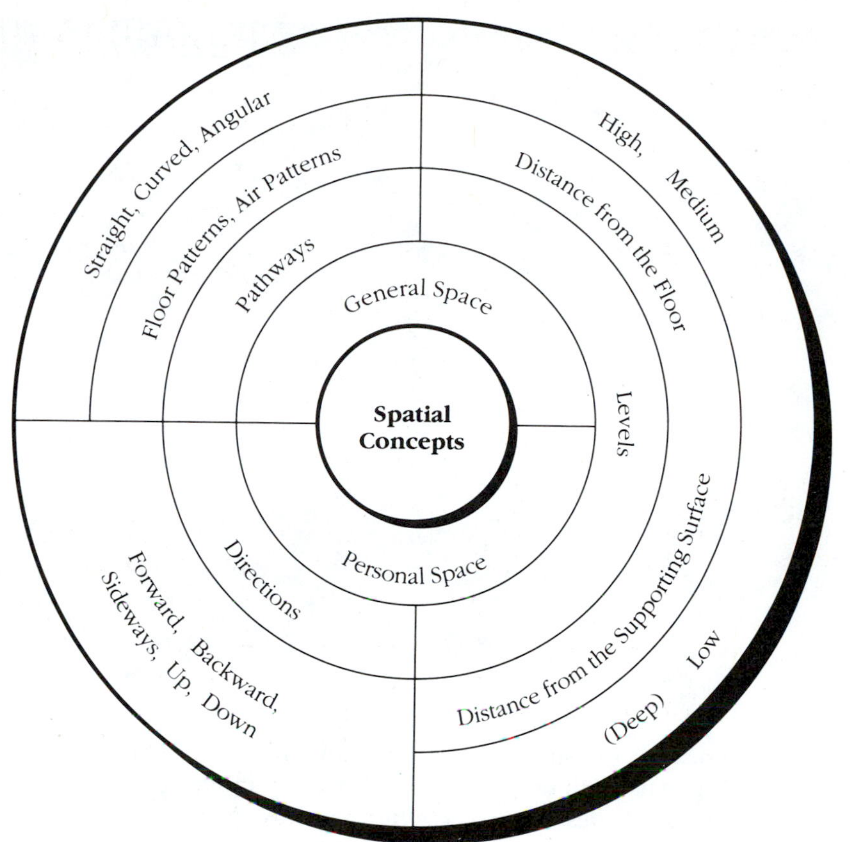

Figure 11.6 Spatial concepts.

Spatial Concepts

As stated in chapter 2, spatial concepts deal with where the body moves (figure 11.6). The body may move on the spot within personal space, or it may travel into open spaces, called general space. We may travel near the ground as we roll or reach high in the air as we leap. The distance we have from the floor or apparatus determines our *level,* which can be low (close to the floor or base), medium, or high (far away from the floor or base). When we travel from one spot to another, we will produce a *pathway.* A floor pattern may take the most direct route possible to our destination (straight pathway), or an indirect, circuitous route (curved or zigzag). We may also create an air pattern as the extremities fill space or as the body travels through the air in flight. When we travel, we have options as to which direction we choose to move. Each of these spatial dimensions (personal space, general space, levels, pathways, and directions) will be discussed with direct reference to gymnastic movement.

A pathway may be seen when one leaves tracks.

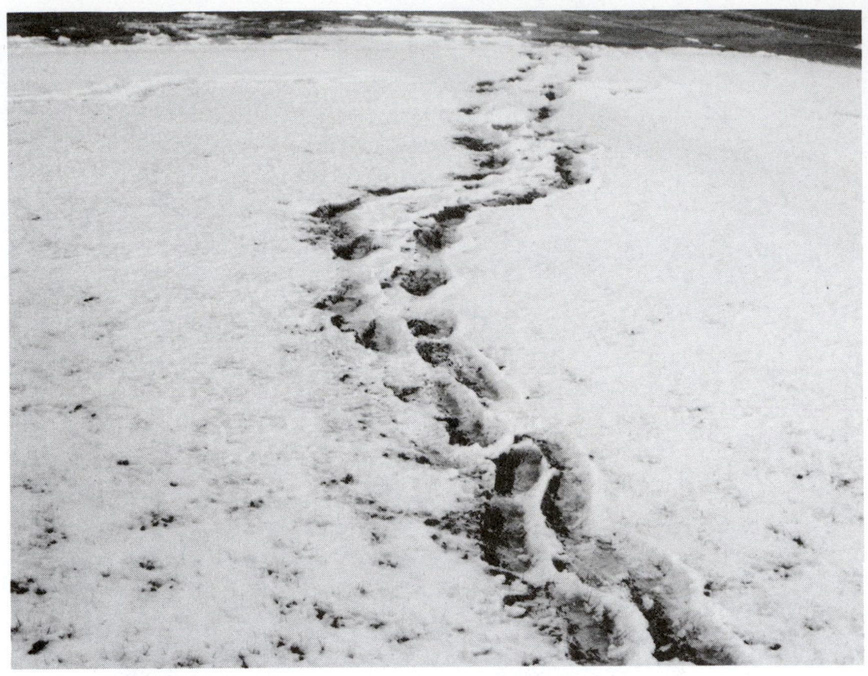

Personal Space

Personal space is the space around the body that may be filled without traveling. We may think of our personal space as a bubble or balloon in which we create shapes. We may reach up into space as we stretch high in preparation for a handstand, or tuck our bodies as we land from jumping. We take the "balloon" of personal space with us wherever we travel. When our body parts are stretched to their limits inside this "balloon" of personal space, a transfer of weight occurs, and we will probably travel to a new spot in the general space.

General Space

General space refers to all the area into which we may travel. It includes any empty space not filled by people, objects, or structures. When we run, jump, swing, or climb, we fill general space.

Pathways

One may illustrate the concept of **pathway** to children by providing the simple analogy of walking on a clean floor with muddy feet or making tracks in freshly fallen snow. When one turns around to look at the footprints made, the pathway will be evident.

Gymnastics apparatus arrangements promote various pathways. Generally speaking, when we travel on the floor, the accent is on the *floor* pathway. When we employ flight and travel through the air (as we do on hanging ropes), the accent in on the *air* pathway. When the teacher asks children to travel around their hoop on the floor, they will follow a circular pathway. The air pathway when swinging on a hanging rope or bar will be curved. When the design of a long skipping rope is manipulated by the child, various floor pathways may result as the child travels along the rope. When benches, beams, and planks are used, the teacher may ask the child to travel along the apparatus. Here the pathway would be straight. However, the teacher may say, "Travel the length of the apparatus touching it only with your hands." In response to this task, many children will travel from one side to the other over a bench, creating a zigzag pathway.

When children work with mats only, their tendency will be to create sequences that travel only in a straight line. You will need to encourage various pathways when transference of weight is developed. "Imagine that you can write your name with your feet on the floor as you travel," and "Repeat your sequence, making sure that corners are sharp if you turn," are examples of tasks that direct the child's concentration to the pathway. Once children have explored various movements and the type of pathway these movements tend to create, you may then introduce letters, numbers, geometrical shapes, and other simple forms as impetus for new pathways.

When planning apparatus arrangements, you will need to consider pathway. If the apparatus is set up in a line, then you can assume children will use a straight pathway. Leaving spaces between large pieces of apparatus, or setting up apparatus in specific designs (e.g., circle) will elicit variety in pathways.

Directions

The concept of direction relates to one's personal space. Direction is relatively simple to children. In early childhood, they learn the concepts of front, back, beside, up, down, forward, backward, and sideways. They will readily understand that they may travel forward (toward their front), backward (toward their back), sideways (to their right or left side), up (toward their head), down (toward their feet), or diagonally, combining three directions that are not opposites (e.g., sideways, up, right).

Some confusion does exist however with respect to the difference between change of direction and change of pathway. A child may perform a forward roll, turn 90 degrees, and perform another forward roll. In this situation, the child is consistently traveling forward into general space and is not changing direction, but creating a zigzag pathway. When you ask children to change direction, where they are facing does not matter, but ***where the action travels in relation to themselves*** is significant.

For further clarification, more examples are provided. A log roll travels to the side of the body, as does a cartwheel. A walkover travels forward. A back arch may be created only by moving down and back or forward and downward.

Children will enjoy discovering which activities are restricted to particular directions and which are flexible in direction. You may be specific in providing guidelines for sequence work. "Create a sequence of traveling forward, traveling up and down, balancing, then traveling sideways." This type of guidance will encourage a great range of possibilities. Older children may be challenged further by guidelines that involve the two spatial concepts of direction and pathway. "Create a sequence of a straight pathway where you travel forward, a curved pathway where you travel diagonally, and finally, in a zigzag pathway, travel backward" is an example of such a task.

Levels

Levels will probably be one of the first spatial concepts you may develop to some degree with children. Children soon learn that flight and instability occur at a high level, speed and mobility are gained at a medium level, and stability is most effective at a low level.

In gymnastics, you will probably begin with familiar traveling actions, such as running, stopping, hopping, and leaping without apparatus. While these actions are performed at a medium to high level, young children will find gaining height difficult and will perform them at a medium level, while older children will employ flight and will use a high level.

Rolling actions occur at a low level. Once children are adept at various types of rolls, the teacher may introduce initiating rolls from various levels. The children may balance at high or medium levels and transfer weight in order to roll. The dive roll is an excellent example of attempting to gain height and flight before tucking to roll. Children may then explore rolling over objects, rolling from apparatus, and rolling onto apparatus, all of which promote change of level.

As apparatus is introduced, the concept of levels may take on new meaning. A child can create a shape at a high level while balancing on a high box. If the child lies down on the box, he or she has created a low shape but is still "high" in relation to the ground. Thus, we may take level to mean both the distance from the ground and the distance from the apparatus that supports our weight.

Relationship Concepts

The concept of relationships is comprised of two subdivisions—relationships to apparatus and relationships to people (figure 11.7). While the former serves as a concept appropriate for gymnastic work with young or inexperienced children, relationships to people is a complex theme appropriate for older children who are socially capable of cooperation with others and have sufficiently developed body management skills.

Relationships to Apparatus

This is an appropriate movement concept for children in kindergarten and first grade, because they are at the stage of grasping spatially oriented words. Such prepositions as in, out, on, off, around, along, through, above, below, in front, behind, beside, over, and under may be explored in relation to small and large apparatus. Such tasks as "Travel over and under

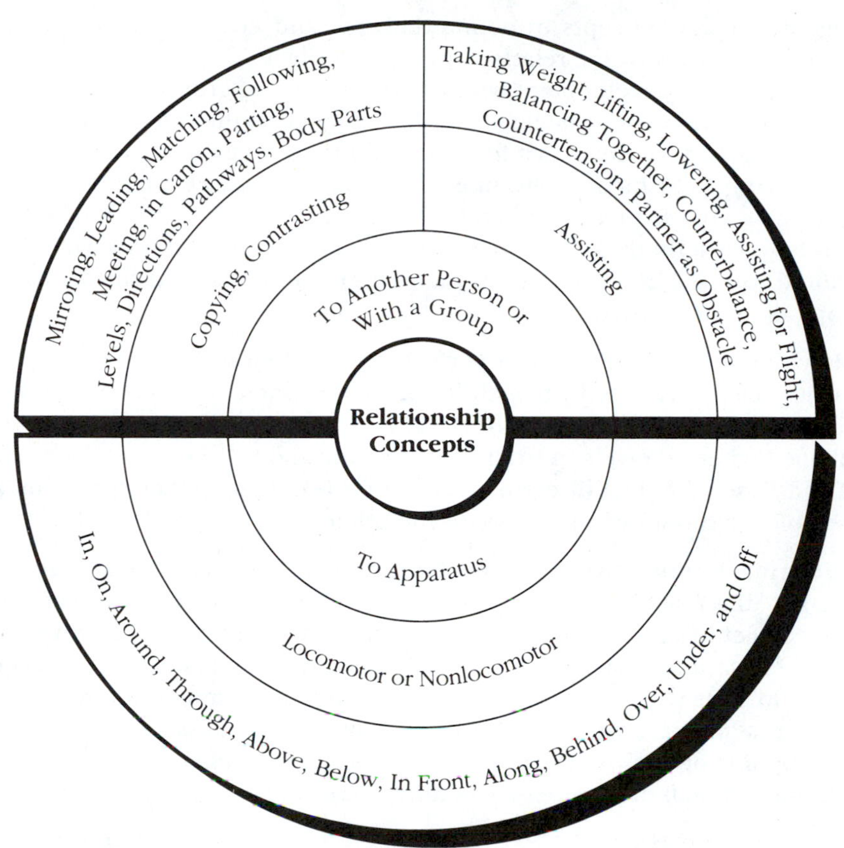

Figure 11.7 Relationship concepts.

the bench,'' and ''Jump in and out of the hoop, then travel through it,'' are simple, yet will challenge young children to problem solve through movement.

Older children in the upper elementary grades should also explore this theme if they are relatively inexperienced. Complex apparatus arrangements demand the ability to relate to the equipment, to ''see'' the possibilities for action. The tasks you give to these older children should be more complex and physically demanding and may involve a combination of spatial prepositions with other concepts, such as pathway, level, body parts, body shape, or time. For example, you may say, ''Travel along the bench backward,'' ''Balance on the box at a high level,'' or ''Try different ways of traveling quickly around your apparatus with emphasis on hands taking the weight.''

Relationships to People

Children will find it helpful, encouraging, and satisfying to develop gymnastic skill with others. They may work with partners or small groups effectively as long as their social ability is sufficient to allow them to cooperate, respect others, solve problems, and safely move in harmony together. (The concepts of counterbalance and countertension previously discussed involve relationships to people.)

Initial skill development with a partner or small group will focus on copying another's movements. Children may combine the best work of their partner with their own to create identical sequences, or they may prefer simply to incorporate one or two movements of their partner's into their own sequence. When children are at different levels of skill, it is important for the teacher to stress that at times the more-skilled child should copy the lesser-skilled, and at others the lesser-skilled child should copy the more-skilled.

Matching

Matching means that children perform exactly the same movements. It is most easily practiced when children face the same way: if *A* points her right foot, *B* must do so as well. However, matching may also be accomplished when *A* travels in front of *B* (leading and following, cannon) or *A* and *B* face different directions. The latter is difficult, since timing may be "off" without one child seeing the other.

Mirroring

Mirroring implies that children face each other, creating a "mirror image." If *A* reaches to the right, *B* will have to reach to the left to create the correct image. Children may need clarification once they begin traveling forward and backward in mirroring. If one travels back, the other must do so as well. If one travels forward, the other travels forward, exactly as a mirror image does. Children may also mirror each other while side by side or back to back; however, this is more difficult because they cannot see each other as easily. A mirror may help in this situation.

Meeting and Parting

Meeting and parting may be performed either in copying or contrasting movements. When children meet, they come together in space. When they part, they move away from one another in space. This concept may be quite challenging if children incorporate apparatus within their sequences because it increases the complexity of the relationship.

Leading and Following

Leading and following, like meeting and parting, may be performed either with similar or differing movements. Here the focus is on the spatial relationship between the two individuals as they follow the same pathway. Children will need to be reminded that once the leader turns 180 degrees, the follower will do so as well and will no longer be in the "following" position. It may also be pointed out that traveling backward is difficult unless planned carefully, for the leader may bump into the follower.

Symmetry and Asymmetry

Symmetry and asymmetry is a body concept as it relates to body shape. However, when two or more people work to form one shape, it may be viewed as a relationship concept. Children will need much cooperation and the ability to visualize what they look like from the "outside" to create symmetrical shapes. If mirrors are not available, the teacher may

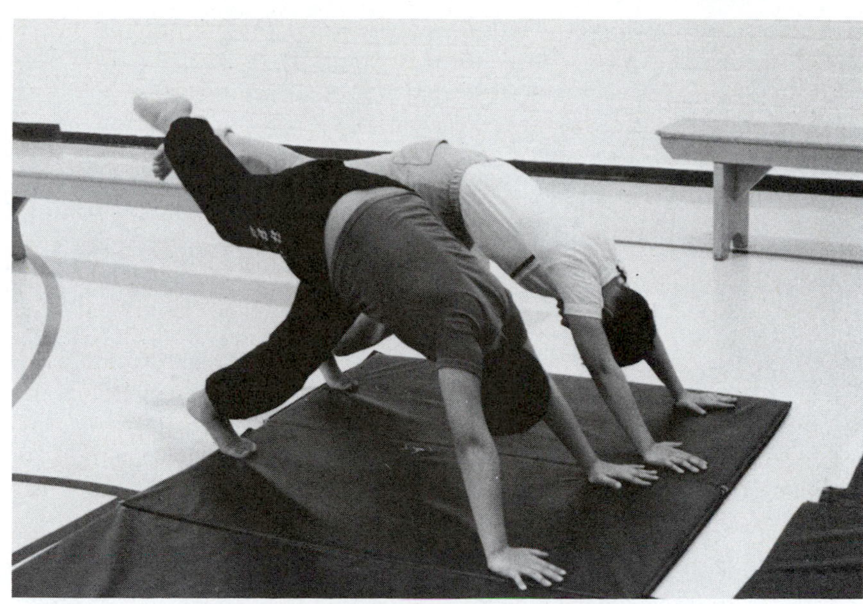

Matching movements are exactly the same.

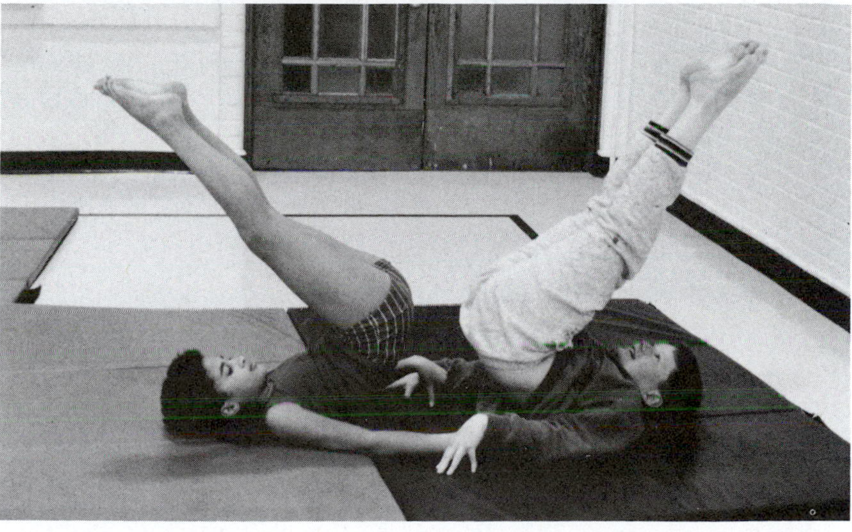

When mirroring, children face each other to create a "mirror" image.

demonstrate with a child or use pictures to help the children grasp this concept. Asymmetry is much easier as one child will create a different shape than the other.

Canon

Movement in canon implies that a particular movement is repeatedly performed by two or more individuals following the same pathway. A typical example of movement in canon is found in classical ballet, where

A symmetrical shape is the same on both sides. These boys have made one shape.

a number of dancers leap across the stage, one after another. In gymnastics, canon may be developed as children roll or transfer their weight in the same way, one after the other (see chapter 5).

Contrasting

Children may also contrast in the sequence work. This contrast may be found in level (one travels high while another travels low), in directions used while transferring weight, in body parts used, or in pathway employed. While the movement one observes in the theme of contrasting with another person may not significantly differ from other themes, it will focus the child's attention on the relationship one may have to another.

Assisting

In partner work, children assist each other in performing gymnastic actions. These actions were discussed in the section of this chapter that dealt with weightbearing, balance, and flight. However, it may be useful to state that children may take partial or total weight of a partner, lift or lower their partner, or assist in creating an extended period of flight.

Application of the Movement Concepts

Many of the movement concepts discussed in this chapter are the focus of the gymnastics lessons presented for you in the accompanying Lesson Plan Manual. The gymnastic themes index (Table 11.5) lists these concepts, and should help you gain a better understanding of gymnastic content and how it may challenge children of all ages. In these lessons, you will find learning sequences for floor work, small equipment, and large apparatus.

Table 11.5

Gymnastics Theme Index

Lessons—Kindergarten	Body concepts	Effort concepts	Spatial concepts	Relationship concepts
1	Locomotion Hands/feet			
2	Locomotion Body parts			
3	Locomotion Body parts		Near/far	
4	Locomotion Shapes			
5	Locomotion Body parts	Fast/slow		
Lessons—Grades 1–2				
6	Locomotion		Directions	
7	Body parts		Directions	
8	Stretched/curled shapes		Directions	
9	Body parts Stretch/curl actions			
10	Transference of weight (Trans. wt.) Rocking/rolling Shapes			
11	Trans. wt.	Fast/slow		
12	Trans. wt.	Contrast Speed		
13	Trans. wt.	Speed changes	Directions	
14	Shapes	Speed changes		
15		Accelerate/decelerate/stillness	Directions Up/down	

Table 11.5 Continued

Gymnastics Theme Index

Lessons—Grades 3–4	Body concepts	Effort concepts	Spatial concepts	Relationship concepts
16	Body parts Trans. wt.		Pathways	
17	Arches Bridges			Partner relationship (rel.)
18	Extension/ contraction	Time		Partner rel. Apparatus rel.
19	Trans. wt. Turning		Directions	
20	Trans. wt. Turning/ twisting			
21			Levels	Partner contrast
22	Turning/ twisting		Levels	
23	Turning/ twisting		Pathways	
24	Geometric shapes		Pathways	Partner copy
25	Shapes		Levels	Matching
Lessons—Grades 5–6				
26	Balance Trans. wt.			
27	Balance Symmetry/ asymmetry			
28	Balance/ overbalance Twisting/ turning			
29	Balance Twisting Symmetry/ asymmetry	Sudden/ sustained		

Table 11.5 *Continued*

Gymnastics Theme Index

Lessons—Grades 5–6	Body concepts	Effort concepts	Spatial concepts	Relationship concepts
30	Flight Trans. wt. Dynamic balance Symmetry/ asymmetry			
31	Trans. wt.	Time changes	Flight	
32	Balance Flight		Flight Levels	
33	Counter-balance	Pull/push	Flight	Flight over a partner Partner Counterbalance
34		Pull/push	Levels	Meeting/parting Counterbalance
35	Symmetry/ asymmetry	Time		Group Work-copy, Canon

Table 11.6

Selecting Appropriate Apparatus for Gymnastic Actions

Gymnastic activity	Possible apparatus
Jumping over	Hoops, skipping ropes, horizontal sticks, benches, low beams, low boxes, planks
From/off	Benches, beams, boxes, horses, planks, trestles, rings, ladder, cargo net, vertical ropes, climber
On	Benches, beams, boxes, horses, planks, trestles, springboard, reuther board, trampette, rings, ladder, vertical ropes, climber, cargo net

Table 11.6 Continued

Selecting Appropriate Apparatus for Gymnastic Actions

Gymnastic activity	Possible apparatus
Rocking and rolling:	
under, through	Hoops, horizontal sticks, benches, trestles
over, on	Benches, trestles, boxes, horses, planks, beams
Sliding	Inclined plank, inclined bench
Stepping actions	Hoops, ropes, horizontal sticks, gymnastic stools, benches, trestles, horses, boxes, rings, ladders, planks, climbers, ropes, cargo net, beam
Climbing	Gymnastic stools, trestles, ladders, horses, boxes, ladders, planks, climbers, vertical ropes, cargo net
Balancing	Hoops, ropes, gymnastic stools, benches, trestles, horses, boxes, rings, ladders, planks, climbers, nets, beams
Hanging	Trestles, horses, boxes, rings, ladders, climbers, vertical ropes, nets, high beams
Swinging	Rings, vertical ropes, horizontal ladders, saddle on bars, climber, cargo net

Summary

Gymnastics plays a vital role in physical education. The focus is on the body and how and where it moves in relation to the floor or apparatus. The movement concepts of the body, effort, space, and relationships are applied similarly in dance, games, and gymnastics with very different results. In gymnastics, the body concepts of weightbearing and weight transference will be stressed more due to the functional, yet aesthetic, nature of gymnastics. Large apparatus will provide exciting possibilities for various actions. Table 11.6 lists appropriate apparatus for gymnastic activities.

Review Questions

1. Discuss the similarities and differences between modern rhythmic gymnastics and educational gymnastics.
2. What are the four body concepts studied in gymnastics?
3. What is the difference between balance and suspension?
4. How are weightbearing, weight transference, and body parts interrelated?
5. How does body shape affect balance?
6. What is the difference between direction and pathway?
7. Older children may enjoy working in pairs. What concepts may be developed?

References

Jordan, D. (1970). *Childhood and movement.* Oxford: Basil Blackwell.

Laban, R., and Lawrence, F. C. (1948). *Effort.* London: Macdonald and Evans, Ltd.

Mauldon, E., and Layson, J. (1965). *Teaching gymnastics.* London: Macdonald and Evans, Ltd.

Morison, R. (1969). *A movement approach to educational gymnastics.* London: Dent and Sons.

Russell, K. (1980). Gymnastics—Why is it in school curricula. *Journal of the Saskatchewan Physical Education Association, 6*(1), 17–19.

Stanley, S. (1969). *Physical education: A movement orientation.* Toronto: McGraw-Hill Ryerson Ltd.

Williams, J. (1974). *Themes for educational gymnastics.* London: Lepus Books.

Wilson, V.J. (1979). Turn on turn off. *Canadian Association of Health, Physical Education and Recreation Journal, 46*(1), 39–41.

Chapter 12
Teaching Gymnastics

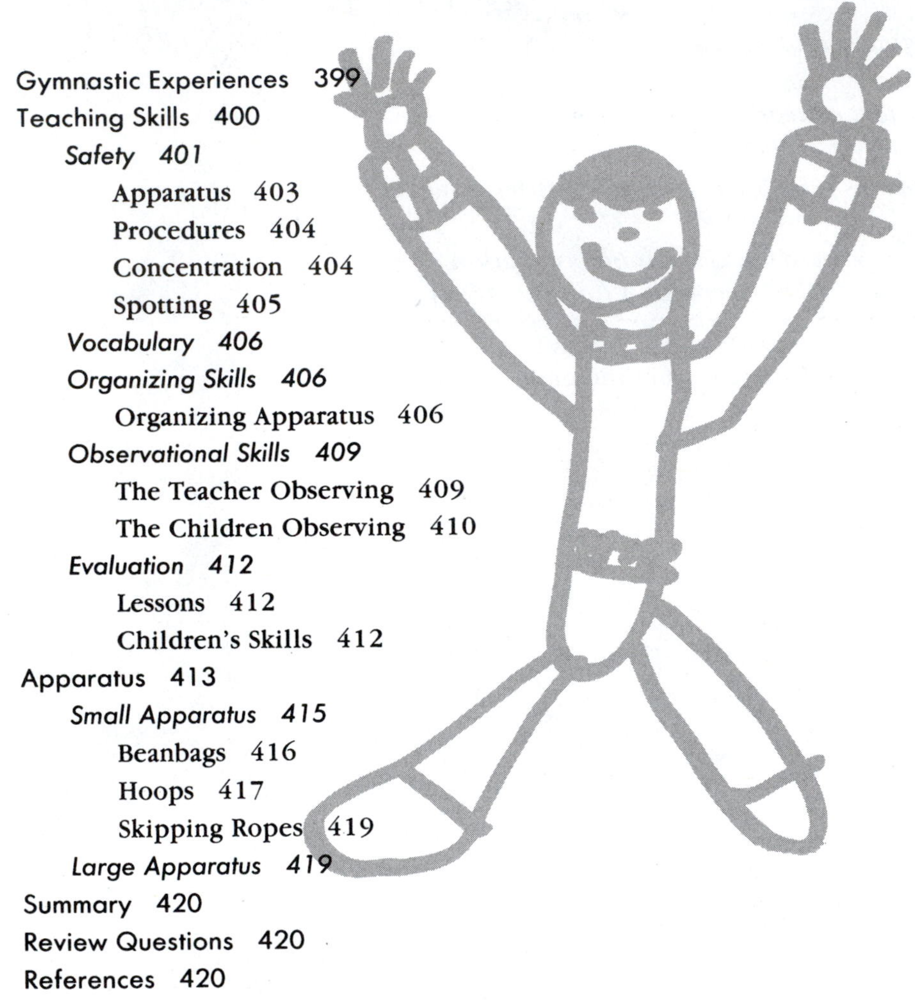

> ***The teacher of educational gymnastics (also) aims to teach bodily skills, but he is equally concerned with knowledge, for his business is education (Williams, 1974).***

As in dance and games, teaching gymnastics is complex and constantly demanding. The tone that you set and the creation of a safe, yet exciting, and positive learning environment is essential for children to feel both secure and challenged in gymnastics.

Gymnastic Experiences

Gymnastics offers opportunities for exciting movement challenges. As children are introduced to jumping, landing, rotating, and balancing on the floor, the addition of apparatus provides new experiences. Children will delight in the adventure that apparatus provides for balancing, climbing, hanging, and swinging.

While there may be a strong tendency to let the children play freely on all apparatus available, you will need to select apparatus that is appropriate for the lesson's objectives and plan tasks that provide a focus for the range of movements from which the child may choose. This does not imply that free play is worthless; it simply means that the child must be taken beyond the stage of free play to that of skill development. If free exploration were the only gymnastic experience offered within the school program, it would be no different from the child's play in the schoolyard.

Because we all enjoy that which we do well, chances are that the children who dislike gymnastics are weak in skill, and those who enjoy it have natural skill. In every class, there will be children who have tremendous difficulty with even the simplest rolls and others who cartwheel or walk on their hands with ease. It is likely that these two groups of children may initially pose concern for you, for how is it possible to cater to the needs of such a diverse group? While one child may require special coaxing merely to get off the bench and participate in the class, another child may seemingly show off by climbing the ropes and perching near the ceiling of the gymnasium. It is only through sensitive guidance in instruction and an environment that caters to the needs of all children that every child will progress in the gymnastic program.

When children are provided with the stimulus of apparatus, open tasks will allow them to discover some of the limitations and potential of that piece. Once children have familiarized themselves with the possibilities, then closed tasks will provide additional challenges. Children may be asked to select one or two movements that they enjoy and then repeat and refine them. In sequence development, the next stage is to find ways of approaching the apparatus, getting on the apparatus, or traveling away from it. Finally, the aim is to join movements so the movements flow smoothly from start to finish. In this way, children create a

Table 12.1

The Gymnastic Experience

The physical experience must be	The social experience must be		The learning experience must promote
Child-oriented	Positive	Encouraging	Concentration
Challenging	Cooperative	Pleasant	Memory
Safe	Helpful	Accepting	Creativity
Clean	Observant	Reinforcing	Inventiveness
Tidy	Supportive	Guiding	Problem solving
Predictable	Advising	Sincere	Analysis
			Observation

movement sequence indicative of their gymnastic ability, and something of which they are proud. Table 12.1 lists the aspects of a successful gymnastic experience.

Teaching Skills

Whatever the children's level of skill, purposeful activity should be maximized. The tasks set and the type of apparatus chosen must be within the children's capabilities. Lessons should occur in sequence, each one building upon the previous one. ***Progression from simple to complex both in tasks and apparatus is vitally important.***

You should initially explore the children's abilities in the area of locomotion on the feet. Traveling and stopping in various body shapes and traveling while changing directions, pathways, and speed will be developed to improve agility and control in running, jumping, hopping, and leaping activities.

New movement concepts are usually introduced on the floor (e.g., body shapes, body parts, time) before small or large apparatus is introduced. With each new movement concept presented, you should provide progressive tasks for the children without apparatus, so the basics of the concepts are mentally appreciated and kinesthetically experienced. Initial exploration and later skill refinement will occur as the children experience balance in relation to the floor. Children should learn to roll immediately upon landing to avoid injury. Discovering effective means of gaining height and appropriate ways to recover upon landing are important. Once you have covered the basic movements required for safety (landing and rolling) and have an appreciation of the movement concept, then apparatus may effectively be introduced.

The arrangement of large and small apparatus will determine the kinds of challenges offered the child. The juxtaposition of pieces should be determined by the movement concept and the tasks you pose. Children may be offered the freedom of repositioning small apparatus to suit their needs or be purposely restricted to a particular arrangement.

> *It is the design, spacing, and stability of apparatus that will determine its usefulness. Different ways of associating separate elements are required, with each arrangement offering particular and distinct opportunities (Department of Education and Science, 1972).*

Remember That

It is only when the task requires skill that the child feels is unattainable or when the child deems the skill useless that children will not participate as fully as possible. When children know that they can succeed in pleasurable activities, all will participate.

To Do

How would you react if your teacher said, "Do a back handspring"? How would you react if the teacher said, "Travel backward using hands and feet"?

The way tasks are worded is extremely important. They must allow for skill development within the movement concept at all skill levels. For instance, less-skilled children may respond to the task "Travel along the bench at a low level" by walking on hands and feet in a crouched position. The highly skilled child may roll forward on the bench, while a child with a lower limb disability may pull himself forward with his arms as he or she slides on his or her stomach. All children are gaining experience and developing skill no matter what their capabilities.

Children should be encouraged to help one another if the opportunity arises. They may offer friendly advice, provide reinforcement for one another, or show their newly acquired skills without apprehension. When children are rewarded for their efforts, the vital support so paramount in skill acquisition will provide tremendous reinforcement.

Safety

Some teachers are hesitant to teach gymnastics for fear of children injuring themselves. Lawsuits resulting from tragic accidents in competitive artistic gymnastics classes have compounded the problem.

Let's examine the cause of such injuries. We know that all children are different. In a class there may be a child who finds gymnastics very difficult and another who finds it very easy. If we expect all children to perform exactly the same movement in exactly the same manner, children will suffer in different ways. Those who have not mastered the prerequisite skills will not be able to perform as expected, while those who

Safety Tip

If you introduced the theme of balance and immediately allowed children to climb to the highest point on apparatus, or hold a shape after jumping off a springboard, injuries may result due to children's lack of control. Teach them first to run, jump, land, and roll.

are capable of learning a much more difficult skill will not be challenged. What will the less skilled group gain by trying to replicate movements too difficult for them? They will gain a sense of failure from practicing the movement incorrectly, and incorrect use of the body may result in injury. The advanced group may become bored and lose concentration when performing the skill. Because concentration is essential for all gymnastic movements, injury may also result if the child is not completely involved. Thus, it is imperative that the activity is structured around the needs of every child in the class. The teaching philosophy of structuring the class to meet the needs of the activity is not only erroneous, it fosters the opportunity for injury.

What Is Wrong with This Situation?

The fourth grade class is participating in the third class of a two month-long unit of gymnastics. The teacher has chosen the movement concept of flight for the lesson because he believes that this is an essential skill to be developed by all children. After a brief gymnastic warm-up, the teacher gives instructions for the children to set up specific gymnastic stations. A group of six children set up a mat, a beatboard, a vault (four feet high), and another mat in a line. The wall prevents the children from placing two mats in a row.

The problems with the situation follow:

1. The movement concept of flight is appropriate only with gymnastically experienced and skilled children. The movement concept of locomotion, balance, body shape, body parts, transference of weight, levels, time (changes in speed), and weight should precede the concept of flight.
2. Every movement concept should be developed on the floor or mats before apparatus is used to challenge the children further. Because the basic principles or ideas pertinent to every theme are applicable both with and without apparatus, the children should develop skill first in its simplest form (without apparatus), then in increasingly complex situations that involve a variety of small, and then large apparatus or with partners or in small groups.
3. Groups of six children will work well if each child is constantly moving and not standing in line. The problem with this apparatus set-up is that it is in a straight pathway where the flow of traffic will progress from one end to the other. Apparatus should be arranged so that children may use any combination of the apparatus and can approach it from a variety of angles.

What is wrong with this apparatus arrangement?

4. The beatboard initially should be used by itself so that children kinesthetically experience the feeling of flight, landing, and rolling. Because the theme of flight is a difficult, advanced theme, it is very dangerous to have a large obstacle placed near it. If a child lacks control in assisted flight, the chances of him or her striking the vault are quite likely and will undoubtedly cause injury.
5. One of the most dangerous aspects of this situation is that the vault is too close to the wall. When a child is flying through the air after take-off from the beatboard, a wall that may stop the motion is certainly not desirable!

Apparatus

Regardless of your preferred style of instruction and the age and experience of the children, the physical environment must be safe and non-threatening. Apparatus that is broken or worn to the point of being unsafe must be repaired. It should also be suitable in size for the children to be safe. Trestles, gymnastic stools, and vaulting boxes should be small enough for children to feel secure yet large enough to be challenging. Placement of apparatus should be such that children's pathways are not "crisscrossing," and there is ample space between pieces of apparatus and the apparatus and the wall.

Children should learn to carry equipment safely.

Procedures

Children must be taught how to lift and carry apparatus so that no injuries occur, either to the floor or the students. Procedures of taking out, setting up, and putting away apparatus should be clearly established and closely followed.

Concentration

Safety also implies a level of concentration by each child. The noise level should be kept at a minimum, though productive chatting is often necessary. Children must be made aware of the importance of concentration when attempting a new movement, refining a previously acquired skill, or joining movements together in a sequence. It is important to establish that children should decide what movement will be attempted before it is begun, because there are times when children change their minds in mid-action. When the difficult concept of flight is being developed, concentration is paramount for children's safety. It is not acceptable to begin one movement and attempt to finish with another! For example, children should not decide to jump *onto* a box and then, after taking off from a springboard, decide to jump *over* the box. Very likely, feet would catch on the box and injury could result.

Spotting

One of the basic premises we believe in is that children are aware of their own limits. It is only when the teacher's expectations are too high or the element of competition is introduced that children go beyond their limits. Thus, spotting (manually helping someone perform an action) should be necessary only when children are attempting actions somewhat beyond their limits. We believe that the onus should be placed on children for their personal safety when they decide what movements will be attempted. You may encourage children to try new and more difficult maneuvers, but children should rarely be forced or manually assisted to perform. The only time that spotting may be helpful is when a child needs assistance to kinesthetically "feel" a new movement. The teacher should be the spotter. For instance, a child may wish to try a back handspring but have no idea where the movement should "go."

> ***Spotting techniques require an understanding of the stunt being performed, knowing how to assist the movement and some degree of strength. . . . The teacher invariably provides the spotting for gymnastics stunts which limits the amount of activity. . . . (Docherty & Morton, 1982).***

Safety Tip

1. Rules for safety should be established and enforced.
2. Children should be responsive to the teacher's command of "rest" or "stop."
3. The teacher should never leave the gymnastic area while children are working.
4. Children should use gymnastic apparatus only when a teacher is present.
5. The activity area should be clean and free of apparatus not in use.
6. Children should only attempt skills that are within their capabilities. They should ask for your help when they plan to do something "scary."
7. Children should never touch one another unless instructed to do so.
8. Children should wear appropriate clothing. Bare feet are most safe as they grip the floor or supporting surface well; socks or sneakers tend to slip on climbing apparatus. When children are hanging by their knees, bare legs should be exposed, so the skin is in contact with the bar. Jewelry, such as dangling earrings and necklaces, should be removed.
9. Mats should be used when children take weight on body parts other than feet in locomotor and nonlocomotor activities. However, children should realize that mats do not prevent injury.
10. Children must lift, carry, and place apparatus as instructed.
11. Wear on apparatus should be monitored by both the teacher and children. Damaged apparatus should be reported immediately.
12. The teacher should establish and adhere to a maximum number of children allowed on the climbing frame and other larger apparatus.

Vocabulary

The vocabulary you use and the energy with which you speak is important. You should convey some of the feeling of the action to the children. Words, such as "spring," "tuck tight," and "lift," need to be said with conviction and strength. The timing of your verbal guidance may also be crucial to how quickly a child learns a new skill. Phrases, such as "Push *now,*" "Tuck *now,*" "Let go *now,*" and "Now *lift,*" require sensitivity to give help at the appropriate moment.

Organizing Skills

The way the class is managed and organized will depend upon the age and gymnastic experience of the children, the apparatus available, and your preferred teaching style. Whatever the situation, good management is imperative for expediency and safety of the children.

In the gymnastic lesson, it should be possible for all of the children to be working at the same time. While line-ups and regimented formations may be pleasing to the eye, they do little to promote maximum activity and maximum skill development. When apparatus is arranged effectively and groups are kept small, waiting will be minimized. The more a child engages in productive movement activities, the more movement skill will result. However, children may also need short periods of rest.

Just as children appreciate the predictability of routine in the classroom, routine in the gymnasium is necessary as well. How you organize the children is up to you, but it is suggested that responsibility is delegated even with the youngest children. When children are given a regular task to perform, such as taking out and setting up a particular piece of apparatus, they will become quite reliable and adept at carrying it out.

Organizing Apparatus

In initial gymnastic lessons, you will find it most helpful to spend a good deal of time reinforcing the importance of safety, care of the apparatus, and how to set up and dismantle specific pieces. Children should be taught always to lift apparatus when carrying it in order to avoid injuring themselves, the apparatus, or the floor. You will need to establish that two, three, or four children (depending on their age) should always carry larger pieces, such as benches, boxes, ladders, and planks. The way that children set up large apparatus should also be checked, so bolts are placed in their designated holes, and clamps, wires, chains, and other interlocking devices are secured. Since apparatus differs considerably from manufacturer to manufacturer, you will need to find out how to safely secure each piece.

When various types of large and small apparatus are used repeatedly, there are various ways the children may be organized to retrieve and set it up. Individuals or small groups of children may be responsible for the same apparatus each day. Once it is carried onto the gymnasium floor, you may direct which pieces will be arranged together. You may be specific as to how the arrangement will be set, or the children may be allowed to arrange it as they wish. Visual aids, such as diagrams or posters

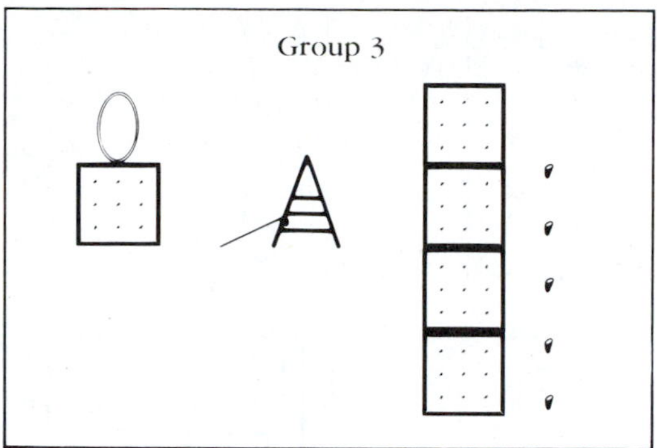

One card per group.

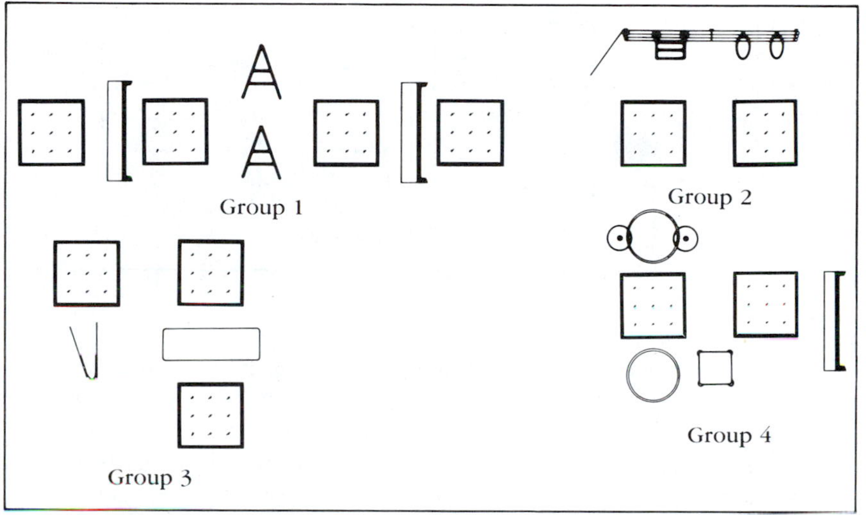

One illustration for the entire class.

Figure 12.1 Visual aids may be used to illustrate apparatus arrangement.

tacked on the gymnasium wall, or cards, given to leaders of small groups may be used to indicate apparatus arrangements for specific stations (figure 12.1).

If light and easily portable apparatus, such as ropes, beanbags, or hoops are used, you may tell the children, "Come and get the apparatus and take it into an empty space." In this situation, all children work with the same apparatus. When there is not enough of one kind for each child, then different apparatus may be used, and children switch apparatus halfway through the class. Stations of various pieces of apparatus will facilitate all children working all of the time. In this type of arrangement, you may allow children to go on to another station when desired, or you may indicate to children when it is time to rotate onto the next area (figure 12.2).

Figure 12.2 (*a*) Everyone works with the same apparatus. (*b*) Half the class works with one type of apparatus; half works with another. The two groups later exchange. (*c*) Children move from station to station as they wish, or when the teacher tells them to move. (*d*) Children take out and set up the apparatus with which they want to work.

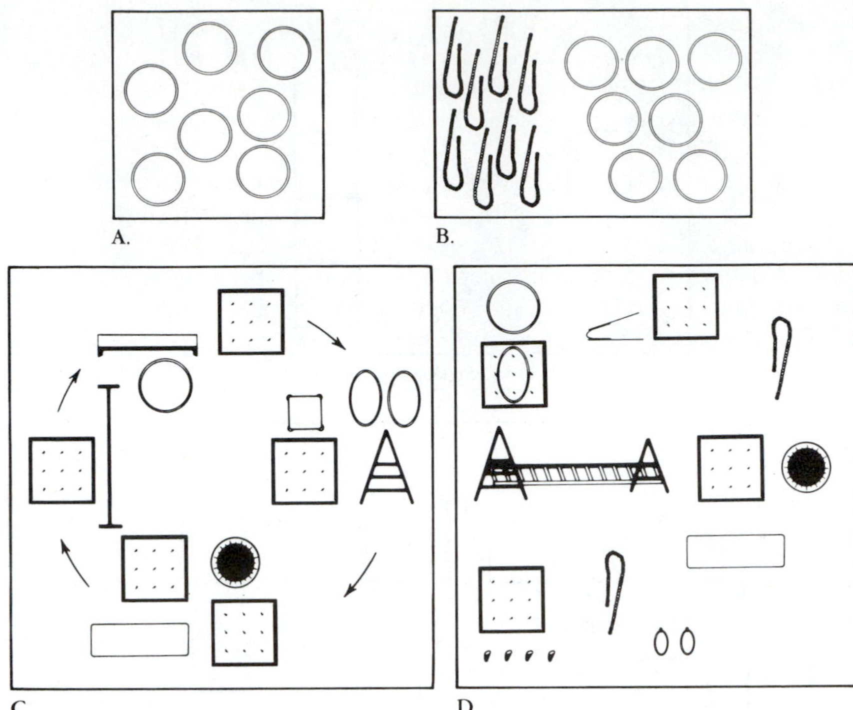

Whether you or the children decide on the precise spatial arrangement of the apparatus, the setting must always be surveyed to ensure adequate space is available for the approach to and travel away from the apparatus. Approaches from various angles should be available so that one particular piece of apparatus is not overcrowded. Mats should be considered apparatus as well, so children practice the full range of their skills in one area. Because children find greatest enjoyment in apparatus that moves, hanging ropes, hanging ladders and bars, springboards, minitramps, and trampettes should be placed at different stations for all to experience. Overcrowding should not be a problem if enough attractive pieces are situated in various spots throughout the gymnasium.

> *Space is essential if vigorous flight and traveling are to be attempted just as stable and firm surfaces are necessary to support robust take-offs and landings (Department of Education and Science, 1972).*

Observational Skills

Being a good observer takes time and experience as a teacher. It is not a skill that can be easily learned overnight or from a book. However, chapters 3, 6, and 9 provide useful information. Some guidelines specific to gymnastics are presented here to help you be a better observer.

The Teacher Observing

Our first concern as we observe children is their safety. If they are carrying, setting up, or putting away apparatus, we should scan the area to ensure that no one is bumping a peer, that apparatus is being lifted and carried properly, and that it is set up in the appropriate place. Once we scan, we should focus on smaller details to further check safety. To focus, we may have to move closer to get a better look at such things as

Sherry's dangling earrings,

the way that Joey is holding the bench,

how far the springboard is from the wall,

if the bolt on the climber is secured properly.

We also observe to check the apparatus arrangement. This will involve both scanning and focusing. You may ask yourself the following questions:

Does each child have a hoop?

Have the children interpreted the diagram of the apparatus arrangement correctly?

Is the arrangement that the children created safe?

Is the apparatus appropriate for the theme of the lesson?

Is it appropriate for the children's level of skill?

When you consider these questions, you will likely visit each station/ apparatus arrangement to find the answer (figure 12.3).

Once you are satisfied that the environment is safe and the apparatus appropriate, you will want to observe the children's movement and how they respond to your tasks. Table 12.2 outlines a simple progression of what you should look for, what you may see, and how you could react.

As you observe the children, you will need to travel throughout the space. Position yourself far enough away from whomever you are observing—it's similar to "missing the forest for the trees." Stand at least ten feet away, so you can see the entire picture and watch the entire movement or movement sequence from start to finish. When you focus on one child, you will likely concentrate on specific body parts, such as knees when landing, the head in balancing, toes in stretching, or the chest in leaping.

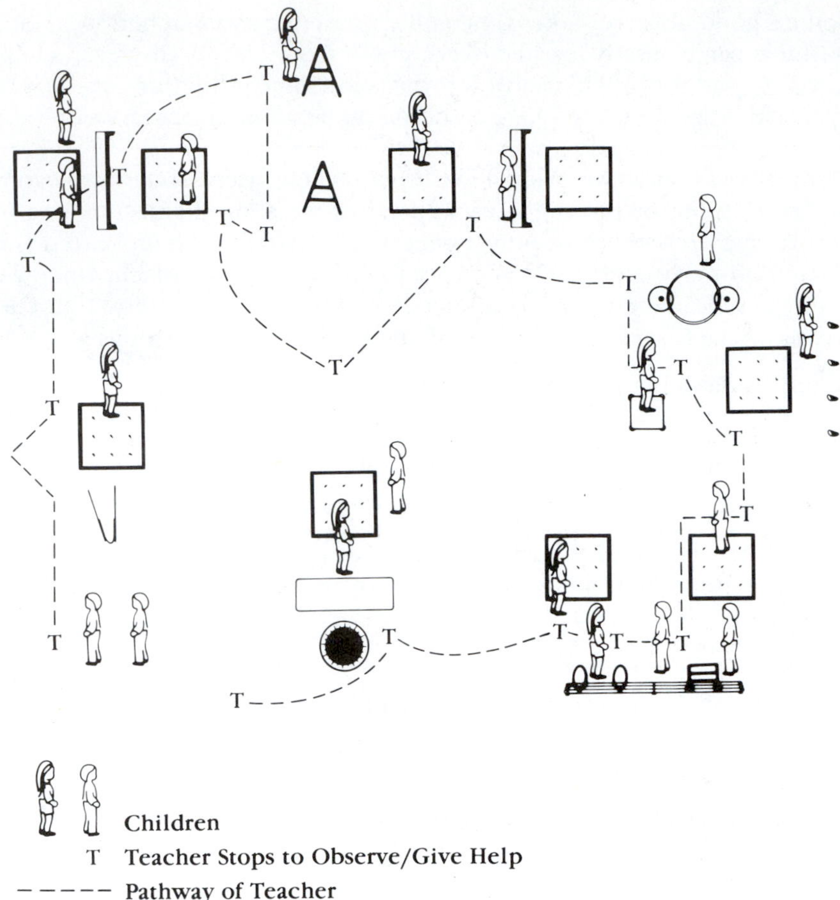

Figure 12.3 The teacher observing the children's movement.

The Children Observing

We believe that children can learn a great deal from observing one another's movements. In gymnastics, peer observation is particularly effective because children are eager to show their work. While peer observation in gymnastics is very similar to that of dance and games, there are some differences largely due to the apparatus.

When children are observing their peers, tell them to do the following:

1. Sit so you can see the "front" of the whole sequence.
2. Concentrate on one or two elements when observing. (These elements should directly result from the task; i.e., "Find three movements showing changes of direction. You should look specifically for changes of direction.")

Table 12.2

Observing Children's Gymnastic Movements

You ask	You see	You respond
1. Is each child trying to answer the task? (on-task behavior)	No; Robbie is playing with his mat.	May I help you fix your mat, Robbie?
2. Is each child answering the task?	No; Jamahl must have misunderstood the task. He is stretching-curling-stretching. I asked for curl-stretch-curl.	Jamahl, can you change the order of your sequence to two curls and one stretch?
3. How could the responses be improved?	The children have a lack of focus; they tend to continually look at the floor.	Public feedback: Meredith, you and Jason are focusing up when you jump. Well done!

Children may learn a great deal from observing one another's movements.

When children are performing, tell them to do the following:

1. Hold their beginning and ending shapes, so the start and finish are clearly defined when they are showing their work.
2. Take their time and avoid rushing through the sequence.

Evaluation

The methods used to evaluate gymnastics will likely be very similar to those used in dance and games. However, remember the difference between gymnastics and dance is that gymnastics focuses on how the body moves in relation to apparatus. How the apparatus is set up and used is important. Gymnastics also focuses on function and design of movement, as well as action, both alone and with others.

There are numerous tests designed to assess competitive gymnastic skills, such as the Ellenbrand Gymnastics Skills Test and the Harris Tumbling and Apparatus Proficiency Test. Because we are concerned with both process and product of skill acquisition (qualitative and quantitative aspects of movement), these tests are usually inappropriate. Our methods of evaluation should reflect what we deem important. We will be evaluating movement pattern and movement skill. Thus, formative rather than summative means should be used, with criterion references established.

Lessons

How much time was spent setting up apparatus? Was there sufficient apparatus for all the children? Should the introduction to the lesson have been longer? Were there too many basic tasks without enough extending and applying tasks?

These and other questions you have may be answered simply by examining your lesson plan. You may critique your lesson by listening to a tape recording or watching a videotape.

Evaluation after each lesson is wise so that you may effectively plan the subsequent lesson. You could assess the appropriateness of progressions from floor work to apparatus, how readily the children grasped the movement concepts (and establish why it was so), variety in skills learned, or the progression from working alone to small groups. A grid may be helpful for you to determine some of the strengths and weaknesses of your lesson (table 12.3).

Children's Skills

When we think of evaluation of children in gymnastics, we first think of evaluating their physical skill level. You will find that some children will quickly develop new skills. Other children may not be quite so talented, or conversely, may be so skilled that they reach a plateau. You will need to come to terms with what you believe is best to evaluate for formal reporting purposes: process, product, or a combination.

Since gymnastics is functional yet includes aesthetic elements, it may be evaluated with respect to either pattern or skill. Was the cartwheel performed with a fully stretched body shape? Did the dive roll reveal a movement of flight? Were the arms neatly tucked into the body during

Table 12.3

Lesson Grid for Ongoing Assessment

Lesson	Experience	Concept(s)	Apparatus	Social	Link
1	Explore	Roll	None	Alone	New
2	Explore/create	Transfer of weight	None/small	Alone	Develop
3	Recall/create	Transfer of weight/body parts	Small/large	Alone/pairs	Develop
4	Imitate	Body parts	Small	Alone/small groups	New
5	Refine	Body parts	Small	Alone/small groups	Develop
6	Create	Body parts/levels	Large	Pairs	Develop

Comments: Children worked well in lesson 1; did not change tasks often enough in lesson 2; large apparatus most challenging but recall needs work in lesson 3; they copy well but head placement weak in lesson 4; concentration poor (due to class party?) in lesson 5; wonderful sequences in lesson 6!

the spin? These questions refer to the movement pattern. When equipment is used in gymnastics, we may evaluate how the body related to the equipment. How high was the box when the child traveled over it? How long did the child walk on the balance beam without looking down? Tables 12.4 and 12.5 will give you ideas about what to evaluate.

Apparatus

Apparatus provides excitement and additional challenge in gymnastics. While small apparatus may be easily manipulated to meet the needs of differing skill levels, large apparatus provides the challenge of new heights. Here the child can swing, balance, hang, and grip. Figure 12.4 illustrates types of gymnastic apparatus.

Children may work with one piece, a combination of small pieces, or both small and large apparatus.

> *When each piece of small apparatus has been used in many different ways the children have built up a considerable movement vocabulary on each, the progression to work with two or three pieces of small apparatus arranged in a circuit will be simple (Mauldon & Layson, 1965).*

Table 12.4

Sample Checklist for Skill Development in Gymnastics

Grade: 3 **Name:** Carl Hardy **Date:** Feb. 3

	Satisfactory	Unsatisfactory	Needs Work On
Running	X		
Jumping	X		
Leaping		X	
Rolling	X		
Balancing		X	
Taking weight on hands			X
Taking weight on other body parts			X
Body shapes	X		
Landing			X
Springing			X
Firm movement	X		
Sudden movement	X		
Sustained movement	X		

Table 12.5

Evaluation of the Child

Date: May 12 **Teacher:** J. Williams **Student:** R. Hill

As compared with peers:

	Stronger	Average	Weaker
Skill level	X		
Recollection, movement memory	X		
Creativity, innovation		X	
Continuity of movement	X		
Cooperation			X
Independence	X		
Conceptual understanding	X		

To Do

Examine the graph in box figure 12.1. On a scale of 1–10, what grade would you assign each child based on their December 20 performance?

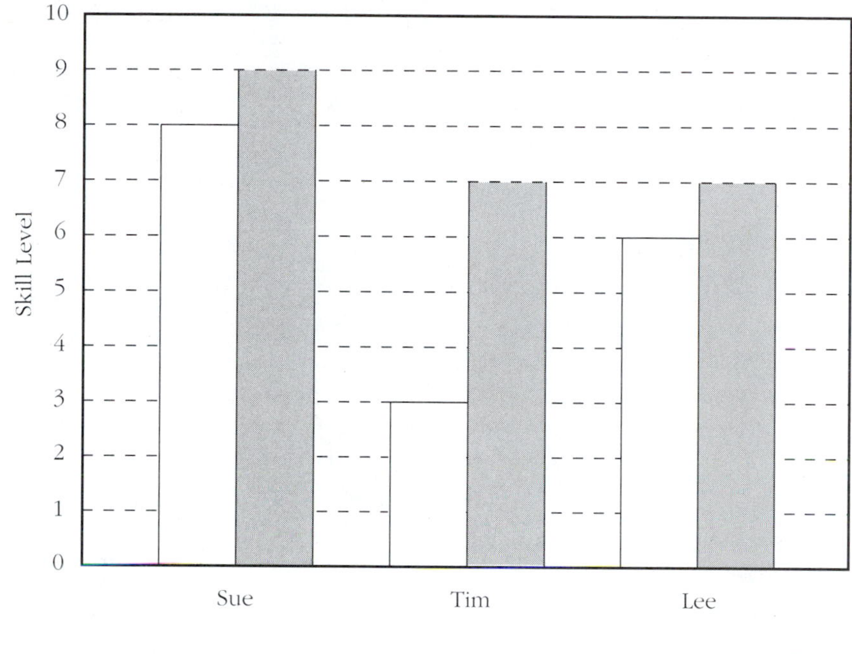

Box figure 12.1 What grade would you assign each child?

Progressive arrangements of apparatus are important, so children develop versatility and skill over a period of time (figure 12.5). As the movement concepts presented progress from simple to complex, so too should the environment. This ensures not only a safe, challenging environment for the child, but also the necessary progression of apparatus arrangements required for effective skill development.

Small Apparatus

Skipping ropes, hoops, mats, and blocks are examples of small apparatus, which is portable and available in most schools. Small apparatus provides additional stimuli, especially for young children who delight in traveling in relation to the apparatus as they jump, travel under and over, around, and through it. Older children may also enjoy using small apparatus because it is a valuable intermediate step between working with large stationary apparatus. They will be challenged to discover the possibilities and limitations of each piece as you set challenging tasks.

Figure 12.4 Gymnastic apparatus.

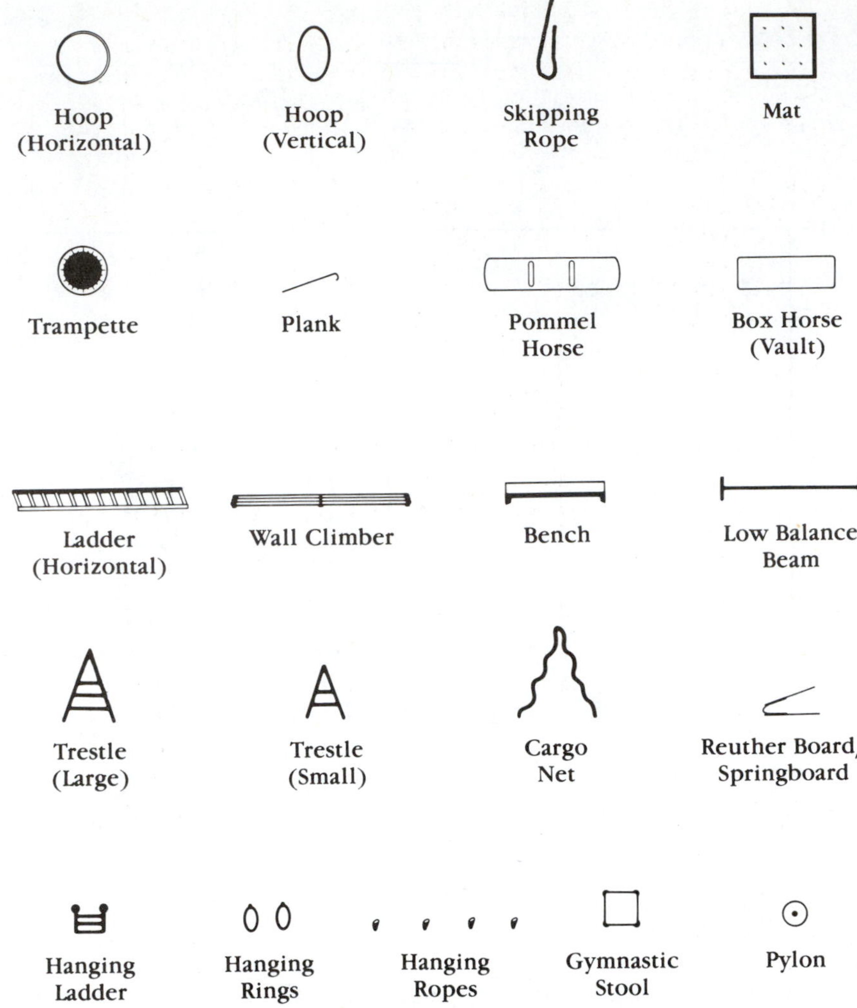

Small apparatus provides a point of reference within the space and may help alleviate problems of line-ups and overcrowding. Children will work within their own space where the apparatus is situated. This will encourage spatial orientation, which is important to develop in the early years. Tasks, such as "Jump across your mat," "Using hands and feet, travel around your hoop," and "Travel along the length of your skipping rope," will clarify the child's conception of space and how it may be filled.

Beanbags

Beanbags may be used effectively in gymnastic lessons. They may be placed between the chin and chest so that children tuck in their heads as they roll forward or backward to maintain a curled shape. They may also be held between the knees if legs tend to separate during rolling. Beanbags may facilitate a symmetrical jumping action by children placing them between their ankles.

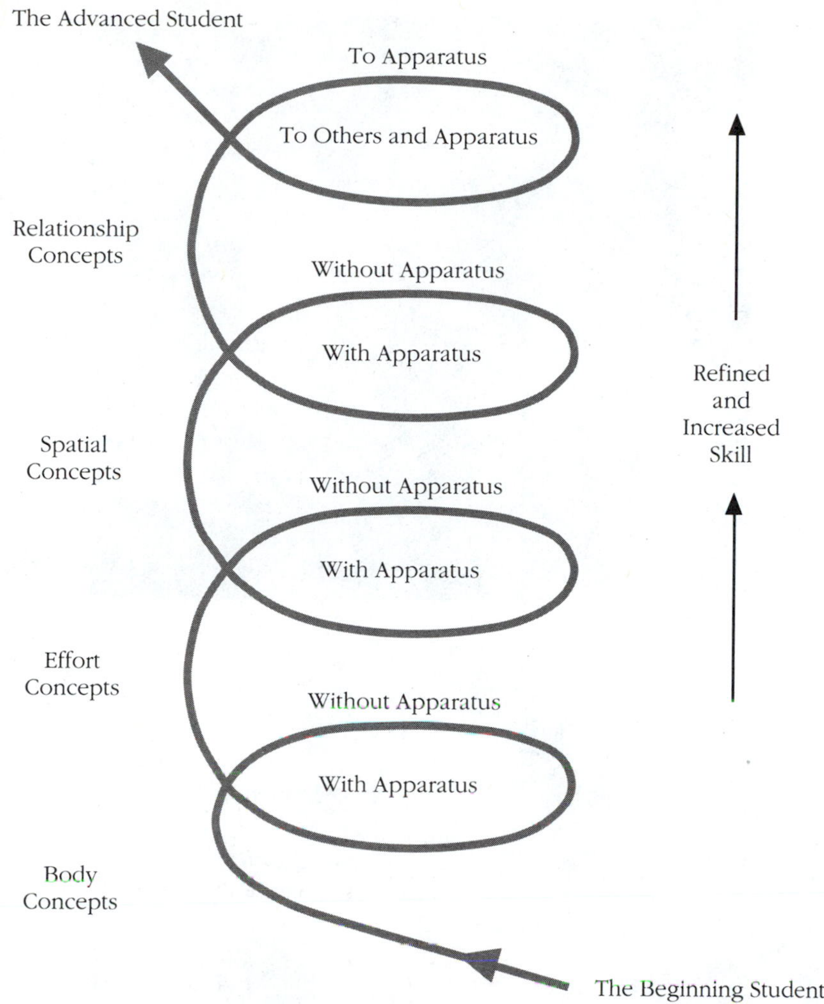

Figure 12.5 When apparatus is initially introduced, there is a decrease in the quality of movement. After apparatus is used for a period of time, skill will surpass previous skill level.

Hoops

Hoops may be used in various ways either as stationary or moving obstacles. Children love to roll hoops and run beside them, jump over them, or step through them as they roll. Hoops may be situated flat on the floor, so children balance or transfer their weight over to the other side using various body parts. They may be walked around to reinforce a circular pathway or traveled along on feet or combinations of hands and feet. A hoop may be balanced vertically by placing a mat through it so that it stays upright. In this situation, children may freely travel over and through as they jump, crawl, and roll in various ways. With additional small apparatus, such as small stools or blocks, hoops, may be raised horizontally to allow traveling over, under, around, and through. Children may also balance inside them. Whichever way hoops are used, consider how much time children spend holding hoops for others.

Large apparatus provides an additional challenge for children.

Skipping Ropes

Skipping ropes are available in most schools, and they provide much challenge for movement. While skipping itself is a worthwhile activity, ropes may be used in ways similar to hoops. They may be placed on the floor in various shapes or attached to chairs or boxes to provide a "high jump" that may be traveled over or under in various ways.

Large Apparatus

Gymnastic stools, ladders, benches, boxes, and vaulting horses are examples of large apparatus. Large apparatus is heavy and cumbersome. Apparatus such as bars, springboards, trestles, ropes, and ladders are often taller, longer, or heavier than the children themselves, who will need to work together to lift, carry, and set them in place. Many schools have large climbing frames that attach to the wall. A "wall climber" usually requires a few children working cooperatively to pull it away from the wall and secure it to the floor.

Although wall climbers and other large apparatus may seem very different from small apparatus, the same basic movements of locomotor and nonlocomotor activities are developed. The numerous small attachments (such as ladders and planks) are designed to add variety and challenge to large climbing frames and will reinforce and extend many of the skills previously acquired. However, large apparatus will provide the additional dimension of being able to support children's total weight at both low and high levels. Skills that were not possible on small apparatus may be performed on large apparatus. These include climbing, swinging, hanging, and rotating around an object at a medium or high level.

Suggestions for apparatus upkeep and storage follow:

- Mats, ropes, and hoops can be hung on a wall to be stored.
- Storage carts are useful for wheeling small apparatus onto the gymnasium floor.
- A portable trolley (the size of your school's mats) allows mats to be stacked and then rolled onto the gymnasium floor.
- Mark one side of each mat to denote a "clean side." Clean sides should be stacked facing one another so that they stay clean.
- Mats should be stacked carefully, not thrown on a pile.
- Hanging ropes should *never* be knotted because they will fray from the friction and pressure of children's weight.

Summary

The teacher's role is complex because children should experience increased skill development and the enjoyment it will bring.

> ***The methods a teacher must utilize to achieve this goal should promote continuous activity and encourage individual exploration and discovery that results in frequent success for the student (Canadian Gymnastics Federation, 1977).***

Review Questions

1. List five factors you will employ to ensure a safe gymnastic environment.
2. What are the advantages and disadvantages of children spotting one another?
3. What is the role of observation in the gymnastics program?
4. On what basis will you evaluate children in the gymnastics program?
5. How does the challenge of small apparatus differ from that of large apparatus?

References

Canadian Gymnastics Federation. (1977). *Coaching certification manual.* Ottawa, Ontario: University of London Press.

Department of Education and Science. (1972). *Movement.* London: Her Majesty's Stationary Office.

Docherty, D., & Morton, A. R. (1982). A focus on skill development in teaching educational gymnastics. *Canadian Association of Health, Physical Education and Recreation Journal, 48*(6), 3–8.

Mauldon, E., & Layson, J. (1965). *Teaching gymnastics.* London: Macdonald and Evans, Ltd.

Williams, J. (1974). *Themes for educational gymnastics.* London: Lepus Books.

Chapter 13 Learning Experiences in Gymnastics

While we do not wish to be restricted by our lesson plan, an effective plan provides us with the initial source of guidance. Once with your class, you will be attending to the children's various needs and cannot expect to remember every task, activity, or arrangement of apparatus within the lesson. You will need time to interact with the children as the particular movement dictates. To be good teachers, we should not be preoccupied with what we'll say next to the whole class when one child requires our undivided attention. The plan should be used for quick reference during the lesson.

The age and previous experience of the children you teach will be the primary factors to consider when you design gymnastic lessons. The expectations you realistically may establish for their level of skill, the vocabulary you select for development, and the tasks you spend the most time extending, applying, and refining are paramount.

If the children have had minimal exposure to gymnastics, you should first teach rolling, for safety reasons, whether they are in kindergarten or grade 6 (as outlined in Lesson Plan 1). However, the development of the tasks and the final stage of the lesson would differ because of the various needs, abilities, interests, and experiences of the children. Older children will progress more rapidly as their grasp of the concepts both cognitively and physically is more advanced. Thus, while each group may begin at relatively the same point on the gymnastic continuum, great divergence should occur over a period of several lessons.

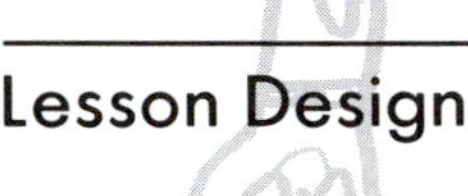

Lesson Design

We must have a general idea of what we wish to cover before we plan a lesson. The general content should be based on a selected movement concept, while considering the needs of the children. While no movement concept can be developed in isolation, it will provide a basic framework within which the children will work. For example, if a class is asked to "Travel any way you like along the bench," locomotion is key, but direction, level, time, and relationships are also employed. The concept of locomotion here will provide the focus for movement development, and for this reason, should be clearly presented to the children at the onset of each lesson.

When planning lessons, you will need to decide how much time the children will spend working on the floor, or small or large apparatus.

> *Whatever the length of lesson, the proportion of time allocated to floor and apparatus work has to be considered. When introducing a new idea the time spent working at floor level will be greater than that on apparatus but in consecutive lessons the working time will probably be equally divided. Once the particular theme has been fully explored at floor level the children will need a greater proportion of time to exploit the possibilities on apparatus (Mauldon & Layson, 1965).*

Movement Concepts

The movement concept should be clearly outlined and discussed with the children if a new concept is being presented. If it has been the focus of previous lessons, then review is probably warranted even if it is a cursory look at the essentials. All tasks and resultant movement exploration and development should involve the application of the concept. True skill development will ensue because the children's focus will be on solving specific movement problems. You should have a preconceived idea of what types of responses will result, so children may be appropriately guided.

Initial lessons should focus on relatively simple and familiar actions for the child. Movements should focus on not only the whole body as in running, jumping, and rolling, but also on various body parts that require preparation for more stressful work. Stretching and curling as weight is transferred from one body part to another work the neck, trunk, and hip regions. Weight taken on the hands, shoulders, hips, and stomach tax the muscles of the upper body. Body parts may be stressed in locomotion with tasks, such as "Travel with knees high," "Travel with springing actions and quiet feet," or "Lift your arms high to accentuate your leap."

If children are older or more advanced in their movement, the teacher may expect more complicated responses to more involved tasks. The additional elements of space and time may be added in initial lessons with such tasks as "Travel backward with springing actions," and "Ensure that you use a sudden take-off as you leap and then balance."

Even when children have had a strong background in gymnastics, it is wise to begin with the more basic concepts of weightbearing and weight transference for review purposes. From there, you may make decisions about the movement concepts that will most effectively stimulate the children to increase their motor competency. For example, students may be adept at traveling and balancing on their hands in various ways. The introduction of apparatus, such as benches, horses, and boxes for traveling on, along, or over, with weight on the hands, will further challenge the children.

In all likelihood, the children you teach will have had some gymnastic experience. They may have used the gymnastic apparatus within the school with little exposure to the movement concepts and vocabulary presented in this text. In this situation, children will require careful guidance during the lessons in order to fully appreciate the movement possibilities within each concept. If you use age-appropriate apparatus and social structures (working alone, with a partner, or small group), the children should find delight in your classes and their developing skill.

Apparatus

Apparatus is introduced to provide further stimulation within the theme. Young children usually require more time to discover the range of movements possible within a theme without apparatus, while older children may quickly indicate to the teacher their readiness for the additional challenge of obstacles.

You must carefully consider which pieces of apparatus will be most appropriate and conducive for the movement concept being developed. After children have explored the range and movement potential of the concept while working on the floor, an additional challenge of small or large apparatus provides further motivation and stimulus. It is extremely important that you select suitable apparatus for the children and that it promotes the range of movements that provide the focus of the lesson. For instance, if you select the theme of levels and tell the child to create a sequence of travel at a high level, then at a low level, and balance at a medium level; the apparatus of a large box, a bench, and skipping rope will encourage appropriate responses. You should always ask yourself how you would respond to the task with the apparatus provided. If you would have difficulty solving the movement problem with the apparatus suggested, then you can anticipate the children will as well. See table 11.5 to help you select appropriate apparatus.

Usually at the beginning of the lesson, little or no apparatus is used, so children will focus their attention completely on the body. Some teachers allow students to take apparatus out and begin work before the class begins. Other teachers are adamantly against introducing apparatus until students are sufficiently limbered. As a teacher, you will find what works best for you and your class. Figure 13.1 outlines the progression we suggest for apparatus use.

Partner and Group Work

While young children may find success in working with another or others only after a good deal of time has been spent working on their own, older children may be physically and mentally prepared to collaborate with their peers in the earlier stages of skill development. This process of cooperation and collaboration may also be a valuable motivating tool for pre-adolescent children in the upper elementary grades. These children are sometimes self-conscious and find tremendous support and encouragement in working with others. The amount of time children may spend working with others, due to their own inclinations or the decision of the teacher, is shown in figure 13.2.

Creating Sequences

Children should be expected to create sequences that reflect the best movement they have performed that day. Sequences may involve the floor or a mat, apparatus, and/or other children. You will need to stress a clear beginning shape, good continuity of actions joined together, and the holding of a clear shape to conclude the sequence.

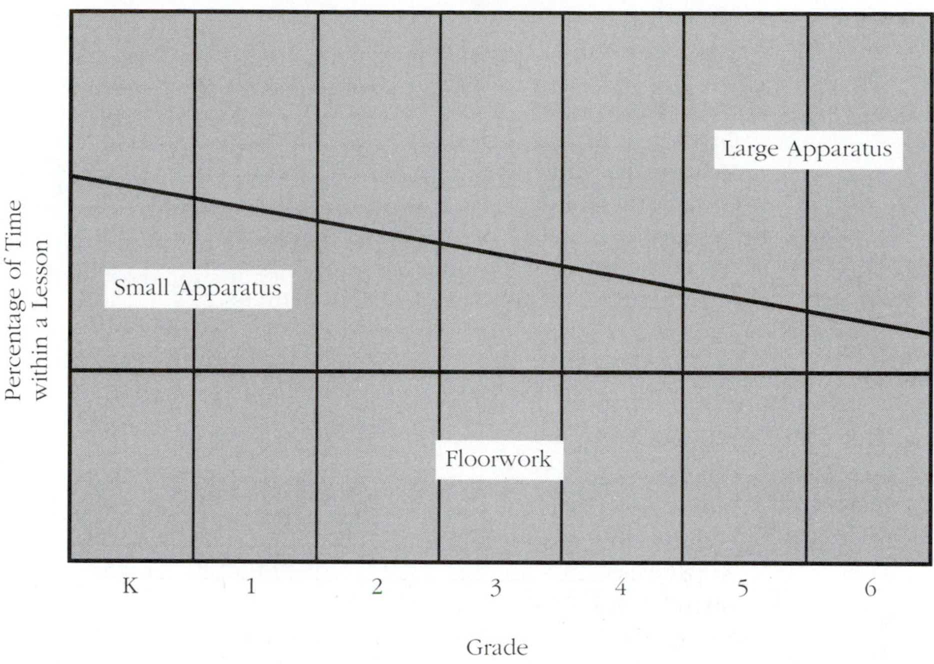

Figure 13.1 Progression in the use of apparatus.

Grade	K	1	2	3	4	5	6
Working Alone		OOOO	OOOO	OOOO	●●●●●●	●●●●●●	●●●●●●
Working in Pairs		oooooo	●●●●●●	●●●●●●	●●●●●●	●●●●●●	●●●●●●
Working in Small Groups			oooooo	oooooo	●●●●●●	OOOO	OOOO

Used Rarely oooooo
Used Often ●●●●●●
Used Extensively OOOO

Figure 13.2 Progression in social structure. Children should be exposed gradually to working with others as they mature through the grades.

Sample Gymnastics Lesson Plan Formats

Format 1

Grade: ______________________________

Movement Concept: ______________________________

Gymnastic Actions: ______________________________

Apparatus: ______________________________

Introduction (3–5 Minutes)

Movement Development (10–15 minutes)

1. Leg work
2. Arm work
3. Whole body work
4. Sequence work

Culmination (10–15 minutes)

Format 2

Grade: ______________________________

Movement Concept: ______________________________

Gymnastic Actions: ______________________________

Apparatus: ______________________________

Introduction (3–5 Minutes)

Movement Development (10–15 minutes)

1. Without apparatus
2. With apparatus

Culmination (10–15 minutes)

(Note that apparatus may be used in any portion of the lesson. Format 1 ensures that weight is taken on all body parts for a well-rounded movement experience.)

Whatever the age and skill level of the class, the most difficult task for the teacher will be to find continuity of action within movement sequences. Children will tend to find a few movements that they enjoy and are successful with, but will probably have difficulty combining them smoothly. Because gymnastics involves the sequencing of various types of locomotor and nonlocomotor movements, you will need to spend much time on ways isolated movements may be combined.

Because children learn effectively from watching others and enjoy performing their work, you may wish to include a few minutes of observation. Some children may be eager to perform their sequences and will readily do so, while others may need your encouragement. "Let's watch all the children in this corner," or "This half of the class show us your sequences," may be all the incentive the children require. However, while you should provide as much encouragement as possible, children should not be forced to display their work, especially if they are not pleased with the result.

Lesson Plan Formats

As you progress as a teacher, you will find particular lesson plan formats more appropriate for your needs than others. Two examples are shown.

Sample Lesson Plans

The sample lesson plans that follow are arranged in order of difficulty from simple to complex. We begin with a basic lesson focusing on rolling and springing with small apparatus and end with a lesson that is challenging in skill, apparatus, and social structure.

These lessons are not designed for a particular age group but are based on an approximate social, cognitive, and skill level of a typical class of children. If you choose to follow these plans, keep in mind that adjustments (in vocabulary and sentence structure) will have to be made to the tasks, so they are appropriate for, and understandable to, your class.

Careful observation of the children as they respond to the tasks will be essential. At times, children will generate new movement ideas that you may not have considered. Sometimes, you may find your lesson digressing from its original intent into a new skill or concept. In order to capitalize on the "teaching moment," encourage this digression and work with the children—not against them. For example, you may follow Lesson Plan 1 but find the children become absorbed with twisting and rolling. Instead of saying, "No, don't do that, do this!", it is wiser to capture their interest and promote further skill development by changing your springing tasks to "twisting" tasks.

Lesson Plan 1 *Safety Training*

- Grade: Any gymnastically inexperienced group of elementary school children
- Length: 20–30 minutes
- Apparatus: One mat per child (if available) or grass
- Objectives: The children will be able to
    1. create stretched shapes in jumping,
    2. create round shapes that roll,
    3. absorb force by rolling after flight for safety reasons,
    4. sequence run, jump, land, roll, with continuity in movement (figure 13.3).

Safety Training		
Body Concepts Activities: Jumping, rolling, transference of weight		
Effort Concepts	**Spatial Concepts**	**Relationship Concepts**
Time-sudden changes in shape	Levels	

Figure 13.3 Safety training—Lesson Plan 1.

Tasks	Teaching Aids
Introduction	
Organizing	
Find a space all by yourself.	
Basic	
Run into empty spaces and jump whenever I clap.	Initially, clap with a predictable time span between claps. Later, claps may become unpredictable. Watch for jumps with good height. Encourage children to move continuously.
Refining	
Swing your arms up to gain height. Bend your knees to land quietly. Keep your head up; don't look at the floor when you jump.	Force should be absorbed by sudden curling of the trunk and knees after stretching in the air. You may want the class to watch someone who jumps with good form.
Push off the floor suddenly, and stretch your body as much as possible when you are in the air. Remember to bend your knees when you land.	Watch children's use of feet and ankles to see if they really stretch in the air.
Extending	
This time, on your own, run, jump, touch the floor with your fingertips, and repeat.	Encourage children to find rhythm in their movement. This will facilitate a smooth sequence of action.
Concept and Skill Development	
Organizing	
Get a mat for yourself and place it on the floor as far away from everyone else as possible.	Establish the most efficient way to get out the mats. Sometimes it is easier for two children to carry their mats together, rather than each child carrying one.
Basic	
Find several curled shapes and see if you can rock back and forth on each one.	Stimulate children's ideas by suggesting various body parts to take their weight (e.g., stomach, back).

Find a curled shape and rock back and forth.

Refining

Make sure your shape is really curled. Tuck in knees, elbows, and head, and hold it tight.

Children may observe one another to check if shapes are curled. A beanbag may be placed between a child's chin and chest to ensure a tucked head if the body is curled toward the stomach.

Extending

Begin with small rocking actions and increase their size to the point that it makes you roll over.

This may be easy for some children and more difficult for others. Assist those who need help.

Raise the level of one good curled shape, so you have a new base of support. Let gravity pull you down to roll. Make that shape again and repeat the action.

Weight may now be on knees or feet. Children will have to shift their center of gravity (hips) off balance so they roll.

Refining

This time make a stretched shape on one or two feet, then curl so that you roll.	Shapes may be stretched long or wide. Point out that elbows, knees, and toes should be stretched.
Again stretch, then curl, but this time quickly bend your head, knees, and elbows before you land.	Stress the importance of not using hands to break the fall. Children should take weight on upper back, hips, and the side of arms and legs, not bony body parts.

Extending

Add a little jump before you roll, so you are really stretched, then tightly curled.	Give children a good deal of time to master this task before you go to the next. (It may take longer than you anticipated!)
Add a small run to your sequence, so you run-jump-land-roll.	Quick tucking of the body is necessary to safely roll. Curling of the knees and back are very important to absorb force.

Refining

Run very lightly, jump, land, and roll forward, backward, or sideways.	Remind children to continue their roll in the direction they were running (see figure 12.1).

Applying

Repeat your sequence over and over again, jumping then rolling into different spaces. Try to create a rhythm in your movement.	Watch children's use of space. Advanced children will roll quickly; slower children will roll with caution. Observation of others may help some children.

Culmination

Because gymnastic apparatus provides a unique challenge in the elementary physical education program, you may wish to expose an inexperienced class to a variety of apparatus at this point. It is a good idea to allow them to freely explore the apparatus before you set specific tasks for them (figure 13.4).

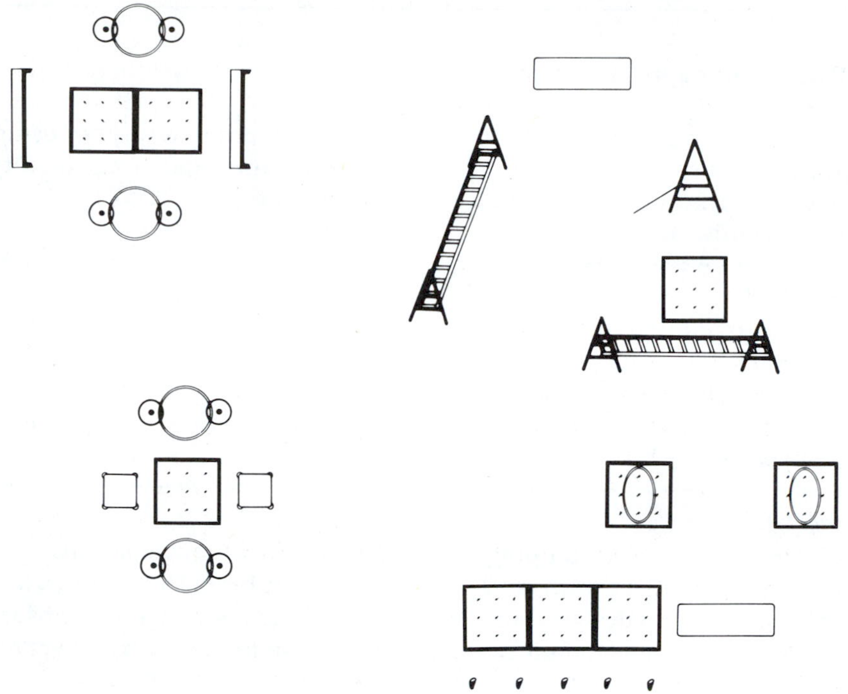

Figure 13.4 Apparatus arrangement for Lesson Plan 1.

Tasks	Teaching Aids
Organizing Please look at the diagram on the board. This is how we'll set up the apparatus today. Sandra's group, please leave your mats where they are, but put away everyone else's. John's group, please get two benches and two hoops and set them up. Terry's group, get the ropes out and set them up. Julie's group, please take out three trestles, two planks, and one box. Brenda's group, you'll need two trestles, a plank, two hoops, and a box.	Assist children in retrieving apparatus. Check to see if it's set up the way you asked.

Basic	
Play on your apparatus as you like.	
Jump over, onto, or off of your apparatus. Remember to really stretch in the air and curl tightly when you land.	Help children find ways of using the apparatus. Encourage quality in jumping.
Organizing	
Do the same thing on different apparatus.	
Now that you have used a variety of apparatus, find a piece that you like.	Ensure that all children are active and no one is waiting for a turn.
Applying	
Create a sequence of jumping, landing, and rolling with your apparatus. Try to design your sequence, so you can do it twice without stopping.	Continuity of movement is important here. Help children design their sequences to ensure quality in jumping, landing, and rolling.
Observing	
Let's watch this group perform their sequences. Watch carefully for good jumps and rolls.	Choose a group of children who are using the apparatus in a variety of ways.

Fitness Fact

Running and jumping repeatedly will promote cardiovascular endurance and muscular endurance of the thighs.

Important Points

In Lesson Plan 1, children may have their first attempt in creating a gymnastic sequence. You should look for the following:

1. ***Truly stretched shapes when they jump.*** Watch particularly for stretching in arms, thighs, knees, ankles, and toes.
2. ***Truly curled shapes with heads especially tucked in.*** You may say to children, "Look at your belly button as you roll" if they are curling forward.

3. *Absorption of force as children land* through bent knees, ankles, and curled backs.
4. *Continuity of movement* (smooth movement) in the sequence of run, jump, land, and roll.

Note that every task within the lesson is naturally related to the previous task. The first task of run and jump requires vigorous activity and warms up the children. It also encourages the kinesthetic experience of stretching and curling so weight transference occurs. The tasks then progress from simple rocking, to rolling, to rolling preceded by traveling on feet, with a moment of flight (in the jump).

Ways in which Lesson Plan 1 may be modified are presented in table 13.1.

Possible Progressions

The lesson as outlined should provide plenty of material for most classes. You may wish to vary the lesson with the following

1. Movement action
   a. Traveling in other ways than running (skip, hop, leap)
   b. Turning in flight during the jump
   c. Focus on pathway during the sequence
   d. Focus on direction during the sequence (i.e., travel sideways, twist to roll forward or backward)
   e. Focus on time-traveling quickly and rolling s-l-o-w-l-y
2. Partner work
   a. Children performing their sequences at the same time, not matching
   b. Incorporating copying in matching, leading, and following, meeting and parting, or contrasting levels, directions, or timing of actions in any part of the lesson
3. Children may be ready to explore the possibilities of incorporating apparatus not suggested in the lesson.
4. Lessons could involve both a partner and apparatus. However, the children should have previously been exposed to either a partner or apparatus, so they are not faced with two new stimuli at once.

Table 13.1

Modifications for Lesson Plan 1

Lesson Plan 1 involved

Running	Curling	Floorwork
Jumping	Rocking	A variety of small
Landing	Rolling	and large apparatus

Kindergarten—Grade 3

Lesson	*Review material*	*New material*	*Apparatus*
1	Running and stopping	Jumping Landing	Free play
2	Jumping Landing	Rocking Rolling	Exploring Jumping Landing Rolling
3	Rocking Rolling	Sequencing run-jump-land-roll	Small and large
		—or—	
1	Running and stopping	Rocking Rolling	Free play on large apparatus
2	Rocking Rolling	Running Jumping Landing	Over, off, and on large apparatus
3	Jumping Landing	Sequencing run-jump-land-roll	Small and large apparatus

Grades 4–6

Lesson	*Review material*	*New material*	*Apparatus*
1	Running and stopping	Jumping Landing	Over Off On
2	Running Jumping Landing	Rocking Rolling	Small apparatus with a partner
3	Rocking Rolling	Run-jump-land-roll	Large apparatus with a partner
		—or—	
1	Running Jumping Landing	Rocking Rolling	Free play
2	Sequencing run-jump-land-roll	Rocking Rolling	Small apparatus with a partner
3	Sequencing run-jump-land-roll		Large apparatus with a partner

Fitness Fact

Traveling and stopping quickly to hold a shape promotes muscular strength, especially in the thighs, hips, back, and shoulders.

Lesson Plan 2 *Stepping Actions*

This lesson focuses on weight transference, where children perform stepping actions. To clarify this concept, steplike transference of weight can take place using a number of body parts; for example, in handstands and cartwheels, hands and feet alternately act as supports for the rest of the body (Mauldon & Layson, 1965).

- Grade: 3 or 4
- Length: 20–30 minutes
- Apparatus: Mats (one for each child if available)
  Option 1: Hoops
  Option 2: Large apparatus (see figure 13.4)
- Objectives: The children will be able to
  1. create narrow, wide, curled and twisted shapes,
  2. transfer weight onto various body parts,
  3. sequence three forms of weight transference showing, different body shapes (figure 13.5).

Stepping Actions		
Body Concepts Activities: Stepping actions with hands and feet, weight transference, body shape		
Effort Concepts	**Spatial Concepts**	**Relationship Concepts**
Flow-continuity of action		On, along, and off apparatus

Figure 13.5 Stepping Actions—Lesson Plan 2.

Tasks	**Teaching Aids**
Introduction	
Basic	
Travel any way you like on your feet. When I clap, stop, make a shape, and freeze. Hold it and travel again.	Stress good use of space and quick response to claps. Point out various shapes children have made, and discuss whether they are primarily stretched, curled, or twisted.

Refining

As you are running think of what type of shape you'll make when you stop. If you make a stretched shape, stretch all your body parts. If you make a curled shape, curl your body tightly. If you twist, twist as much as you can.	You may demonstrate a weak shape and then have a child demonstrate a good shape. Point out the difference (e.g., placement of head, hands, feet). Also point out that a stretched shape may be wide or tall and thin (narrow).

Extending

Travel and freeze making shapes on your own. After you've made your shape, twist it so that you face a new place to travel.	Sequence work is beginning here. Continue to encourage clarity of shape. You may have to clarify twisting (feet fixed, body rotates) with the children.

Basic

Travel, using body parts other than your feet to take your weight.	Children may take weight on combinations of hands, head, knees, and back.

Extending

This time focus on the shape of your body as you travel. First, try making round or curled shapes, then try making wide shapes.	Children may arch, spring from feet to hands to feet, roll, or cartwheel.
Now have only your hands and feet take your weight. First, see what different ways you can find, then repeat the good ones, concentrating on the shape of your body.	Observe and help children clarify their body shapes.

Refining

Place your hands on the floor shoulder-width apart. Spread your fingers apart as far as possible.	Observe the hand positions of the children.

Concept and Skill Development

Option 1: Hoops

Tasks	Teaching Aids
Basic	
Transfer your weight from feet to hands to feet. Only your hands may go inside the hoop. What kind of shapes can you make when you do this?	Children should begin standing, so they create momentum for their hips to go up as their hands go down.
Refining	
Try really stretching your shape, as you take your weight on your hands and make your feet travel over the hoop.	You may tell children that stretched shapes are best when shoulders and hips are placed above the hands (in a line). Children should look at their hands.
Extending	
Place your hands in the hoop and make your feet go to the other side, but now sequence it: hand-hand-foot-foot.	Analogies, such as "Stretch your toes to the ceiling," "Think of yourself as spokes of a wheel stretching out," and "Imagine you are a puppet with someone pulling the strings on your legs," may help the children achieve a true stretch.
You can also try placing both hands together on the floor, then landing both feet together.	Placing the hands far away from the feet may encourage a moment of flight before the hands touch the ground.
Experiment with placing your hands close to or far away from your feet.	Children may experiment with placing the hands in front of and behind their feet. This will encourage a front or a back walkover.

Place your hands in the hoop and make your feet go to the other side.

Basic

Find other ways of transferring your weight as you travel over or across the hoop. You may use feet only, or a combination of hands and head, knees and elbows, or any other combinations that work for you.

Having children observe each other may help them gain some new ideas. If quality movements are beginning to emerge, you may choose some for the class to observe.

Refining

Find some good ways of traveling over or across the hoop accentuating your body shape.

Stress smooth weight transference and clear body shape. Encourage twisted and wide shapes, as well as more common stretched and curled shapes.

Culmination

Applying

Create a sequence of three ways of transferring your weight over or across your hoop, showing at least two different body shapes.

Expect variety in skill level but quality in clarity of shape. Final observation will reinforce satisfaction of accomplishments.

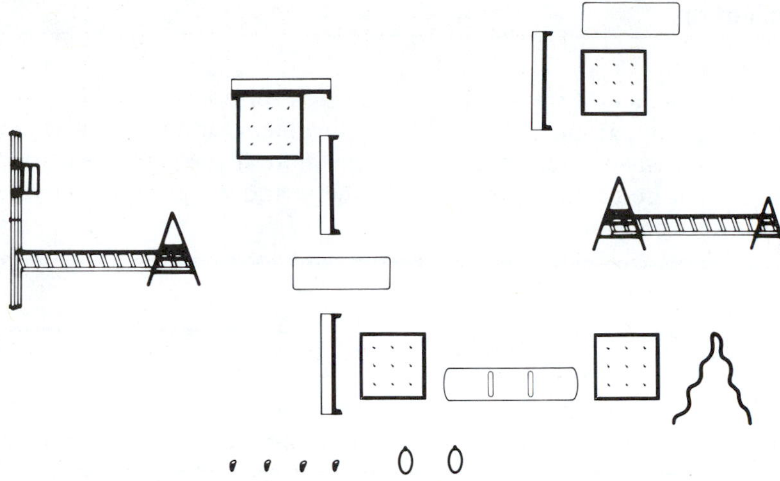

Figure 13.6 Possible apparatus for Lesson Plan 2, Option 2.

Concept and Skill Development

Option 2: Large Apparatus

Tasks	Teaching Aids
Basic	
Explore getting onto or over your apparatus using stepping actions with feet and hands. Travel along or off your apparatus using a pattern of hands-feet-hands or feet-hands-feet.	Check foot and hand pattern of the children.
Extending	
Try to take a number of steps with your hands as you travel along or off your apparatus.	Some apparatus may not be conducive to this task. Children may take some or all of their weight on their hands (e.g., their feet may still be on the apparatus).
Now focus on curled body stepping actions as you travel on, along, over, or off your apparatus.	You may mention that when the body is curled, the center of gravity is lowered and balance is easier than when the body is stretched.
This time make stretched shapes using feet and hands to travel on, along, over, or off the apparatus.	Make sure that children really stretch their bodies.

Culmination

Applying

Create a sequence of stepping action to get on, along, and off your apparatus. Show at least two different body shapes in your stepping action.	Watch for continuity of movement, and suggest ways to promote it through use of body shape and weight transference.

Fitness Fact

Weight on hands promotes muscular strength. If repeated long enough, this will promote muscular endurance in the arms and trunk.

Important Points

In Lesson Plan 2, children are exposed to weight transference with emphasis on stepping actions and body shape. The concept of body shape should have been at least briefly introduced in dance, games, or gymnastics prior to this lesson. However, since weight transference may be new to the children, Lesson Plan 2 will provide an introduction for further work in weight transference that is linked with other apparatus and other movement concepts.

You will notice that in the first option (using hoops) the tasks are more closed in that they lend to the specific movements of a handstand, cartwheel, back walkover, front walkover, and round-off. These skills are given less emphasis in option 2. If you desire to have greater emphasis on these skills, the lesson may be modified through more closed teaching methods. (One can achieve this through tasks, such as "Take your weight on hands only in a stretched shape.")

As you observe children working, take special notice of the following:

1. ***Students who are especially weak or especially talented in their skill.*** They may need extra encouragement, alternative ideas, or time for refinement.
2. ***Use of hands.*** When hands are placed on the floor to receive the body's weight, the whole palm and all fingers should contact the floor to create as large a surface area as possible. Hands should be placed shoulder-width apart for greatest stability.
3. ***Children's shape.*** Clarity of shape is a major objective.

As in Lesson Plan 1 and in all lessons you plan, tasks should be arranged from general to specific and simple to more complex, always reinforcing the movement concept of the lesson.

Ways in which Lesson Plan 2 may be modified are found in table 13.2.

Possible Progressions

It is suggested that you repeat this basic lesson with some changes so that the concept of weight transference may be fully appreciated. Remember that all concepts may be developed through partner or group work and/or variation of apparatus. The concept of body shape may be replaced by other movement concepts so that lessons could focus on weight transference of ***body parts, pathway, level, direction,*** and ***time.***

Table 13.2

Modifications of Lesson Plan 2

Lesson Plan 2 involved

Traveling with different body shapes
Transferring weight onto hands and feet in curled and stretched shapes
Sequencing stepping actions with stretched and curled body shapes
Option 1: Floorwork and hoops
Option 2: Floorwork and large apparatus
The following progressions are modifications of Lesson Plan 2. If you are teaching kindergarten to grade 3, the children should spend most of their time working alone. In grades 4 through 6, partner and small group work will provide additional challenge.

Lesson	***Review material***	***New material***	***Apparatus***
1	Weight transference	Stretching Curling Twisting	Hoops
2	Stretching Curling	Stepping actions	Benches
3	Stepping actions	Twisting Curling Stretching —or—	Large apparatus
1	Stretching Curling Twisting	Weight transference	None
2	Weight transference	Stepping actions	Hoops
3	Stepping actions	Stretching Curling Twisting	Large apparatus

The movement concept of body shape will also warrant further study. If you wish to explore and develop this concept in further lessons, then a natural progression will move into other areas, such as body shape and ***balance, locomotion, stressing body parts,*** and ***level.***

To gain further ideas for the development of the above concepts, refer to chapter 11.

Lesson Plan 3 *Balancing*

- Grade: 4 (with previous experience with partner work)
- Length: 30–45 minutes
- Apparatus: One mat per child
- Objectives: The children will be able to
    1. balance with three different bases of support,
    2. match a partner's balances,
    3. create a movement sequence with a partner that matches and involves three balances (figure 13.7).

Figure 13.7 Balancing—Lesson Plan 3.

Balancing		
Body Concepts Activities: Balancing, body parts to balance on		
Effort Concepts	**Spatial Concepts**	**Relationship Concepts**
Weight		Matching a partner

Tasks	**Teaching Aids**
Introduction	
Organizing	
Find a space by yourself.	Make sure that the children are as far apart as possible.
Basic	
Travel and freeze as quickly as you can in your own time.	Every child should repeat this at least five times.
Refining	
Travel and freeze again, making sure you really concentrate on holding your freeze.	Ensure that children spread their arms, bend their knees, and place their feet shoulder-width apart to step quickly.
Extending	
Travel, jump, and land on only one foot and freeze. Try again, landing on your other foot.	You may have to discuss the necessity of a lowered center of gravity and absorption of force (bending of knees, arms wide) for children to be successful.

Balance on your head with one or two other body parts.

Organizing

Find a partner who is wearing the same color shirt as you are. Decide who will be *A* and who will be *B*.

Applying

B, match *A*'s running, jumping, landing, and freezing, and follow closely behind. This is cooperative, so *A* don't travel too fast and be careful when you travel backward. When I tell you, *B* will lead and *A* will follow.

You will have to tell children that the leader should never turn around to face the follower, because the follower will have to turn his or her back on the leader. Children may tend to make this competitive rather than cooperative. Stress quality in pairs. Groups of three are acceptable if there is an odd number of children in the class.

Concept and Skill Development

Organizing

Group 1, please pull out the mats. The rest of you, line up behind Tim. Group 1, hand each person a mat. Place your mat as far away from anyone as possible.

Basic

Explore balancing on different body parts. You can try balancing on combinations of feet, knees, seat, stomach, shoulders, head, elbows, and hands.

Encourage children to try unusual combinations of body parts, such as head and knees or elbows and seat.

Extending

Continue balancing on different body parts, but increase the challenge by balancing on as few body parts as you can (i.e., one elbow and one knee, your head and one foot).

Concentrate now on balancing on combinations of hands and feet. You could try both hands and both feet, both hands and one foot, both feet and one hand, or one hand and one foot.

Balance with your stomach facing the wall, floor, and ceiling.

Remind children that their base of support will need to be wide if they have two or three body parts on the ground. The lower the center of gravity, the more stable the body will be.

The children may benefit from observing one another or you may need to give them ideas by demonstrating yourself.

Applying

Find your best balance on hands and feet.

Balance on your head with one or two other body parts.

Watch carefully that children do not injure their necks. There is diversity of opinion as to whether weight should be taken on the top of the head or near the hairline. However, children should never take their weight on their foreheads, because this is dangerous to their necks.

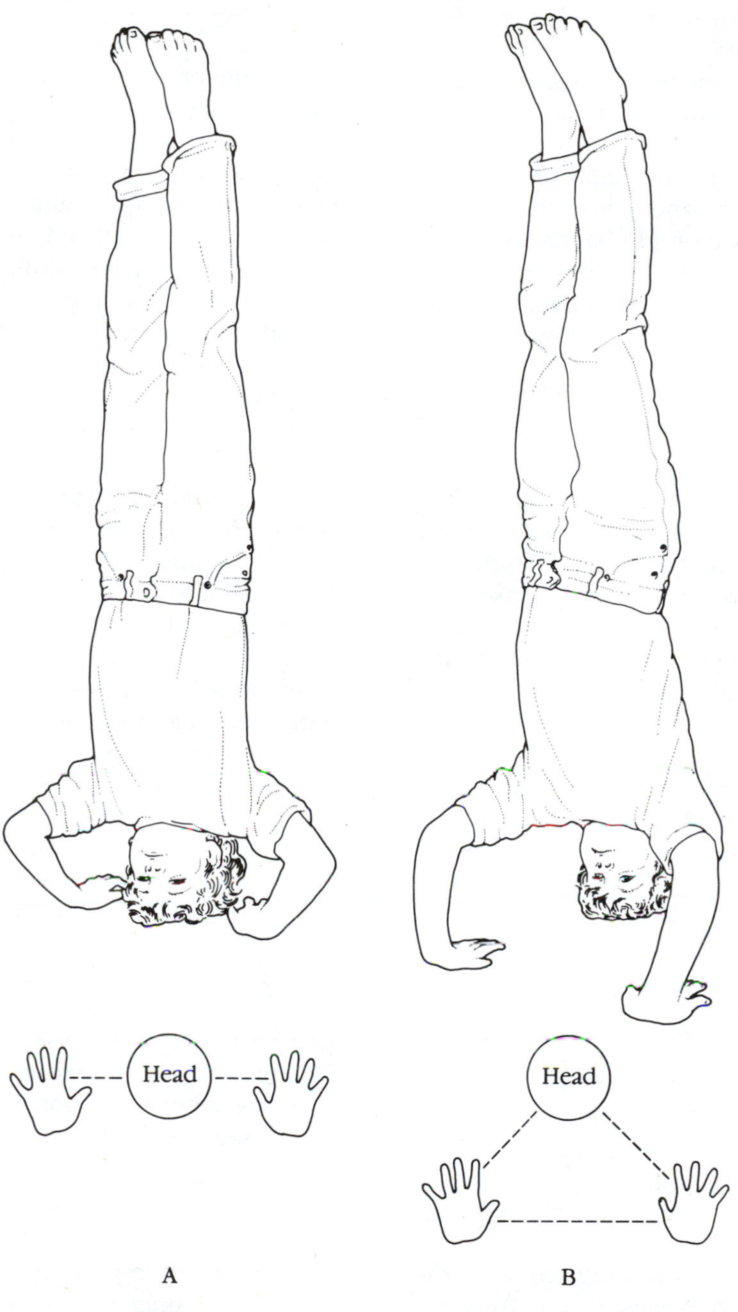

Figure 13.8 Which person's hands show better placement and result in more stability?

Extending

Balance on head and hands only. Where should your hands be placed in relation to your head? (figure 13.8)

Children's fingers should be spread apart with palms on the floor. The head and hands should form a triangle.

Applying	
Find your best balance on your head with one or two body parts. Create a movement sequence of three balances: your best balance on (1) hands and feet, (2) head and other body parts, and (3) any other balances. Put them in any order you like.	Encourage children to hold very still. You may have to circulate throughout the space and provide public feedback to children who are challenging themselves. Discourage simplistic balances on one or two feet. Encourage interesting shapes.
Refining	
You'll need to figure out how you can move from one balance to another. (This task could be the basis of a lesson in itself.) Will you travel (e.g., roll) in between balances or do all three balances on one spot?	Variety is desired, with purposeful movement in between shapes. Children's bodies should be "tight" throughout the sequence, rather than "shape-relax-shape." Look for continuity of movement where the shape is held because of its aesthetic interest.
Organizing	
Find a partner that you haven't worked with. We can have a group of three if there is an odd number. Show your sequence of three balances to your partner.	Point out that there could be a group of three. This eliminates the problem of one child feeling left out. Children should sit far enough (10 feet) away from their partner to clearly see the balances. Stress that those showing their work should take their time.

Culmination

Applying	
Create a matching sequence of three balances. One is your partner's favorite from your sequence, one is your favorite from your partner's sequence, and the third can be a new balance or one from either sequence.	You may need to present or review the concept of matching (see chapters 2 and 11). Be sure the children understand the directions. You may want to use one pair as an example.

Tasks	Teaching Aids
Refining	
Be sure that you have a beginning shape and a way to get into your first, second, and third shape. Usually, matching sequences are performed side by side. Decide if this is how you want to do it or if you want to face each other, face different directions, etc. Practice your sequence over and over until it is polished.	Students will need to be told to take their time and hold their shapes clearly. Observation of various spatial combinations will help children appreciate how movement looks different with a variety of "fronts."

Option 1

The teaching method at this point could become quite closed. You may believe it is very important for children to develop some specific, "traditional" gymnastic skills. Thus, these tasks are presented with little choice for the student; however, they are still intended to accommodate a diversity of skill levels.

This sequence of tasks is designed to develop the students' skill in both the headstand and the handstand.

The movement concepts are body parts (head and hands) and body shape in the action of (static) balancing.

Tasks	Teaching Aids
Basic	
Take your weight on your head and both hands, forming a triangle with these three body parts.	Make sure the children's fingers are spread and their palms are on the floor. Check students' head placement. Their weight should be in between their foreheads and the tops of their heads.
Simplifying	
Keep your body curled as you take the weight onto your head and hands. You may want to try a frog stand, where your elbows rest on your knees.	Students will have greater success if they try this slowly. First, one elbow goes on one knee, then the other. Reinforce the concept of "strong hands."

You may want to try a "frog stand," where your elbows rest on your knees.

Extending

You were working on a curled shape balancing on your hands and head. Now try slowly raising your toes to the ceiling, so you form a stretched shape as you balance.

Reinforce the stretching of the trunk and leg muscles to the ceiling. Tight muscles are extremely important.
Can they perform the action with variation in time?
Children who can easily do a headstand may be challenged by creating twisted or wide shapes as they balance on their head and hands, or by moving into a headstand with straight legs.

Basic

Take your weight on your hands only. Remember hands should be shoulder-width apart.

Children should not lock their elbows, yet their arms must be strong.

Extending

Is it easier to do a handstand starting with your weight on your hands and feet or just your feet? Try it both ways and see if you can figure out the answer and a reason for it.

You could put children in pairs to observe one another for hand placement.

Since our center of gravity is in our hip area, we want to use the momentum of our hands going down to get our hips to go up. Students should not begin with hands and feet on the floor; it requires more strength to get their feet up.

Children will also need to be told to place their hands near where their feet were so that the downward momentum is used. Otherwise, the momentum is down and forward—a waste of energy.

Refining

Take your weight on your hands again, but imagine that someone is pulling your toes up to the ceiling, like a puppet. Really stretch! Make sure your stomach is tight; point your toes!

You may wish to physically pull a student's ankles upward.

Children who have learned the handstand may work on creating various shapes as they balance: walking on their hands (dynamic balance), traveling sideways as in a cartwheel to "get into" the handstand, rolling backward into a handstand (back extension), or moving from a headstand into a handstand.

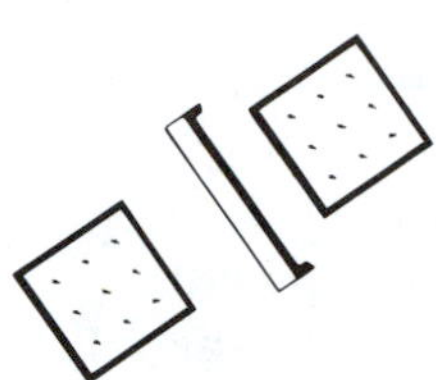

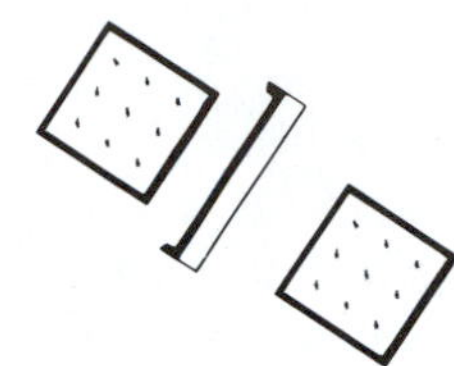

Figure 13.9 Benches and mats for balancing sequence.

Option 2

- Apparatus: One bench for 4–5 children

Task	Teaching Aids
Organizing	
Find a partner whom you've never worked with before. We may have a group of three.	Stating that you may have a group of three will alleviate the problem of someone feeling left out.
Join another pair, so you have a group of four or five. Two of you get a bench and bring it back to your space. The other two or three, place your mats on either side of the bench (figure 13.9).	Be sure that children carry the benches properly. The groups should be well spread apart and the benches far away from the walls.

Basic	
By yourself and using the bench, try some of the balances you or your partner created.	Children may place some body parts on the bench and others on the floor (i.e., head on the floor, feet on bench) or all body parts on the bench (i.e., head and hands).
Extending	
Working with your partner again, adapt the sequence you did on the floor, matching one another, so you now use the bench. One balance must be totally on the bench, another off the bench, and the third balance some weight should be on the bench and some weight on the floor.	You will have to observe, circulate, and provide guidance when children need help.
Refining	
Work on matching your movements as closely as possible.	

Important Points

In Lesson Plan 3, balancing is first explored alone, then with a partner, then applied through matching on the floor and finally on large apparatus. This lesson is not intended to serve as the initial experience in balance but rather to illustrate how balance, partner work, and apparatus may be interrelated.

Take notice of how the tasks are arranged. While each basic task offers new guidelines, the refining tasks involve a partner and extending tasks require matching movements. Thus, the first applying task is a basic review and requires synthesis of what has previously been accomplished. The final applying task again involves matching movements but with the additional challenge of apparatus.

Make a balance with the bench.

As you observe children within this lesson, take special notice if they are cooperating as they are matching. Matching may occur as children travel and balance beside or behind/in front of one another (traveling beside is the easiest). Timing is important when matching and may be very difficult in some actions.

Table 13.3

Modifications of Lesson Plan 3

Lesson Plan 3 involved

Floorwork
Partner work
Partner work on small apparatus

Kindergarten–Grade 3

Lesson	*Modification*
1	Floorwork → partner work
2	Floorwork → small apparatus
3	Floorwork → small apparatus → large apparatus
	—or—
1	Floorwork → small apparatus
2	Floorwork → large apparatus
3	Floorwork → partner work

Grades 4–6

Lesson	*Modification*
1	Floorwork → small apparatus → large apparatus
2	Floorwork → partner work → alone on small apparatus → partner work on small apparatus
3	Floorwork → partner work → alone on large apparatus → partner work on large apparatus

Possible Progressions

Lesson Plan 3 could be used as it is written. However, there is probably too much material for one lesson. It could be modified for children in kindergarten through grade 3 by simply omitting the partner work. If you use this lesson with children in the upper elementary grades, you may conclude the lesson when children have created matching balances, and involve the benches in later lessons. You could develop many progressions, as outlined in table 13.3.

Lesson Plan 4 *Gaining Flight*

- Grade: 5 (experienced, relatively skilled children)
- Length: 30–45 minutes
- Apparatus: Large apparatus such as boxes, benches, horses, reuther boards/beatboards, trampettes, ropes
- Objectives: The children will be able to
  1. show flight with no apparatus,
  2. show flight with flight-assisting apparatus,
  3. show flight with flight-assisting apparatus adjacent to other small and large apparatus,
  4. sequence movements that involve flight,
  5. use good judgment in selecting movements to perform (figure 13.10).

Figure 13.10 Gaining flight—Lesson Plan 4.

Gaining Flight		
Body Concepts Activities: Jumping, springing, swinging		
Effort Concepts	**Spatial Concepts**	**Relationship Concepts**
Time-sudden movement	Levels	On, over, off apparatus

Tasks | **Teaching Aids**

Introduction

Organizing

Take a mat into your own space.

Basic

Tasks	Teaching Aids
Travel around the room using flight to get over the mats as you come to them. Change your method of traveling when you like.	Stress good height, through use of arms and legs in take-off and landing. Encourage quality movement.

Refining

Tasks	Teaching Aids
Try to stay in flight as long as possible by keeping your head up when you are in the air and when you land.	Children tend to look at the floor when they jump.

Extending

This time after you land with flight, roll. You should jump or hop before the mat so that you can roll on it.	Note children's use of space. They should use whatever mats are free.

Refining

Try to spring and land with light feet.	Stress good use of knees and ankles.

Basic

Travel across your mat by rolling forward, but precede the roll with a small jump before your hands contact the floor.	This is the basis of the dive roll. Stress good spring in knees and stretching of the body during flight.

Refining

Make sure your chin is tucked into your chest, so the back of your head touches the floor first. Aim for height, not distance.	Children may practice this by rolling over a crouched partner.

Extending

This time take a small run before you roll and finish your roll with a jump.	Stress quick curling and stretching, with lots of spring in knees and ankles.

Concept and Skill Development

Basic

Find a movement you can do well where you quickly transfer your weight from feet to hands to feet in some way.	Children may perform a headstand, handstand, cartwheel, or other movement.

Refining

Make the movement very quick, so your hands are in contact with the floor for as short a time as possible.	Children will have to use their arms and shoulders effectively to produce spring.

Figure 13.11 Possible apparatus arrangement for Lesson Plan 4.

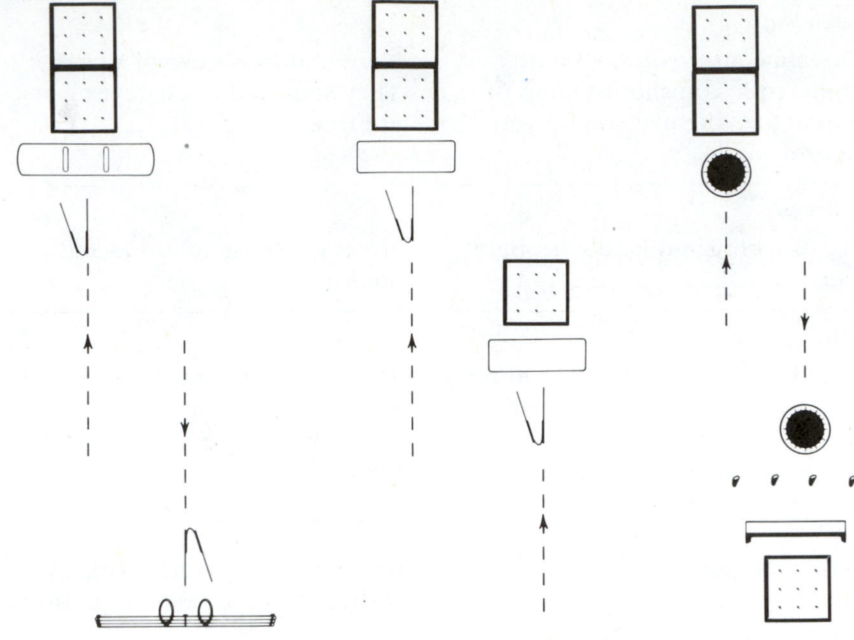

Extending

Take a short run before you perform your movement and delay putting your hands on the floor for as long as possible, so that you have flight. This may come before, during, or after the movement.

Stress quick stretching and curling and "tight" bodies. Children may require quite a long time to develop this skill. Observation of others may illustrate important points.

Culmination

Organizing

Get into your groups of five. When I hand you a card, please set up the apparatus as shown in figure 13.11.

Check that apparatus is in good condition and that "runways" are all going the same direction.

Basic (with flight-assisting apparatus only)

There are different types of flight-assisting apparatus: the reuther board, the springboard, the trampette, and ropes and bars. All of these will help you gain flight to different extents. Try the boards and trampette with two-foot take-offs, placing your feet in various points on the apparatus, and trying to gain height or distance (up or out).	Point out that force must be projected down, so the body will be sent up. Try to go to the shortest line up.

Refining

What things did you discover? (Allow time for discussion.) Go back to the apparatus, trying to incorporate what we've talked about.	Taking off with both feet is best because more force is projected down. The reuther board tends to project the body forward, the springboard up and forward, and the trampette, up.

Extending

At your station, use the apparatus. Use it to gain height, and find a movement you can do after you land. Think about what you are going to do before you begin the movement.	Stress safe, thoughtful movement. Children's variation in skill level may be dramatically different. A crash mat may be used here if you think this will help the children progress.

Basic (with flight-assisting and other large apparatus)

Find a station that you'd like to work on. Work on ways of using the flight-assisting apparatus to get on or over the other apparatus.	Apparatus may be set up in a variety of ways. See figure 13.11.

Use your flight-assisting apparatus to gain height.

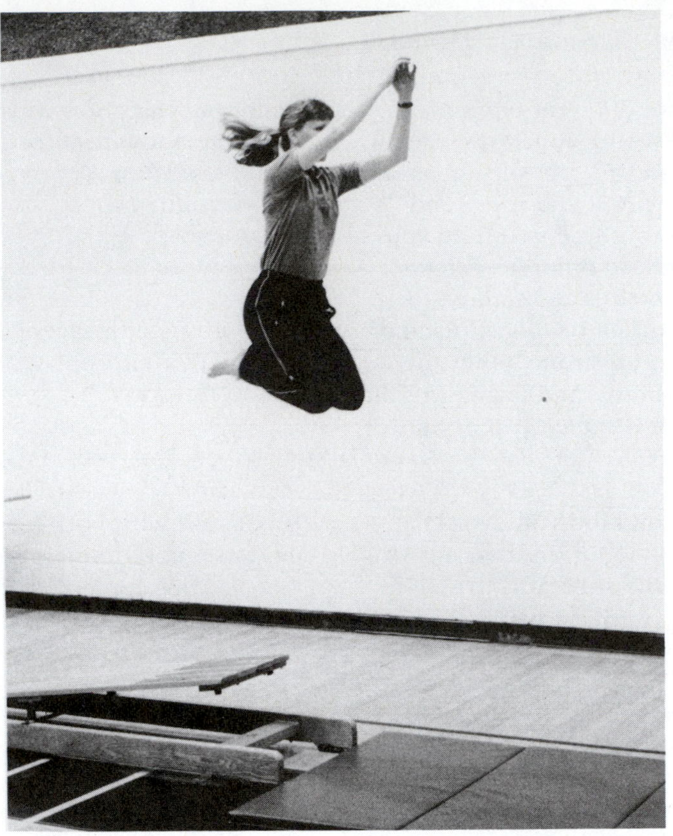

Refining

Note which body parts you are using. Keep hips and trunk ''tight'' as you try to gain more flight.

Give assistance to children, providing ideas and guidance for improved movement.

Extending

Find a good movement as you travel onto or over the apparatus. Add another movement either before or after you have gained flight.

Children with lower skill levels will likely add movements before their flight (i.e., they may roll to the trampette). Children with higher skill levels will likely add movements after flight (i.e., cartwheel after vaulting a box).

Applying

Create a movement sequence where you use at least three pieces of apparatus and employ flight at least twice.	Stress continuity of movement and how children travel from one piece of apparatus to another. Observation may occur so that children may see each other's work.

Important Points

In Lesson Plan 4, children are exposed to the advanced concept of flight. It cannot be stressed too heavily that this concept is appropriate only for older students or students who have already acquired a good deal of bodily control in gymnastic movement.

You will note that the lesson provides a gradual progression from flight on the feet, to flight on various body parts (primarily hands and feet), to flight assisted by apparatus, and finally, flight in relation to large apparatus. The important things for you to stress as children progress in flight follow:

1. Children are constantly mindful of safety in all situations.
2. Children have "tight" bodies during flight.
3. Children in fact, are, ready to progress to the next stage before you offer additional challenges.

Possible Progressions

As was the case in Lesson Plan 3, Lesson Plan 4 was written with a great deal of material, so you may use the lesson in whole or in part. The lesson could conclude before flight-assisting apparatus is introduced or before flight-assisting apparatus is used with other large apparatus.

Ways the lesson could progress from the applying task follow:

Flight in partner work/matching

Leading and following

Contrasting

Meeting and parting

Assisting flight

If you have reached this point with your children, they are well-skilled and a class of whom you should be proud.

Summary

Finding the "right" progression of concepts for your class will require your sensitivity and good observational skills. At times, you may find repetition of tasks and practice will most benefit the children; at other times, the children will "feed you" what guidance they are ready for. Above all, share the success and pride in the work of the children!

Review Questions

1. Discuss the purpose of each of the three parts of the gymnastics lesson plan.
2. Write a progression of tasks for run, jump, land, and roll.
3. Which will you teach first—weightbearing or weight transfer? Provide your rationale.
4. What types of gymnastic actions will increase arm strength?

References

The British Journal of Physical Education. (1991). 22(3), the entire volume is devoted to gymnastics.

Mauldon, E., & Layson, J. (1965). *Teaching gymnastics.* London: Macdonald and Evans, Ltd.

Rikard, I. (1992). Developmentally appropriate gymnastics for children. *JOPERD, 63*(6), 44–46.

Related Readings

Capel, S. (1986). Educational Gymnastics Meeting Physical Education Goals. *Journal of Physical Education, Recreation and Dance.* 57:2, 34–38.

Docherty, D., & Morton, A. (1982). Focus on Skill Development in Teaching Educational Gymnastics. *CAHPER Journal.* 48:6, 3–8.

Williams, J. (1974). *Themes for Educational Gymnastics.* London: Lepus Books.

Sources for Gymnastic Themes and Progressions

Canadian Gymnastics Federation. (1977). *Coaching certification manual.* Ottawa, Ontario: University of London Press.

Mauldon, E., & Layson, J. (1979). *Teaching gymnastics.* London: Macdonald and Evans Ltd.

Williams, J. (1974). *Themes for educational gymnastics.* London: Lepus Books.

Index

Q

R

S

T

U

V

W

Y